Mormon Feminism

Mormon Feminism

ESSENTIAL WRITINGS

EDITED BY JOANNA BROOKS,

RACHEL HUNT STEENBLIK,

and

HANNAH WHEELWRIGHT

OXFORD
UNIVERSITY PRESS

OXFORD
UNIVERSITY PRESS

Oxford University Press is a department of the University of Oxford. It furthers
the University's objective of excellence in research, scholarship, and education
by publishing worldwide. Oxford is a registered trade mark of Oxford University
Press in the UK and certain other countries.

Published in the United States of America by Oxford University Press
198 Madison Avenue, New York, NY 10016, United States of America.

Library of Congress Cataloging-in-Publication Data
Mormon feminism : essential writings / edited by Joanna Brooks, Rachel Hunt Steenblik, and Hannah
Wheelwright.
pages cm
Includes index.
ISBN 978-0-19-024803-1 (hardback : alk. paper); 978-0-19-084838-5 (paperback : alk. paper)
1. Feminism—Religious aspects—Church of Jesus Christ of Latter-day Saints.   I. Brooks, Joanna, 1971–
editor.   II. Steenblik, Rachel Hunt, editor.   III. Wheelwright, Hannah, editor.
BX8643.W66M67 2016
289.3082—dc23
2015004452

for those who came before
for those who will follow
fresh courage take

Contents

IV. RESURGENCE: Mormon Feminism in the Early 2000s   226

A Note on the Cover

Nikki Hunter (1969–) "The Pants Quilt" (2012)

On December 16, 2012, inspired by a call to action by blogger Stephanie Lauritzen, Mormon feminists around the world took action to raise the visibility of feminist issues by wearing pants to local LDS church services. (Male allies and others who supported the cause but did not wish to wear pants demonstrated solidarity by wearing purple.) Although not officially prohibited, pants-wearing by women at Sunday services jarred with deeply-held gendered dress customs in many Mormon communities around the globe. Wearing pants proved to be an especially transformative experience for many participants who had never openly discussed their concerns about gender in their home congregations. Hundreds donated the pants they wore to be joined in a commemorative quilt sewn by Feminist Mormon Housewives blogger Nikki Hunter of Idaho. "One time, as I pondered how much black and gray and purple I was likely to receive as the color scheme of the quilt," Hunter recalls, "I was overcome by the need for a nap, and as I awoke, I was given in a dream-state not only how the quilt should look—a rising sun coming through a grove of trees at dawn—but the name of the quilt: 'Sunday Morning.'" Hunter pieced together 143 pants in all shades and textures of black, grey, and purples. The quilt honors the legacy of handcraft in Mormon women's culture and captures a sense of momentum and optimism about the future of Mormon feminism.

Acknowledgments

This book has been blessed by many hands. We are grateful to all of the authors who have contributed and granted permission to republish their essays, speeches, petitions, and poems, and often sent notes of encouragement and offered editorial input as well. Claudia Bushman, Laurel Thatcher Ulrich, and Margaret Toscano provided definitive guidance from the inception of this project and continued to support it through its completion. We were honored to have the input of the women who attended our book workshop—including several contributors to this volume and founding figures of contemporary Mormon feminism—at the Fortieth Anniversary *Exponent II* retreat in New Hampshire in September 2014. Andrea Radke-Moss, Stacy Burton, Elouise Bell, Lynn Matthews Anderson, Judith Dushku, and Kristine Haglund also provided valued scholarly and editorial perspective. This manuscript has been touched by the legendary editorial hand of Mary Lythgoe Bradford. We thank Fara Sneddon for developing our list of additional resources, and Kristiina Sorenson and Shelley Hoffmire who not only developed the topical guide and book group questions but also carefully line-edited the entire manuscript.

Joanna Brooks: At every step of the way in this project, I have felt the presence—sometimes palpable—of Mormon feminists past, present, and future. I am deeply grateful to have been born to this legacy, to all the Mormon feminists who have cared for me and taught me, to my co-editors for their intelligence, dedication, reliability, energy, and grace, and to my family for giving me the time. Ella and Rosa, I am so proud to have feminist daughters.

Rachel Hunt Steenblik: I am immeasurably grateful for the opportunity to have participated in this project. It was a gift to work with Joanna and Hannah, as it was a gift to consciously and consistently turn my heart (and mind) to my spiritual foremothers and sisters. The work of remembering felt at times both harrowing and holy. I am thankful for *The Exponent* bloggers who offered continual support and suggestions, and for my husband, Spencer, and my daughter, Cora, who offered their patience and love, as well as their listening ears.

Hannah Wheelwright: I am grateful to witness the words of Mormon women and to partake of their rich living history side by side with such unwavering editors. I thank my five generations of Mormon pioneer ancestors, especially my parents, for instilling in me a strong moral compass and a faith that inspires the courage to act on it. Lastly, I thank all those who supported me in my time at BYU, and particularly the dear friends always close by.

Contributors

Allred, Janice Merrill: independent scholar and theologian

Anderson, Lavina Fielding: editor, author, and co-founder, Mormon Alliance

Anderson, Lynn Matthews: independent scholar

Bell, Elouise: Professor Emeritus of English, Brigham Young University

Bradford, Mary Lythgoe: former editor, *Dialogue: A Journal of Mormon Thought*

Brooks, Joanna: author and Professor of English and Associate Vice President, San Diego State University

Bushman, Claudia Lauper: Professor of American Studies, Columbia University; former director, Joseph Fielding Smith Institute for Church History

Butterworth, Lisa: Idaho State University; founder, Feminist Mormon Housewives blog

Cassler, Valerie Hudson: George Bush Professor of Political Science, Texas A&M University

Colvin, Gina: Lecturer, College of Education, University of Canterbury (New Zealand)

Dushku, Judith Rasmussen: Professor of Political Science, Suffolk University

Farnsworth, Sonja

Farr, Cecilia Konchar: Professor of English, St. Catherine University

Graham-Russell, Janan: Howard University

Hammond, Elizabeth: independent scholar

Hansen, Nadine McCombs: attorney

Hawkins, Lisa Bolin: author

Howe, Susan Elizabeth: Associate Professor of English, Brigham Young University

Huefner, Dixie Snow: Professor Emeritus of Education, University of Utah

Johnson, Sonia: activist and author

Kelly, Kate: activist and attorney

Kimball, Violet Tew: author

Madsen, Carol Cornwall: Professor Emeritus of history, Brigham Young University, and former associate director, BYU Women's Research Institute

McBaine, Neylan: founder, Mormon Women Project, media consultant, and author

Munk, Margaret Rampton

Nelson, Trine Thomas

Newell, Linda King: Past president, Mormon History Association

Okazaki, Chieko Nishimura: educator and religious leader

Pearson, Carol Lynn Wright: author of more than thirty books and plays, including *My Turn on Earth* and *Goodbye, I Love You*

Pedersen, Cherie: educator

Peterson, Claire Whitaker: Screenwriter, *Man's Search for Happiness, Johnny Lingo,* and *The Waltons*

Raynes, Meghan: University of Colorado, Denver

Russell, RevaBeth: educator and activist

Sillitoe, Linda: Pulitzer Prize–nominated journalist

Steenblik, Rachel Hunt: Claremont Graduate University

Strayer, Chelsea Shields: Consultant and doctoral student, Boston University

Stromberg, Lorie Winder: Editor of the *Mormon Women's Forum Quarterly*

Taylor, Kynthia: independent scholar and theologian

Toscano, Margaret Merrill: Associate Professor of Humanities, University of Utah

Ulrich, Laurel Thatcher: Professor of History, Harvard University, and author of the Pulitzer Prize–winning *A Midwife's Tale*

What Women Know Collective

Wilcox Desimone, Linda P.: author, editor, and independent scholar

Young, Lani Wendt: author

Mormon Feminism

Mormon Feminism

An Introduction

JOANNA BROOKS

This book offers an introduction to the Mormon feminist movement through the words of the women who have lived and built it. It includes writings that capture key ideas, questions, concerns, and events in Mormon feminist experience from the movement's organizing moments in the early 1970s to the present. Never before have core Mormon feminist writings—from the movement's beginnings to the present—been compiled in one place. In doing so, we hope to provide a historical overview of the ways in which Mormon women have engaged with questions about gender in the Church of Jesus Christ of Latter-day Saints (the LDS Church). Today, due to increasingly visible Mormon feminist activism and some positive changes in LDS Church policies, the status of women in the LDS Church has become front-page news.* This book is for anyone who wants to go deeper than the headlines and understand what it means to be a Mormon feminist. This book is for Mormon women and men who have questions about gender dynamics within Mormonism. Maybe you have wrestled with these questions personally. Maybe you have witnessed a friend or relative struggle with these questions, or have read or heard about Mormon feminist activism and want to understand it better. Maybe you are not Mormon but are curious about how contemporary Mormons live our vibrant and demanding faith and reconcile ourselves to its challenges. Maybe you are a fellow feminist of faith, a scholar of religion and gender, or a student learning about women in Mormonism. We welcome you to learn from our experience, in our own words. (Non-Mormon readers may benefit from

---

* See, for example, Laurie Goodstein and Jodi Kantor, "Missions Signal a Growing Role for Mormon Women," *New York Times* (March 1, 2014), A1; Kristen Moulton, "Mormon Women Again Turned Away from Priesthood Meeting," *Salt Lake Tribune* (April 5, 2014), A1; William Harless, "Group Seeks Ordination for Mormon Women," *Wall Street Journal* (April 6, 2014), http://www.wsj.com/articles/SB10001424052702303910404579485782242824574.

the Glossary of Mormon terms and historical figures, one of the appendices of this book.)

What is Mormon feminism? To begin with, let's define some key terms. Mormonism is an American-born religious movement founded in the 1820s in upstate New York by a young farm worker named Joseph Smith. Smith participated in a wave of nineteenth-century Protestant revivals that emphasized that common people could know God directly through experience. In the process of his own religious search, Smith by his own account experienced a series of direct encounters with God the Father, Jesus Christ, and ancient prophets. These encounters led to Smith's translation and publication of the *Book of Mormon*, which he presented as a scriptural account of an ancient Judeo-Christian civilization in the Americas, and to his founding of the Latter-day Saint movement. Today, the largest branch of that movement is the Church of Jesus Christ of Latter-day Saints, which claims more than 15 million members worldwide. A Mormon is anyone who identifies with the Latter-day Saint movement by virtue of his or her church membership, religious beliefs, or family or cultural heritage.

Like other Christians, Mormons believe that a benevolent God sent his son Jesus Christ to atone for the sins of humankind and thus make it possible for souls to reunite with God in heaven; Mormons practice baptism by immersion as a saving rite and regard the Bible as holy scripture. Additional dimensions of Mormon theology developed by Joseph Smith in the 1830s and 1840s go beyond these basic tenets of Christianity, reflecting the Latter-day Saint movement's view of itself as a form of Christianity that, through a process of "continuing revelation" from God to Church leaders, has "restored" essential doctrines, practices, and books of scripture lost to contemporary Christendom. Consequently, in addition to the Bible, Mormons regard three additional books revealed to Joseph Smith—the *Book of Mormon, Doctrine and Covenants,* and *Pearl of Great Price*—as holy scripture. In addition to viewing baptism as a saving rite and participating in weekly worship services structured around the Christian sacrament, observant adult Mormons also participate in a set of sacred temple rituals developed by Smith to vest believers with the sacred knowledge necessary to return to the presence of God. Marriage to a fellow Mormon in a Latter-day Saint temple is believed to be eternally binding and necessary to share in the highest levels of God's glory—indeed, as Joseph Smith taught, to become like God in the eternities. Joseph Smith's vision of eternal marriage entailed polygamy; contemporary Mormonism teaches us that we have both a Heavenly Father and a Heavenly Mother who are the parents of the souls of humankind. With its view of a female God and its celebration of Eve as an exemplar of the principle of agency for her decision to eat the fruit of the tree of knowledge, Mormon theology offers in some respects a more progressive gender theology than the more conservative forms of Judeo-Christianity.

A Mormon feminist is anyone who identifies both with the Mormon movement and with the centuries-old struggle for women's equality, dignity, well-being, and full participation that we call feminism. Pulitzer Prize–winning historian Laurel Thatcher Ulrich, one of the founding figures of the contemporary Mormon feminist movement, defines Mormon feminism as follows:

> A feminist is a person who believes in equality between the sexes, who recognizes discrimination against women and who is willing to work to overcome it. A Mormon feminist believes that these principles are compatible not only with the gospel of Jesus Christ but with the mission of the Church of Jesus Christ of Latter-day Saints.[*]

Claudia Bushman, another Mormon feminist founding mother, wrote in the debut 1974 issue of the Mormon women's newspaper *Exponent II* that the movement was "poised on the dual platforms": "to strengthen the Church of Jesus Christ of Latter-day Saints, and to encourage and develop the talents of Mormon women."[†] She continued, "That these aims are consistent we intend to show by our pages and our lives." Twenty years later, Brigham Young University professors Mary Stovall Richards and Kent Harrison wrote in the journal *BYU Studies*: "The gospel . . . clearly proscribes unequal unrighteous treatment of anyone by anyone. 'Feminism' . . . simply espouses fair and equal treatment for all of our Heavenly Parents' children as wonderful holy potentially divine beings."[‡] Forty years later, Neylan McBaine, a self-described "moderate" Mormon feminist, wrote:

> If you care about the spiritual, emotional and intellectual development opportunities available to you, your wife, your sister or your daughter, you are a feminist. Period. Based on this definition, the doctrine of The Church of Jesus Christ of Latter-day Saints is inherently feminist. The Lord cares about women, our leaders care about women and we as a people care about women.[§]

Throughout the forty years of the contemporary Mormon feminist movement, Mormon feminists have again and again asserted the compatibility of Mormonism and feminism.

But there are also aspects of Mormon doctrine and practice that offer mixed or contradictory messages about gender, equality, and power. First, there is the issue of the gendered identity of God. Mormon theology envisions God as a Heavenly

---

[*] See Ulrich, "The Pink *Dialogue* and Beyond," anthologized in this volume.

[†] See Bushman, *"Exponent II* Is Born," anthologized in this volume.

[‡] Kent Harrison and Mary Stovall Richards, "Feminism in the Light of the Gospel of Jesus Christ," *BYU Studies* 36.2 (1996–1997): 181–99.

[§] Neylan McBaine, "A Moderate Mormon's Manifesto," *Feminist Mormon Housewives* (October 1, 2013): http://www.feministmormonhousewives.org/2013/10/a-moderate-mormons-manifesto/.

Father married to Heavenly Mother, but there is virtually no role for, reference to, or depiction of the Heavenly Mother in Mormon liturgy and practice, and among some Mormons it is still considered taboo to talk about her. If God is both male and female, why is the female aspect of God not recognized in contemporary Mormonism? Second, and closely related, is the unresolved issue of the spiritual value of gender roles. In the 1970s through the first decade of the 2000s, LDS Church leaders assigned increasing spiritual value to what Europeans and Euro-Americans regarded as "traditional" gender roles, with women defined by mothering and caregiving responsibilities and men defined as "presiders" in home and church; in 1995, the Church's "Proclamation on the Family" declared that these gender roles were eternal and an essential feature of the soul, even though LDS scripture provides little information on this subject. Are the "traditional" European and Euro-American gender roles that order the operations and culture of the contemporary LDS Church a reflection of the essential nature of God and godliness, or a projection of our own human understanding onto the divine? Is it possible, as LDS Church leaders state, for men and women to have different forms of access to power and different levels of authority within the Church and yet be equal? Third, there is the unresolved issue of polygamy. The LDS Church officially stopped performing plural marriages in 1890 under tremendous pressure from the United States government. However, the Church has never renounced the *doctrine* of eternal polygamy—that in the highest levels of heaven a man may be married to more than one woman—as introduced by Joseph Smith. Eternal plural marriages, with one man "sealed" to more than one woman in the afterlife, continue to be performed in Mormon temples. Is this a remnant of a rejected theology, or are Mormons to believe that polygamy will be the order of the heavens? Fourth, the question of women's access to priesthood also remains unresolved. When he developed Mormon temple liturgies in the 1840s, Joseph Smith incorporated ritual elements that suggest he viewed women as holders of a form of priesthood. But this vision was never fully realized, owing in part to Smith's early death, and many Mormon women reject the notion that they hold the priesthood, even though temple rites symbolically vest them with priesthood authority. Do Mormon women hold the priesthood, and if so, how will they use it? Fifth, there is the unresolved issue of racial privilege and bias within the LDS Church. From the late nineteenth century through 1978, Mormons of Black African descent were excluded from full participation in the lay priesthood and in LDS temple ceremonies. Since that time, LDS leaders have renounced racism but have never fully rejected theologies generated by Mormon leaders and laypeople to justify the segregation. If Mormonism was wrong to exclude Black women and men from full participation, why have leaders been so reluctant to acknowledge and address the fallibility of the tradition?

These paradoxes, inconsistencies, and ambivalences around gender, equality, and power in Mormon theology produce a palpable tension that Mormon women process in a number of different ways. Mormon feminists have taken pains to assert that core principles of the Mormon faith—including the love of God for all humankind, the creation of men and women in the divine image of Heavenly Parents, the capacity of the individual to exercise free will, or "agency," after the example of a courageous Eve, and to receive immediate knowledge of truth through personal revelation—are essentially "consistent" and "compatible" with feminism's core emphases on every human being's right to dignity, well-being, opportunity, and full participation in society, regardless of gender. Still, it is common to find Mormon feminism characterized as an "oxymoron": a contradiction in terms. Some point to the patriarchal quality of the Mormon tradition, which since its founding has been led by an all-male hierarchy and administered by an all-male lay priesthood that empowers every observant male LDS Church member aged twelve and above to preside over and conduct the essential rituals of the faith. The LDS Church's twentieth- and twenty-first-century history of opposition to the women's movement, epitomized in its organized efforts to defeat the Equal Rights Amendment in the 1970s and 1980s, is also seen as evidence of Mormonism's anti-feminism. At the same time, some within the Mormon faith view feminism as essentially incompatible with the doctrines of the LDS Church, perceiving contemporary feminism to be critical of or even hostile to the role of the family in Mormon doctrine. Laurel Thatcher Ulrich observes that in this way Mormon feminists share a common experience of an identity "double bind" with feminists of color and feminists of faith from other religious traditions who "[found] themselves stigmatized within their own group when they advocated for change and dismissed by other feminists when they defended their heritage."[*] Mormon feminists often hear from both conservative Mormons and progressive non-Mormons that ours is an impossible position—that one simply cannot be *both* a Mormon and a feminist.

This polarization is not new. For almost two centuries, the situation of Mormon women has been imagined in stark and strongly polarized terms. In the nineteenth century, Mormon polygamy captured the American imagination and became the subject of national anti-polygamy crusades. Sensational anti-polygamy literature depicted Mormon women as voiceless, submissive dupes of an exploitative and radical religious sect. In truth, the lives of Mormon women were far more complicated. From its beginnings, the Mormon movement attracted and produced women who were leaders, thinkers, and visionaries, women who found purpose in building a new civilization—a Zion—premised on ideals of cooperation, knowledge-seeking, and personal and collective transformation. Women in Utah were the first in the territorial United States to enjoy the right to vote. Many nineteenth-century Mormon women participated in the movement for women's

---

[*] Laurel Thatcher Ulrich, "Mormon Women in the History of Second-Wave Feminism," *Dialogue: A Journal of Mormon Thought* 43.2 (2010): 56.

suffrage and were welcomed as colleagues and sisters by national suffrage leaders like Elizabeth Cady Stanton and Susan B. Anthony. Some even stood up to affirm polygamy as freeing women from the bonds of traditional marriage and allowing them to focus on spiritual pursuits; in the 1870s, Mormon women held "Great Indignation Meetings" to demonstrate their political will to fight anti-polygamy legislation.

After the LDS Church officially stopped authorizing new plural marriages in the 1890s and with Utah's admission to statehood, the Mormon people began a slow movement toward assimilation within mainstream American society. With this assimilation, the position of Mormon women shifted as Mormons themselves sought to shed their radical nineteenth-century image and to emphasize their common ties to mainstream American Protestant "family" values. At the same time, the LDS Church was adopting a modern bureaucratic structure that contracted traditional avenues for women's participation and emphasized women's vocational role in the home. Mormon scholars have described this as a period of "retrenchment."* By the 1970s, the image of the Mormon woman ascendant in the American imagination was that of the perfectly contented and submissive housewife. Once again, the image did not capture the complexity of Mormon women's lives. Many Mormon women worked out of necessity, and some worked by choice, pursuing careers in education, public service, medicine, and the arts. Others found themselves dreaming and hungering for realms of influence beyond the domestic sphere and found ways to voice their dissatisfaction with the contracted role of women in the LDS Church.

Mormon feminism affirms the complexity and diversity of the lives of Mormon women, even as it acknowledges historic and contemporary tensions around issues of gender in the LDS Church. Many of us share a common experience of growing up feeling affirmed by Mormon teachings about the infinite worth and divine potential of individual souls, encouraged to obtain a personal knowledge of truth through study and experience, and supported in warm and nurturing Mormon communities, before confronting in adolescence and young adulthood the pressure to conform to strictly demarcated gender roles and the limitations placed on women's participation in the institutional church. Some of us grow up knowing from experience that the bonds of Mormon community life and the principles and standards of the faith do not prevent physical, sexual, and emotional abuse, violence against women, or denial of opportunity, education, and resources, and

* See Armand L. Mauss, *The Angel and the Beehive: The Mormon Struggle with Assimilation* (Urbana: University of Illinois Press, 1994); Armand L. Mauss, "The Mormon Struggle with Assimilation and Identity: Trends and Developments Since Midcentury," *Dialogue: A Journal of Mormon Thought* 27.1 (1994): 129–49; Armand L. Mauss, "Rethinking Retrenchment: Course Corrections in the Ongoing Campaign for Respectability," *Dialogue: A Journal of Mormon Thought* 44.4 (2011): 1–42.

that Mormonism's patriarchal power structures may in fact compound abusive power dynamics and situations. Some of us, when we are still quite young, recognize inequality in the leadership and programmatic opportunities the LDS Church offers girls and boys, women and men. Many of us identify as feminists because the feminist movement's hunger for justice and positive change aligns with our own religious feelings as Mormons that the purpose of life is to work for the betterment of humankind, the creation of a Zion community of equals.

Mormon feminists also learn to live with tensions around gender issues they may experience in their family relationships and local congregations. Mormons live our faith day by day in the context of close-knit communities. Given this intimacy, unity has been a key value in contemporary Mormon communities; expressing a differing point of view or assuming a minority identity—especially one like feminism, which has been criticized by Church leaders—can yield consequences ranging from mild discomfort to open disapproval and hostility. As Algie Ballif, a wise elder voice of Mormon feminism, said in 1980, "We do have opposition. It is a difficult opposition. It is an opposition that hurts, sometimes very deeply, because you know you are not understood by those that have probably known you all your life." But she encouraged Mormon feminists to find joy and purpose in the tensions they lived: "How we need to support each other, to know that you and I and all of us are having struggles. And we don't want to give up those struggles. They are very valuable. We want to have them."[*]

Both Mormonism and feminism—as Algie Ballif's words exemplify—value struggle or work as necessary to growth. Feminism urges men and women not just to accept conventional thinking about gender and power but to live more conscientiously meaningful lives. Similarly, Mormon doctrine emphasizes the deep meaningfulness of life and stresses that the purpose of mortality is to gain experience and understanding. In this spirit, Mormon feminists are united by their disposition to think critically about gender-related ideas and conventions in Mormonism and to search out answers to unresolved doctrinal questions. For example, we ask, if "all are alike unto God," as the Book of Mormon teaches,[†] why does the LDS Church present men and women with different opportunities for service and participation based on their gender? Why is the LDS Church leadership hierarchy entirely male at every administrative level above local congregations? Is this a reflection of the will of God, of core principles of Mormon doctrine, or of the cultural and historical contexts in which Mormonism developed? How does the institutional preponderance of male leadership impact the lives of Mormon women? How does the exclusion of women from leadership, theological decision-making, and Church policy development impact the priorities and practices of the LDS Church? How

---

[*] Maxine Hanks, *Women and Authority: Re-emerging Mormon Feminism* (Salt Lake City: Signature Books, 1992), 112.

[†] See 2 Nephi 26:33.

might the Church change if women had an equal say in shaping its budgets, bureaucratic operations, curriculum, and standards, and an equal role in articulating prophetic truths? How do we explain gender inequality in Mormonism to our sons and daughters? What is the most effective way to develop fuller opportunities for Mormon women's participation? If Mormonism has from its earliest periods affirmed the reality of a Heavenly Mother, why have contemporary LDS Church leaders forbidden Mormons from praying to or worshipping Her, and why is She entirely absent from Mormon theology and liturgy? Why did traditions of women's spirituality like women's healing by laying on of hands disappear from contemporary Mormonism? Why has polygamy *not* disappeared from the scripture, theology, and marriage-related policies of the contemporary LDS Church? How have historical emphases within Mormonism on the self-sacrificing role of women impacted our lives and well-being? What dimensions of Mormon women's lives are we afraid or ashamed to talk about? Is it okay to be angry, mournful, or frustrated with a faith we care deeply about? How can we create safe spaces for disagreement, struggle, fear, anger, and complication in a culture that seems to value uniformity, obedience, and perfection? What happens to women whose lives diverge from the models of family and womanhood idealized in Mormon doctrine and culture? How are divorce, infertility, sexuality, body issues, and depression handled in Mormon communities? Conversely, what strengths can women draw from Mormon theology and tradition as they give birth, breastfeed, and raise children? Will we be welcomed in our families and communities if we articulate feminist commitments or concerns? How can we dismantle or persist despite political polarization and the stigmatization of feminism in Mormon culture? What are the differences between Mormon women—differences of race, class, nationality, sexuality—that we must acknowledge, appreciate, or address if we are to become a Zion people? How have racial and class privilege distorted the spirituality and piety of white Mormon women, and how have racial and economic oppression impacted the lives of Mormon women of color?

Mormon feminism is the name for the community where we can explore these questions openly and together. Each Mormon feminist finds herself coming into these questions at a different moment in her life. This can be a disorienting experience, especially given the deep confidence many Mormons place in our faith's ability to answer most of life's challenges and questions. But Mormon feminism offers the welcome message that none of us is alone in our questions, nor are we the first to ask them. We can learn much from those who have been living, researching, and writing about these questions for the last forty years.

This book offers a collection of influential and significant writings from the contemporary Mormon feminist movement, from 1970 to the present. While the historical foundations of Mormon feminism date back at least to the generation of Mormon women who founded the *Woman's Exponent* in the 1870s, if not to the earlier generation of women who founded the LDS Relief Society in the 1840s, we have chosen to focus only on the last four decades, when Mormon women consciously elected to use the term "feminist" to characterize their perspectives on their faith and organize together for change. While many others have written about Mormon women's issues with care and insight, we have opted to focus on writings by Mormon women so as to allow readers to understand Mormon women's experiences in our own words. We have selected writings that have played a historic role in developing Mormon feminist history and theology or that have articulated key issues, tensions, and dimensions of Mormon women's lives. Most appear here in condensed or excerpted form with information that can guide readers to their fuller original versions, many of which are available online. This is the first anthology of Mormon feminist writing published since Maxine Hanks's landmark *Women and Authority: Re-emerging Mormon Feminism* (1992), a book that crystallized a new surge of feminist energy in the early 1990s and educated a generation of feminists that followed. A few of the most crucial essays from that book are republished here. Whereas *Women and Authority* was organized topically and was designed for a primarily Mormon audience, we have organized this anthology chronologically and have prepared it for a broad audience of non-Mormons and Mormons, scholars and laypeople. We hope that by presenting works chronologically we can trace the historical development of Mormon feminist viewpoints, deepen conversations within Mormonism about the gains and setbacks of the last forty years, and foster conversations and comparisons with people of faith and scholars in other traditions.

Mormon feminists have been coming together to address questions about our faith since the late 1960s and early 1970s, just as the women's movement was making impact in communities across America. During these years, many women organized "consciousness-raising groups"—discussion circles held in homes, colleges and universities, community centers, synagogues, or churches—where they could speak honestly and openly about their lives and identify common points of experience for reflection and analysis. Often drawing from strands of progressive thought endemic to their belief systems, religious women applied explicitly feminist frames of analysis to their own traditions and cultures. Inspired by the legacy of Catholic social justice reformers like Dorothy Day and the progressive spirit of the Second Vatican Council (1962–1965), Catholic feminists in 1969 staged the "Easter Bonnet Rebellion" protest against policies requiring women to cover their heads in church. In 1970, Catholic feminist Elizabeth Farians organized a joint meeting between the National Council of Catholic Bishops and the Joint Committee of Organizations Concerned with the Status of Women in the Church, a coalition of Catholic feminist groups that demanded that leaders condemn sexism and end gender discrimination within the church. Progressive Jewish religious leaders like Mordecai Kaplan had been advocating greater equality for women in Jewish religious practice since the late nineteenth and early twentieth centuries, and many Jewish-identified women like Betty Friedan and Alix Shulman had been leaders in the mainstream feminist movement. But it was in the early 1970s that religious Jewish feminism found a voice through writers who criticized gender inequalities in Jewish religious law, like Trude Weiss-Rosmarin, in her 1970 essay "The Unfreedom of Jewish Women" in the *Jewish Spectator*, and Rachel Adler, in her 1971 essay "The Jew Who Wasn't There: Halacha and the Jewish Woman."

At the same historic moment, in June 1970 in Newton, Massachusetts, a group of Mormon women met in the home of Laurel Thatcher Ulrich to convene their own weekday morning consciousness-raising group. "I had encountered 'the problem with no name' long before Betty Friedan described it,"* Ulrich remembers. "I was ambivalent about solutions. By 1970, I had begun to make small adjustments in my own life, but I still believed that my deepest conflicts were personal rather than general. If I were a better person, I reasoned, a more Christ-like and less-neurotic person, I would not find it so difficult to 'live for others.' "† Together, women like Ulrich, Judith Rasmussen Dushku, and Claudia Bushman discussed the religious and cultural pressures they bore, as well as issues like birth control and the role of women in church leadership and administration. In 1971, the group produced a special women's issue of *Dialogue: A Journal of Mormon Thought* featuring essays on Mormon women's history and contemporary lives. Next, they developed a Mormon women's history class for the local LDS Church Institute of Religion. Their research led them to discover lost worlds of nineteenth-century Mormon women's experience and achievement, including histories of Mormon women's activism as suffragettes, social reformers, artists, and institution builders that had disappeared from contemporary Mormon consciousness. During these same years, thousands of miles away, a group of women researchers, including Jill Mulvay Derr, Linda King Newell, Carol Cornwall Madsen, Lavina Fielding Anderson, and others hired by LDS Church historian Leonard Arrington to work in the Church Historical Department, were discussing similar personal and historical discoveries over weekly lunch meetings in downtown Salt Lake City. Derr and Newell, while working in the LDS Church Historical Department, hand copied minutes from the original 1842 meetings of the women's Relief Society that offered revolutionary insights into the expansive potential of Mormon theology on gender, including evidence that Joseph Smith himself had promised to make of Mormon women a "kingdom of priests."‡ Copies of these minutes circulated and were read aloud in gatherings of Mormon feminists across the country. Susan

---

* In *The Feminist Mystique* (1963), Betty Friedan characterized the discontent and existential unease of women in mid-twentieth-century America as "the problem with no name."

† See Ulrich, "The Pink *Dialogue* and Beyond," anthologized in this volume.

‡ Joseph Smith, *The Beginning of Better Days: Divine Instruction to Women from the Prophet Joseph Smith*, intro. Sheri Dew and Virginia Pearce (Salt Lake City: Deseret Book, 2013), 100.

Kohler's discovery in Harvard's Widener Library of the *Woman's Exponent*, a progressive newspaper produced by and for Mormon women in the late nineteenth and early twentieth centuries, also stunned Mormon feminists in the 1970s with their trenchant, unapologetic declarations of support for women's rights. Laurel Ulrich remembered, "These women were saying things in the 1870s that we had only begun to think."* Just as Jewish feminists were undertaking efforts to recover lost histories of women's significance to the Jewish tradition, just as Catholic feminists were organizing conferences on ordination, Mormon women, too, were organizing themselves and taking a fresh look at their shared history. "Mormon women," Ulrich writes, "weren't passive recipients of the new feminism. We helped to create it."† Our anthology's Part I includes foundational essays from this first decade of Mormon feminism.

These efforts came at a moment when the religious authority and culturally approved roles of Mormon women had significantly contracted. An LDS Church initiative known as "Priesthood Correlation," first launched in 1908, had over the course of the twentieth century brought all Church operations under the bureaucratic management of exclusively male priesthood offices.‡ The women's Relief Society, which was founded in 1842 as an autonomous body with powers parallel to those of the LDS Church's male priesthood quorums, had by 1971 surrendered its organizational and financial independence and even terminated publication of its own magazine. The limiting effects of correlation were compounded by the gendered side effects of Mormonism's efforts to assimilate within the American mainstream. Viewed with suspicion as religious radicals and deviants in the nineteenth and early twentieth centuries, LDS people in the 1930s to 1950s sought to redefine themselves as exemplars of conservative middle-class American "family" values, placing extra stress on women's roles as mothers, wives, and homemakers. Within the faith, these were also years of theological retrenchment, which brought renewed fundamentalism, literalism, conservatism, and, for women, a new emphasis in over-the-pulpit messaging on their domestic role. One study of articles written about women in LDS Church magazines finds that during the late nineteenth and early twentieth centuries *all* of the articles in the Church's youth magazine the *Era* "advocate[d] nontraditional, or extra-domestic, activities for women"—a reflection of the hands-on

---

* See Ulrich, "The Pink *Dialogue* and Beyond," anthologized in this volume.

† Ulrich, "Second Wave," 45.

‡ On correlation, see Thomas Alexander, *Mormonism in Transition: A History of the Latter-day Saints, 1890–1930* (Urbana: University of Illinois Press, 1986), 93–124; Marie Cornwall, "The Institutional Role of Mormon Women," *Contemporary Mormonism: Social Science Perspectives* (1994): 239–64; Jill Mulvay Derr and C. Brooklyn Derr, "Outside the Mormon Hierarchy: Alternative Aspects of Institutional Power," *Dialogue: A Journal of Mormon Thought* 15.4 (1982): 21–43; and Jennifer Huss Basquiat, "Reproducing Patriarchy and Erasing Feminism: The Selective Construction of History within the Mormon Community," *Journal of Feminist Studies in Religion* (2001): 5–37.

roles that Mormon women played in the economic lives of Utah communities as well as in national politics, social reform, the building of institutions like hospitals and schools, and LDS Church life. But this shifted dramatically over the course of the twentieth century. In the 1910s, about 66 percent of the articles appearing in youth magazines continued to advocate nontraditional women's roles, while about 33 percent emphasized motherhood and domesticity. By the 1970s, the dynamic was entirely reversed: 73.7 percent of the articles in LDS youth magazines defined women in relationship to domestic roles.[*] The expansive spiritual boldness and activist disposition of Mormonism's nineteenth- and early twentieth-century women had all but disappeared from memory, as had traditional woman-centered Mormon religious practices like women's healings and washings and anointings before childbirth, which declined after modest discouragement from LDS Church leaders.[†]

The contrast between Mormon women's activist history and the constriction of roles for women in contemporary Mormon church policy and culture was thrown into high relief by the LDS Church's opposition to the Equal Rights Amendment (ERA) and other feminist initiatives in the late 1970s. Many Mormons had initially supported the ERA, which proposed to amend the US Constitution to include the pledge that "equality of rights under the law shall not be denied or abridged by the United States or any state on account of sex." In fact, the ERA had already been ratified by the state of Idaho, home to a large Mormon population, and was poised for ratification in Utah when, in early 1975, LDS Church leaders declared in a *Church News* editorial their concerns that the amendment would undermine traditional gender roles for men and women, roles that, according to Church leaders, reflected the will of God. Mormon feminists watched with concern as LDS congregations in Utah, Hawaii, and Washington were mobilized in 1977 to disrupt conventions held in honor of International Women's Year, as described by Dixie Snow Huefner in her essay in this volume. From 1978 to 1980, the LDS Church used print media and over-the-pulpit messaging to organize Church members nationwide to donate money, write letters, and distribute literature in opposition to ERA ratification. The Church's anti-ERA mobilization was deeply distressing to Mormon feminists. Some organized counter-efforts to document the scale of the Church's political involvement and offer an alternative LDS perspective on women's rights. Mormons for ERA (MERA), founded by Maida Rust Withers, Teddie Wood, Hazel Rigby, and Sonia Johnson in Virginia in 1978, grew into a national organization, and Johnson (see her speeches anthologized in this volume) rose to national visibility as its president and lead spokesperson.

---

[*] Laura Vance, "Evolution of Ideals for Women in Mormon Periodicals, 1897–1999," *Sociology of Religion* 63.1 (2002): 57.

[†] See Linda King Newell, "A Gift Given, a Gift Taken," anthologized in this volume.

Her plainspoken, hard-hitting, and often provocative criticisms of LDS Church opposition to the ERA led to her excommunication in 1979.*

These difficult years deepened political polarization and gender role retrenchment within Mormon communities and attached a lasting stigma to Mormon feminism. Lawrence Foster, a non-Mormon scholar of Mormon life, wrote in 1979, "The activities and range of personal options for women in the Mormon church may never have been so narrowly circumscribed as in the present."† Elder voices in the Mormon feminist movement expressed concern. Esther Eggertson Peterson, a Utah-born Mormon who rose to national prominence as a labor, consumer, and women's rights advocate and served in the administrations of Presidents Kennedy, Johnson, and Carter, observed wistfully the narrowing of Mormon perspective: "When I was at BYU, our thinking was so broad and so big; our faith could encompass these things. Now you hear, 'Don't read it; don't think about it. Accept what we tell you.' That I can't stand—the narrowing. It's the broadness that we need and I think our religion is—my interpretation is—that it is broad and big."‡ Peterson's sisters Algie Eggertson Ballif and Thelma Eggertson Weight were among the founders of the Alice Louise Reynolds Forum, an association of older Mormon feminists in Provo, Utah, who expressed dismay about anti-feminism within the Church in a March 1979 letter to LDS Church president Spencer W. Kimball:

> Dear President Kimball:
>
> We speak for a sizeable minority of LDS women whose pain is so acute that they must try to be heard. Does the First Presidency really know of our plight? We cannot believe that anyone deliberately seeks to destroy us; nevertheless that is the signal we are receiving. We feel that we are the victims of a deliberate and punishing ultra-conservative squeeze to force us out of fellowship. In a classic example of guilt by association, Mormon feminists are being linked to the destruction of the family, homosexual marriages, and abortion. We are accused of rejecting family responsibility and of abandoning moral values. Women who work are publicly labeled as selfish and worldly. Suddenly many devoted Mormon women are being treated like apostates. . . . We

* See Martha Sonntag Bradley, *Pedestals and Podiums: Utah Women, Religious Authority, and Equal Rights* (Salt Lake City: Signature Books, 2005); Sonia Johnson, *From Housewife to Heretic* (New York: Doubleday, 1981); Neil J. Young, " 'The ERA Is a Moral Issue': The Mormon Church, LDS Women, and the Defeat of the Equal Rights Amendment," *American Quarterly* 59.3 (2007): 623–44; D. Michael Quinn, "The LDS Church's Campaign Against the Equal Rights Amendment," *Journal of Mormon History* 20.2 (1994): 85–155.

† Lawrence Foster, "From Frontier Activism to Neo-Victorian Domesticity: Mormon Women in the Nineteenth and Twentieth Centuries," *Journal of Mormon History* 6 (1979): 4.

‡ Hanks, *Women and Authority*, 91–92.

desperately need to know whether, after serious consideration, soul-searching, and prayer, you indeed and in fact find us unworthy, a minority open to attack, and ultimately expendable. If not *can the word get out* that Mormon feminists are not to be subjected to intimidations, rejection for Church assignments, loss of employment, and psychological excommunication. Every difference of opinion or sincere question should not be answered with a threatening indictment of one's testimony. We are women who love the Lord, the Gospel, and the Church; we have served, tithed, and raised righteous children in Zion. We plead for the opportunity to continue to do so in an atmosphere of respect and justice. For decades we have been part of the solution, whatever the need has been; we are saddened to be now considered part of the problem.[*]

In the 1980s, a decade represented by this anthology's Part II: "Lived Contradictions," Mormon feminists endeavored to create spaces where they could take shelter from the intense judgment they sometimes encountered in their home congregations, develop supportive networks, and deepen their ongoing conversations about gender in the LDS Church. The first Mormon feminist retreats were convened in 1982 at Provo Canyon, Utah, and Nauvoo, Illinois, a historic Mormon community and site of the founding of the LDS Relief Society. Invitation-only women-only retreats allowed women to share their experiences and undertake study and discussion in spaces protected from anti-feminism. Independent publications like *Sunstone* magazine and *Dialogue: A Journal of Mormon Thought* also served as important venues for Mormon feminist thought and writing. Peggy Fletcher (Stack) became the first woman editor of *Sunstone* in 1980. Mary Lythgoe Bradford, who in 1978 became the first woman editor of *Dialogue: A Journal of Mormon Thought*, championed the personal essay as a space where Mormon women could explore complicated truths about their lives. Having such spaces felt even more crucial given persistent over-the-pulpit rhetoric—including LDS Church president Ezra Taft Benson's high-profile 1987 address "To the Mothers in Zion"—that presented stay-at-home motherhood as a religious obligation for Mormon women. Personal essays by Carol Lynn Pearson, Elouise Bell, Cherie Taylor Pedersen, and Reva Beth Russell (anthologized in this volume) pushed back at the perfectionist pressures that the exaltation of stay-at-home motherhood placed on Mormon women, critically examined the costs of the self-sacrificing Mormon female ideal, and satirized the lopsided gender participation that characterized Sunday church meetings. *Dialogue* and *Sunstone* also featured historical and theological studies by Mormon feminists like Nadine

---

[*] Amy L. Bentley, "Comforting the Motherless Children: The Alice Louise Reynolds Women's Forum," *Dialogue: A Journal of Mormon Thought* 23.3 (1990): 50.

Hansen, Linda King Newell, and Carol Cornwall Madsen (anthologized in this volume) that investigated shifting patterns of women's leadership and authority in the LDS Church, as well as evidences of women's connection to priesthood in the Judeo-Christian tradition in general and Mormonism specifically. In 1984, speaking at a symposium hosted by *Sunstone* magazine, Margaret Toscano broke new theological ground in her essay "The Missing Rib: The Forgotten Place of Queens and Priestesses in the Establishment of Zion" (anthologized in this volume) by making the claim, based in historical church documents, that Joseph Smith had envisioned women's participation in Mormon temple rites as a form of priesthood ordination. The publication of Maureen Ursenbach Beecher and Lavina Fielding Anderson's *Sisters in Spirit: Mormon Women in Historical and Cultural Perspective* (1987), the first university-press published book of essays written by Mormon women about Mormon women's history, offered important feminist perspective and scholarly validation of our shared experience.[*]

Nourished by this body of writing and scholarship and energized by the surge of mainstream feminism's "third wave," Mormon feminism rebuilt momentum and critical mass as it entered the 1990s, a decade represented in Part III, "Defining Moments." Scholars like Margaret Toscano, Janice Allred, and Maxine Hanks produced important new explorations of feminist theology, epitomized in the publication of Hanks's *Women and Authority: Re-emerging Mormon Feminism* (1992), a book that would shape the consciousness of Mormon feminist generations to come.[†] In addition to groundbreaking essays on Heavenly Mother and women and priesthood (including D. Michael Quinn's "Mormon Women Have Held the Priesthood since 1843"), Hanks's anthology included the voices of hundreds of historic Mormon women, from excerpts from the *Woman's Exponent* in the 1870s to clippings from newsletters and letters to the editor documenting the 1980s fight over the Equal Rights Amendment. Hanks developed an essential resource that helped frame contemporary Mormon feminism and educate a rising generation of Mormon feminists. New feminist organizations, such as the Salt Lake City–based Mormon Women's Forum and VOICE: The Committee to Promote the Status of Women at Brigham Young University, were founded in 1988. The Mormon Women's Forum sponsored regular meetings, symposia, and a newsletter that addressed theological and social issues, provided forums for important Mormon feminist thinkers and writers like Linda Sillitoe, Carol Lynn Pearson, Lynn Matthews Anderson, and many others, and connected feminist-identified Mormon women across the country. VOICE brought a new level of feminist organization, visibility, and activism on women's issues to the

---

[*] Maureen Ursenbach Beecher and Lavina Fielding Anderson, eds., *Sisters in Spirit: Mormon Women in Historical and Cultural Perspective* (Urbana: University of Illinois Press, 1987).

[†] Maxine Hanks, ed., *Women and Authority: Re-emerging Mormon Feminism* (Salt Lake City: Signature Books, 1992).

Brigham Young University campus, hosting speakers like Margaret Toscano, convening campus speakouts on sexual violence, and organizing Take Back the Night marches that filled the quiet streets of downtown Provo. Newly hired, openly feminist faculty members like Cecilia Konchar Farr, Tomi-Ann Roberts, Martha Sontag Bradley, Susan Howe, and Gail Houston and a newly energized BYU Women's Research Institute, which introduced a women's studies minor on campus in 1991, also raised the profile of Mormon feminism. Significant works of Mormon women's literature published during these years included Carol Lynn Pearson's one-woman play *Mother Wove the Morning* (which debuted in 1989 and was published in 1992), exploring the reality of the divine feminine through the perspectives of women across history and civilizations, and Terry Tempest Williams's *Refuge: An Unnatural History of Family and Place* (1991), an ecofeminist exploration of loss, conscience, and grief.[*] Williams describes the impacts of environmental destruction on the landscapes of Utah and the bodies of women, including her own mother, who died in 1983 from breast cancer linked to exposure to fallout from nuclear testing—one of thousands of so-called "downwinders" in southern Utah. Reflecting on how their obedience to authority increased the vulnerability of southern Utah's Mormons to government abuses, Williams wrote, "As a Mormon woman of the fifth generation of Latter-day Saints, I must question everything, even if it means losing my faith, even if it means becoming a member of a border tribe among my own people. Tolerating blind obedience in the name of patriotism or religion ultimately takes our lives."[†] Her words reflected a renewed willingness in the 1990s among Mormon feminists to act and speak boldly and to join their commitments with broader currents and initiatives in the mainstream feminist movement.

The decade also brought new visibility to Mormon women of color with the appointment in 1990 of Chieko Okazaki as a member of the LDS Church's general Relief Society Presidency under President Elaine Jack. Okazaki, a professional educator who grew up as the daughter of Japanese-American farmworkers in Hawaii, knew the impacts of racism both inside and outside the LDS Church. She spoke out gracefully, unapologetically, and memorably on the importance of recognizing diverse ways of being Mormon—a crucial message at a time when the LDS Church had grown to a global membership above 7 million but remained in its core institutions deeply imbricated in the white middle-class culture of its western North American center. She was also beloved for using her position of authority to hear and bear witness to the experiences of Mormon women who had struggled with or had overcome hardships including sexual abuse, modeling

---

[*] Carol Lynn Pearson, *Mother Wove the Morning* (Walnut Creek: Pearson Press, 1992); Terry Tempest Williams, *Refuge: An Unnatural History of Family and Place* (New York: Random House, 1991).

[†] Williams, *Refuge*, 286.

an openness to hearing and speaking hard truths so important to Mormon feminism.* Staci Ford describes Okazaki's impact:

> Okazaki assumed multiple burdens of representation modeling how a woman of Japanese American ancestry could repeatedly confront racism and sexism in the post-World War II US (including in the LDS Church) and shatter stereotypes. . . . She graciously but firmly rebuked the ignorance, anxiety, smugness, and shame surrounding sensitive topics ranging from depression and abuse to racism and gender inequality. She gracefully bore a particular burden of representation over several decades, often very publicly. †

White Mormon feminists, too, were making some conscious efforts toward improving their understanding of the intersections of race and gender, even as they processed the embarrassment of the LDS Church's historic racial segregation of priesthood and temple worship, which had ended only in 1978. BYU professor Cecilia Konchar Farr in her essay "Dancing Through the Doctrine" (1995) gently criticized the homogeneity and insularity of white Mormon feminism. But it would be at least another decade before white Mormon feminists would begin to seriously examine the intersections of racial privilege, sexuality, class, and gender, to re-examine the priorities of the Mormon feminist movement, and to actively seek to learn from the perspectives of Mormon women of color.

A new critical mass of Mormon feminism in the 1990s met with reaction from LDS Church officials. In 1991, wary of increased discussion of the doctrinal reality of the divine feminine, LDS Church Apostle Gordon B. Hinckley cautioned Mormon leaders that praying to Heavenly Mother was a sign of nascent "apostasy."‡ Feminist faculty at Brigham Young University in the early 1990s faced mounting opposition from conservatives on campus and off, who were emboldened by a national anti-feminist backlash that positioned feminists as enemies in a "culture war" threatening the pillars of American civilization.§ LDS Church Apostle Boyd K. Packer, speaking in May 1993 to a gathering of Church leaders, identified Mormon feminists, intellectuals, and gays and lesbians as "dangers"

---

* See Gregory A. Prince, "'There Is Always a Struggle': An Interview with Chieko N. Okazaki," *Dialogue: A Journal of Mormon Thought* 45.1 (2012): 112–40.

† Staci Ford, "Crossing the Planes: Gathering, Grafting, and Second Sight in the Hong Kong China International District," paper delivered at Mormonism & Asia conference, Graduate Theological Union, Berkeley, California (March 22, 2014), 17.

‡ Gordon B. Hinckley, "Cornerstones of Responsibility," Regional Representatives Seminar, Salt Lake City, Utah (April 1991), 3–4.

§ See Bryan Waterman and Brian Kagel, *The Lord's University: Freedom and Authority at BYU* (Salt Lake City: Signature Books, 1998); for the broader national context, see Susan Faludi, *Backlash: The Undeclared War Against American Women* (New York: Vintage, 1991).

to the faith.* Professor Cecilia Konchar Farr was fired from Brigham Young University in June 1993 over her feminist activism. Lavina Fielding Anderson, who had criticized the LDS Church's surveillance of unorthodox, feminist, and intellectual members, was excommunicated in September 1993, as were feminist scholars Maxine Hanks, feminist activist Lynn Kanavel Whitesides, and feminist-allied scholars D. Michael Quinn and Paul Toscano. Janice Allred was heavily monitored by LDS Church leaders as she wrote theology about Heavenly Mother and was excommunicated in 1995 after she elected to publish that theology in *Dialogue: A Journal of Mormon Thought*. Her sister Margaret Toscano was also closely monitored and was excommunicated in 2000. For its part, the LDS Church responded to new theological pressures around conventional notions of gender and laid a foundation for its coming involvement in the legal fight against same-sex marriage with its release of "The Family: A Proclamation to the World" in September 1995. The Proclamation, composed without input from Mormonism's highest-ranking women leaders—the general Relief Society Presidency†—declared that "gender is an essential characteristic of individual premortal, mortal, and eternal identity and purpose." Men and women, it continued, have different divinely appointed responsibilities predicated on biological sex: "Fathers are to preside over their families in love and righteousness and are responsible to provide the necessities of life and protection for their families. Mothers are primarily responsible for the nurture of their children. In these sacred responsibilities, fathers and mothers are obligated to help one another as equal partners." Although not canonized as scripture or presented as revelation, the Proclamation gave new theological legitimacy to folk doctrinal arguments paralleling priesthood for men and motherhood for women that had emerged in Mormon discourse in the 1950s to rationalize women's diminished role in LDS institutional life and leadership. It also crystallized a powerful contradiction in Mormon thought and life—the assertion that men could both "preside" over women and be their "equal partners."

By the end of the 1990s, firings, excommunications, and theological retrenchment caused many Mormon feminists to reconsider or discontinue their participation in LDS Church life and exerted a powerful chilling effect on Mormon feminist activism, research, and writing. Fearing institutional reprisals that could threaten their Church membership, marriages, and family life, and, for some, their employment and livelihood, many women scaled back their feminist activism or took their commitments underground. Younger Mormon women turned away from the prospect of developing careers in feminist scholarship or from Mormonism altogether. Key feminist institutions like the Mormon Women's Forum lost energy

---

* Boyd K. Packer, "Talk to the All-Church Coordinating Council," May 18, 1993; typescript in possession of author.

† Prince, "There Is Always a Struggle," 136.

and focus as women retreated to safer, more private spaces like Internet discussion groups to process their feelings of fear, loss, and anger. Even as seasoned a Mormon feminist as Claudia Bushman wondered in a 2003 interview with journalist Peggy Fletcher Stack whether the movement would survive into a new generation.[*]

But the situation was not as bleak as it seemed. Claudia Bushman, Carol Cornwall Madsen, and Cherry Silver launched women's history summer seminars at Brigham Young University that sustained the crucial and long-standing Mormon feminist project of writing Mormon women's history and nourished the careers of younger Mormon women scholars. And no one could yet envision the incredible impact that the Internet would have on the Mormon feminist movement. In 2004, an Idaho Mormon stay-at-home mother named Lisa Butterworth found herself seeking refuge from the polarized election-year rhetoric at church in the online world of the Mormon "bloggernacle," a constellation of Mormon-authored blogs named after the historic Mormon Tabernacle at Temple Square in downtown Salt Lake City. Inspired by the quality of civil conversation she found there but hungry for content that spoke specifically to women, Butterworth launched the *Feminist Mormon Housewives* (FMH) blog. FMH attracted a dedicated community of contributors and commentators who felt freed by the anonymity the Internet afforded to express and explore their questions and concerns about gender dynamics in Mormonism without fear of reprisal. Mormon women who felt isolated in their families and congregations found a sense of community on FMH and blogs like *Zelophehad's Daughters* and the online edition of the historic feminist publication the *Exponent*, founded in 2005 and 2006. The blogs brought Mormon feminism roaring back to life, offering writers immediate access to thousands of readers, and offering a newly accessible stream of content and a global community to a new generation of Mormon women raising questions about gender and equality. This resurgence is represented in Part IV of this anthology. In 2007, despite personal fears of reprisals, a group of veteran Mormon feminists posted an online petition challenging Church leaders' statements that defined the value of women in terms linked only to motherhood and homemaking. Younger Mormon feminists also pushed through fear to found new activist organizations like LDS Women Advocating Voice and Equality, launched in 2010, and social-media backed initiatives like Wear Pants to Church Day (2012) and Ordain Women (2013) that made national media headlines and generated intense discussion about women's roles within the LDS Church.[†] Forty years after the beginnings of the first Mormon feminist consciousness-raising groups, thirty years after the profound discouragements

[*] Peggy Fletcher Stack, "Where Have All the Mormon Feminists Gone?" *Salt Lake Tribune* (October 4, 2003).

[†] On the impact of the Internet on Mormon Feminism, see Jessica Finnegan and Nancy Ross, " 'I'm a Mormon Feminist": How Social Media Revitalized and Enlarged a Movement," *Interdisciplinary Journal of Research on Religion* 9.12 (2013).

of the Equal Rights Amendment era, twenty years after the excommunications and firings of leading Mormon feminists, ten years after the movement had been declared all but dead by its own founders, Mormon feminism in the 2010s attained an unprecedented level of visibility, activity, and impact. Just as they had in the 1970s and 1990s, the most public and vocal Mormon feminist leaders once again found themselves facing discipline from the LDS Church and regarded as enemies by more conservative LDS Church members. The June 2014 excommunication of Kate Kelly, one of the leaders of the Ordain Women movement, was deeply felt among Mormon feminists. But it has done virtually nothing to deter or dampen the Mormon feminist movement, nor has it lessened the impact of the women's ordination movement and other Mormon feminist activism in pushing forward conversations about gender equality among leaders and laity alike.

We hope that this book will support conversations about gender and equality among the Mormon people and will deepen our collective understanding of our faith tradition. Most Mormons are not aware of the vital historical and theological work done by earlier generations of Mormon feminists, work that offers transformative perspectives on the Mormon past, present, and future. Many Mormon feminists have not had access to LDS Church-owned venues for sharing our work, often due to conservative retrenchment and suspicion of feminist viewpoints. Since the 1970s, Mormon feminists have self-published our own books or have relied on small independent Mormon publications and publishers or, more recently, blogs and podcasts; we have convened to talk Mormon feminist theology and theory not at academic conferences but at community-based symposia, retreats, and family camps. This independence has given Mormon feminism a distinctly vernacular and accessible character. But institutional support is needed to collect, preserve, foster the continuity, and ensure the longevity of Mormon feminist thought. We hope this book, by collecting and preserving the work of earlier Mormon feminist generations, will serve each new wave of young Mormon men and women who ask questions about faith, power, and gender.

We also hope this book will foster better understanding of Mormon women's issues among non-Mormon readers and scholars. Early feminist scholarship on gender and Mormonism tended to overstate the voicelessness of Mormon women or catastrophize Mormon feminist experience in a way that rendered us unrecognizable to ourselves. In 1978, historian Marilyn Warenski published *Patriarchs and Politics: The Plight of the Mormon Woman*, a book that argued that Mormonism as a patriarchal religion was essentially incompatible with feminism and that Mormon women who participated in the women's movement did so as patriarchy's "pawns." *Patriarchs and Politics* drew criticism from Laurel Thatcher Ulrich for its "polemic[ism]" and its neglect of historical sources,* and

---

* Laurel Thatcher Ulrich, "Out of the Slot: Review of Marilyn Warenski's *Patriarchs and Politics*," *Dialogue: A Journal of Mormon Thought* 12.2 (1979): 127.

it motivated LDS historians Maureen Ursenbach Beecher and Lavina Fielding Anderson to assemble the groundbreaking *Sisters in Spirit: Mormon Women in Historical and Cultural Perspective* (1987) so as to present a richer picture of Mormon women's agency and motivation. Writing in 1995, Cecilia Konchar Farr called on mainstream feminist activists and scholars to consider critically their own secularist assumptions and to acknowledge the rich experiences and feminist legacies of women of faith including Mormon feminists (see her essay "Dancing Through the Doctrine" anthologized in this volume). Like feminist scholars from communities of color, colonized and indigenous communities, and communities of faith like evangelical Christianity and Islam, we hope that our efforts will enrich feminism by expanding its frames of analysis and action.

We also hope this volume will contribute to the growing field of Mormon Studies. Mormon Studies programs at secular universities like Claremont Graduate University, Utah Valley University, and the University of Virginia have created new spaces of possibility for feminist research, like the Claremont Mormon Women's Oral History project and the Mormon Women's History Initiative. New scholarship by Mormon feminists emphasizes the complexity and diversity of Mormon women's lives and the agency of Mormon women as interpreters and shapers of their religious worlds. Amy Hoyt asserted in a groundbreaking 2007 article in *Feminist Theology*: "Beyond the paradigm of victim/empowerment, . . . LDS women may be understood as subjects who are actually engaged in intricate, highly gendered theological worldviews" (90).[*] Historians Andrea Radke-Moss, Kate Holbrook, Lisa Olsen Tait, Kristine Wright, Kathryn Daynes, Merina Smith, Christine Talbot, and Lindsay Hansen Park have researched and written about our shared past in ways that illuminate Mormon women's complex lives and motivations, even under challenging circumstances like polygamy.[†] Psychologist Jennifer Finlayson Fife has shed light

---

[*] Amy Hoyt, "Beyond the Victim/Empowerment Paradigm: The Gendered Cosmology of Mormon Women," *Feminist Theology* 16.1 (2007): 89–100.

[†] See Andrea G. Radke-Moss, *Bright Epoch: Women and Coeducation in the American West* (Lincoln: University of Nebraska Press, 2008); Lisa Olsen Tait, "The Young Woman's Journal: Gender and Generations in a Mormon Women's Magazine," *American Periodicals: A Journal of History, Criticism, and Bibliography* 22.1 (2012): 51–71; Lisa Olsen Tait, "The 1890s Mormon Culture of Letters and the Post-Manifesto Marriage Crisis: A New Approach to Home Literature," *BYU Studies Quarterly* 52.1 (2013): 98–124; Jonathan A. Stapley and Kristine Wright, "Female Ritual Healing in Mormonism," *Journal of Mormon History* 37.1 (2011): 1–85; Kathryn M. Daynes, *More Wives than One: Transformation of the Mormon Marriage System, 1840–1910* (Urbana: University of Illinois Press, 2001); Merina Smith, *Revelation, Resistance, and Mormon Polygamy: The Introduction and Implementation of the Principle, 1830–1853* (Logan: Utah State University Press, 2013); Christine Talbot, *A Foreign Kingdom: Mormons and Polygamy in American Political Culture, 1852–1890* (Urbana: University of Illinois Press, 2013); and Lindsay Hansen Park's series on polygamy at the Feminist Mormon Housewives podcast: Feministmormonhousewivespodcast. org. See also Jennifer Huss Basquiat, "Reproducing Patriarchy and Erasing Feminism: The Selective

on both the limited and the empowered dimensions of Mormon women's sexuality, psychologist Verlyne Nzojibwami has explored the psychological strategies that Mormon women adopt to deal with patriarchy in the faith, theologian Caroline Kline has addressed the contradictions of Mormonism's rhetoric on gender roles, and Nancy Ross and Jessica Duckett Finnegan have written about Mormon feminists' savvy use of social media to navigate their religious lives.*
Mormon feminist scholars and writers like Janan Graham-Russell, Elise Boxer, Moana Uluave, Gina Colvin, Grace Ka Ki Kwok, Melissa Inouye, Caroline Kline, Trine Russell Nelson, Lani Wendt Young, and Staci Ford are also introducing the viewpoints of Mormon women of color and women in the global LDS church.† Colvin, for example, works from an indigenous (Maori) womanist perspective to offer trenchant critiques of how the LDS Church's origins and administrative and cultural centering in white middle-class North America inflicts its operations worldwide with elements of racism, classism, and colonialism that run counter to the core theological principles of the Latter-day Saint movement. Grace Kwok explores how Mormon women in global contexts interact with Mormonism's conservative gender dynamics, which also privilege white middle-class North American women, experiencing a "triple marginalization" as minority women within a minority faith. Feminist research now in progress engages how Mormon women of color and LGBT Mormons create meaning and manage such tensions in their religious lives.‡

We hope this book will also help Mormon feminism reflect on its history as it strives to become a more globally conscious movement in the twenty-first century.

Construction of History Within the Mormon Community," *Journal of Feminist Studies in Religion* (2001): 5–37.

* Jennifer Finlayson-Fife, "Female Sexual Agency in Patriarchal Culture: The Case of Mormon Women," *Boston College Dissertations and Theses* (2002): AAI3043412; Verlyne Nzojibwami, *Creating Space: How Mormon Women Reconcile Their Feminist Attitudes within a Patriarchal Religion* (Ph.D. dissertation, University of Calgary, 2009); Caroline Kline, "The Mormon Conception of Women's Nature and Role: A Feminist Analysis," *Feminist Theology* 22.2 (January 2014): 186–202; Jessica Finnigan and Nancy Ross, " 'I'm a Mormon Feminist': How Social Media Revitalized and Enlarged a Movement," *Interdisciplinary Journal of Research on Religion* 9.12 (2013).

† Grace Ka Ki Kwok, *Mormon Women Identities: The Experiences of Chinese Mormon Women* (MA thesis, Department of Comparative Literature, University of Hong Kong, 2012); Melissa Inouye, "The Oak and the Banyan: The 'Glocalization' of Mormon Studies," *Mormon Studies Review* 1 (2014): 70–79; Melissa Inouye, "How Conference Comes to Hong Kong," *Patheos*, "Peculiar People," March 4, 2013, http://www.patheos.com/blogs/peculiarpeople/2013/03/how-conference-comes-to-hong-kong/; Melissa Inouye, "Culture and Agency in Asian Mormon Women's Experience in North America and the Rise of Global Mormonism," in Kate Holbrook and Matthew Bowman, eds., *Mormon Women in Historic and Contemporary Perspectives* (Salt Lake City: University of Utah Press, 2016).

‡ See, for example, Taylor G. Petrey, "Toward a Post-Heterosexual Mormon Theology," *Dialogue: A Journal of Mormon Thought* 44.4 (2011): 106–41.

It will be important to continue the foundational work of Mormon feminist theologians like Margaret Toscano so that we can address points of irresolution and potential within our own theology and join with other feminist theologians of other faiths in the larger project of analyzing what Rosemary Radford Ruether calls "God talk." It will also be important to continue to address racial inequality in our own movement and tradition, and especially for white Mormon feminists to take stock of and responsibility for the damaging effects of historic racial privileges and biases within the LDS Church, joining in solidarity with and supporting Mormon feminists of color in this effort, and aligning ourselves with the broader feminist movement's efforts to acknowledge the intersectionality of race, class, gender, and sexuality. While the first generations of Mormon feminists developed analyses of power disparities between Mormon men and women, there is additional work to be done in analyzing modes of power that have been available to Mormon women, including the use of public piety, submission, ostracization, and other forms of microaggression to establish hierarchies among Mormon women and to manage our relationship with the non-Mormon world. In this, we can learn much from religion scholars like R. Marie Griffith, who has studied submissive gender roles in evangelical Christian communities, and Saba Mahmood and Leila Ahmed, who write about the politics of piety and the veil in Islam.* We can also join broader conversations in feminism and religion by thinking carefully about Mormonism and globalization. The global growth of the LDS Church has been scaffolded on colonial and neocolonial economic power structures that disadvantage many of the world's indigenous and Southern Hemisphere peoples. What can Mormonism contribute to the economic well-being and self-determination of these communities? What can we as Mormon feminists share from our rich tradition of faith and struggle to contribute to movements seeking greater economic and educational equality for women and girls around the world? We offer the first forty years of Mormon feminist writing as a place of refuge, reflection, and preparation as we look to the work that lies ahead.

* R. Marie Griffith, *God's Daughters: Evangelical Women and the Power of Submission* (Berkeley: University of California Press, 1997); Saba Mahmood, *Politics of Piety: The Islamic Revival and the Feminist Subject* (Princeton, NJ: Princeton University Press, 2005); Leila Ahmed, *A Quiet Revolution: The Veil's Resurgence, from the Middle East to America* (New Haven, CT: Yale University Press, 2011).

Key Events in Contemporary
Mormon Feminism

1940 to Present

During the late nineteenth and early twentieth centuries, Mormon women established a solid record of participation in the women's movement. White Mormon women enjoyed the right to vote in territorial Utah, were encouraged by LDS Church leaders to seek education and participate in economic development and self-sufficiency projects, and used their political might to defend polygamy, a practice some Mormon women viewed as freeing them from the bondage of traditional marriage. Meanwhile, Mormon women of color, like the African-American pioneer Jane Manning James, contended with the compound challenges of economic survival in the American West as well as with Mormonism's racist theology, which denied African Americans participation in sacred LDS temple rites and thus access to the highest levels of heaven.

Many of the proto-feminist energies of the time were channeled through and into the Relief Society, a voluntary association of women sponsored by the LDS Church. Emmeline B. Wells, the second editor of the Woman's Exponent *(1872–1914), a newspaper for Mormon women that championed women's rights, including suffrage, became general president of the Relief Society in 1910. Her appointment coincided with the rise of correlation, an LDS Church bureaucratic initiative that aimed to streamline Church administration under the authority of male-only priesthood offices and in so doing curtailed the independence and initiative of women leaders. Wells was released from her position in 1921 at age 93: the first Relief Society president to be released rather than passing from office at the time of her death, as had been customary and has continued to be the pattern for the presidents of the LDS Church. Her deposal and death a few weeks later marked the beginnings of decades of declining institutional power for Mormon women. During these middle decades of the twentieth century, equality- and advocacy-minded Mormon women sought and found in the world outside the LDS Church a role as activists, scholars, and authors—and became important forerunners to the emergence of the contemporary Mormon feminist movement in 1970.*

These are moments in the pre-history and history of the Mormon feminist movement, including breakthrough publications by leading Mormon women writers and scholars.

1940   General Relief Society President Amy Lyman Brown seeks to re-establish the Relief Society's historic agenda of collective activism on community issues despite opposition from some LDS Church authorities; Brown delivers "Some Challenges to Women" speech at Utah State University, advocating that "women becom[e] more interested in politics and government, both local and national" and take a collective activist approach to challenges in social welfare, education, economic development, and public health.

1942   Virginia Sorenson, *A Little Lower Than the Angels*

1942   Maureen Whipple, *The Giant Joshua*

1944   Under the direction of Amy Lyman Brown, *Relief Society* magazine addresses global policy and peace issues; Esther Peterson becomes first lobbyist for National Labor Relations Board in Washington, D.C.

1945   Fawn Brodie, *No Man Knows My History*

1946   LDS Church officials formalize end to women's ritual healings, washings, and anointings for the sick and preparatory to childbirth.

1950   Juanita Brooks, *Mountain Meadows Massacre*

1954   LDS Church Apostle John Widtsoe issues revised edition of his book *Priesthood and Church Government*, in which he appears to be the first LDS Church authority to parallel priesthood for men with motherhood for women: "the man who . . . feels he is better than his wife because he holdsthePriesthood. . .hasfailedtocomprehendthemeaning. . .ofpriesthood. . .becausewomanhashergiftofequalmagnitude—motherhood. . . motherhood is an eternal part of the priesthood."

1955   Leonard Arrington publishes "The Economic Role of Pioneer Mormon Women," *Western Humanities Review* 9 (Spring 1955): 145–64.

1957   Esther Peterson becomes first woman lobbyist for the American Federation of Labor-Congress of Industrial Organizations (AFL-CIO).

1961   President John F. Kennedy appoints Esther Peterson head of the Department of Labor's Women's Bureau; Peterson organizes President's Commission on the Status of Women, which produces report that sparks national debate on equal pay for equal work.

1963   LDS author Helen Andelin publishes *Fascinating Womanhood*; Esther Peterson is driving force behind passage of the federal Equal Pay Act.

1966   Laurel Thatcher Ulrich, Carolyn Peters (Person), and other Boston-area Mormon women publish *A Beginner's Boston* as a Relief Society fundraiser; *Dialogue: A Journal of Mormon Thought* is founded as independent venue for Mormon scholarship, inquiry, and theology, with Frances Menlove as only woman founder.

1967   LDS Church *Priesthood Bulletin* announces policy recommending that only Melchizedek and Aaronic priesthood holders offer prayers in sacrament meeting (July–August).

1968–   General Relief Society President Belle Spafford serves as president of
1970   National Council of Women.

1969   LDS Church First Presidency releases statement opposing birth control (April); Church Social Services Department takes over Relief Society programs for unwed mothers, youth, and Native Americans (October).

1970   LDS Church introduces policy prohibiting wives of non-endowed Church members or non-members from receiving the endowment, a key LDS temple rite; *A Beginner's Boston* cohort initiates Mormon feminist consciousness-raising group in Boston; under program of Priesthood Correlation, Relief Society loses its financial independence: assets of $2 million turned over to LDS Church, dues and fundraisers discontinued (June–July); *Utah Historical Quarterly* publishes special issue on women; *Relief Society* magazine discontinued (December).

1971   LDS Church First Presidency issues message (in print and on a vinyl record insert to the *Ensign*) that criticizes "the more radical ideas of women's liberation" (January); "Pink" issue of *Dialogue* edited and produced by Boston-area Mormon feminists.

1972   Equal Rights Amendment passes Congress and heads for state-by-state ratification—in the House, the vote among Mormon representatives is 4–1–2 in favor of ratification; in the Senate, the vote among Mormon senators is 2–1 in favor of ratification; Leonard Arrington is appointed LDS Church historian and hires Jill Mulvay Derr, Maureen Ursenbach Beecher, and Carol Cornwall Madsen; Boston Mormon feminist cohort begins research for Mormon women's history class at LDS Institute—Susan Kohler discovers complete set of the nineteenth-century *Woman's Exponent* in the stacks at Harvard's Widener Library; Young Men and Young Women Mutual Improvement Association reorganized, with Young Women's reclassified as an auxiliary to the Aaronic priesthood (November); Idaho legislature overwhelmingly ratifies the Equal Rights Amendment.

1973   Carol Lynn Pearson, *Daughters of Light*; Boston-area Mormon feminists organize first annual "Exponent Day" dinner featuring visiting Mormon women role models as speakers; Susan Sessions Rugh chairs "Women in Academics" week and lecture series at BYU, an event organized as a response to a bridal conference held on campus.

1974   *Exponent II* begins publication (July), reaching a subscriber list of 4,000 by the end of its first year; *Sunstone* begins publication; *Deseret News* poll finds that 63 percent of Utah Mormons favor ratification of ERA (November); Relief Society President Barbara Smith announces her opposition to ERA at University of Utah Institute of Religion (December).

1975   Editorial opposing the ERA appears in the *Church News*, citing different divine "roles" for men and women (January); Elouise Bell delivers BYU forum address on the "Implications of Feminism at BYU" (September).

1976   First Presidency states opposition to ERA: "We recognize men and women as equally important before the Lord, but with differences biologically, emotionally, and in other ways.... The ERA, we believe, does not recognize these differences" (October); Boston-area Mormon women self-publish *Mormon Sisters*, ed. Claudia Bushman; students organize first BYU Women's Conference, featuring openly feminist-identified Mormon women speakers.

1977   After campaigning by Elder Boyd K. Packer and General Relief Society President Barbara Smith (January), ERA is rescinded in Idaho (February); Mormons organize in Florida (March) and Virginia (April) to defeat ERA; Mormon women in Utah (June), Hawaii (July), and Washington (July) attend IWY conferences and defeat proposals; Alice Louise Reynolds Forum founded (September) by women in support of Utah IWY organizers; Claudia Bushman, under pressure from General Authorities as a stake president's wife, steps down from editorship of *Exponent II*.

1978   Sonia Johnson, Hazel Rigby, Maida Rust Wither, and Teddie Wood organize Mormons for ERA; led by Professor Reba Keele, Alice Louise Reynolds Forum begins to meet on campus at BYU; first women's meeting convened at the LDS Church's semi-annual global General Conference; documentary on Mormon women and depression by Louise Degn aired on Salt Lake City, Utah, television station KSL (February); BYU Board of Trustees creates Women's Research Institute (April); Ida Smith hired as founding director of the Women's Research Institute; priesthood and temple ban lifted for LDS Church members of African descent (June); Mary Sturlaugson Eyer becomes first African-American woman to serve a full-time LDS proselytizing mission; Sonia Johnson testifies before Senate subcommittee on compatibility of ERA and Mormon theology (August); prohibition against women praying in sacrament meeting lifted (September); Relief Society turns over wheat reserves valued at $2.5 million to General Church Welfare Committee (September); LDS Church campaigning against ERA continues, including fundraising to defeat ERA supporters running for office (October–November), printing and distribution of *Why Mormon Women Oppose ERA* brochure (October), and LDS Church-backed anti-ERA mobilization in Nevada and Virginia (November); Marilyn Warenski, *Patriarchs and Politics: The Plight of the Mormon Woman* inspires Wednesday Salt Lake City lunch group of Mormon women historians to initiate book project that would become *Sisters in Spirit*—Warenski's major argument was that all major efforts by Mormon women had been orchestrated by LDS hierarchy; Vicky Burgess-Olson publishes *Sister Saints*; Irene Bates, Lynda Taylor, and others produce *Reflections*, a documentary on Mormon women; Mary Lythgoe Bradford becomes first woman editor of *Dialogue: A Journal of Mormon Thought*.

1979   Members of Alice Louise Reynolds Forum write to LDS Church president Spencer Kimball to express grave concern over anti-feminist intimidation in LDS Church settings and to ask for his assistance in "getting the word out" that Mormon feminists are not to be excluded from full fellowship (March); Alice Louise Reynolds Forum barred from meeting in Harold B. Lee Library at BYU due to pro-feminist content of meetings (May); Virginia Mormons lobby state legislature, generating 85 percent of anti-ERA mail; Mormons in Missouri organize against ERA (October); Sonia Johnson excommunicated (December); Sunstone Symposium begins.

1980   Mormons for ERA charters airplanes to fly over SLC Temple Square during General Conference, the Hill Cumorah pageant in upstate New York, and other major Mormon events, towing banners carrying slogans like "Mother in Heaven Loves the ERA"; LDS Church publishes *The Church and the Proposed Equal Rights Amendment: A Moral Issue* (March) as an insert in *Ensign* magazine; 21 ERA supporters (two who chained themselves to gates, including Sonia Johnson) arrested after protesting Bellevue, Washington, temple open house (November); red *Dialogue*—follow-up to 1971 "Pink" issue on women's issues—published; Peggy Fletcher becomes first woman editor of *Sunstone*; Mary Sturlaugson Eyer, *A Soul So Rebellious*.

1981   Sonia Johnson, *From Housewife to Heretic*; MERA member Nadine Hansen publishes "Women and Priesthood" in *Dialogue*; Boyd K. Packer address "The Mantle Is Greater than the Intellect" critiques New Mormon history, the movement among feminist and feminist-allied historians like Leonard Arrington toward a more scholarly accounting of the Mormon past.

1982   ERA supporters picket LDS Church buildings and meetinghouses in California; Leonard Arrington removed from his post as LDS Church historian; Mary Bradford, ed., *Mormon Women Speak*; Mormon feminists convene "Pilgrims" retreat at Nauvoo, Illinois, on May 15–17—first 1842 minutes of the Relief Society "very much a topic of discussion"; Provo Canyon retreat organized.

1983   Sonia Johnson resigns as president of MERA (February); attendees of Nauvoo celebration organize first annual "Midwest Pilgrimage" retreat (June).

1984   Alice Louise Reynolds Forum renamed Algie Ballif Forum; annual BYU Women's Conference co-sponsored by LDS Church; Margaret Toscano delivers "The Missing Rib" at Sunstone Symposium, described by Laurel Thatcher Ulrich as "first public exposure of the claim to women's priesthood" based on the words of Joseph Smith and the design of the LDS temple ceremony.

1985   Linda King Newell and Valeen Tippett Avery, *Mormon Enigma*; Avery and Newell and *Mormon Enigma* "blacklisted" (June); RLDS Church elects to ordain women; BYU WRI delegated to organize BYU Women's Conference.

1986   Speaking ban on Newell and Avery lifted (April); LDS-net, first email listserv for Mormons, organized.

1987   LDS Church president Ezra Taft Benson delivers "To the Mothers in Zion" address (February); Maureen Ursenbach Beecher and Lavina Fielding Anderson, *Sisters in Spirit* published.

1988   Mormon Women's Forum established by Karen Erickson Case and Kelli Frame; BYU Committee to Promote the Status of Women founded by Kristin Rushforth and four other students—renamed "VOICE" in 1989; Mormon-L Internet listserv created and becomes site for first online LDS feminist discussions.

1989   Carol Lynn Pearson debuts *Mother Wove the Morning* in Walnut Creek, California; Margaret Toscano fired from Brigham Young University (July); Marie Cornwall named director of BYU WRI.

1990   Revisions to LDS temple ceremony change women's covenants from "obey" to "hearken" to their husbands and improve the portrayal of Eve; "Electronic Latter-day Women's Caucus, plus men" (ELWC+) organized by Lynn Matthews Anderson for the purpose of "advancing discussions about LDS feminism and women's issues"; Carol Cornwall Madsen gives first ever presidential address of Mormon History Association focused on women's history (June); Chieko Okazaki is first woman of color appointed to General Relief Society Presidency.

1991   BYU WRI sponsors first scholarly conference on Gender and the Family (February); BYU WRI establishes women's studies minor; BYU student prays to "Our Father and Mother in Heaven" at university event; Apostle Gordon B. Hinckley warns Regional Representatives to be "alert" to "small beginnings of apostasy," including prayer to Heavenly Mother (April); President Hinckley repeats remarks on prayer to Heavenly Mother at Relief Society general fireside (September); Terry Tempest Williams, *Refuge: An Unnatural History of Family and Place.*

1992   Cecilia Konchar Farr delivers pro-choice speech at NOW rally in Salt Lake City (January); first Take Back the Night demonstration at BYU (April); Carol Lynn Pearson publishes *Mother Wove the Morning*; Maxine Hanks publishes *Women and Authority: Re-emerging Mormon Feminism*;

existence of LDS Church "Strengthening the Members" committee conducting surveillance of Mormon writers, intellectuals, feminists, and progressives revealed and confirmed (August); Maureen Ursenbach Beecher, Janath Russell Cannon, and Jill Mulvey Derr publish *Women of Covenant: The Story of the Relief Society*; BYU Women's Research Institute sponsors conference on Mormon women, which is met with letters of protest from anti-feminists across the country (October); BYU Women's conference invitation to Laurel Thatcher Ulrich vetoed without comment by BYU board of trustees.

1993   Elder Packer tells All Church Coordinating Council that feminists, intellectuals, and gays and lesbians are dangers to church (May); Cecilia Konchar Farr fired from BYU (June); long-time BYU Women's Conference organizer Carol Lee Hawkins removed from her position (July); excommunication of six feminists and intellectuals known as the "September Six": D. Michael Quinn, Lavina Fielding Anderson, Maxine Hanks, Lynn Whitesides Kanavel, Paul Toscano, and Avraham Gileadi (September); White Roses demonstration organized by Mormon feminists expresses hope for reconciliation between LDS Church and progressives (October); MWF creates Counterpoint Conference (October).

1994   VOICE launches Clothesline project at BYU; first Rocky Mountain Retreat organized by Paula Goodfellow, Jerrie Hurd, and Lisa Ray Turner.

1995   Janice Allred excommunicated for writings about Heavenly Mother (May); *The Family: A Proclamation to the World* read in General RS meeting (September); LDS Church begins anti-same sex marriage (SSM) activism in Hawaii.

1996   *MWF Quarterly* discontinues publication; Professor Gail Turley Houston fired from Brigham Young University for publicly expressing her feminist beliefs (July); Clothesline Project banned at BYU (October); BYU professors Kent Harrison and Mary Stovall Richards publish "Feminism in the Light of the Gospel of Jesus Christ" in *BYU Studies*, affirming common elements of feminism and LDS belief and practice.

1998   LDS Church launches campaign to oppose SSM in Alaska.

2000   Margaret Toscano excommunicated; LDS Church backs ballot initiative to prevent SSM in California.

2003   Claudia Bushman convenes younger women historians for summer seminar "Latter-day Saint Women in the Twentieth Century" at Brigham Young University's Joseph Fielding Smith Institute, with former Relief Society General Presidency members Elaine Jack and Aileen Clyde in attendance; Peggy Fletcher Stack writes article in *Salt Lake Tribune* querying "Where Have All the Mormon Feminists Gone?" (November).

2004   Carol Cornwall Madsen and Cherry Silver convene second seminar on twentieth-century Mormon women's history at BYU Joseph Fielding Smith Institute; historian Andrea Radke-Moss addresses FAIR conference, "The

Place of Mormon Women: Perceptions, Prozac, Polygamy, Priesthood, Patriarchy, and Peace" (August); Claudia Bushman publishes papers from 2003 summer seminar as *Latter-day Saint Women in the Twentieth Century; Lisa Butterworth launches Feminist Mormon Housewives blog.*

2005 Kathryn Lynard Soper launches *Segullah,* a literary journal by and for LDS women; Caroline Kline, Jana Remy, and Deborah Farmer establish *The Exponent* blog; Carol Cornwall Madsen and Cherry Silver publish papers from 2004 seminar as *New Scholarship on Latter-day Saint Women in the Twentieth Century.*

2006 Claudia Bushman addresses FAIR Conference on "The Lives of Mormon Women" (August); *Zelophehad's Daughters* blog launched.

2007 Julie Beck, "Mothers Who Know" (October) General Conference address followed by What Women Know collective statement (November).

2008 LDS Church backs "Yes on 8" campaign in California; Mormon feminist veterans of ERA fight organize effort to document extent of LDS involvement in Yes on 8.

2009 Jessica Oberon Steed organizes first Sophia Gathering (May); Claudia Bushman launches Mormon Women's Oral History Project at Claremont Graduate University (May); BYU Women's Research Institute dissolved by university officials; Zandra Vranes and Tamu Smith launch *Sistas in Zion* blog.

2010 Neylan McBaine organizes *Mormon Women Project,* an online archive of interviews with Mormon women around the world (January); Meghan Raynes, Chelsea Shields Strayer, Susan Christiansen, Emily Clyde Curtis, Tresa Edmunds, Jenne Alderks, Stephanie Snyder, Elisabeth Calvert Smith, Kaimi Wenger, and Caroline Kline organize advocacy group LDS Women Advocating Voice and Equality (March).

2012 LDS Church announces age change for women missionaries (October); FMH temple baptisms campaign (March); FMH podcast launch; "All Are Alike Unto God" statement launched (September); first Pants to Church day (December 16).

2013 "All Enlisted," a Facebook-based group for "active LDS men and women" who wish to "engage in acts of peaceful resistance to gender inequality in the LDS church" launch Let Women Pray letter-writing campaign (January); Anya Tinajero, Jill Anderson, and Azul Uribe convene first meeting of Mormon feminists in Mexico (February); Ordain Women launches (March 17); Jean Stevens is first woman to pray in General Conference (April); first Ordain Women direct action (October); Claudia Bushman and Caroline Kline, *Mormon Women Have Their Say: Essays from the Claremont Oral History Collection.*

2014 Ofa Kaufusi becomes first woman of color to pray at LDS General Conference; second Ordain Women direct action (April);

excommunication of Ordain Women's Kate Kelly (June); Dorah Mkhabela becomes first Black woman to pray at LDS General Conference (September).

Sources

Anderson, Lavina Fielding. "The LDS Intellectual Community and Church Leadership: A Contemporary Chronology." *Dialogue: A Journal of Mormon Thought* 26.1 (1993): 7–64.

Bentley, Amy L. "Comforting the Motherless Children: The Alice Louise Reynolds Women's Forum." *Dialogue: A Journal of Mormon Thought* 23.3 (1990): 39–61.

Bradley, Martha. *Pedestals and Podiums*. Salt Lake City: Signature Books, 2005.

Bushman, Claudia L., et al. "My Short Happy Life with *Exponent II*." *Dialogue: A Journal of Mormon Thought* 36.3 (2004): 179–92.

Hall, Dave. "A Crossroads for Mormon Women: Amy Brown Lyman, J. Reuben Clark, and the Decline of Organized Women's Activism in the Relief Society." *Journal of Mormon History* 36.2 (2010): 205–49.

Hanks, Maxine, ed., *Women and Authority: Re-emerging Mormon Feminism*. Salt Lake City: Signature Books, 1992.

Remy, Jana. "Mormon Women's History Timeline." http://www1.chapman.edu/~remy/MoFem/mormonwomen.html.

Ulrich, Laurel Thatcher. "Mormon Women in the History of Second-Wave Feminism." *Dialogue: A Journal of Mormon Thought* 43.2 (2010): 45–63.

Waterman, Bryan, and Brian Kagel, *The Lord's University: Freedom and Authority at BYU*. Salt Lake City: Signature Books, 1998.

Additional Sources

Carol Lynn Pearson, Lavina Fielding Anderson, Aimee Hickman, Andrea Alexander, Anya Tinajero, Lynn Matthews Anderson, Cindy Le Fevre, Paula Goodfellow, Margaret Blair Young, Janeanne Peterson, Andrea Radke-Moss, Judy Dushku, Karen Rosenbaum, Tamu Thomas-Smith, Caroline Kline, Andrea Radke-Moss, Laurel Thatcher Ulrich, Susan Howe, Claudia Bushman, Colleen Goodsell, Margaret Moore, Mary Lythgoe Bradford.

I

Foundations

Mormon Feminism in the 1970s

"We began as a group of women talking about our lives." This is how Claudia Lauper Bushman described the circle of Boston-area Mormon women—including Laurel Thatcher Ulrich, Grethe Ballif Peterson, Carolyn Durham Peters, and Judith Rasmussen Dushku—who gathered in June 1970 for what their contemporaries in the women's liberation movement would have called a "consciousness-raising group." The women in Boston were not alone: Mormon women in Washington, D.C., Salt Lake City, and Los Angeles also found themselves in the early 1970s examining the feminist legacies and possibilities of the Mormon faith.

From its nineteenth-century beginnings, Mormonism had attracted and produced its share of intellectually curious, spiritually ambitious, and politically progressive women. With the support of a theology that offered potentially expansive ways to think about the spiritual value of gender, early Mormon women often resisted nineteenth-century cultural norms that valued submissive piety. Many instead embraced active public roles as lay leaders and healers in the early life of the Church of Jesus Christ of Latter-day Saints (the LDS Church), in the building of new homes, communities, and institutions after the migration to Utah, and in national efforts for women's suffrage. With the turn of the twentieth century, as Mormonism transitioned from a frontier sect to a mainstream American church, some of the independent energies of early Mormon women were curtailed, especially as the LDS Church brought formerly independent women's organizations under the supervision of male Church leaders.

Still, a tradition of Mormon women's leadership, education, and activism survived in social reform efforts led in the early twentieth century by women like Amy Lyman Brown, Louie B. Felt, and Louise Robinson, who under the auspices of the Church's historically woman-led Relief Society founded hospitals, social programs, and welfare services. It also survived mid-century in the intellectual and political lives of women like Juanita Brooks, who produced clear-eyed histories of controversial events in the Mormon past, Maurine Whipple, who wrote novels reflecting critically on Mormon patriarchy and polygamy, and labor and women's rights activist Esther Eggertson

Peterson. In 1956, a University of Utah master's student named Mary Lythgoe Bradford wrote her thesis on Esther's cousin Virginia Eggertson Sorensen, a celebrated and accomplished member of Mormonism's "Lost Generation" of artists and writers whose novels thoughtfully rendered conflicts between individual conscience and collective story in Mormon towns like Nauvoo and Manti in terms that found a broad American audience.

Bradford's scholarly attention to Sorensen marked the beginnings of an effort in the 1960s and 1970s to recover Mormon women's history. This Mormon feminist history movement was encouraged by the LDS Church's official historian, Leonard Arrington, and an emerging generation of Mormon feminist historians, including Bushman, Ulrich, Maureen Ursenbach Beecher, Jill Mulvay Derr, and Linda King Newell. Their research shed light on past eras when Mormon women had exercised a fuller range of spiritual, administrative, and expressive powers. Carol Lynn Pearson made a key contribution to this remembering of the lost worlds of Mormon women with her book Daughters of Light (1973). This compilation of excerpts from Mormon historical sources documented a rich nineteenth-century past during which Mormon women had prophesied and laid on hands to heal; Pearson's book reached a wide LDS audience. After Boston-area Mormon feminists volunteered to teach a class on Mormon women's history at the local LDS Institute of Religion, Susan Kohler discovered in the stacks of Harvard's Widener Library the Woman's Exponent (1872–1914), a progressive nineteenth-century newspaper produced by and for Mormon women; taking its inspiration from this historic forerunner, the Mormon feminist publication Exponent II was launched by Bushman, Ulrich, Carrell Hilton Sheldon, and others in 1974.

But even as these Mormon feminist intellectual energies crested, the LDS Church was mobilizing members nationwide to disrupt regional conventions of women's rights activists and to prevent the ratification of the Equal Rights Amendment. At the International Women's Year Conference of June 24–25, 1977, in Salt Lake City, thousands of conservative LDS women, organized by their local Mormon leaders, disrupted the convention, defeating every measure on the platform—including simple measures to protect consumer and children's rights. But LDS Church mobilization spurred Mormon feminists to organize. In Provo, Utah, in September 1977, writer Helen Candland Stark, activist Algie Eggertsen Ballif, her sister Thelma Eggertsen Weight (sisters to Esther Eggertsen Peterson), Fern Smoot Taylor, Wanda Scott, Anna Taylor, and Alice Jensen organized a lunch meeting to show support of IWY Utah convention chair Jan Tyler; from this first meeting came the foundations of the Alice Louise Reynolds Women's Forum, which would grow over the decades into a Utah Valley feminist institution. Women in and around Washington, D.C., started Mormons for ERA. By the end of the 1970s, Mormon feminists found themselves—as they often would in decades to follow—in a contradictory position between a faith whose histories and teachings they cherished and a church whose political priorities they questioned or, in the case of activists like Sonia Johnson, openly challenged.

Claudia Lauper Bushman (1934–), "Women in *Dialogue*: An Introduction" (1971)

The contemporary Mormon feminist movement dates one of its points of origination to a historic home gathering of Mormon women in Boston, Massachusetts, in June 1970. "The world was turning upside down," Claudia Bushman would later remember, "as groups demonstrated against the Vietnam War, as the civil rights movement brought exposure and new respect for black citizens, as college students turned insurgent and occupied their campuses, and as women showed surprising spunk and backbone. Our group of LDS women began to discover their history and to discuss authority, birth control, housework, and additional possibilities for their lives. Most of this group had student husbands, straitened incomes, and young children. We didn't expect to be taken seriously." But the women took themselves seriously, as did tens of thousands of other women across the United States who were encouraged by the burgeoning women's movement to organize similar consciousness-raising groups in the early 1970s. One evening, while walking with her husband, historian Richard Bushman, and Eugene England, a literature professor and editor of *Dialogue: A Journal of Mormon Thought*, Bushman proposed that the Boston Mormon feminist group produce its own issue of *Dialogue* centering on the perspectives of Mormon women. England immediately welcomed the idea. The issue appeared in the summer of 1971 with a bright pink cover, strikingly original Mormon feminist art and graphics by Carolyn Durham Peters, essays by a diverse group of Mormon women, including the historian Juanita Brooks, photographs of rural Mormon women by the Depression-era photographer Dorothea Lange, reviews of plays and books written by and about Mormon women, and an overview of Mormon women's history by LDS Church historian Leonard Arrington. On the back cover, it featured a quote from Brigham Young proclaiming the usefulness of Mormon women in spheres beyond the domestic, a powerful rejoinder to a growing emphasis within mid-twentieth-century Mormon culture linking women's essential purpose to home and family. The "Pink Issue" of *Dialogue*, as it would later be known, struck a warm, frank, and bold note to mark the beginning of a new era in Mormon women's history.

Source

Bushman, Claudia L. "Women in *Dialogue*: An Introduction." *Dialogue: A Journal of Mormon Thought* 6.2 (1971): 5–8.

References and Further Reading

Bushman, Claudia. "Should Mormon Women Speak Out? Thoughts on Our Place in the World." *Dialogue: A Journal of Mormon Thought* 41.1 (2008): 171–84.
Frederickson, Kristine Wardle. "There Is Always Something You Can Do: A Conversation with Claudia Bushman." *Mormon Historical Studies* (April 2013): 91–118.

"WOMEN IN *DIALOGUE*: AN INTRODUCTION"

In June of last year a dozen or so matrons in the Boston area gathered to discuss their lives. The Women's Liberation movement was then in full flower, making converts and causing all women to search their souls before reaffirming their traditional commitments. While to all outward appearances we had nothing to complain of, the first meeting was an impassioned exchange of frustrations, disappointments and confessions. We had expected some serious confrontations because all attending are not in complete agreement on various issues, and there were some. More notable, though, were the shared feelings and mutual support that emerged. The effect was cathartic.

The original dozen or so are women in their thirties, college-educated with some graduate degrees, mostly city-bred, the wives of professional men and the mothers of several children.[1] While this group remains, we have added another dozen or so, including several young professional wives without children and some singles. This amorphous group is officially open to anyone interested and we try never to mention it without proffering an invitation. Although we sometimes refer to ourselves as the L.D.S. cell of Women's Lib, we claim no affiliation with any of those militant bodies and some of us are so straight as to be shocked by their antics. We do read their literature with interest. Several people who have been invited to join us have declined, and rumors persist that we are involved in heretical activities. One doubter who visited admitted she saw no harm but felt the meetings were a grievous waste of time. Others who came to scoff have stayed to join in. While some members admit that they return home shattered and with headaches, others consider the meetings positively therapeutic and rely on them for mental health.

We try to speak honestly and openly, but otherwise the scene resembles a Primary preparation meeting or morning brunch with ladies chatting together while toddlers trip over their feet and infants demand attention. In truth these are the same ladies who man the Church auxiliaries and volunteer for clean-up committees. Several women are involved extensively in community and educational programs as well as in Church work. We currently have no working mothers among us, but those who are now childless definitely plan to combine work and childcare. Although it is poor form to identify wives by their husbands today, three of our group are married to bishops.

We spend no time railing at men. In general, members affirm the family as the basic unit in society and hope to work out strong partnerships with husbands to provide the best possible upbringing for their children. The programs of the Church are appreciated in working toward these goals.

The standard model for Mormon womanhood is the supportive wife, the loving mother of many, the excellent cook, the imaginative homemaker and the diligent Church worker, a woman whose life is circumscribed by these roles. This model has been so clearly presented to us in sermon and story that we feel strong responsibility to cleave to that ideal and guilt when we depart. And so our group, largely made up of supportive wives and loving mothers who are also excellent homemakers and Church workers, has discussed the genesis of that model, how much of it is scriptural and how much traditional, and whether other models have met with acceptance in Church history.

We looked for diversity because, in all honesty, we are not always completely satisfied with our lives as housewives. Our families are of primary importance to us, but they do not demand all our time. We benefit from outside interests and can usually manage them without skimping on the baked goods. Our educated intelligence, which we have been taught is the glory of God,* sometimes cries out for a little employment. Does it undercut the celestial dream to admit that there are occasional Japanese beetles in the roses covering our cottages?

We have also been concerned with the problems of single women and of women with strong career orientations. The Church emphasis on the standard model makes deviants defensive. Our society puts terrible pressures on single girls to marry while allowing them very little initiative in the process. Career women pursue their special interests but feel frowning disapproval from on high. Although these women may build happy and satisfactory lives, they continually need to justify their positions. Housewives may complain of their tedious treadmill, but at least they have official approval. The singles chastise them for not counting their blessings.

While doctrinally it is perfectly clear that wives should support their husbands, indeed are pledged to them as their husbands are pledged to the Lord, and that having children and lots of children is a good rather than a bad thing, we question whether these priorities preclude other varieties of behavior. Looking for help in pronouncements from Church leaders and in Church history, we were delighted to discover that women have always played a vital role in our society, often outside the house. Brigham Young, pained by the sight of strong young louts doing light work instead of clearing sagebrush, pressed women into jobs. More interested in utilizing every available pair of hands than giving women fulfillment and satisfaction, he required that they make themselves useful in shops, schools and telegraph offices. And it was he who made this revolutionary pronouncement:

> As I have often told my sisters in the Female Relief Societies, we have sisters here who, if they had the privilege of studying, would make just as good mathematicians or accountants as any man; and we think they ought to have the privilege to study these branches of knowledge that they may develop the powers with which they are endowed. We believe that women are useful, not only to sweep houses, wash dishes, make

---

* See LDS scripture Doctrine and Covenants 93:36, "The glory of God is intelligence, or, in other words, light and truth."

beds, and raise babies, but that they should stand behind the counter, study law or physic, or become good bookkeepers and be able to do the business in any counting house, and all this to enlarge their sphere of usefulness for the benefit of society at large. In following these things they but answer the design of their creation. (*Discourses of Brigham Young*, pp. 216–217)

The heritage of Mormon women is impressive in its complexity. How ironic that polygamous wives, the very epitome of mistreated and downtrodden femininity in the eyes of the world, should have been among the most independent, liberated women of their time. Those poor women whose husbands courted sweet things beneath their eyes and married them with or without the wife's permission were also the managers of their own farms, the sole support of their children and sometimes professional women as well. The frequent government crackdowns on the oft-wed elders gave some ambitious women a chance to skip town and to be educated in the East, leaving their children with their sister wives in the day care centers of the past.

We can say of polygamy that we wouldn't want to live it, and that it was probably as hard on the men as women, yet the dedication of those early saints is impressive indeed. And if many polygamous wives suffered bitter torments, others apparently schooled their feelings and genuinely accepted the other wives as loved sisters. While a woman's role as a mother was increased, her wifely duties were lessened, and she was forced to manage her own family as head of the household. Few Mormon wives lead such autonomous lives today.

The independent lives of nineteenth century Mormon women give us pause, but we don't argue that women should be "freed" from their traditional home-centered commitment. All women should not be out working at careers, and those who choose to stay at home probably need more support today than their working sisters. In our day the career woman is increasingly justified for her good use of her faculties and her service to mankind, while the housewife is depicted as dowdy and dull; not only oppressed, she is so dumb she doesn't know it. Housewives deserve our unqualified defense. As members of the Church we have knowledge of eternal priorities, and surely housewives are devoted to these. If some women find themselves in prison at *home,* others consider it heaven on earth and make it that for their little angels. It is as serious a fault for women who need outside involvements to berate housewives as for housewives to feel threatened by working women.

We argue then for acceptance of the diversity that already exists in the life styles of Mormon women. We have too many native differences to fit comfortably into a single mold. Though the ladies of our group love each other dearly and have much in common, we are unable to agree on many things. Our major achievement, if we can claim any, is that ordinarily silent women have examined their lives and written about what they have seen. For a woman eager to do something unique and meaningful, but bogged down with the minutia of everyday life, the pattern of another woman who has surmounted the same obstacles has real worth. Women have always been valued in the Church but not encouraged to say much. We hope that now and in the future more ladies will speak out and, what is more, be heard.

Notes

1. Of those families with children, the current average age is three and two-thirds each. Of the four children born to group members this year, one increased the family's children to five, one to six, and one to eight.

Claudia Lauper Bushman (1934–), *"Exponent II is Born"* (1974)

Not long after they began to meet to discuss their lives as Mormon women, the Mormon feminists of Boston turned their attention to Mormon history. It was a natural choice: Claudia Bushman was working on a Ph.D. in American Studies at Boston University, and Laurel Thatcher Ulrich was studying for her Ph.D. in history at the University of New Hampshire. Encouragement came from Leonard Arrington, the forward-thinking LDS Church historian, who had done pioneering work recovering the stories of historical Mormon women and conscientiously recruited female colleagues to join the endeavor. In 1972–1973, Boston's feminists developed a Mormon women's history lecture series for the LDS Institute of Religion, an off-campus Church-sponsored resource center for Mormon college students. Claudia Bushman would later recall, "I grew up in the Church but knew nothing of LDS women's history. I did not know that the Relief Society operated cooperative stores, spun and wove silk fabric (including hatching the silkworms from eggs and feeding them on mulberry leaves that they gathered by hand), gleaned the fields to save grain for bad times, and trained as midwives and doctors. I didn't know that they were the first women in the United States to vote, even though Wyoming's women were first to receive the right to vote. I didn't know that they edited their own excellent newspaper or that they had large meetings where they spoke up for their rights and beliefs as citizens and as Mormons. Finding all this out was part of our Boston women's study." While conducting research to prepare for the lecture series, a Mormon feminist named Susan Kohler had discovered in the stacks at Harvard's Widener Library a complete set of the *Woman's Exponent* (1872–1914), a boldly progressive newspaper produced by and for Mormon women. The discovery electrified Mormon feminists, who read hand-copied excerpts to one another aloud at meetings of their consciousness-raising group and circulated them to other Mormon feminists around the country. "These women were saying things in the 1870s that we had only begun to think!" Laurel Thatcher Ulrich later remembered. Wrote Claudia Bushman: "We found in our foremothers who spoke out the models we were searching for in our own lives." In July 1974, the Boston feminists launched *Exponent II*, proclaiming it "the spiritual descendant of the *Woman's Exponent*." The first issue ran a masthead with the slogan "Am I Not a Woman and a Sister?" and featured articles on the Equal Rights Amendment; profiles of Mormon women divinity students, civic leaders, and business owners; announcements for Mormon feminist study groups, retreats, and seminars; and poetry by Carol Lynn Pearson (anthologized in this volume). *Exponent II* continues in print today as the longest-running independent publication by and for Mormon women.

Source

Bushman, Claudia L. "*Exponent II* Is Born." *Exponent II* 1.1 (July 1974): 2.

References and Further Reading

Bennion, Sherilyn Cox. "The *Woman's Exponent*: Forty-Two Years of Speaking for Women." *Utah Historical Quarterly* 44 (Summer 1976): 222–39.

"*EXPONENT II* IS BORN"

One hundred and two years ago a group of Mormon women began publication of a forthright newspaper called the *Woman's Exponent*. This ambitious paper circulated worldwide women's news, reports of the Church auxiliaries, feminist editorials, suffrage progress, household tips, letters, humor, and more to sisters from Salt Lake to St. George and throughout the territories. The *Exponent* was published until 1914.

The discovery of this newspaper has meant a lot to women today. Our foremothers had spirit and independence, a liveliness that their daughters can be proud of. Devoted mothers and wives, they tended their homes and children, helped support the family, and turned out a dynamic newspaper on the side. Can we do the same?

The Mormon women of the Greater Boston area have been thinking and talking about Mormon women's issues for five years now. Our network of sisterhood grows constantly. Sisters write us from far off and come to visit our meetings. These relationships have enriched us all, and we hope to catch more of our sisters in this net of common experience and understanding.

To that purpose we begin publication of *Exponent II*, a modest but sincere newspaper, which we hope will bring Mormon women into closer friendship. Faithful but frank, *Exponent II* will provide an open platform for the exchange of news and life views. *Exponent II*, poised on the dual platforms of Mormonism and Feminism, has two aims: to strengthen the Church of Jesus Christ of Latter-day Saints, and to encourage and develop the talents of Mormon women. That these aims are consistent we intend to show by our pages and our lives.

Carol Lynn Wright Pearson (1939–), "Millie's Mother's Red Dress" (1974)

"Our educated intelligence, which we have been taught is the glory of God, sometimes cries out for a little employment," Claudia Bushman wrote in her introduction to *Dialogue* in 1971. Even Mormon women who viewed parenthood as a sacred responsibility wondered to what extent Mormonism's late-twentieth-century model of self-sacrificing motherhood reflected the will of God who, as LDS scripture taught, created women and men so that they might progress eternally in knowledge and experience. These themes are explored further in a poem by Carol Lynn Pearson. In 1974, Carol Lynn Pearson was living in Provo, Utah, her hometown, a mother of three young children and author of two books of poems, a play, a screenplay for the LDS Church educational film *Cipher in the Snow*, and the popular historical anthology *Daughters of Light* (1973). She would, over the course of a career spanning five decades, become a major voice in Mormon life. "Millie's Mother's Red Dress" is based on a true story shared with Pearson by Millie herself. "During the years in which I did a lot of speaking to Relief Society and Mormon women's groups, I often used this poem," Pearson recalled. "Watching the women listen to it was always very moving: pain on so many faces, sometimes tears. I knew they had been Millie, or their mother had been Millie." These poems gently push their readers to reflect more carefully on whether all sacrifices are necessary and sacred ones, and what discouraging women's individuality and intellectual and creative pursuits may cost not only the individual but her family and community as well.

Source

Pearson, Carol Lynn Wright. "Millie's Mother's Red Dress." *Exponent II* 1.2 (October 1974): 7.

References and Further Reading

Pearson, Carol Lynn. *Daughters of Light.* Salt Lake City: Bookcraft, 1973.

"MILLIE'S MOTHER'S RED DRESS"

It hung there in the closet
While she was dying, Mother's red dress
Like a gash in the row
Of dark, old clothes
She had worn away her life in.

They had called me home
And I knew when I saw her
She wasn't going to last.

When I saw the dress, I said
"Why, Mother—how beautiful!
I've never seen it on you."

"I've never worn it," she slowly said.
"Sit down, Millie—I'd like to undo
A lesson or two before I go, if I can."

I sat by her bed
And she sighed a bigger breath
Than I thought she could hold.
"Now that I'll soon be gone
I can see some things.
Oh, I taught you good—but I taught you wrong."

"What do you mean Mother?"

"Well—I always thought
That a good woman never takes her turn,
That she's just for doing for somebody else.
Do here, do there, always keep
Everybody else's wants tended and make sure
Yours are at the bottom of the heap.
Maybe someday you'll get to them,
But of course you never do.
My life was like that—doing for your dad,
Doing for the boys, for your sisters, for you."

"You did—everything a mother could."

"Oh, Millie, Millie, it was no good—
For you—for him. Don't you see?
I did you the worst of wrongs.
I asked for nothing—for me!

"Your father in the other room,
All stirred up and staring at the walls—
When the doctor told him he took
It bad—came to my bed and all but shook
The life right out of me. 'You can't die,
Do you hear? What'll become of me?
What'll become of me?'
It'll be hard, all right, when I go.
He can't even find the frying pan, you know.

"And you children.
I was a free ride for everybody, everywhere.
I was the first one up and the last one down
Seven days out of the week.
I always took the toast that got burned,
And the very smallest piece of pie."
"I look at how some of your brothers treat their wives now
And it makes me sick, 'cause it was me
That taught it to them. And they learned.
They learned that a woman doesn't
Even exist except to give.
Why, every single penny that I could save
Went for your clothes or your books
Even when it wasn't necessary.
Can't even remember once when I took
Myself downtown to buy something beautiful—
For me.

"Except last year when I got that red dress.
I found I had twenty dollars
That wasn't especially spoke for.
I was on my way to pay it extra on the washer.
But somehow—I came home with this big box.
Your father really gave it to me then.
'Where you going to wear a thing like that to—
Some opera or something?'
And he was right, I guess.
I've never, except in the store,
Put on that dress.

"Oh Millie–I always thought if you take
Nothing for yourself in this world
You'd have it all in the next somehow.
I don't believe that anymore.
I think the Lord wants us to have something—
Here—and now.

"And I'm telling you, Millie, if some miracle
Could get me off this bed, you could look
For a different mother, 'cause I would be one.
Oh, I passed up my turn so long
I would hardly know how to take it.

But I'd learn, Millie.
I would learn."

It hung there in the closet
While she was dying, Mother's red dress,
Like a gash in the row
Of dark, old clothes
She had worn away her life in.

Her last words to me were these:
"Do me the honor, my dear,
Of not following in my footsteps.
Promise me that."

I promised.
She caught her breath
Then Mother took her turn
In death.

Claire Whitaker Peterson (1928–),
"Hide and Seek" (1974–1975)

The early Mormon feminists who held house meetings in Boston in the 1970s to "discuss their lives" were engaging in the powerful feminist practice of convening "consciousness-raising groups"—small meetings where women could take turns reflecting aloud on the truths of their individual and shared experiences. In a world centered on the lives, perspectives, and concerns of men, women's "consciousness raising" constituted a revolutionary act. For Mormon women, the challenge of this kind of truth-speaking was compounded by pressure within the LDS community to measure up to models of ideal Mormon womanhood and to publicly share only life stories that affirmed the power of faith to surmount life's difficulties or projected positive images of Mormons to a sometimes prejudicial public. A poem by Claire Whitaker published in *Exponent II* encourages new openness among Mormon women in acknowledging their losses, regrets, and imperfections. Born in Chicago to a family with Utah Mormon pioneer roots, Whitaker graduated from Northwestern University in 1949. "Growing up Mormon in the thirties in Chicago I had no idea that women needed liberating," she remembers. "All the adult sisters I knew there took their liberation for granted, including my mother, who put my father through school and landed him his first job. They were all free to work, study, get degrees, raise children or not. It was only after a couple of years at Brigham Young University when unsettling orders began coming down from 'authorities' that I became aware that attitudes toward women were changing in the LDS Church." Whitaker was a mother of five living in small-town Midway, Utah, when, in 1969, two uncles who worked for Brigham Young University's film studio invited her to write the screenplays for the LDS Church film *Man's Search for Happiness* (1964), screened at the New York World's Fair, and for the now-classic LDS short film *Johnny Lingo* (1969). Her sister Susan Kohler, an early member of Boston's Mormon feminist community who discovered lost copies of the *Woman's Exponent* in the Harvard library, encouraged Whitaker to publish her poems in *Exponent II*.

Source

Peterson, Claire Whitaker. "Hide and Seek." *Exponent II* 2.1 (September 1975): 16.

"HIDE AND SEEK"

Sisters,
Open your windows wide for me;
Let me come to your fences
And look in your yards.
Show me how your roses rust.
Point to where your attics leak.
Trust me with your unpaid bills.

Are there days when all the colors in your rooms run drab
And you take out a tarnished hurt and put a fresh shine on it?
Do you envy young girls with their long smooth necks,
And have you ever dreamt of lying naked in the rain?

I only see your faces creamy-bland
And smiling.
The outsides of your lives are neatly bricked
Like east bench houses
And if somewhere you have a closet where roaches lurk,
I do not know it from your
Awninged eyes.

My front stoop too is swept,
My avocado carpet freshly raked and footprint-free,
And all my clocks are wound.
But truth has a dark side, like the moon—
A sock kicked under the bed,
Two lines of a poem yellowing under the shelf paper,
And somewhere in the shrubbery a regret
Rustling and illusive:
What if? what if?

Sisters,
Are not our gardens planted in the same soil?
Let us not hide from each other any more.
Look in your mirrors;
You will find my face, entreating,
And I will turn to see your shadows
Trembling at my side.
Perfect, we have no need of each other;
Groping, we might touch hands
And never be alone again.

Elouise Bell (1935–), "The Implications of Feminism for BYU" (1975)

In its inaugural 1974 issue, Claudia Bushman proclaimed that a goal of *Exponent II* was to demonstrate in life and writing the complementarity of the "dual platforms of Mormonism and feminism": "to strengthen the Church of Jesus Christ of Latter-day Saints, and to encourage and develop the talents of Mormon women." One year later and thousands of miles west, Brigham Young University English professor and Relief Society General Board member Elouise Bell presented the same case in a historic campus-wide forum at Brigham Young University on September 30, 1975. Bell was the first BYU woman faculty member to deliver a forum address. She arrived, she remembers, having broken both ankles in a fall, in a wheelchair and wearing a pantsuit—even though pantsuits were forbidden for female faculty under the campus dress code—and was introduced by university president Dallin H. Oaks. Reaching into Mormon women's activist nineteenth-century history, Bell encouraged BYU women students to take their education more seriously and urged her entire audience to recognize the women's movement as one of history's most significant advances and worthy causes. Bell would have a thirty-five-year career as a BYU faculty member and administrator. "Looking back on my career at BYU—which I absolutely loved, all things considered—I feel now that perhaps I was too cautious," Bell now believes. But her words on September 30, 1975, would prove to have tremendous impact. A young BYU graduate student in the classics named Margaret Merrill (later Toscano) was in the audience for Bell's forum that day. "I was on fire. I had been so worried about gender issues and I was going through this huge spiritual struggle about whether there was a place for me in the Mormon Church because I didn't feel like what I cared about mattered. And I had always been an intellectual woman. All my friends I talked ideas to were men. I wondered, where are the other women who are intellectual, who are interested in ideas?"

Source

Bell, Elouise. "The Implications of Feminism for BYU." *BYU Studies* 16.4 (1976): 527–40.

"THE IMPLICATIONS OF FEMINISM FOR BYU"

A feminist is a person, whether a man or a woman, who believes that historically there have been inequities in the education and treatment of women in several or many spheres of society and who is interested in correcting those inequities as he or she sees them. That's about the extent of my definition of feminism.

What is a feminist at BYU concerned about? First of all, that women have equal opportunities for scholarships and admissions. And in that regard I might say that BYU is moving ahead. The president's scholarship, named after the current president of the Church, and so currently titled the Spencer W. Kimball scholarship, is now, for the very first year, available to women as well as to men. The feminist is also concerned that when women come to college, they are counseled wisely, that they are told about a full range of options for career choices, that they are not channeled into two or three traditional majors only, that they are not, for instance, directed only into education, into home economics, into nursing. In April 1975, BYU granted 1,510 degrees to women. Of that total, 1,180 were in two colleges—740 in Child Development and Family Relations and 440 in Education. While these are fine fields for women, there are many other opportunities. There are as many opportunities for women as for men, and it's this message that the feminist wants to communicate to the young college woman. The feminist is concerned also that at a university, a young woman have [*sic*] many strong and positive female role models. That is to say, she ought to see women in positions of authority, in positions of success, in positions of achievement, and she ought to get the message, indirectly as well as directly, that there are opportunities for women and there are many options open.

Another aspect of higher education which has been sorely neglected and will take considerable effort to reverse has to do with the whole presentation of knowledge, the whole organization of knowledge. While I do not have time to present this case here, let me just explain briefly. Nearly all of the disciplines—history, art, economics, agriculture, medicine, literature—nearly all of these disciplines have been organized by men, developed by men, the textbooks have been written by men, and they are, by and large, about men. Many scholars now say if we look at history from the perspective of the other half of the human race, we might ask different questions about history, and we might gain entire new insights if we ask a different set of questions. So the feminist is concerned with a scholarly, rational review of the actual fundamental underpinnings of most disciplines.

Let me voice [another] concern as a feminist at BYU, and please keep in mind my definition of feminism. I wonder, in some cases, if the young women are receiving equal educations, or if they are not really receiving educations of quite a different character than the young men, educations in some senses quite inferior. I would ask the young women in the audience today: How eager are you for knowledge; how thirsty are you for wisdom and the learning that is available to you? What kind of priority do you put on your classes? Do they come rather far down on the list after your church activities, your social activities, your relationships with your roommates and a number of other interests? No one could ever accuse BYU young women of being slothful playgirls, but I sometimes feel there is not the active intellectual involvement that there should be. A bright young man at BYU usually realizes that there is a certain amount of knowledge and a number of ideas he must get into himself, that he must interiorize and make part of himself, before he's equipped to go out into the world and make his contribution. Sometimes the bright young woman takes a more passive attitude.

Now let me ask a third question which may be of concern to many of you as you hear me, or anyone, talking about feminism, and that is the question, stated very directly: "Don't the objectives of feminism threaten the family as an institution? Isn't feminism at its heart inimical to many of the principles of the gospel, especially the principles of home and family?" It is true that a central thrust of feminism is a reexamination of many of society's institutions: the family, the school, the penal institutions, the church. Many different institutions are being reevaluated, that is true. But reevaluation does not necessarily mean rejection, and in fact as I have read the writings of many feminists and talked with some of them, I have found that as a result of their reevaluation they are going back to family values and family traditions with a renewed zest and a renewed appreciation of what they mean. I find many people expressing a renewed determination to spend more time with their children, to spend less time "getting and spending"; less time after the material goods, and more time with the family. Many women feminists are not only spending more time with their children themselves, but urging and helping their husbands to find time to be with their children, to do things together as families, to work together as a family, play together as a family, get close to nature together as a family.

A question that I am asked very often when I'm away from campus and rather frequently when I'm on campus is this: "Can a person be a devoted member of the Church, a devoted Latter-day Saint, and a feminist at the same time?" Our pioneer foremothers here in the State of Deseret in the last century were very much aware of what was going on in the feminist movement. They were in touch with the great feminist leaders of America like Susan B. Anthony and Elizabeth Cady Stanton. They not only corresponded with these women, but had them out here to Utah, talked with them, stumped with them from meeting to meeting. They were very active, very much concerned. They wrote essays, editorials, letters, and pamphlets; they worked vigorously for women's causes in those days and, at the same time, they went about their work in building up the kingdom. I'm talking about such leaders as Emmeline B. Wells, Susa Young Gates, and many other women whose names should be better known than they are. So there is great precedent for Mormon feminism.

But when people ask me that question, what they usually mean is this: "Is it possible to be an active, devoted member of the Church, and an active, concerned feminist when you know that sometimes there's going to be a seeming paradox in the principles and teachings and goals of these two parts of your life? There are going to be some questions raised by feminism that seem to be contradictory to gospel principles. There are going to be some things that are taught in the gospel that seem to go contrary to the objectives of feminism."

As I have attempted to live the commandments and to live my religion, and also to be a concerned feminist, there have been questions come up to which I do not know the answers. There have been problems and puzzles and enigmas. I have found that clear thinking and the use of the tools that a good education can provide, utilized under the influence of the Holy Spirit, which one must seek, and which has province over all matters of the intellect and all matters of learning, that these in combination, the Holy Spirit and the process of clear thinking, can solve many problems and answer many questions. But where they do not supply the answers, I am content to wait.

I truly believe that the righteous goals of feminism, the wise goals as opposed to the unwise goals, will help us prepare a generation of women more fit than ever before to bear their joint responsibility in establishing the kingdom of God. Let it not be said that BYU or the Latter-day Saint people stood on the sidelines while great and needed social reforms were taking place in the twentieth century. Rather let it be said that we took our rightful positions in the forefront of that movement. That we were agents for directing it. That we used discernment to know worthy objectives from pernicious ones. That we became teachers and leaders for every righteous aim of self-fulfillment, growth, and high achievement. To all those in the BYU community, I extend the challenge to examine the issues of feminism, to make decisions about them individually on the basis of reason and the light of truth within you, to welcome a new day when women can hold on to all that is traditionally fine and right and God-given and God-ordained, and to encompass as well new alternatives, new options, greater fulfillment of potential, and an ever-increasing responsibility and desire and willingness to do our share in building the kingdom of God.

Judith Rasmussen Dushku (1942–), *Mormon Sisters*: "Feminists" (1976)

After publishing their special 1971 issue of the journal *Dialogue* and launching *Exponent II*, the Mormon feminists of Boston set to work on a new publishing endeavor: converting the lectures they had developed for a Mormon women's history course at the Cambridge, Massachusetts, LDS Institute of Religion into a groundbreaking collection of essays. Encouraged and supported by LDS Church historian Leonard Arrington and members of the LDS Church Historical Department, including Maureen Ursenbach Beecher, Chris Rigby Arrington, and Jill Mulvay Derr, a collective of twelve women authors and additional editors and researchers produced *Mormon Sisters: Women in Early Utah*. Contributor Laurel Thatcher Ulrich would later recall, male scholars who reviewed the manuscript thought it "lame" and "nothing new," and publishers rejected it. But the Boston collective pressed on, publishing the book themselves under the label "Emmeline Press Limited," in honor of Emmeline B. Wells (1828–1921), editor of the *Woman's Exponent*, a nationally known advocate for women's suffrage, and general president of the LDS Relief Society (1910–1921). Wrote editor Claudia Bushman in the book's introduction, "The Boston women are spiritually and often physically descended from the women who figure in this book. Writing about them has been a trial equivalent to crossing the plains. That an untrained, grass-roots group of sisters should have come this far at all is a modern spiritual experience. The authors feel that they have made history by making history." Among the contributors was Judith Rasmussen Dushku, an Idaho-born Brigham Young University graduate, mother of three, political scientist, activist, and faculty member at Suffolk University. Her contribution to *Mormon Sisters* documents the extensive activism of Mormon women in the nineteenth century as advocates for women's equality and suffrage, not only in Utah but on the national stage. In recovering this vital chapter of Mormon women's history, the spirited and activism-inclined Judy Dushku assured Mormon feminists that they had not been the first generation to find the core principles of their faith compatible with women's emancipation, nor were they the first to raise their voices and join their efforts with a national women's movement.

Source

Dushku, Judith Rasmussen. "Feminists." *Mormon Sisters: Women in Early Utah*. Cambridge, MA: Emmeline Press Limited, 1976.

"FEMINISTS"

In a letter to the editor dated August 1877, a Philadelphia woman confessed that until she read the *Woman's Exponent* she had not looked upon "woman suffrage in Utah as worth a fillip." Under polygamy, she had assumed, "each man has not merely his own vote, but just as many votes as he owns wives, and that each woman is either an oriental doll or a domestic drudge, with neither impulse nor impetus towards an individualized existence." The outspoken feminism of the *Exponent* changed her mind and she acknowledged that "the women of the States have jumped at very unjust conclusions in regard to their sisters in Utah."[1]

In the 1870s Utah's women were indeed misunderstood. In important respects, they still are. In most histories of the movement, female suffrage in Utah has been treated as a curiosity strangely unrelated to feminist agitation elsewhere. Historians have been unable to explain why the "last outpost of barbarism" should have extended the vote to women in 1870, fifty years before the nation adopted the Nineteenth Amendment and decades before women's suffrage had acquired respectability elsewhere. Some writers have suggested that the male hierarchy simply saw a chance to enlist the help of women against threats from anti-polygamists in Washington and at home.[2] Mormon writers have more often seen the suffrage act as a logical extension of the law of common consent,* which had included both sexes from the earliest years of the Church.[3] But neither group has paid enough attention to the women themselves and to their relationship with the wider equal rights movement of the nineteenth century. While Utah women first received the vote without petitions or demonstrations, they still spoke out, freely and frequently, in behalf of the extension of that right to women elsewhere. They campaigned in favor of the other causes motivating eastern feminists—wages, educational opportunities, and legal status. In 1887, when Congress took away their right to vote with the passage of the Edmunds-Tucker Act, their feminism acquired a new urgency. By 1895 they were prepared, organizationally and ideologically, for victory in the suffrage controversy which erupted in Utah's statehood convention. For twenty-five years Utah's independent women showed their dedication to the cause. They demonstrated their feminism in three major areas—in publishing, in grass-roots organizing, and in personal association with national women's rights leaders.

The Woman's Exponent, a bi-monthly paper produced in Salt Lake City from 1872 until 1914, did not significantly alter its focus on women's issues through more than forty years of publication. Its tone was neither self-conscious nor cautious, and it firmly and directly discussed feminist ideas and explained how they enhanced gospel ideals. Modern readers are often surprised at its forthrightness. "Woman feels her servitude, her degradation, and she is determined to assert her rights," said an editorial of the 1870s.[4] For more than twenty years the subtitle of the paper was, "The Rights of Women of Zion and the Rights of Women of all Nations."[5] The history of the *Exponent* testifies both to the vigor with which Mormon women agitated for the goals of the national movement and to the widespread official support which made such agitation possible.

Significantly, the *Exponent* was first published on Brigham Young's birthday, 2 June 1872, and every June thereafter tribute was paid to him. The anniversary

---

* "law of common consent": In the Doctrine and Covenants 26:2, revelation to LDS Church founders Joseph Smith and John Whitmer establishes that the administrative business of the Church should be decided by the "law of common consent," with sustaining votes from the membership.

issue for 1881, for example, praised his efforts in behalf of the Relief Society and of women's suffrage and went on to explain his role in the founding of the paper:

> President Young was also desirous the women of Zion should publish a paper in their own interest, and was solicitous that it should be extensively circulated, and that the sisters should preserve their volumes and have them bound, for, he said, "It will contain a portion of Church history, the record of the works and experiences of women."[6]

From its inception then, the *Exponent* had the good wishes of the brethren. Yet the *Exponent* was neither owned nor directly controlled by the Church, and it was financed by subscriptions. It did, however, publicize activities of the Relief Society and was widely regarded as the Society's voice. An editorial in the 15 November 1889 issue claimed that for over seventeen years the *Exponent* had been "the official organ of the women of Zion." It was entitled to this distinction, the author went on to say, because it had published reports from all women's organizations: the Relief Society, the Young Ladies' Associations, and the Primary Associations; because it had "always given information on the suffrage question"; because it had advocated the "woman's side of all vexed questions"; because it had published biographical sketches of the leading women of the Church; and because it had publicized the activities of the Woman Suffrage Association in Utah.[7]

As the voice of Utah's women, the *Exponent* exemplified the three defining qualities of feminism in any age: a desire to encourage women to speak for and to women, a sense of injustice and inequality of opportunity, a conviction of the absolute equality of the sexes. An editorial in the 1 March 1878 issue defended women against the charges of "an eminently popular and learned man" who had written that "the greatest nuisance in society . . . is a woman who thinks she has a special mission." Women do have a special mission, the author asserted, a mission that cannot be fulfilled through her influence on her family alone:

> If woman has so much wisdom to counsel others, if her advice is judicious and her influence salutary, then why may she not be capable of acting out her own nature, expressing her own views, instead of doing so by proxy through her husband, her brother, or some friend?[8]

Neither vicarious influence nor coat-tail salvation was sufficient for the Latter-day Saint woman. "Girls don't be afraid of the term 'strong-minded,'" another column had cautioned, "for of such there is certainly a necessity; the stronger you are in mind and body the better for you . . . do not wait for any other person to bring you forward."[9] A correspondent from Manti North Ward noted that it was customary for "the lords of creation" to quote the Apostle Paul in denying women the right to speak. While acknowledging the many good things in the writings of Paul, this sister questioned whether he was qualified to define the position of women:

> Now let us ask, Who was Paul? In the first place Paul was a Roman, second an educated lawyer, third he was a bachelor as we learn from reading, 1st. Cor., 7th Chap, 7th and 8th verses, fourth he tells us in his defense before Agrippa that he was "raised a Pharisee" in the strictest sense of the word, and last we know, he did not enjoy that constant and elevating association with Jesus, which the other apostles were privileged to enjoy, and, which might have softened, or slightly ameliorated his views toward women.[10]

After this venture into higher criticism, the writer went on to testify of the coming role of women in Christ's plan, urging her sisters to become Marys, not Marthas.*

Zion's women had good reason to complain of injustice. They were held in derision by most of the world. But the *Woman's Exponent* was as ready to expound the common grievances of women everywhere as to defend their own cause. There are examples in every issue. A letter from Grantsville in the 1870s, for instance, decried the sexual exploitation of young women and the double standard of judgment applied to seducer and seduced.[11] A long article in an 1890 paper documented the need for equal pay for equal work,[12] while a poem from the 1880s vowed to "strike" for better working conditions in the home:

> In the daylight shall be crowded all the work that I will do:
> When the evening lamps are lighted, I will read the papers too.[13]

Emmeline Wells was particularly concerned with the constraints of the pedestal:

> See the manner in which ladies—a term for which I have little reverence or respect—are treated in all public places! . . . She must be preserved from the slightest blast of trouble, petted, caressed, dressed to attract attention, taught accomplishments that minister to man's gratification; in other words, she must be treated as a glittering and fragile toy, a thing without brains or soul, placed on a tinseled and unsubstantial pedestal by man, as her worshipper.[14]

---

* "Marys, not Marthas": a reference to the New Testament story of Jesus's visit to the home of two sisters, Martha, who works in the kitchen to prepare to feed their guest, and Mary, who instead sits to listen to his teachings (Luke 10:38–42). When Martha criticizes her sister for declining to help, Jesus defends Mary for choosing "the better part."

Like feminists in the eastern states, authors in the *Woman's Exponent* urged exercise, sensible clothing, and general improvement of health as part of a total platform for the improvement of women's position.[15] They were concerned with the same grievances—sexual, economic, and legal; and they frequently reprinted pertinent articles from women's publications in other parts of the country.

Emmeline B. Wells, writing later about the *Exponent,* said, "From its first issue it was the champion of the suffrage cause, and by exchanging with women's papers of the United States and England it brought news of women in all parts of the world to those of Utah."[16]

In recording the achievements of women in other places, Utah's women did not forget their own. In fact, they occasionally had cause to gloat. "It was in Utah that the right of women to support themselves as clerks, telegraph operators, and so on, was first publicly and practically acknowledged," claimed an editorial note of 1873.[17] They could also note their own right to vote. No reader of the *Exponent* could mistake the pride of these Mormon women in their own achievements. Said an early issue:

> It was telegraphed east and west that two ladies had been admitted to the bar of Utah as practicing lawyers, and the local press has had considerable to say in regard to it; yet it might with equal justness and more force have been telegraphed that here in Utah, decried, abused and maligned as it has been, women enjoy more of what is contended for as woman's rights than they do in any State in the Federal Union; and that they appreciate their position and are seeking to qualify themselves for spheres of usefulness to which their sisters in other parts of the country can only yet look in prospective.[18]

While the citizens of Utah Territory were aware of a wide variety of women's issues, political equality seems to have been the goal which attracted the broadest support. This was particularly true after the [Utah territorial] female suffrage law of 1870 came under attack from Washington. Initially critics of polygamy had hoped that Utah women would use their vote to change the marital system. When they did not, eastern reformers began pressuring Congress to take the vote away. Zion's feminists soon learned that publishing was not enough. If they were to defend their rights, they had to become involved in organizing and educating their sisters at the local level.

At first this was done through the Relief Society, probably on a semi-official basis. Susa Young Gates wrote that:

> The captain of Utah's woman-host, Eliza R. Snow, was foremost in all this labor as in every other during her period of public activity; yet she turned over the active direction of this suffrage movement

to that champion of equal rights, Sarah M. Kimball. For many years Mrs. Kimball was the "Mormon" suffrage standard bearer. It would be less than justice if it were not here recorded that her active brain, her unselfish devotion to the work of God, and her magnificent organizing powers bore rich fruit during this vital period (1868–1893) in the history of woman's development in the Church. Following her leadership of the suffrage forces was that other indomitable pioneer, President Emmeline B. Wells. Then in later years came that no less splendid patriot, Mrs. Emily S. Richards, who ably conducted suffrage affairs in this state in the later years.[19]

Incorporating suffrage goals into the program of the Relief Society turned political work into Church work. Many women pursued suffrage work as diligently as they did their religious callings. Edward Tullidge reported that Relief Society President Eliza R. Snow appointed Bathsheba W. Smith as a missionary to go "all through the South" and preach retrenchment. Sister Snow added that Sister Smith could "preach woman's rights on her mission," if she wished.[20]

Sister Wells recalled that Sarah M. Kimball, "leader in the Relief Society and later a nationally known woman's rights advocate," began programs for civic education for women in Utah." She used the Relief Society to promote activities which increased the knowledge of the sisters in matters of government and law. "Relief Society meetings became . . . mock trials, and symposia on parliamentary law."[21]

Not all the organized suffrage activity was within the Relief Society. In 1889, two years after the Edmunds-Tucker Act disfranchised Utah's women, the Territorial Suffrage Association was organized with one hundred members. The *Woman's Exponent* dealt with news of Woman Suffrage Association conferences in the same way it reported news of the Relief Society, Primary, and YLMIA, giving complete accounts of talks given and changes in officers. Reports of regular WSA meetings in Juab County, in Sanpete County, in Ogden City, in Sevier County, and in other smaller towns and counties fill the pages of the *Exponent*, especially between 1875 and 1896, and indicate that there were active chapters all over the territory.[22] Most places that had active Relief Societies in the 1880s and 90s had some kind of WSA organization, or at least were encouraged to do so by Relief Society leaders.[23] The Territorial Suffrage Association chapters were officially linked to the NWSA and afforded some Utah women the opportunity to travel to other states and to Washington to lobby Congress for changes in federal legislation that affected them. At a gathering in Washington in 1891, Utah had the second largest number of delegates participating.

Although territorial branches of the Woman Suffrage Association were not organized until after the disfranchisement crisis of 1887, influential Mormon women had established ties with the national women's movement long before that. In 1871, a large group of sisters had turned out to greet Elizabeth Cady Stanton and Susan B. Anthony on their first trip west. She seized the opportunity to speak to a large assembly, of Mormon women on "polyandry, polygamy, monogamy, and prostitution":

> After this convocation the doors of the Tabernacle were closed to our ministrations, as we thought they would be, but we had crowded an immense amount of science, philosophy, history, and general reflections into the five hours of such free talk as those women had never heard before. As the seceders had just built a new hall, we held meetings there every day, discussing all the vital issues of the hour; the Mormon men and women taking an active part.[24]

In a time of schism, Mrs. Stanton's flirtation with [William Godbe's "Godbeite"] seceders might have alienated the Church leadership. Apparently this did not happen, for the long involvement of Emmeline Wells and her associates in the national suffrage movement dated from this period. Mrs. Stanton found much to praise in Mormon life, while Sister Wells found a new calling in the women's movement. In an account written much later for Susan Anthony's history, Sister Wells pointed with pride to the large number of Utah women who became active in the suffrage movement in the 1870s:

> The fact that the women of Utah were so progressive in the suffrage question and had sent large petitions asking for the passage of the Sixteenth Amendment to the Federal Constitution to enfranchise all women, resulted in an invitation for [Mrs. Wells] to attend its annual convention at Washington in January, 1879.

She went on to note that the Utah delegates were invited to speak at the convention and selected to go before Congressional committees and the President of the United States "as well as to present important matters to the Lady of the White House."[25]

Since Mormons were regarded as a strange and dishonorable sect by many Americans at this time, and their polygamous marriages were abhorrent to most of those who allied themselves with the cause of women's rights, it is particularly interesting that within one branch of the women's movement a relationship of tolerance, and even respect, developed between Mormon and gentile women. Susan B. Anthony's letters home during her first visit to Utah show her own initial repugnance. "The system of the subjection of woman here finds its limit, and she touches the lowest depths of her degradation," she wrote. Still, she could see polygamy as only a more advanced form of the abuses of monogamy:

> When I look back into the States, what sorrow, what broken hearts are there because of husbands taking to themselves new friendships, just

as really wives as are these, and the legal wife feeling even more wrong and neglected.[26]

If Utah's women did not convince her of the values of polygamy, they at least demonstrated their own interest in female rights. According to one biographer, Miss Anthony "formed several friendships with Mormon women and decided to regard them as she regarded her conventionally married friends. There were no obvious signs of difference between them and these intelligent Mormon ladies."[27]

In 1890, the participation of Mormon women in the national women's movement became a divisive issue in the East. The National Woman Suffrage Association, under the leadership of Miss Anthony and Mrs. Stanton, had always been considered too radical by the more conservative American Woman Suffrage Association led by Lucy Stone and Julia Ward Howe. In the 1880s, great efforts had been made to unite the two groups, but the latter faction had refused to join an organization to which Mormon women belonged and which endorsed women's trade unions, both acceptable to the NWSA. In 1889, a conference was held in Washington and the groups tried to work out their differences. Pressure was put upon Elizabeth Cady Stanton, president of the National group, to compromise her position. She did not. She would not be a part of any organization that did not make *all* women feel welcome if they shared common goals.[28] She made it particularly clear that "Mormon women, black women, and Indian women" must not be excluded from the Association or she would sever her connection with it. With Susan B. Anthony's support, she prevailed, and the two groups were joined.[29]

Soon after, Elizabeth Cady Stanton, then seventy-seven years old, stepped down from the leadership of the organization and Susan B. Anthony became president. Miss Anthony traveled to Utah to meet with Mormon women on several occasions, and she became an important link with the women there. To the Latter-day Saint women, her visits to Utah were special events, and her statements were widely discussed in the press. In 1896, when Utah became a state and women's suffrage was restored, she joined her friends in Utah in the celebrations honoring their victory. As she traveled through the state, she was "honored in every possible way."[30] Miss Anthony wrote that she felt a spirit of warmth and openness when she was with the Mormon women, and that she counted some of them among her close friends.[31] In 1900, Mrs. Wells and several other Mormon women traveled to Atlanta, Georgia, to attend the Susan B. Anthony eightieth birthday celebration. Miss Anthony was given a length of silk produced in the Utah [women's] sericulture project.

Mormon women were aware that most outside observers did not take their feminism seriously because of their participation in plural marriage. Many Latter-day Saint women saw themselves as not only part of the women's emancipation movement, but beyond or ahead of it. Today's radical feminists might not endorse plural marriage as the solution to some of these problems, but Mormon women did. Polygamy, they said, relieved women of the loneliness and drudgery of monogamous, single-family living, offering opportunities for a variety of intimate friendships, and for shared household and child-care responsibilities. It also emancipated them from other marital duties, if Mrs. Stanton's report is correct: "The women who believed in polygamy had much to say in its favor, especially in regard to the sacredness of motherhood during the period of pregnancy and lactation; a lesson of respect for that period being religiously taught all Mormons."[32] In a day when even the outspoken Mrs. Stanton dared speak of no other form of birth control than abstinence, the Mormon system had its appeal.

But feminist advocacy of polygamy went beyond these issues to a more fundamental problem. An article in an 1874 issue of the *Woman's Exponent* had defended the virtue and integrity of plural wives and had gone on to ask:

> Is there then nothing worth living for, but to be petted, humored and caressed, by a man? That is all very well as far as it goes, but that man is the only thing in existence worth living for I fail to see. All honor and reverence to good men; but they and their attentions are not the only sources of happiness on the earth, and need not fill up every thought of woman. And when men see that women can exist without their being constantly at hand, that they can learn to be self-reliant or depend upon each other for more or less happiness, it will perhaps take a little of the conceit out of some of them.[33]

The "ultimate degradation" became the path of liberation. Plural marriage showed women they could live their lives without the continual attention and adulation of a spouse. Or at least so it seemed from the editorial offices of the *Woman's Exponent*.

In publishing, in grass-roots organization, and in personal association with women's rights leaders, Utah feminists accomplished much in the years from 1870 to 1896. They encouraged thoughtful discussion in their own society of issues regarding the worth and responsibilities of the sexes, they demonstrated that feminist ideals could be compatible with Mormon doctrine, and they forged a direct and active link with the wider movement for equal rights.

Notes

1. *Woman's Exponent* 6 (1 September 1877), 49
2. Eleanor Flexner, *A Century of Struggle* (New York: Atheneum, 1972), 163.
3. Thomas G. Alexander, "An Experiment in Progressive Legislation: Woman Suffrage in Utah in 1870," *Utah Historical Quarterly* 38 (Winter 1970), 21, 29–30.

4. *Woman's Exponent* 6 (1 July 1877), 20.
5. This slogan appeared on the masthead of the *Woman's Exponent* from 1 November 1879 to 15 December 1896.
6. *Woman's Exponent* 10 (1 June 1881), 4.
7. Ibid., 18 (15 November 1889), 92.
8. Ibid., 6 (1 March 1878), 148.
9. Ibid., 3 (15 January 1875), 123.
10. Ibid., 18 (1 June 1889), 1.
11. Ibid., 1 (1 August 1872) 13.
12. Ibid., 18 (15 February 1890), 136.
13. Ibid., 18 (15 August 1889), 43.
14. Ibid., 1 (15 July 1872), 29.
15. Ibid., 1 (31 January 1873), 131; also 1 (15 August 1872), 46; 6 (1 February 1878), 132.
16. Susan B. Anthony and Ida Husted Harper, eds., *The History of Woman Suffrage*, 6 vols. (Rochester, New York: Susan B. Anthony, 1902) 4:936–37.
17. *Woman's Exponent* 1 (1 April 1873), 161
18. Ibid., 1 (1 October 1872), 68.
19. The General Board of the Relief Society, *A Centenary of Relief Society: 1842–1942* (Salt Lake City: The Deseret News Press, 1942), 67.
20. Edward W. Tullidge, *The Women of Mormondom* (Salt Lake City: n.p., 1965), 505.
21. Thomas G. Alexander, "An Experiment in Progressive Legislation: Woman Suffrage in Utah in 1870," *Utah Historical Quarterly* 38 (Winter 1970), 28.
22. *Woman's Exponent*, see especially issues from 1887–89.
23. *A Centenary of Relief Society*, 65–67.
24. Anthony and Harper, 4:937–38.
25. Ida Husted Harper, *Life and Work of Susan B. Anthony*, 3 vols. (Indianapolis: The Hollenback Press, 1908), 1:390.
26. Katherine Anthony, *Susan B. Anthony: Her Personal History and Her Era* (Garden City, NY: Doubleday & Co., 1954), 262.
27. Flexner, 153.
28. Alma Lutz, *Created Equal: A Biography of Elizabeth Cady Stanton* (New York: The John Day Co., 1940), 281–82.
29. Anthony and Harper, 4:944.
30. Theodore Stanton and Harriet Stanton Blatch, eds., *Elizabeth Cady Stanton: As Revealed in Her Letters, Diary and Reminiscences*, 2 vols. (New York: Harper & Brothers, 1922), 1:66.
31. Harper, 2: 1, 202.
32. Louise Noun, *Strong-Minded Women* (Iowa City: The Iowa State University Press, 1969), 184.
33. *Woman's Exponent* 3 (30 September 1874), 6.

Margaret Rampton Munk (1941–1986), "First Grief" (1978)

From its beginnings, Mormon feminism has shown a willingness to ask difficult questions and to abide with the uncertainty they may produce. Poet Margaret Rampton Munk voiced this willingness in her poem "First Grief," first published in *Exponent II* in the fall of 1978. The daughter of Utah governor Calvin Rampton and Lucy Beth Cardon, Munk was an honors student and editor of the student newspaper at the University of Utah who earned a Ph.D. in political science at Harvard University and taught at universities in Asia and the United States. She died from ovarian cancer in 1986. "First Grief" describes Munk's efforts to comfort her adopted daughter; it is among the first pieces of contemporary Mormon women's writing to voice hunger for a Heavenly Mother whose existence is established by nineteenth-century Mormon doctrine but whose presence had been virtually absent from modern Mormon liturgy, teachings, practice, and culture.

Source

Munk, Margaret Rampton. "First Grief." *Exponent II* 5.1 (Fall 1978): 17.

References and Further Reading

Munk, Margaret Rampton. *So Far: Poems*. Potomac, MD: Greentree, 1986.
Rosenbaum, Karen. "For Meg—With Doubt and Faith." *Dialogue: A Journal of Mormon Thought* 24.2 (1991): 83–92.

"FIRST GRIEF"

Last night, my daughter
Mine by right of love and law,
But not by birth
Cried for her "other mother."

Accountable
And duly baptized she may be,
But eight is young,
So young,
For grownup grief,
The first I cannot mend
With Bandaids,
Easy words,
Or promises.

I cannot tell her yet
How I have also cried
Sometimes at night
To one whose memory
My birth erased;
Who let me go
To other parents
Who could train and shape the soul
She had prepared,
Then hid her face from me.

Dixie Snow Huefner (1936–), Excerpts from "Church and Politics at the Utah IWY Conference" (1978)

Mormon feminists like Elouise Bell and Claudia Bushman insisted on the coherence of core principles of Mormonism and feminism in their shared reverence for human freedom and emancipation. But the LDS Church announced its opposition to the Equal Rights Amendment with an editorial in the Church-owned *Deseret News* in January 1975. At the time, thirty-three states, including the heavily Mormon-populated state of Idaho, had already ratified the Amendment, which stated, "Equality of rights under the law shall not be denied or abridged by the United States or by any State on account of sex." The Church's announcement surprised many Mormons—surveys showed that a majority of Utahns had previously supported the ERA—and marked the beginning of a new era of high-profile and high-pressure LDS Church activism on issues of gender and sexuality. Beginning in 1976, high-ranking LDS Church leaders traveled to give anti-ERA stump speeches, and local congregational leaders, including bishops and stake presidents, followed LDS Church orders in organizing rank-and-file Mormons in seven states to work to prevent its passage. During the summer of 1977, LDS Church officials organized thousands of members in Utah, Hawaii, and Washington to disrupt statewide women's conventions held in honor of the "International Women's Year" declared by the United Nations. Martha Sonntag Bradley experienced a feminist awakening as she witnessed the openly contentious Utah IWY proceedings firsthand as a young mother of three. "Confused, I read over the list of resolutions on the ballot I was supposed to vote for or against, but I realized I had not even begun to think about what my position as a woman in the world should be." Marilyn Curtis White, a self-described "Traditionalist" and a leader of the LDS delegation to the Hawaiian IWY later recalled,

> I saw Mormon women chosen as leaders, who over the pulpit and in the name of Jesus Christ told their sisters to watch their lead and vote "no" as a bloc on every issue. I saw sisters so ignorant of the issues that they couldn't do anything but blindly follow their leaders. I saw LDS women so afraid of those who did not hold their point of view that they refused to engage in honest debate. And afterward, I saw Mormon women go back into their houses and shut the doors on a world they had only glimpsed and had refused to confront.

Dixie Snow Huefner, a Mormon with Utah roots who had graduated from Wellesley College with a degree in political science, attended the IWY as a young mother of two. Huefner had lived in the Boston area and had participated in the earliest years of Mormon feminist organizing there, contributing an essay to the

"Pink" issue of *Dialogue*. She went on to earn a master's degree in special education and later a law degree, to clerk for the US Court of Appeals for the Tenth Circuit, and teach special education law as a University of Utah faculty member. Her 1978 essay on the IWY conference captures the moment when Mormon feminists realized that no matter how deeply they themselves felt the coherence of core principles of Mormonism and feminism, their own church would in fact be a formidable opponent of the contemporary women's movement.

Source

Huefner, Dixie Snow. "Church and Politics at the Utah IWY Conference." *Dialogue: A Journal of Mormon Thought* 11.1 (1978): 58–76.

References and Further Reading

Bradley, Martha. *Pedestals and Podiums: Utah Women, Religious Authority, and Equal Rights* (Salt Lake City: Signature Books, 2005).
Sillitoe, Linda. "Women Scorned: Inside the IWY Conference." *Utah Holiday* 6.2 (August 1977): 63–65.

EXCERPTS FROM "CHURCH AND POLITICS AT THE UTAH IWY CONFERENCE"

When my Relief Society President asked me to recruit 10 women from our ward to attend the International Women's Year Utah Women's Conference, she assured me that the Church was not instructing Mormon women how to vote but was merely encouraging them to be present and to reflect "church standards" when appropriate. She shared a comment from the stake Relief Society leadership expressing concern that the conference would be too "liberal" without the presence of Mormon women. She also passed on a copy of the conference pre-registration form, on which a stake leader had checked those workshops she thought Mormons ought to attend; they included, among others, workshops on the Equal Rights Amendment (ERA), reproductive health (which was to discuss abortion), teenage pregnancy and young women. The Relief Society President and I concurred in the decision that the most appropriate way to involve ward sisters would be to share factual information about the conference and to invite them officially, on behalf of the Relief Society, not only to attend but to share their individual values and viewpoints.

The week of the conference, two phone calls made me wonder if Church desire to involve its women in the IWY Conference had gone beyond mere community participation. The first call was from a friend in a Salt Lake City east bench ward. She had been asked by her official Relief Society "recruiter" to attend as a ward delegate and vote against the Equal Rights Amendment and other resolutions seen as contrary to church positions. The second call was from a woman in my ward who had attended sacrament meeting in another ward the Sunday before the conference. The woman thought I would like to know that the bishop in that ward had read from the pulpit a letter alleged to be from Ezra Taft Benson, in which women were urged to attend the conference to defend church positions and to prevent feminists and radical leftists from dominating the conference. (A check in my own ward revealed no such letter.)

That the Church's quota system was effective was shown by the presence at the convention's opening song and prayer of some 9,000 registrants. The conference organizers had originally planned for 3,000 participants; ultimately attendance was to swell to over 13,000. A clue to the mood of the conference came as introductions of dignitaries were made. While polite applause greeted the introduction of Mary Anne Krupsak, New York State's Lieutenant Governor and the IWY federal observer assigned to the Utah conference, rousing cheers greeted the introduction of Relief Society President Barbara Smith. Most of the audience were clearly LDS and eager to demonstrate their loyalty.

From Friday morning's proceedings it was clear that the majority of conference registrants were openly hostile toward the Utah Coordinating Committee and the federal regulations guiding the state women's conference. The source of the enormous groundswell of distrust for the Utah IWY Coordinating Committee was puzzling to me. I knew a number of the Committee members and several members of task forces. From past experience I knew them to be responsible people; from conversations with several of them I knew the Committee had tried to be both fair and moderate in all conference preparations. The vast majority of the Committee was made up of women from all parts of the Wasatch Front (the state's urban core, where the majority of its population resides.) Half were LDS. Some were young, some elderly. Some were homemakers; some were professional women. Most had records of community involvement. Ethnic minority women were represented. The committee chairperson was an active member of the LDS Church and a BYU faculty member.

To judge by remarks heard from the floor of the convention, the fact that organizers and nominees were generally interested in the women's movement seemed both perverse and conspiratorial to most conference participants—who were not similarly interested and had therefore passed up chances to become involved until the Church had rallied them. It was not until after the conference was over and their control secure that the majority would acknowledge that the Coordinating Committee had run the conference fairly and had not used dirty tricks on unwitting conference goers.

Different workshops produced differing experiences for conference goers. Some were constructive and even peaceful. Other workshops were quarrelsome and chaotic. In the Friday afternoon ERA workshop, which I attended (and which was repeated Saturday morning), the audience listened to the two proponents of the ERA politely and quietly for the most part, but frequently interrupted the speeches of the two opponents to shout enthusiastic approval. The ensuing parliamentary debate produced some of the conference's most "anti" militant resolutions. The audience did not support the task force's "neutral" resolution urging dissemination of information, pro and con, on the ERA. Instead it voted down not only support for the ERA but also support for any public funding for discussion of the issue. Saturday's participants went further and advocated abolition of all future funding for International Women's Year.

By Saturday the results of the national resolutions, voted on by secret ballot the day before, had been tallied by the computer. Every one of the national resolutions had been defeated. In addition to rejecting unpopular resolutions supporting the ERA, the right of a woman to control her own body (abortion on demand), enforcement of non-discrimination in education on the basis of sex (Title IX), and day-care programs, the registrants defeated a host of more moderate resolutions, examples of which are quoted below:

Child Care: Education for parenthood programs should be improved and expanded by local and state school boards with technical assistance and experimental programs provided by the Federal government.

Credit: The Federal Equal Credit Opportunity Act should be vigorously, efficiently, and expeditiously enforced by all the Federal agencies with enforcement responsibilities.

Employment: The Executive Branch of the Federal government should abide by the same standards as private employers.

Female Offenders: Federal and state governments should cooperate in providing more humane, sensible, and economic treatment of young women who are subject to court jurisdiction because they have run away from home, have family or school problems, or commit sexual offenses ("status offenders").

Legal Status of Homemakers: More effective methods for collection of support should be adopted.

Older Women: Public and private women's organizations should work together to give publicity to the positive roles of women over 50 and to provide the services that will enable elderly women to function comfortably in their own homes instead of moving to institutions.

Rape: State and local governments should revise rape laws to provide for graduated degrees of the crime to apply to assault by or upon both sexes; to include all types of sexual assault against adults; and to otherwise redefine the crime so that victims are under no greater legal handicaps than victims of other crimes.

Women in Elective and Appointive Office: The President, Governors, political parties, women's organizations, and foundations should join in an effort to increase the number of women in elective and appointive office, including especially judgeships.

A major factor in the negative vote was obviously the acknowledged philosophical opposition of the majority of the participants to both feminism and to the women's movement. They had no wish to examine individual issues on their merit but rather were present to make a political statement in opposition both to the very legitimacy of the need for the conference, and to the role of the federal government in establishing state coordinating committees and the upcoming convention in Houston. But an explanation for the defeat of *all* the resolutions, even supposedly noncontroversial ones, must go beyond this. Great numbers of conference participants had attended pre-conference caucuses and were heavily swayed by the judgments and attitudes of caucus leaders. Attendees stated that caucus leaders had urged the defeat of the national resolutions, had voiced fear of radical feminist control of state and national conferences, had cited "horror stories" from other state conventions about homosexual life-style support and pornographic movies, had expressed open distrust of the IWY Coordinating Committee in Utah and had distributed anti-ERA, anti-abortion delegate slates. Every vagueness in the wording of the national resolutions was seen as conspiratorial and devious. Some caucuses were told not to bother to read the resolutions because some of them might "sound good" and therefore might deceive the reader. Caucus leaders had represented the politically conservative forces opposed to abortion, the ERA and the women's movement in general. They had used the Church's organizational mechanisms and their own Church affiliation to encourage attendance at the caucuses. Many persons in attendance accepted such representations unquestioningly, neither challenging the sources of the information nor checking its accuracy.

Another contributing factor was that for many participants the conference was the first introduction to the women's movement and its concerns. The complexity of many of the issues may have made many women feel too ignorant to make sound judgments; under these circumstances, they simply adopted the old adage which has defeated many another political issue: "When in doubt, vote no."

How much of the results of this conference, either good or bad, can be laid at the doorstep of the Church? Certainly the large turnout at the conference can be attributed to the Church's calling of 10 women from each ward. The church's organizational mechanisms are superb. Use of both the priesthood authority and the quota system made the invitation to attend acquire the nature of a call, with the intended result: people came.

What transpired after the initial phone calls from President Benson's office is unclear, but it is clear that messages farther down the line (from stake Relief Society Presidents to ward presidents to ward members) stated over and over again that the Relief Society wanted women at the conference to defend Church positions and to prevent domination by radical feminists. Concern about the nature of the conference, rather than the desire to encourage community participation by LDS women, was the dominant theme of countless messages relayed down the chain. Given the IWY Committee's personal request to the Relief Society to support the IWY Conference by inviting its women to attend, some may question whether the actual way in which the Church chose to accept the invitation was either generous or gracious.

Both before and after the conference the Church insisted that it had not told its women how to vote; it had only encouraged them to attend. It seems obvious that members did not need to be told explicitly how to vote. Their attitudes about the conference had already been shaped.

The behavior of conference participants in reaching their decisions is also something with which the Church ought to be concerned. The conference was too often characterized by distrust, self-righteousness and a battlefield mentality which demanded unconditional victory. For women with Judeo-Christian roots, too many behaved in unchristian fashion.

We in the Church often cite with pride Joseph Smith's pronouncement: "I teach the people correct principles and they govern themselves." When we are gullible, unquestioningly believing persons who are acting in secular capacities and trading on their Church ties, one may ask whether we have indeed been taught correct principles. When we are unable to participate in the political arena with love, courtesy, compassion and respect for all persons, including those whose beliefs are different from our own, can we say we have learned correct principles? Perhaps we ought to address some hard social issues in Relief Society, and other church meetings, with clear church sanction and clear church acceptance of divergent solutions among its members. If church members do not practice correct principles under conditions of stress, how can we say with assurance that we know how to govern ourselves?

Sonia Johnson (1936–), "My Revolution": Excerpt, *From Housewife to Heretic* (1981)

Church leaders first brought their anti-ERA fight to Washington, D.C.-area LDS congregations in April 1977, hoping to mobilize the relatively small but well-connected and politically aware Mormon community to lobby Virginia legislators to defeat the extension of the ratification deadline for the Amendment. One of the members of the congregations targeted for anti-ERA mobilization was Sonia Johnson, a forty-one-year-old mother of four and devout Church member who played the organ and taught in the Sunday School and Relief Society as well. A Utah-born Mormon with pioneer roots and a doctorate in education from Rutgers University, Johnson had experienced a very personal feminist awakening earlier that spring. The launch of the LDS Church anti-ERA campaign in Virginia made her an activist. In this excerpt from her 1981 memoir *From Housewife to Heretic*, Johnson describes her feminist transformation as a process taking her from a deeply felt spiritual unease, through an intense encounter with darkness and an earnest plea to God, to an answer that arrives with an overwhelming spiritual witness—a narrative formula that has defined the conversion narratives of Mormons from Joseph Smith to the present.

Source

Johnson, Sonia. *From Housewife to Heretic*. 1981. Albuquerque, NM: Wildfire Books, 1989.

References and Further Reading

Bradford, Mary L. "The Odyssey of Sonia Johnson." *Dialogue: A Journal of Mormon Thought* 14.2 (1981): 14–26.

FROM HOUSEWIFE TO HERETIC

One afternoon I sat on the basement stairs and wondered why I felt so depressed. We had a lovely house, I had a part-time editing job (which I didn't enjoy much, but I could do it at home and it left plenty of time for the children and church work); the house was clean, supper was ready to go into the oven, and I had several free hours before everyone came home. Ordinarily all this, plus the fact that we were all well and our lives were going smoothly, should have given me a feeling of contentment. But there I was, swamped with despair and praying aloud, "Why, Father, why do I feel so awful? What's wrong with me?" I prayed on and on, aloud, as is my wont when I'm alone, but the deadly, leaden feeling refused to budge. And then I remembered a talk I'd heard in church the Sunday before, which suggested that since we don't always understand ourselves well enough to know what we should pray for, we should ask God.

So I did. And no sooner had I done so than I surprised myself by saying, still in vocal prayer: "Father, I know there's something I've been trying to avoid knowing for a very long time—probably all my life—because I've been too afraid to face it, afraid of what it might do to my life and family, afraid I couldn't handle it, that it might overwhelm me and maybe even drive me insane. But I have become so unhappy by not dealing with it, that doing so could not make me any more miserable. So no matter what it is, I am ready to know it. I want to know it. I must know it!"

Immediately, I heard my own voice in my mind say clearly, "Patriarchy is a sham."

In the Mormon church, patriarchy is sacred; it is held to be the principle of organization by which a male God created and governs the world through other males like himself. It is the masculine glue that holds the world together. I had been taught this all my life, and had had it reinforced one hundredfold in the temple, that most sacred Mormon structure in which the divinity of patriarchy—of maleness—is the basic message.

To keep God and to learn to trust again, that was the first requisite of my revolution. To do that, I had to establish first that he was not sexist—which is a good deal easier said than done. I said no—intellectually—to God's sexism. Gradually, stroke by stroke, I redrew deity, piece by piece I reorganized heaven, because I wanted neither to give them up nor to fight against them.

I began to understand that God is not going to punish women for thinking, for questioning, for seeing through the myths that bind us, for being angry about what so richly deserves our anger, for going forth boldly to fight against the injustices that have been visited upon us so casually and so cruelly for so long. I began to understand that women are, in fact, going to be blessed and strengthened and comforted for this. I began to understand that we are going to be made joyful.

Also soon after that fateful night, I made the totally un-unique discovery one day that men had made God in their own image to keep control of women. Why then could not women remake God in a way that would, instead of disenfranchising and dehumanizing half the human race, empower everyone, make everyone whole? It was clearly time for women to desegregate the club and reorganize heaven.

Thinking about this, I remembered Mother in Heaven, the divine being to whom Mormon doctrine attests (and who was put there, appropriately enough, by a female prophet—probably when the men were away at some Old Boys' meeting). Remembered, sought her, and found her. And loved her. Oh, how I loved and continue to love her! As I gradually reinstated her in her rightful position in my new heaven as equal in power and glory to Father—not in subordination, as the churchmen so wishfully think (and won't they be surprised!)—I began to feel a wholeness and a personal power that transcended any happiness I had ever known. With Mother on her throne as a model for me in heaven, I felt wonderful. I felt wonderful knowing that femaleness is as divine, as desirable, as powerful as maleness.

Sonia Johnson (1936–), "The Church Was Once in the Forefront of the Women's Movement": Speech to the Senate Constitutional Rights Subcommittee (1978)

As the LDS Church's covert efforts to mobilize Virginia members to prevent the ERA's passage intensified in 1978, Mormons who supported the Equal Rights Amendment organized their own grassroots efforts. About twenty men and women, including Mormons for ERA founders Hazel Davis Rigby, Teddie Wood, Maida Withers, and Sonia Johnson, joined a pro-ERA march down Pennsylvania Avenue in July 1978. On August 4, 1978, after Mormons for ERA received an invitation from Senator Birch Bayh to participate in a panel on religious views of the Equal Rights Amendment, Sonia Johnson appeared before the Senate Constitutional Rights Subcommittee. Johnson was chosen to represent the cause,

she later recalled, because "I hadn't sullied my reputation in the church by protesting against its treatment of Blacks. (I was in Africa most of the time!)" (Rick
Johnson's career had taken the family abroad.) Several of the original Mormons
for ERA members had vocally opposed the LDS Church's ban on full participation
by Black men and women, which had only been rescinded in June 1978; Withers,
a Georgetown University dance professor, also had a history of civil rights
activism stemming from her tenure as one of the few white faculty members at
Washington, D.C.'s Howard University. With no public activist record, Johnson,
the group believed, might best reflect the conservative ideals of Mormon womanhood. She arrived at the Senate Office Building "with my big round A MORMON
FOR ERA card on my bosom, fasting, and so frightened I could get through it
only with the help of the Lord." Physically trembling, she delivered her testimony
on the compatibility of women's equality and LDS beliefs, citing the history of
Mormon women's activism recovered by Boston-area Mormon feminists a few
years before and interrupted by what Hazel Davis Rigby described as "spontane-
ous outbursts of applause" from the 350-member audience. Afterward, Johnson
was subjected to what one reporter described as a "mean" and "denigrat[ing]"
interrogation from Utah Senator Orrin Hatch, who said, "I would be surprised if
the Mormon women who are for ERA would comprise one-tenth of one percent."
Johnson replied, "You yourself belong to a church of only 3 million members
which purports to be the only true church in the world. That is a pretty precarious
position. I am accustomed to being one of few and in the right."

Source

Johnson, Sonia. "The Church Was Once in the Forefront of the Women's Movement."Sonia
Johnson Collection, Box 6, folder 1, Special Collections Department, J. Willard Marriott
Library, University of Utah.

"THE CHURCH WAS ONCE IN THE FOREFRONT
OF THE WOMEN'S MOVEMENT"

Wherever we go with our bumper stickers, our buttons, our signs and banners that
proclaim us Mormons who support the ERA, we are greeted with disbelief and
amazement. This, in turn, amazes us. So few people remember that the church
was once in the forefront of the equal rights movement, and that Mormon feminists played a significant part in that movement. Women of great prominence in
the church—Eliza R. Snow, wife of Joseph Smith, and, after his death, of Brigham
Young; Susa Young Gates, daughter of Brigham Young; Emmeline B. Wells and
many others—addressed themselves, in their *Woman's Exponent*, to the woman
question. The *Woman's Exponent* was an unofficial Mormon magazine begun at
the instigation of Brigham Young. It was the first magazine published by and for
women west of the Mississippi.

Early Mormon feminists demonstrated that the movement for equal rights could be compatible with Mormon doctrine. That they are compatible is eminently clear to us. Joseph Smith, the founder of the church, once remarked that his method of governing the members was to teach them correct principles and let them govern themselves. In doing so, he was acting in accord with one of the most profound doctrines of the church—the human right to, and necessity for, free agency. Mormon scriptures are replete with assurances that this is an eternal principle. As one highly respected Mormon theologian writes:

> We believe that the entire human race existed as spirit beings in the primeval world and that . . . they were endowed with the powers of agency or choice while yet but spirits; and the divine plan provided that they be free-born in the flesh, heirs to the inalienable birthright of liberty to choose and to act for themselves in mortality. . . .[1]

Behind such a doctrine lies great love and trust. The church teaches us that our Father in Heaven knows that many of us will make self-limiting and destructive choices, but that his greatest desire is that we should one day become like him. He understands that for such tremendous growth it is essential for us to have full options, to take responsibility for choosing, to live somehow through the consequences of our choices, and to learn from them what constitutes full humanity. He trusts us with this precious gift, not because he thinks we will all use it wisely, but because he loves us so much he is willing to take the risk.

The leaders of the church, though great and good men, are nevertheless mortal and not yet like our Father in the fullness of love. Because they love us less, they are less willing to risk, less willing to trust us to make wise decisions. They have chosen instead to tamper with our agency, to attempt to compel us to do what they believe is right through the use of fear and of their considerable authority. Unlike the Lord, they are afraid now, having taught us correct principles, to let us govern ourselves.

The rhetoric of the modern church sounds much like that of former times, but there is one critical difference—women are supported in word only, not in deed, a practice which confuses and blinds many church members. In their official statement opposing the ERA, the leaders of the church affirm the "exalted role of woman in our society," and then proceed to withdraw support from an amendment which would give her equal protection under the law. In church publications and practices, despite the lofty sentiments expressed, women are almost always regarded as "roles" rather than as individual human beings with interests and capacities as varied and significant as men's. A fine example of this appeared in the Congressional Record, May 26, 1978, page S8441, the church's statement opposing extension: "Because all human life begins with her, the Church of Jesus

Christ of Latter-day Saints has always held her in revered light." It is our biological functions, our "role" as mothers which alone gives us value. We can express our dismay at this equivocation no better than one Mormon sister expressed hers in 1880: "Is this all, this shadow without the substance, that our brethren can afford to give us?"[2]

She would have been angered to learn that less than a hundred years hence—in the late 1960's—our brethren would suddenly consider us too exalted to offer prayers in our sacrament meetings, a right inherent in church membership from the very beginning, so exalted that they abolished the magazine which had been published in some form since 1872 by and for the women of the church.

We are so exalted that young women must be several years older than their male peers in order to serve a mission for the church, and are not encouraged to do so at any age.

So exalted that we are not allowed to manage the budget for our own women's auxiliary, to organize, plan, or conduct major church services that are not primarily for females or children.

So exalted that we cannot stand in the circle where our own babies are being christened by our husbands and male friends.

So exalted that we are encouraged to sacrifice our educations to support our husbands in obtaining theirs, so exalted that we should do by far the greater share of the difficult tasks of parenting because our husbands are too busy with the "important" matters of church and business.

Where equality does not even pertain, the word "exalted" is a mockery. One wonders if the leaders of the church would gladly exchange their sex and become so exalted, and if not, what has happened to a church which professes to be the church of Jesus Christ and has forgotten his central teaching: "What you would that others would do unto you, do ye even so unto them."

Mormon women do not wish to be exalted in this or any real way. As one of our courageous foremothers wrote:

> We want an open field and no favor; we want you to decide upon the merits of our case and not out of a spirit of chivalry to our sex. We want equal and exact justice, we want for our girls the same chances in the race that are provided for our boys. We want our colleges to admit young women to the same course and on the same conditions as they do young men. We want to be allowed to decide what our sphere is. . . . All these things and many more, we ask in the name of common humanity, and we will not be contented with the half loaf. . . .[3]

We firmly believe that what our early sisters would have wanted, what they would be working for if they were here today, what constitutes the whole loaf with which they would be contented, is ratification of the Equal Rights Amendment. They left us a mighty heritage of courage and conviction, and we rejoice, as they did, that:

> This is a momentous age. Art and science are making wonderful strides. Everything, it would seem, which can benefit and interest the human family is being developed and improved. Woman cannot help feeling the impulse given to this generation. It is the spirit of God, and woman shares this influence. She is bound to rise, and no human power can stop her progress.[4]

Notes

1. See James E. Talmage, *Jesus the Christ* (Salt Lake City, Deseret Book, 1957), 17.
2. See "Equal Rights," *Woman's Exponent* 8 (March 1, 1880), 146.
3. See "An Address," *Woman's Exponent* 8 (February 15, 1880), 143.
4. See Flora S. Hill, "The Impulse of the Hour," *Woman's Exponent* 8 (April 15, 1880), 171.

Sonia Johnson (1936–), "Patriarchal Panic: Sexual Politics in the Mormon Church" (1979)

The LDS Church–backed campaign against the ERA intensified in preparation for the opening of the Virginia legislative session in January 1979, when regional Church leaders quietly orchestrated the organization of a purportedly "independent" LDS Citizens Coalition to raise funds, distribute anti-ERA political literature, and lobby legislators to oppose ratification. "Mormons constituted only 0.5 percent of the population of Virginia," historian Martha Sonntag Bradley would later write, "but were responsible, at least in the northern part of the commonwealth, for 85 percent of the anti-ERA mail received by legislators." Mormons for ERA intensified its efforts as well, requesting that the secretary of the Virginia commonwealth investigate whether the LDS Citizens Coalition had violated state lobbying regulations and chartering a plane to fly overhead Temple Square during the LDS Church's General Conference in April 1979 towing a banner that read "Mormons for ERA are everywhere!" Sonia Johnson also continued to speak to the press and the public, her speeches growing sharper in their indictment of the LDS Church's political operations and patriarchy. The fieriest was Johnson's September 1, 1979, speech to a meeting of the American Psychological Association in New York City. Journalist and Mormon feminist Linda Sillitoe (see her poem anthologized in this volume) would later reflect that Johnson's "use of hyperbole and sometimes startlingly vivid language [was] usually humorous or ironic" but in this case expressed a sense of "pain or anger" that struck many Mormons as "polemic and harsh." Copies of the "Patriarchal Panic" speech were circulated widely in Mormon circles, including by the campus student government at Brigham Young University, ostensibly as evidence of the dangers of supporting the ERA.

On November 14, 1979, Sonia Johnson was called to a church disciplinary court on charges that in her public speeches she had "spoken evil of the Lord's anointed," a violation of religious vows she had taken as a temple-attending Mormon. The all-male body of local Mormon Church leaders who served as judges and jury focused particularly on her "Patriarchal Panic" address, which they misconstrued as accusing LDS Church leaders of "savage misogyny." Candle-holding supporters—including Congresswoman Pat Schroeder and Esther Eggertson Peterson, a Utah-born Mormon, member of a noted Mormon progressive family, and a consumer, labor, and women's rights advocate who had served in the Kennedy, Johnson, and Carter administrations—gathered in the church parking lot during the hearing. On December 1, 1979, Sonia Johnson received notice by letter that she had been excommunicated from the Church of Jesus Christ of Latter-day Saints. She would continue as the president of Mormons for ERA through December 1980, devote herself for another few years to the fight for ERA ratification, write and publish a memoir, run for the presidency of the National Organization for Women, and, eventually, open her own feminist commune in New Mexico. Tens of thousands of Mormon women identified with the feminist movement during the 1970s. Thousands supported the Equal Rights Amendment. Only one was excommunicated. But her story sent an outsized message to Mormon feminists in the 1980s that their activism could cost them their religious home.

Source

Johnson, Sonia. "Patriarchal Panic: Sexual Politics in the Mormon Church." Sonia Johnson Collection, Box 6, folder 1, Special Collections Department, J. Willard Marriott Library, University of Utah.

"PATRIARCHAL PANIC: SEXUAL POLITICS IN THE MORMON CHURCH"

Sexual politics is old hat in the Mormon Church. It was flourishing when my grandparents were infants, crossing the plains to Utah in covered wagons. Although different generations have developed their own peculiar variations on the theme, I believe my generation is approaching the ultimate confrontation, for which all the others were simply dress rehearsals. Mormon sexual politics today is an uneasy mixture of explosive phenomena: the recent profound disenfranchisement of Mormon women by Church leaders, the Church's sudden strong political presence in the anti-ERA arena and the women's movement.

Saturated as it is with the anti-female bias that is patriarchy's very definition and reason for being, the Mormon Church can legitimately be termed "The Last

Unmitigated Western Patriarchy." (I know you Catholics and Jews in this audience will want to argue with that but I will put my patriarchs up against yours any day!) This patriarchal imperative is reinforced by the belief that the President of the Church is a Prophet of God, as were Isaiah and Moses, and that God will not allow him to make a mistake in guiding the Church. He is, therefore, if not doctrinally, in practice "infallible"—deified. Commonly heard thought-obliterating dicta in my Church are "When our leaders speak, the thinking has been done" and "when the Prophet speaks, the debate is ended." They forget to mention that the debate probably never even got started since in the Church there is little dialogue or real education. Indoctrination is the prime method of instruction because obedience is the contemporary Church's prime message.

The political implications of this mass renunciation of individual conscience for direction from "God" are not clearly enough understood in this country. The Mormons, a tiny minority, are dedicated to imposing the Prophet's moral directives upon all Americans and they may succeed if Americans do not become aware of their methods and goals. Because the organization of the Church is marvelously tight and the obedience of the members marvelously thorough-going, potentially thousands of people can be mobilized in a very short time to do—conscientiously—whatever they are told, without more explanation than "the Prophet has spoken."

But Mormon anti-ERA activity, though organized and directed by the hierarchy of the Church from Salt Lake down through regional and local male leaders, is covert activity, not openly done in the name of the Church. Members are cautioned not to reveal that they are Mormons or organized by the Church when they lobby, write letters, donate money and pass out anti-ERA brochures door-to-door through whole states. Instead, they are directed to say that they are concerned citizens following the dictates of their individual consciences. Since they are, in fact, following the dictates of the Prophet's conscience and would revise their own overnight if he were to revise his, nothing could be further from the truth.

In addition, Mormon women, who make up most of the anti-ERA Mormon army (and the leaders refer to it as an army in true patriarchal style), are advised not to tell people that the men of the Church have organized them, but to maintain that they voluntarily organized themselves. "People won't understand," their male leaders explain which in patriarchal doublespeak means: "People will understand only too well that this is the usual male trick of enlisting women to carry out men's oppressive measures against women, hiding the identity of the real oppressors and alienating women from each other."

So many of us in the Church are so unalterably opposed to this covert and oppressive activity that one of the major purposes of MORMONS FOR ERA has become to shine light upon the murky political activities of the Church and to expose to other Americans its exploitation of women's religious commitment for its self-serving male political purposes.

The reaction of the Church fathers to the women's movement and women's demand for equal rights has produced fearful and fascinating phenomena. In the mid-1960s, Utah's birthrate was almost exactly the same as the national rate, but by last year it was double the national average—evidence of a real patriarchal panic, a tremendous reaction against the basic feminist tenet that women were meant by their Creator to be individuals first and to fulfill roles second—to the degree and in the way they choose, as men do. In almost every meeting of the Church (and Mormons are noted for their much meeting), there is some message designed to reinforce the stereotype of the "good" Mormon woman, acceptable to the Brethren and therefore to God; messages calculated to keep women where men like them best: "made" (created) to nurture husband and children, housebound, financially and emotionally dependent, occupationally immature, politically naive, obedient, subordinate, submissive, somnambulant and bearing much of the heavy and uncredited labor of the Church upon their uncomplaining shoulders.

Encyclicals from the Brethren over the past ten years such as those which took away women's right to pray in major Church meetings (this right has since been restored but women will not be safe from the Brethren's capricious meddling with our inalienable human rights until we attain positions of power and authority in our Church); to control our own auxiliary money and program and to publish our own magazine for communication among ourselves have put women under total male control, requiring us to ask permission of men in even the smallest of matters. These rulings—which have seriously harmed women's self-esteem, lowered our status, made us bootlickers and toadies to the men of the Church and destroyed what little freedom of choice we had—those rulings reveal the depth of the Brethren's fear of independent, non-permission-asking women, the kind of women which are emerging from the women's movement. And it is no accident that they were enacted just as the feminist tide in the United States began to swell.

But we have other, more direct, ways of knowing how badly threatened and angry our brethren are by the existence of women who are not under their control. In April, we hired a plane to fly a banner over Temple Square in Salt Lake City during a break in the world-wide Conference of male leaders being held in the Tabernacle. The banner announced that MORMONS FOR ERA ARE EVERYWHERE. A reporter phoned the [press secretary] of the Church to ask how the Brethren were taking this little prank and was told that they found it "amusing." Then the [press secretary] suggested that the reporter put a cartoon in the next day's paper showing our plane flying over the Angel Moroni atop the Temple (as the actual newspaper had) but instead of a trumpet, picture Moroni brandishing a machine gun. One does not need to be a psychoanalyst to understand how "amusing" the Brethren found our "little prank." More recently, when an *Associated Press* reporter interviewed President Kimball on the subject of uppity Mormon women, the Prophet warned that Church members who support the Equal Rights Amendment should be "very, very careful" because the Church is led by "strong men and able men. . . . We feel we are in a position to lead them properly." The threat here is open and clear. We had better be very, very careful because the men at the head of the Church are strong and the patriarchs have for millennia crushed those women who escaped from their mind-bindings. President Kimball is further quoted as saying, "These women who are asking for authority to do everything that a man can do and change the order and go and do men's work instead of bearing children, she's just off her base"—a truly appalling revelation of ignorance about the realities of women's lives.

But perhaps the image of greatest terror crawled from the psyche of Hartman Rector, one of the General Authorities of the Church, in response to my testimony before the U.S. Senate Subcommittee on Constitutional Rights:

> *In order to attempt to get the male somewhere near even, the Heavenly Father gave him the Priesthood, or directing authority for the Church and home. Without this bequeath, the male would be so far below the female in power and influence that there would be little or no purpose for his existence. In fact (sic) would probably be eaten by the female as is the case with the black widow Spider.*

Given this view of women, it should come as no surprise that despite the carefully calculated public relations campaign which portrays the Mormon Church as the last bastion (and probably the inventors!) of the happy family and fulfilled womanhood, all is not well in Zion: all is particularly not well among Zion's women.

In recent years, considerable hue and cry has arisen over the subject of depression among Mormon women, inspiring a spate of documentaries and articles. The *Salt Lake Tribune* in December of 1977 quoted local therapists as stating that up to three-quarters of their Mormon patients were women and that the common denominator was low self-image and lack of fulfillment outside the home. This depression is endemic and begins at an early age: the incidence of suicide among teenaged females in Utah is more than double the national average and rising. Seven of 10 teenaged brides are premaritally pregnant and 40 percent of Utah's brides are teens. The proportion of teenage marriages in Utah has been greater than for the nation each year since 1960, which might partially account for Utah's divorce rate being higher than the national average. (The time of the beginning of the increase is also significant, as I have pointed out earlier). Alcoholism and drug abuse among women are problems in Mormon culture, as are child and wife abuse. In the last 14 years, rape in Utah has increased 165 percent and the local index of rape is 1.35 percent higher than the national average. Add to this the significant fact that attendance at Relief Society, the Church's women's auxiliary, and at the Young Women's organization meetings has dropped off drastically nationwide.

What all this says to the patriarchs is anyone's guess, they are either afraid to talk with those of us who are alarmed at their opinions and treatment of women or they do not consider us worth their time. But what it says to those of us who have survived being Mormon women is that our sisters are silently screaming for help and that they are not only NOT finding it at Church, but that at Church they are being further depressed and debilitated by bombardment with profoundly demeaning female sex-role stereotypes. Their Church experience is making them sick.

Because Mormon women are trained to desire above all else to please men (and I include in this category God, whom all too many of us view as an extension of our chauvinist leaders), we spend enormous amounts of energy trying to make the very real but—for most of us—limited satisfactions of mother- and wifehood substitute satisfactorily for all other life experiences. What spills over into those vacant lots of our hearts where our intellectual and talented selves should be vigorously alive and thriving are, instead, frustration, anger and the despair which comes from suppressing anger and feeling guilty for having felt it in the first place. Last summer, a Utah woman wrote to Senator [Orrin] Hatch of Utah: "A sea of smoldering women is a dangerous thing." And that's what the Mormon patriarchy has on its hands: a sea of smoldering women. Those whose anger is still undifferentiated, who do not realize how thoroughly they are being betrayed their rage is exploited by Church leaders who subvert it into attacks against feminist causes such as the Equal Rights Amendment, making scapegoats of women and their righteous desires, identifying women as the source of women's danger (a patriarchal tactic for maintaining power that has its roots in antiquity) and trying to distract us from recognizing that where our real danger as women lies, and always has lain, is in patriarchy.

But women are not fools. The very violence with which the Brethren attacked an Amendment which would give women human status in the Constitution abruptly opened the eyes of thousands of us to the true source of our danger and our anger. This open patriarchal panic against our human rights raised consciousness miraculously all over the Church as nothing else could have done. And revealing their raw panic at the idea that women might step forward as goddesses-in-the-making with power in a real—not a sub- or through men—sense, was the leaders' critical and mortal error, producing as it did a deafening dissonance between their rhetoric of love and their oppressive, unloving, destructive behavior.

I receive phone calls and letters from Mormon women all over the country and each has a story or two to tell: how two Mormon women in one meeting independently stood and spoke of their Mother in Heaven, how they met afterwards and wept together in joy at having found and named Her; how a courageous Mormon woman is preparing to make the first public demand for the priesthood.

"The time has come," she says calmly, "for women to insist upon full religious enfranchisement." This statement is the Mormon woman's equivalent of the shot heard 'round the world! Our patriarchy may be The Last Unmitigated but it is no longer unchallenged. A multitude of Mormon women are through asking permission. We are waking up and growing up and in our waking and growing can be heard—distinctly—the death rattle of the patriarchy.

Linda P. Wilcox Desimone (1939–), "The Mormon Concept of a Mother in Heaven" (1980)

At roughly the same historical moment as the Mormon feminists of Boston organized, another group of Mormon women convened lunchtime meetings at Temple Square in downtown Salt Lake City, often gathering under Eliza R. Snow's gable window in the garden of the Lion House, Brigham Young's historic home. All were observant members of the Church; most were working mothers, and a few had positions in the Church Office Building or in the LDS Church Historical Department under the direction of LDS Church historian Leonard Arrington, a champion of Mormon women's history and historians. The Wednesday Lion House lunch group—which included Maureen Ursenbach Beecher, Linda King Newell, Lavina Fielding Anderson, Carol Cornwall Madsen, Jill Mulvay Derr, and others—talked, as did Boston's Mormon feminists, about the burgeoning women's movement and its points of coherence and conflict with Mormon belief and culture. "We watched as outsiders accused Mormon culture of chauvinism, sometimes with justification; we observed how insiders defended the faith, sometimes with sophistries we could not accept," recalled Maureen Ursenbach Beecher. "We recognized the joy of many Mormon women whose lives in the pattern of wife- and motherhood fulfilled them; we saw also the pain of others caught between the Scylla of poverty-level, stay-at-home mothering and the Charybdis of out-of-home employment. We saw our sisters serving energetically in church and community; we recognized that they were often pressed into unproductive roles when they had potential for dynamic leadership." As tensions between the LDS Church and the women's movement mounted, the Wednesday lunch group watched with concern as non-LDS people wrote about Mormon women and their faith in a way that reduced both to flat caricatures. They resolved to recover a fuller version of Mormon history and theology that would honor the potential of faith as a source of women's emancipation, including the uniquely Mormon doctrine of an embodied and coequal Heavenly Mother, early Mormon women's practices of healing, and the feminist significance of LDS temple rites as a form of female ordination. Among the group was Linda Wilcox, a Stanford University–educated historian and working mother of three. At the suggestion of Maureen Beecher, Wilcox wrote this essay chronicling the development of Mormon belief in the Heavenly Mother, a subject that had by the 1970s acquired a curious sense of mystery and even taboo in LDS communities. Wilcox later recalled, "I did not anticipate those people who have told me how they were moved by it." This and other essays written by the Wednesday lunch group were later published in the groundbreaking volume *Sisters in Spirit: Mormon Women in Historical and Cultural Perspective* (1987).

Source

Desimone, Linda P. Wilcox. "The Mormon Concept of a Mother in Heaven." *Sunstone* 5.5 (September–October 1980): 9–15.

References and Further Reading

Beecher, Maureen Ursenbach, and Lavina Fielding Anderson, eds. *Sisters in Spirit: Mormon Women in Historical and Cultural Perspective*. Urbana: University of Illinois Press, 1987.

"THE MORMON CONCEPT OF A MOTHER IN HEAVEN"

The idea of a mother in heaven is shadowy and elusive, floating around the edges of Mormon consciousness. Mormons who grow up singing "O My Father" are familiar with the concept of a heavenly mother, but few hear much else about her. She exists, apparently, but has not been very evident in Mormon meetings or writings. And little if any theology has been developed to elucidate her nature and characterize our relationship to her.

By the end of the nineteenth century, Elizabeth Cady Stanton in her *Woman's Bible* was explaining Genesis 1:26–28 ("And God said, Let us make man in our image, after our likeness") as implying the "simultaneous creation of both sexes, in the image of God. It is evident from the language," she writes, "that the masculine and feminine elements were equally represented" in the Godhead which planned the peopling of the earth. To Stanton, as in the gnostic texts, a trinity of Father, Mother, and Son was more rational, and she called for "the recognition by the rising generation of an ideal Heavenly Mother, to whom their prayers should be addressed, as well as to a Father."[1]

Half a century before Stanton's bible, the Mormon religion had begun to develop a doctrine of a heavenly mother—a glorified goddess, spouse to an actual Heavenly Father, and therefore the literal mother of our spirits. The Mother in Heaven concept was a logical and natural extension of a theology which posited both an anthropomorphic god, who had once been a man, and the possibility of eternal procreation of spirit children.

The origins of the Heavenly Mother concept in Mormonism are shadowy. The best known exposition is Eliza R. Snow's poem, "O My Father," or "Invocation, or the Eternal Father and Mother"—the title it was known by earlier. When the poem was first published in the *Times and Seasons* it carried the notation, "City of Joseph, Oct. 1845," but the actual date of composition is not known. It does not appear in Eliza's notebook/diary for the years 1842–44.[2]

President Wilford Woodruff gave Snow credit for originating the idea: "That hymn is a revelation, though it was given unto us by a woman."[3] President Joseph F. Smith claimed that God revealed that principle ("that we have a mother as well as a father in heaven") to Joseph Smith; that Smith revealed it to Snow, his polygamous wife; and that Snow was inspired, being a poet, to put it into verse.[4]

Other incidents tend to confirm this latter view. Susa Young Gates told of Joseph Smith's consoling Zina Diantha Huntington on the death of her mother in 1839 by telling her that not only would she know her mother again on the other side, but "More than that, you will meet and become acquainted with your eternal Mother, the wife of your Father in Heaven." Susa went on to say that about this same time Eliza Snow "learned the same glorious truth from the same inspired lips" and was then moved to put this into verse.[5] Since Huntington and Snow were close friends as well, it was a likely possibility that they spoke of this idea.[6] David McKay recorded that during a buggy ride on which he accompanied Eliza Snow, he asked her if the Lord had revealed the Mother in Heaven doctrine to her. She replied, "I got my inspiration from the Prophets teachings[;] all that I was required to do was to use my Poetical gift and give that Eternal principal in Poetry."[7]

Women were not the only ones acquainted with the idea of a mother in heaven during Joseph Smith's lifetime. There is a third-hand account of an experience related by Zebedee Coltrin:

> One day the Prophet Joseph asked him [Coltrin] and Sidney Rigdon to accompany him into the woods to pray. When they had reached a secluded spot Joseph laid down on his back and stretched out his arms. He told the brethren to lie one on each arm, and then shut their eyes. After they had prayed he told them to open their eyes. They did so and saw a brilliant light surrounding a pedestal which seemed to rest on the earth. They closed their eyes and again prayed. They then saw, on opening them, the Father seated upon a throne; they prayed again and on looking saw the Mother also; after praying and looking the fourth time they saw the Savior added to the group.[8]

Church leaders of the nineteenth century, although they did not speak much about a mother in heaven, seemed to accept the idea as commonsensical, that for God to be a father implied the existence of a mother as well. Brigham Young said that God "created man, as we create our children; for there is no other process of creation in heaven, on the earth, in the earth, or under the earth, or in all the eternities, that is, that were, or that ever will be"—an indirect reference to the necessity of a mother for the process of creation.[9] He also quoted his counselor Heber C. Kimball's recollection of Smith's saying "that he would not worship a God who had not a Father; and I do not know that he would if he had not a mother; the one would be as absurd as the other."[10]

Apostle Erastus Snow also used indirect inference in explaining the logic of the Heavenly Mother concept:

> Now, it is not said in so many words in the Scriptures, that we have a Mother in heaven as well as a Father. It is left for us to infer this from what we see and know of all living things in the earth including man. The male and female principle is united and both necessary to the accomplishment of the object of their being, and if this be not the case with our Father in heaven after whose image we are created, then it is an anomaly in nature. But to our minds the idea of a Father suggests that of a Mother.[11]

Snow's position was somewhat distinct from those of other Mormon leaders in that he described God as a unity of male and female elements, much like the Shakers' Father-Mother God:

> "What," says one, "do you mean we should understand that Deity consists of man and woman?" Most certainly I do. If I believe anything that god has ever said about himself, and anything pertaining to the creation and organization of man upon the earth, I must believe that Deity consists of man and woman . . . there can be no god except he is composed of the man and woman united, and there is not in all the eternities that exist, nor ever will be, a God in any other way. . . . There never was a God, and there never will be in all eternities, except they are made of these two component parts; a man and a woman; the male and the female.[12]

To Snow, God was not a male personage with a heavenly mother as a second divine personage; both of them together constituted God.

One reason little theology was developed about a heavenly mother is that the scriptural basis for the doctrine was slim. Joseph Fielding Smith noted that "the fact that there is no reference to a Mother in Heaven either in the Bible, Book of Mormon or Doctrine and Covenants, is not sufficient proof that no such thing as a mother did exist there."[13] As a possible reason for this gap in the scriptures, an LDS seminary teacher offered his explanation in 1960: "Considering the way man has profaned the name of God, the Father, and His Son, Jesus Christ, is it any wonder that the name of our Mother in Heaven has been withheld, not to mention the fact that the mention of Her is practically nil in scripture?"[14]

In looking next at statements by church leaders in the twentieth century, I would like to concentrate briefly on three time periods: the first decade of the new century, the 1920s and 1930s, and finally the more recent decades of the 1960s to the present. I would also like to take note of some themes which are apparent in these time periods—themes which may illustrate developments in the larger society as well.

For example, immediately after the turn of the century one noticeable thread which ran through several comments about Mother in Heaven was an association of that doctrine with the movement for women's rights, a major issue in the last years of the nineteenth century, especially in Utah. Apostle James E. Talmage in discussing the status and mission of women spoke of the early granting of the franchise to women in Utah and the Mormon church's claim that woman is man's equal. In this context he then went on to say, "The Church is bold enough to go so far as to declare that man has an Eternal Mother in the Heavens as well as an Eternal Father, and in the same sense 'we look upon woman as a being, essential in every particular to the carrying out of God's purposes in respect to mankind.' "[15] An article in the *Deseret News* noted that the truthfulness of the doctrine of a mother in heaven would eventually be accepted by the world—that "it is a truth from which, when fully realized, the perfect 'emancipation' and ennobling of woman will result."[16] To many the concept of a mother in heaven was a fitting expression of a larger movement which aimed at raising the status of women and expanding their rights and opportunities.

Also in that first decade of the twentieth century the Mormon church's Mother in Heaven doctrine was criticized and challenged by the Salt Lake Ministerial Association as being unchristian.[17] B. H. Roberts, of the Council of the Seventy, responded by claiming the ministers were inconsistent. They objected to the idea of Jesus having a literal heavenly father, he said, but then they also complained because

> We believe that we have for our spirits a heavenly mother as well as a heavenly father! Now observe the peculiar position of these critics: It is all right for Jesus to have a mother; but it is all wrong for him to have a father. On the other hand, it is all right for men's spirits to have a Father in heaven, but our reviewers object to our doctrine of their having a mother there.[18]

Two years later the church's First Presidency issued a statement entitled "The Origin of Man." Although much of this message explicated their view of man's (including woman's) earthly origins, the statement also took up the question of spirit beginnings as well. While couching the doctrine partially in abstract generalities such as that "man, as a spirit, was begotten and born of heavenly parents," the statement also made a clear and explicit reference to a mother in heaven: "All men and women are in the similitude of the universal Father and Mother and are literally the sons and daughters of Deity."[19] By 1909 if not before, the Mother in Heaven doctrine had become an officially recognized tenet of Mormon belief. Apostle Joseph Fielding Smith later described this as one of presumably several "official and authoritative statements" about this doctrine.[20]

In the 1920s and 1930s there seemed to be emphasis on the idea of "eternal" or "everlasting" motherhood. It seemed important to emphasize that motherhood was as ongoing and eternal as godhood. Apostle John A. Widtsoe, for example, found a "radiant warmth" in the "thought that among the exalted beings in the world to come we shall find a mother who possesses the attributes of Godhood. Such conceptions raise motherhood to a high position. They explain the generous provision made for women in the Church of Christ. To be a mother is to engage in the eternal work of God."[21]

Since the 1960s, we can see some widening out, with a greater variety of images presented by church authorities who speak about a mother in heaven. Joseph Fielding Smith, much like Elizabeth Cady Stanton, quoted Genesis 1:26—"Let us make man in our image after our likeness" (his italics)—and suggests, "Is it not feasible to believe that female spirits were created in the image of a 'Mother in Heaven'?"[22] His emphasis implies that a female goddess was involved in the planning and decision making, was part of whatever group of exalted beings decided to create earthly men and women.

In 1974 H. Burke Peterson of the Presiding Bishopric emphasized the Heavenly Mother's role as producer of spirit offspring. In asking church members to count the cost of a mother working outside the home, he warned about the danger of becoming "a mother whose energy is so sapped that she is sometimes neglecting her call from the Lord, a call that will one day prepare her to become an eternal mother—a co-creator of spiritual offspring."[23] One supposes that by "her call" Peterson means the care of her children and that he is suggesting nurturing and guiding one's children prepares one to become an exalted goddess-mother.

Four years later President Spencer W. Kimball expressed his view of the Mother in Heaven as "the ultimate in maternal modesty" and "restrained, queenly elegance." He emphasized her great influence on us: "Knowing how profoundly our mortal mothers have shaped us here," he said, "do we suppose her influence on us as individuals to be less if we live so as to return there?"[24] Here we have both maternal nurturing and exalted goddess qualities in the Mother in Heaven.

A question to which there is no definitive answer—but much speculation—is whether there is more than one Mother in Heaven. The Mormon church's doctrinal commitment to celestial (plural) marriage as well as the exigencies of producing billions of spirit children suggests a probability of more than one mother in heaven. Apostle John Taylor, writing in answer to a question reportedly raised by a woman in the church, said in 1857 in a newspaper he was publishing in New York City: "Knowest thou not that eternities ago thy spirit, pure and holy, dwelt in the Heavenly Father's bosom, and in his presence, and with thy mother, one of the Queens of heaven, surrounded by the brother and sister spirits in the spirit world, among the Gods?"[25] He implied one Heavenly Father with many "Queens."

There has been no encouragement from contemporary Mormon church leaders to worship a heavenly mother. Still there has been evidence of female desire to reach out to a mother in heaven in some way. A letter to the editor of *Dialogue: A Journal of Mormon Thought* in 1974 told of a Mormon woman spending preparatory time in meditation, kneeling privately to pray, and then calling out for the first time, "'Mother in Heaven, I believe you may exist. Are you there? We know the Father and the Son, but why have you not revealed yourself?' And a wondrous voice clearly answered, 'Good daughter, until this time, no one asked. The men have not thought to ask.'"[26]

Notes

1. Elizabeth Cady Stanton, *The Woman's Bible*, pt.1 (1895–98; rprt. ed., New York Arno Press, 1972), 218.

2. Maureen Ursenbach Beecher, "The Eliza Enigma: The Life and Legend of Eliza R. Snow," in *Charles Redd Monographs on Western History*, 6 (Provo, UT: Brigham Young University Press, 1976): 34; *Times and Seasons* 6 (15 Nov. 1845): 1039

3. Wilford Woodruff, "Discourse," *Latter-day Saints' Millennial Star* 56 (Apr. 1894): 229

4. Joseph F. Smith, "Discourse," *Deseret Evening News*, 9 Feb. 1895. I am indebted to Maureen Ursenbach Beecher for much information on Eliza R. Snow and the Mother in Heaven doctrine. As Boyd Kirkland has noted, a number of sources suggest that Snow and Brigham Young believed Eve to be the Mother in Heaven. Letter to the editor, *Sunstone* 6 (Mar.–Apr. 1981): 4–5

5. Susa Young Gates, *History of the Young Ladies' Mutual Improvement Association* (Salt Lake City: Deseret News, 1911), 15–16

6. The debate has continued, however. Church leader B. H. Roberts spoke of "that splendid hymn of ours on heavenly motherhood, the great throbbing hunger of woman's soul, and which was given to this world through the inspired mind of Eliza R Snow." *Answers to Ministerial Association Review*, delivered at two meetings of the M.I.A. Conference, 9 June 1907 (Salt Lake City: Church of Jesus Christ of Latter-day Saints, 1907): 18. Apostle Melvin J. Ballard, however, considered the Mother in Heaven concept a revelation given by Jesus Christ through Joseph Smith, in his Mother's Day address in the Tabernacle, Journal History, 8 May 1921, typescript, archives, Historical Department, Church of Jesus Christ of Latter-day Saints, Salt Lake City, 1–3 (hereafter LDS archives). Apostle Milton R. Hunter in 1945 claimed the doctrine of a mother in heaven originated with Smith, ascribing to him revelation by which "a more complete understanding of man—especially regarding his person and relationship to Deity—was received than could be found in all of the holy scriptures combined." Among such new understandings was the "stupendous truth of the existence of a Heavenly Mother" and the "complete realization that we are the offspring of Heavenly Parents." Hunter said that these ideas became "established facts in Mormon theology" and an "integral part of Mormon philosophy," *The Gospel Through the Ages* (Salt Lake City: Stevens and Wallis, Inc., 1945), 98–99.

7. David McKay to Mrs. James Hood, 16 Mar. 1916, photocopy of holograph in possession of Maureen Ursenbach Beecher, courtesy of Shirley Bailey.

8. Abraham H. Cannon Journal, 25 Aug. 1880, LDS archives.

9. Brigham Young, *Journal of Discourses*, 18 June 1865, 26 vols. (Liverpool: Latter-day Saints' Book Depot, 1855–86), 11:122; hereafter JD.

10. JD, 23 Feb. 1862, 9:286.

11. JD, 31 May 1885, 26:214.

12. JD, 3 Mar. 1878, 19:269–70.

13. Joseph Fielding Smith, *Answers to Gospel Questions* (Salt Lake City: Deseret Book, 1960), 3:142.
14. Melvin R. Brooks, *LDS Reference Encyclopedia* (Salt Lake City: Bookcraft, 1960), 309–10.
15. James E. Talmage, *Deseret News*, 28 Apr. 1902.
16. "The Divine Feminine," *Deseret News*, 4 Feb. 1905.
17. "Ministerial Association's Review of Mormon Address to the World," *Salt Lake Herald*, 4 June 1907, 8.
18. B. H. Roberts, "Answer to Ministerial Association Review," 9 June 1907, in *An Address: The Church of Jesus Christ of Latter-day Saints to the World* (Salt Lake City, 1907), 18–19.
19. First Presidency, "The Origin of Man," *Improvement Era* 13 (Nov. 1909): 80
20. Joseph Fielding Smith, "Mothers in Israel," *Relief Society Magazine* 57 (Dec. 1970): 884.
21. John A. Widtsoe, "Everlasting Motherhood," *Latter-day Saints' Millennial Star* 90 (10 May 1928): 298.
22. Smith, *Answers to Gospel Questions*, 3:144.
23. H. Burke Peterson, *Ensign* 4 (May 1974): 32.
24. Spencer W. Kimball, *Ensign* 8 (May 1978): 6.
25. John Taylor, "Origin, Object, and Destiny of Women," *The Mormon*, 29 Aug. 1857.
26. Letter to the Editor, *Dialogue: A Journal of Mormon Thought* 9.3 (1974): 7.

Lisa Bolin Hawkins (1954–), "Another Prayer" and "Let My Sisters Do for Me" (1980)

As Linda Wilcox Desimone wrote in her 1980 essay recovering historical references to the Heavenly Mother in the Latter-day Saint tradition, Heavenly Mother's presence had remained "shadowy and elusive." Even though talking about her in LDS Church contexts seemed, by the late twentieth century, to be taboo, poets reached for language to describe the human longing to know her. In her poem "Another Prayer," Provo, Utah–based poet Lisa Bolin Hawkins interrogates the silence surrounding Heavenly Mother. Her poem "Let My Sisters Do for Me" was written out of the frustration she experienced as a participant in International Women's Year programming in Utah. (See Dixie Snow Huefner's essay on the IWY this anthology.) Hawkins recalls,

> I was 22 years old, a newlywed, and a convert to the LDS Church of almost six years. I had just graduated from BYU and was about to start BYU Law School. I was dismayed that, after many faithful LDS women had spent months carefully preparing for the IWY meetings, the meetings were swamped and co-opted by hundreds of LDS women who knew nothing about IWY but were there to undermine the meetings regardless of the substance of the agenda. These women admitted that they had attended the meetings at the direction of their Church leaders and had not studied the proposals, which made the false conflicts that had been created between the groups even more frustrating. Most disturbing was the unkind and even hateful way in which the women,

my sisters, responded to anyone (including me) who tried to persuade them to allow reasoned discussion of the IWY proposals or to speak at all. Their behavior was contrary to gospel teachings in so many ways; it was a faith-shaking experience. At the time, I was angry with those who had concluded that the women who had planned for the Utah IWY meetings were a threat. I was a card-carrying, testimony-bearing LDS woman (I still am), and they were calling me the enemy. My poem expressed my feelings that any priesthood leaders who—contrary to LDS Church doctrine—were not going to treat women as equals and true sisters should allow women to rely upon and minister to each other at life's essential moments.

Sources

Hawkins, Lisa Bolin. "Another Prayer," *Exponent II* 6 (Winter 1980): 16.

Hawkins, Lisa Bolin. "Let My Sisters Do for Me," in Linda Sillitoe, "New Voices, New Songs: Contemporary Poems by Mormon Women," *Dialogue: A Journal of Mormon Thought* 13.4 (1980): 47–61.

"ANOTHER PRAYER"

Why are you silent, Mother? How can I
Become a goddess when the patterns here
Are those of gods? I struggle, and I try
To mold my womanself to something near
Their goodness. I need you, who gave me birth
In your own image, to reveal your ways;
A rich example of Thy daughters' worth;
Pillar of Womanhood to guide our days;
Fire of power and grace to guide my night
When I am lost. My brothers question me,
And wonder why I seek this added light.
No one can answer all my pain but Thee.
Ordain me to my womanhood, and share
The light that Queens and Priestesses must bear.

"LET MY SISTERS DO FOR ME"

If we must preserve our differences,
Then let my sisters do for me.
Let my sister tear my last resistance

From my mother's womb, let her
Cradle me and give me my name,
Let her baptize me and call me forth
To receive the Spirit, let her
Teach me of the world, let her
Ordain me to womanhood, let her
(She does wash, anoint and clothe)
Be my god beyond the veil, let her
Heal my sickness, hold my baby, be my friend.
Let her dig my grave, let her robe me,
Let her bless my empty bones.
If you will not have me for your sister,
Then let my sisters do for me,
And let me greet my Mother on the far shore.

Carol Lynn Wright Pearson (1939–), "Motherless House" (1980)

Mother in Heaven was also on the mind of poet Carol Lynn Pearson, who in the late 1970s began work on a book entitled *Letters from a Motherless House*. This was, Pearson recalls, "a collection of letters to the Mother, describing for her what life is here on earth without her and asking her to come home." The book would never be published, but the material Pearson gathered about the ancient and historic role of female divinity in the world's religious traditions made its way into her 1992 one-woman play *Mother Wove the Morning*, which is excerpted in this anthology. Her poem "Motherless House" was written in 1980 but did not appear in print until 1993.

Source

Maxine Hanks, ed. *Women and Authority: Re-emerging Mormon Feminism*. Salt Lake City: Signature Books, 1992, 232.

"MOTHERLESS HOUSE"

I live in a Motherless house
A broken home.
How it happened I cannot learn.
When I had words enough to ask
"Where is my mother?"
No one seemed to know
And no one thought it strange

That no one else knew either.
I live in a Motherless house.
They are good to me here
But I find that no kindly
Patriarchal care eases the pain.
I yearn for the day
Someone will look at me and say,
"You certainly do look like your Mother."
I walk the rooms
Search the closets
Look for something that might
Have belonged to her—
A letter, a dress, a chair,
Would she not have left a note?
I close my eyes
And work to bring back her touch, her face.
Surely there must have been
A Motherly embrace
I can call back for comfort.
I live in a Motherless house,
Motherless and without a trace.
Who could have done this?
Who would tear an unweaned infant
From its Mother's arms
And clear the place of every souvenir?
I live in a Motherless house.
I lie awake and listen always for the word that never comes, but might.
I bury my face
In something soft as a breast.
I am a child
Crying for my mother in the night.

Linda King Newell (1941–), "A Gift Given, a Gift Taken: Washing, Anointing, and Blessing the Sick among Mormon Women" (1981)

In addition to the doctrinal history of Heavenly Mother, the feminists of Salt Lake City's Wednesday lunch group also explored the expansive spiritual lives of early Mormon women, who had, they discovered, exercised powers and conducted rituals that had disappeared from contemporary LDS culture. Linda King Newell was at work with Valeen Tippets Avery researching what would be a revolutionary biography of Emma Smith, when she and other researchers, including Vella Evans and Carol Cornwall Madsen, discovered in the LDS Church Historical Department archives evidence that Mormon women in the nineteenth and early twentieth centuries had given one another healing blessings, claiming priesthood powers they believed had been conferred upon them during LDS temple ceremonies. Practices of washing, anointing, and healing the sick, and similarly consecrating the bodies of women preparing for childbirth had been a cherished part of Mormon women's lives but slowly had disappeared. Newell brought this history back, painstakingly reaching into the diaries of Mormon women and restoring their names and experiences. Her essay "A Gift Given, a Gift Taken" also presented what would become a core idea of the Mormon feminist movement: that LDS Church modernization and bureaucratization had incurred losses for Mormon women and constricted what had once been a more expansive world of Mormon women's spiritual authority and practice. Her argument that asking for permission to exercise spiritual authority actually led to a loss of power serves as a touchstone of Mormon feminist thought to the present day.

Source

Newell, Linda King. "A Gift Given, a Gift Taken: Washing, Anointing, and Blessing the Sick among Mormon Women." *Sunstone* 6.4 (September–October 1981): 16–25.

References and Further Reading

Stapley, Jonathan A., and Kristine Wright. "Female Ritual Healing in Mormonism." *Journal of Mormon History* 37.1 (2011): 1–85.

"A GIFT GIVEN, A GIFT TAKEN: WASHING, ANOINTING, AND BLESSING THE SICK AMONG MORMON WOMEN"

For members of the modern Church of Jesus Christ of Latter-day Saints, the term "washing and anointing" is synonymous with the initiatory ordinances of the temple endowment. Joseph Smith first introduced the practice to male members of the LDS church in the Kirtland Temple; he included women when he gave the endowment and sealing ordinances to his select "Quorum of the Anointed" in Nauvoo.[1] By the time the Mormons had established a refuge in the Great Basin, washing and anointing had also been combined with healing. Although it grew out of the temple ordinances in Nauvoo, the practice by women was carried on outside the temple.[2] Even after the establishment of the Endowment House in Salt Lake in 1855 and the later dedications of the St. George, Manti, and Logan temples, the ordinance took place both within the confines of those sacred structures and in the privacy of individual homes.

That women could and did participate in blessing and healing the sick was a clearly established and officially sanctioned fact by the time the Saints had established a refuge in the Great Basin. Women like Sarah Leavitt and Edna Rogers left records of their experiences with healing others in Kirtland[, Ohio]. In Nauvoo[, Illinois], the Prophet Joseph Smith not only formed the Relief Society as an essential part of the Church, but he also introduced the ceremony of the temple endowment, including washings and anointings. With the coming of the Relief Society, the women had an organization through which they manifested the gifts of the spirit. Of this period, Susa Young Gates, a daughter of Brigham Young, wrote: "The privileges and powers outlined by the Prophet in those first meetings [of the Relief Society] have never been granted to women in full even yet." Then Susa asked, "Did those women, do you and I, live so well as to be worthy of them all?"[3]

There is considerable evidence within the minutes of the Nauvoo Relief Society meetings to suggest that Joseph Smith seemed to envision the Relief Society as an independent organization for women parallel to the priesthood organization for men.[4] Yet both seemed to come under the aegis of the priesthood as a power from God, not as an administrative entity.

The women themselves saw their organization as more than a charitable society. Spiritual gifts such as speaking in tongues and healing the sick were not only discussed in their meetings—the sisters openly practiced them. With Joseph's approval, Emma [Hale Smith] and her counselors laid hands on the sick and blessed them that they might be healed. The fifth time the Relief Society convened, Sarah Cleveland invited the sisters to speak freely and women stood one at a time in this testimony meeting. Sister Durfee was among those who spoke. She "bore testimony to the great blessing she received, when administered to after the last meeting by Emma Smith and [her] Counselors Cleveland and Whitney, she said she never realized more benefit through an administration." She added that she had been healed and "thought the sisters had more faith than the brethren." Following the meeting, Sarah Cleveland and Elizabeth Whitney administered to another Relief Society sister, Mrs. Abigail Leonard, "for the restoration of health."[5]

In the intervening week, someone apparently reported to Joseph that the women were laying their hands on the sick and blessing them. His reply to the question of the propriety of such acts was simple. He told the women in the next meeting "there could be no evil in it, if God gave his sanction by healing . . . there could be no more sin in any female laying hands on the sick than in wetting the face with water." He also indicated that there were sisters who were ordained to heal the sick and it was their privilege to do so, "If the sisters should have faith to heal," he said, "let all hold their tongues."[6]

In 1857, Mary Ellen Kimball recorded her visit to a sick woman in company with Presindia, her sister wife. They washed and anointed Susannah, cooked her dinner, and watched her "eat pork and potatoes" with a gratifying appetite. "I felt to rejoice with her for I shall never forget the time when I was healed, by the power of God through faith in him which power has again been restored *with* the priesthood" (a phrase that indicates a distinction in Mary Ellen's mind).

> But after I returned home I thought of the instructions I had received from *time* to time that the priesthood was not bestowed upon woman, I accordingly asked. Mr. [Heber C.] Kimball if women had a right to wash and anoint the sick for the recovery of their health or if it is a mockery in them to do so. He replied inasmuch as they are obedient to their husbands, they have a right to administer in that way in the name of the Lord Jesus Christ but not by authority of the priesthood invested in them for that authority is not given to woman.

Mary Ellen [*sic*], then noted an argument that would calm apprehensions for the next four decades: "He also said they might administer by the authority given to their husbands in as much as they were one with their husband."[7]

At the same time, strong official encouragement for women to develop and use their spiritual powers is evident. Brigham Young, speaking in the Salt Lake Tabernacle on 14 November 1869, scolded both men and women for not improving themselves. The example he cited, was of "Why do you not live so as to rebuke disease?" he demanded. "It is your privilege to do so without sending for the Elders." He laid down some practical advice; if the child is ill of a fever or of an upset stomach, treat those symptoms by all means, beware of too much medicine, and remember that prevention is better than cure. He ended by addressing himself specifically to mothers: "It is the privilege of a mother to have faith and to administer to her child; this she can do herself, as well as sending for the Elders to have the benefit of their faith."[8] Having enough faith to heal was clearly, for Brother Brigham, "practical religion" like having enough food on hand.

The previous year in Cache Valley, Apostle Ezra T. Benson had called on all the women who had been "ordained to wash and anoint to exercise their powers to rebuke an unspecified disease which had so destructively coursed, its way through the valley."[9] This record neither identifies the ordained women nor who ordained them. It says only that they were "ordained to wash and anoint." Zina Huntington Young's journal mentions several healings. On Joseph Smith's birthday in 1881, she washed and anointed one woman "for her health" and administered to another "for her hearing." She remembered the Prophet's birthday and reminisced about the days in Nauvoo when she was one of his plural wives: "I have practiced much with My Sister Presindia Kimball while in Nauvoo & ever since before Joseph Smith's death. He blest Sisters to bless the sick." Three months later: "I went to see Chariton [her son] & administered to him, felt so sad to see him suffer." The next year she notes with satisfaction hearing an address by Bishop Whitney in the Eighteenth Ward wherein he "blest the Sisters in having faith to administer to there [sic] own families in humble faith not saying by the Authority of the Holy priesthood but in the name of Jesus Christ. . . ."[10]

Still, healing by women caused some confusion; this quiet, routine practice on the local level occasionally raised questions that, when answered publicly by Church leaders or the Relief Society, seemed to start a ripple of uneasiness that sooner or later set off another inquiry. Church leaders began to issue general cautions about women blessing the sick. Angus Cannon, president of the Salt Lake Stake, included the following in his answer to a question about women holding the priesthood: "Women could only hold the priesthood in connection with their husbands; man held the priesthood independent of woman. The sisters have a right to anoint the sick, and pray the Father to heal them, and to exercise that faith that will prevail with God; but women must be careful how they use the authority of the priesthood in administering to the sick."[11] Two years later, on 8 August 1880, John Taylor's address on "The Order and Duties of the Priesthood" reaffirmed that women "hold the Priesthood, only in connection with their husbands, they being one with their husbands."[12]

A circular letter sent from Salt Lake that October "to all the authorities of the Priesthood and Latter-day Saints" described the organization of the Relief Society, its composition, its purposes, the qualifications for its officers, and their duties. The letter includes a section called "The Sick and Afflicted":

> It is the privilege of all faithful women and lay members of the Church, who believe in *Christ,* to administer to all the sick or afflicted in their respective families, either by the laying on of hands, or by the anointing with oil in the name of the Lord; but they should administer in these sacred ordinances, not by virtue and authority of the priesthood, but by virtue of their faith in Christ, and the promises made to believers; and thus they should do in all their ministrations.[13]

It seems clear that the First Presidency was answering one question: anointing and blessing the sick is not an official function of the Relief Society, since any faithful member may perform this action. However, by specifying women's right to administer to the sick "in their respective families," the Church leaders raised another question: what about administering to those outside the family circle? They gave no answer, although the practice of calling for the elders or calling for the sisters had certainly been established.

Another question also bears on the topic: "Is it necessary for sisters to be set apart to officiate in the sacred ordinances of washing, anointing, and laying on of hands in administering to the sick?" Eliza R. Snow used the columns of the *Woman's Exponent* in 1884 to answer:

It certainly is not. Any and all sisters who honor their holy endowments, not only have the right, but should feel it a duty whenever called upon, to administer to our sisters in these ordinances, which God has graciously committed to His daughters as well as to His sons, and we testify that when administered and received in faith and humility they are accompanied with all mighty power.

Inasmuch as God our Father has revealed these sacred ordinances and committed them to His Saints, it is not only our privilege but our imperative duty to apply them for the relief of human suffering.

Eliza Snow, in 1884, then echoed the language of Joseph Smith in his 28 April 1842 instructions to the Relief Society: "thousands can testify that God has sanctioned the administration of these ordinances [of healing the sick] by our sisters with the manifestation of His healing influence."[14]

In answering the question of who should "officiate, in the sacred ordinances," Eliza Snow's language is instructive. By limiting its performance to those who have been endowed, she definitely places the source of their authority under the shelter of those ordinances in the temple. In other words, she saw washing and anointing the sick as an *ordinance* that could and did take place outside the sacred confines of the temple. Women, through their endowment, had both the authority and obligation to perform them.

Two differing points of view were now in print. Eliza Snow and the First Presidency agreed that the Relief Society had no monopoly on the ordinance of administration by and for women. The First Presidency, however, implied that the ordinance should be limited to the woman's family without specifying any requirement but faithfulness. Eliza Snow, on the other band, said nothing of limiting administrations to the family—indeed, the implication is clear that anyone in need of a blessing should receive it—but she said that only women who have been endowed may officiate.

As the washings and anointings continued, women attending an 1896 Relief Society conference in the Logan Tabernacle heard a Sister Tenn Young urge: "I wish to speak of the great privilege given to us to wash and to anoint the sick and suffering of our sex. I would counsel every one who expects to become a Mother to have these ordinances administered by some good, faithful sister." She later gave instructions on how it should be done. Her counsel was endorsed by Mary Ann Freeze, who "said she attended to this and the curse to bring forth in sorrow was almost taken away."[15]

But doubts kept surfacing among women whose desire for approval from their presiding brethren inevitably led to questions of propriety. Answers varied, however, depending on who provided them.

In 1888, Emmeline B. Wells, editor of the *Exponent* and soon to be general president of the Relief Society, sent Wilford Woodruff a list of questions on the topic of washing and anointings. Her questions, and his response follow:

> *First: Are sisters justified in administering the ordinance of washing and anointing previous to confinements to those who have received their endowments and have married men outside the Church?*
>
> *Second: Can anyone who has not had their endowments thus be administered to by the sisters if she is a faithful Saint in good standing and has not yet had the opportunity of going to the temple for the ordinances?*
>
> To begin with I desire to say that the *ordinance* of washing and anointing is one that should only be administered in Temples or other holy places which are dedicated for the purpose of giving endowments to the Saints. That *ordinance* might not be administered to any one whether *she has* received or has not received her endowments, in any other place or under any other circumstances.
>
> But I imagine from your questions that you refer to a practice that has grown up among the sisters of washing and anointing sisters who are approaching their confinement. If so, this is not, strictly speaking, an ordinance, unless it be done under the direction of the priesthood and in connection with the ordinance of laying on of hands for the restoration of the sick.
>
> There is no impropriety in sisters washing and anointing their sisters in this way, under the circumstances you describe; but it should be understood that they do this, not as members of the priesthood, but as members of the Church, exercising faith for, and asking the blessings of the Lord upon their sisters, just asking the blessings of the Lord upon their sisters, just as they and every member of the Church, might do in behalf of the members of their families.[16]

President Woodruff's careful distinctions between the *temple ordinance* of washing and anointing, the *church member's practice* of washing and anointing, and the *priesthood ordinance* of anointing in connection with a healing blessing does not directly address the position Eliza R. Snow had taken earlier that only endowed women should administer to others. Inevitably, the issue became more confused. When precisely the same act was performed and very nearly the same words were used among women in the temple, among women outside the temple, and among men administering to women, the distinction—in the average mind—became shadowy indeed.

In 1889, Zina D. H. Young, addressing a general conference of the Relief Society, gave the sisters advice on a variety of topics. Between wheat storage and silk culture came this paragraph: "It is the privilege of the sisters, who are faithful in the discharge of their duties and have received their endowments and blessings in the house of the Lord, to administer to their sisters, and to the little ones, in time of sickness, in meekness and humility, ever "being careful to ask in the name of Jesus, and to give God the glory."[17]Although she does not specify whether the "privilege" refers to washing and anointing or both, she reaffirms—without saying so—that it is not a priesthood ordinance. She also reiterates Eliza's position that it was a privilege of the endowed.

As the last decade of the nineteenth century closed, procedural refinements were being added, both officially and in the wards and stakes. In 1893, the *Young Women's Journal* published a spritely article advising girls to get enough faith to be healed, since it is "much easier . . . much less troublesome and expensive withal" than obtaining medical treatment. The writer then offered a program for increasing faith:

> Do not wait until you are sick nigh unto death before making a trial of your faith and the power of God. The next time you have a headache take some [consecrated olive] oil and ask God to heal you. If you have a touch of sore throat, try the oil and a little prayer before you try a single thing besides. Go to bed and see if you are not better in the morning. If you are, then go on adding experience to experience until you have accumulated a store of faith that will all be needed when your body is weak, and you are sick unto death. . . . [A]nd if you still feel sick ask your mother or your father to administer to you. Try that; then if that fails, and they wish to call in elders, let, them do so, and thus exhaust the ordinances of the priesthood before you take the other step [of calling a doctor].[18]

The brisk matter-of-factness echoes Brigham Young's practical heartiness—there is nothing mysterious or mystical here about faith and spiritual gifts. But perhaps most revealing is the attitude of spiritual self-sufficiency and the interchangeability of the mother and father as administrators. If this article reflects practice among the membership at large, administrations were far from being confined to the men ordained with the priesthood.

In the twentieth century, controversy continued over the traditions and policies touching on women's administrations to the sick in general and washing and anointing specifically. On 16 September 1901, a Relief Society general board meeting discussed "whether the sisters should seal the anointing after washings and anointings. Pres. [Elmina S.] Taylor said that she thought it was all right. She had received just as great benefit from the sealing of the sisters as from the brethren, but thought it wise to ask the Priesthood to seal the anointing when it was get-at-able." Her own testimony that she had been as greatly benefitted from the sisters as from the brothers suggests that she did not believe that a man with priesthood ordination might be more efficacious, only that she thought there was wisdom in including the priesthood holders as much as possible. This interpretation is borne out by her next statement: "And if the brethren decided that women could not seal the anointing then we should do as they say" but she could not see any reason why women could not, since "Aunt Zina did."

Over five years earlier, Ruth Fox recorded a discussion with that same gently redoubtable Zina Young. "When asked if women held the priesthood, in connection with their husbands, [she said] that we should be thankful for the many blessings we enjoyed and say nothing about it. If you plant a grain of wheat and keep poking and looking at it to see if it was growing you would spoil the root. The answer was very satisfying to me."[19]

But always someone was eager to poke, and each time the spiritual roots of the women were imperiled. Some, like Louisa Lulu Greene Richards, former editor of the *Women's Exponent*, responded indignantly. On 9 April 1901, she wrote a somewhat terse letter to Church President Lorenzo Snow concerning an article she read in the *Deseret News* the previous day, which stated: "priest, Teacher or Deacon may administer to the sick, and so may a member, male or female, but neither of them can seal the anointing and blessing, because the authority to do that is vested in the Priesthood after the order of Melchizedek." The question of sealing was thus added to the long list of ambiguities. Lulu says, "If the information given in the answer is absolutely correct, then, myself and thousands of other members of the Church have been misinstructed and are laboring under a very serious mistake, which certainly should be authoritatively corrected." She gives a hint of the kind of authority that would be necessary by stating firmly,

> Sister Eliza R. Snow Smith, who received the instructions from the Prophet Joseph Smith, her husband, taught the sisters in her day that a very important part of the sacred ordinance of administration to the sick was the sealing of the anointing and blessings, and should never be omitted. And we follow the pattern she gave us continually. We do not seal in the authority of the Priesthood, but in the name of our Lord and Saviour Jesus Christ.[20]

Over the next few years, however, an emerging definition of priesthood authority, and an increased emphasis on its importance, would remove more and more spiritual responsibilities from women and cluster them to the priesthood. The very statements authorizing the continuance of women's blessings only signaled their dependence on that permission. One month later, the Relief Society general presidency sent President Lorenzo Snow a copy of President Woodruff's 1888 letter to Emmeline B. Wells. This letter, discussed earlier, distinguished between washings and blessings as an ordinance (and hence confined to the temple under priesthood authority) and as a sisterly act.[21] As president of the Church, Lorenzo

Snow reaffirmed the position explained in that letter with the exception that blessings should be "confirmed" rather than "sealed."[22]

Sometime during the first decade of the new century the Relief Society circulated a letter on Relief Society letterhead, called simply "Answers to Questions." Undated, it ended with the notation: "Approved by the First Presidency of the Church." This two-page letter was the most complete document on the subject thus far.

Depending on the extent to which this letter was circulated, it may have been a response to an unsigned 1903 *Young Woman's Journal* lesson that asserted: "Only the higher or Melchizedek Priesthood has the right to lay on hands for the healing of the sick, or to direct the administration . . . though to pray for the sick is the right that necessarily belongs to every member of the Church."[23] This may be the earliest published claim that only the Melchizedek Priesthood had authority to heal. But the Relief Society's approved letter directly countered that position.

This letter clarified some issues that had previously been ambiguous or contradictory. Administrations by women to the sick were not necessarily a Relief Society function, but the letter clearly indicated that women did not need priesthood permission to participate in the performance of these duties. It quoted Eliza R. Snow's position that any endowed woman may perform such services. It said that confining blessings to one's own family was not necessary. The letter also cautioned women to avoid resemblances in language to the temple forms, and although the blessings should be sealed, the sisters did not need a priesthood holder to do it.[24]

Nephi Pratt, the mission president in Portland, Oregon, wrote Church President Joseph F. Smith in 1908 to inquire if he should, in setting Relief Society sisters apart, give them the authority to wash and anoint sisters for their confinement and also whether there were any forms they should follow in carrying out these services. President Smith, answered that the washings and anointings in question were practices that

> [s]ome of our Relief Society Sisters appear to have confounded . . . with one of the temple ordinances. . . . We desire you therefore to impress upon the sisters of your Relief Society that this practice is in no sense whatever an ordinance, and must not be regarded as such, unless it be attended to under the direction of proper authority in connection with the ordinance of laying on of hands for the healing of the sick.

He emphasized, however, that even women who had not received their endowments could participate in the washing and anointing

> as there is no impropriety whatever in their doing so, inasmuch as they do it in a proper way, that is, in the spirit, of faith, and prayer, and without assumption of special authority, no more in fact than members of the church generally need to be barred from receiving a blessing at the hands

of faithful women.... As to the particular form of words to be used, there is none, not any more than there is for an elder to use in administering to the sick.[25]

On 17 December 1909, the First Presidency again endorsed President Woodruff's 1888 letter to Emmeline B. Wells, making one correction:

> Namely in the clause pertaining, to women administering to children, President [Anthon H.] Lund had said those sisters need not necessarily be only those who had received their endowments, for it was not always possible for women to have that privilege and women of faith might do so [give blessings].[26]

Apparently for the first time, directly and decisively a president of the Church had enunciated a policy about who could give and receive such blessings, separating such actions clearly from the temple ceremony and making the rites accessible to any member of the household of faith, male or female. But the matter was not yet laid to rest; the quiet practice of washing and anointing among women went on, but it was accompanied by greater uneasiness by more questions, and by greater uncertainty about the propriety of such actions.

The Oakley (Idaho) Second Ward Relief Society minute book contains a rare, undated item: the written-out blessing to be pronounced in a washing, anointing, and sealing before childbirth. Even though Joseph F. Smith had said that there was no special form for such occasions, it seems that the sisters were more comfortable with one written out. To what extent they followed the pattern, or deviated from it, is not known, but the very existence of the document bespeaks an insistence that it be done, that it be done in a certain way and that it be linked to the Relief Society. They did follow earlier counsel to avoid the wording used in the temple.

The first two blessings follow each other closely with only minor changes in the wording here and there. The blessings were specific and comprehensive.

> We anoint your spinal column that you might be strong and healthy no disease fasten upon it no accident belaff [befall] you, your kidneys that they might be active, and healthy and preform [sic] their proper functions, your bladder that it might be strong and protected from accident, your Hips that your system might relax and give way for the birth of your child, your sides that your liver, your lungs, and spleen that they might be strong and preform their proper functions, ... your breasts that your milk may come freely and you need not be afflicted with sore nipples as many are, your heart that it might be comforted.

They continued by requesting blessings from the Lord on the unborn child's health and expressed the hope that it might not come before its "full time" and that

> the child shall present right for birth and that the afterbirth shall come at its proper time ... and you need not flow to excess.... We anoint ... your thighs that they might be healthy and strong that you might be exempt from cramps and from the bursting of veins.... That you might stand upon the earth [and] go in and out of the Temples of God.[27]

The document combines practical considerations, more common to women's talk over the back fence, with the reassuring solace and compassion of being anointed with the balm of sisterhood.[28] The women sealed the blessing:

> Sister _____ we unitedly lay our hands upon you to seal this washing and anointing wherewith you have been washed and anointed for your safe delivery; for the salvation of you and your child and we ask God to let his special blessings to rest upon you, that you might sleep sweet at night that your dreams might be pleasant and that the good spirit might guard and protect you from every evil influence spirit and power that you may go your full time and that every blessing that we have asked God to confer upon you and your offspring may be literally fulfilled that all fear and dread may be taken from you and that you might trust in God. All these blessings we unitedly seal, upon you in the name of Jesus Christ Amen.[29]

The tender attention to both the woman's psychological and physical state is an example of loving service and gentleness. That this widespread practice continued in similar form for several more decades is illustrated by the account written by a Canadian sister.

> In the years from the early 1930s on, in the Calgary Ward R.S. under presidents—Bergeson, Maude Hayes, Lucile Ursenbach, the sisters often asked for a washing and blessing before going into the hospital for an operation or childbirth. In this ordinance two sisters washed the parts of the body, pronouncing appropriate words of prayer and blessing, being advised to avoid similarity to expressions used in a temple ordinance, and at the conclusion put their hands on the head of the recipient and, in the name of the Lord pronounced a further blessing.[30]

In Cache Valley, a 1910 Relief Society meeting was given over to testimonies of healing. President Lucy S. Cardon "read some instructions to the sisters on the washing and anointing the sick and how it should be done properly," adding a testimony of the importance of having the Spirit of the Lord. One sister "asked a question on the subj." of washing and anointing, and Sister Martha Meedham, with a brisk earthiness that comes off the page, answered that

> she had done as much washing and anointing as anyone in this Stake. Related an experience of a blessing which she had given while she was in Salt Lake. Said she wanted to spend the rest of her life in doing good to others and blessing and confirming them. Related of experiences where all had blessed and anointed people. Said she had written Pres. J. F. Smith on the sub. and he told her to keep on and bless & comfort as she had done in the past. It was a gift that was only given to a few, but all sisters who desired and are requested can perform this.

Along with a number of other women, the local Relief Society president, Margaret Ballard, "spoke of her exp[erience] in washing and anointing and said they had carried out these instructions given." The next sentence speaks volumes, not only for the independence of the Relief Society but perhaps also of mingled pride and trepidation: "The sisters felt that the Bishop should be acquainted with the work we do."[31] Sister Ballard continued, telling the sisters, "how she had been impressed to bless and administer to her father who was *sick* and suffering and he had been healed. Had also been impressed to bless her husband and he was healed." The meeting closed, appropriately with singing, "Count Your Many Blessings."

This rare glimpse into a Relief Society group discussing anointings and blessings is revealing. In addition to the strong associations with faithfulness, the gift of the Holy Ghost, and the importance of personal worthiness, there were other kinds of teachings. One was the irreplaceable testimony of personal experience. The document also shows a sharing of information the sisters had about current policy, former policy, and folklore, along with asking: how do these experiences relate to the priesthood? This, after all, was the crucial question.

In October 1914, President Joseph F. Smith and his counselors sent a letter to bishops and stake presidents establishing official policy on "Relief Society Sisters Regarding Anointing the Sick." For the first time, such a document did not come from the Relief Society itself.[32]

Little of the information was new. It formalized policy that had taken shape over the years: Lorenzo Snow's stipulation that the blessing must be confirmed rather than sealed, Wilford Woodruff's that it was neither a Relief Society function nor an ordinance. The only new policy seems to be that such work comes under "the direction of" the bishop. At the 13 April 1921 general conference, First

Presidency Counselor Charles W. Penrose reported women asking "if they did not have the right to administer to the sick," and he, quoting Jesus' promise to his apostles of the signs that will follow the believers, conceded that there might be

> Occasions when perhaps it would be wise for a woman to lay her hands upon a child, or upon one another sometimes, and there have been appointments made for our sisters, some good women, to anoint and bless others of their sex who expect to go through times of great personal trial, travail and "labor;" so that is all right, so far as it goes. But when women go around and declare that they have been set apart to administer to the sick and take the place that is given to the elders of the Church by revelation as declared, through James of old, and through the Prophet Joseph in modern times, that is an assumption of authority and contrary to scripture, which is that when people are sick they shall call for the elders of the Church and they shall pray over them and officially lay hands on them.[33]

Even though he cited the authority of Joseph Smith, and even though Joseph Smith certainly taught the propriety and authority of elders to heal the sick, President Penrose also contradicted the extension of healing privileges to women by Joseph Smith. In fact, Joseph Smith had cited that same scripture (James 5:14) in the 12 April 1842 Relief Society meeting but, ironically, had made a far different commentary: "These signs . . . should follow all that believe whether male or female."[34]

Throughout the 1920s, Church leaders increasingly drew bolder lines between spiritual gifts and priesthood powers. With the clarification of the priesthood role came restriction in the women's sphere. Church leaders made it clear that women did not have right to priesthood power. Further definition of priesthood included healing, anointing with oil, etc., as exclusive functions of elders.

By 1928, President Heber J. Grant defended the priesthood against "complaint . . . about the domination of the people by those who preside over them." He quoted the description of the ideal way in which priesthood authority is to function, found in Doctrine and Covenants 121, then asked, somewhat rhetorically, "Is it a terrible thing to exercise the priesthood of the living God in the way that the Lord prescribes: 'By kindness and gentleness' "?[35] The pattern had now been established, clarified, and validated.

The strength of that pattern can be seen through a letter from Martha A. Hickman of Logan, who wrote to Relief Society General President Louise Yates Robison, asking:

> Is it orthodox and sanctioned by the Church today to perform "washing" and "anointings" for the sick (sisters) especially in preparation for confinement in childbirth?

Some have advocated that the proper procedure would be to have a special administration by some member bearing the Priesthood for those desiring a special blessing at this time.

Some years ago when our temples did away with this ordinance for the sick and expectant mothers, in many of our wards in this stake, as well as adjoining stakes, committees of sisters, generally two or three in each committee, were called and set apart for this work of "washing" and "anointing" in their respective wards, wherever this ordinance was desired.

I happen to be the head of this committee in the First Ward of Logan Stake. We have officiated in this capacity some ten years, have enjoyed our calling, and have been appreciated. However, since above questions have arisen we do not feel quite at ease. We would like to be in harmony, as well as being able to inform correctly those seeking information. Our Stake Relief Society, nor our Stake President seem to have nothing definite on this matter.[36]

Sister Robison sent the letter back to the stake Relief Society president with an attached letter explaining:

In reference to the question raised, may we say that this beautiful ordinance has always been with the Relief Society, and it is our earnest hope that we may continue to have that privilege, and up to the present time the Presidents of the Church have always allowed it to us. There are some places, however, where a definite stand against it has been taken by the Priesthood Authorities, and where such is the case we cannot do anything but accept their will in the matter. However, where the sisters *are* permitted to do this for expectant mothers we wish it done very quietly, and without any infringement upon the Temple service. It is in reality a mother's blessing, and we do not advocate the appointment of any committees to have this in charge, but any worthy good sister is eligible to perform this service if she has faith, and is in good standing in the Church. It is something that should be treated very carefully, and as we have suggested, with no show or discussion made of it.

We have written to Sister Hickman and told her to consult you in this matter, as it is always our custom to discuss matters of this kind with our Stake Presidents, and have them advise the sisters in their Wards.[37]

There is an air of almost wistful timidity about Sister Robison's letter that bespeaks near-resignation toward the change that was happening, not necessarily because the policy against blessings had changed *per se,* but because policy about the priesthood had changed the environment in which they occurred. Non-priesthood blessings were now suspect. One of the last documents on the subject is a little notebook containing a record of "Washing[s] and Anointing[s] done by sisters in 31st Ward" in Salt Lake City. It begins in 1921: "Sister Dallie Watson for confinement, Dec. 1, 1921—by Emma Goddard and Mary E. Creer. 1033 Lake Street." Every few weeks there is another entry, usually for childbirth, but sometimes for illness. The last entry is 2 July 1945, to a Jane Coulam Moore who had officiated twenty-four years earlier at the first anointing.[38]

The next year brought the official death knell of this particular spiritual gift. On 29 July 1946, Elder Joseph Fielding Smith of the Quorum of the Twelve wrote to Belle S. Spafford, the Relief Society general president, and her counselors, Marianne C. Sharp and Gertrude R. Garff.

> While the authorities of the Church have ruled that it is permissible, under certain conditions and with the approval of the priesthood, for sisters to wash and anoint other sisters, yet they feel that it is far better for us to follow the plan the Lord has given us and send for the Elders of the Church to come and administer to the sick and afflicted.[39]

It would certainly be difficult for a sister to say that she did *not* wish to follow "the plan the Lord has given us" by asking for administration from her sisters rather than from the elders. One Relief Society worker in Canada recalled: "This ordinance was a comfort and strength to many. But it was discontinued and the sisters were asked to call for administration by the Priesthood instead when necessary and desirable."

Elder Smith's pronouncement ended the practice where it had not already stopped. There is no further evidence of such blessings being given by women.

Susa Young Gates's statement still rings clear: "The privileges and powers outlined by the Prophet [Joseph Smith] . . . have never been granted to women in full even yet." When the lives of Latter-day Saint women—their faith, spirituality, devotion, and sacrifice—are seen across the history of the restored Church, we find a record as venerable as that of men. We must respond to Susa's question, "Did those women . . . live so well as to be worthy of them all?" in the affirmative.

Notes

1. For the most comprehensive studies to date of the history of the temple ordinance, see D. Michael Quinn, "Latter-day Saint Prayer Circles," *BYU Studies* 19 (Fall 1978), and David John Buerger, *The Mysteries of Godliness: A History of Mormon Temple Worship* (Salt Lake City: Signature Books, 1994).

2. For examples of women participating in healing in Kirtland, see Linda King Newell and Valeen Tippetts Avery, "Sweet Counsel and Seas of Tribulation: The Religious Life of the

Women in Kirtland," *BYU Studies* 20 (Winter 1980), and Linda King Newell, "Gifts of the Spirit: Women's Share," to be published in a collection of essays edited by Lavina Fielding Anderson and Maureen Ursenbach Beecher, hereafter cited as "Gifts of the Spirit" manuscript. For additional accounts, see Carol Lynn Pearson, *Daughters of Light* (Salt Lake City: Bookcraft, 1973).

3. Susa Young Gates, "The Open Door for Women," *Young Women's Journal* 16 (1905): 117.

4. See Newell, "Gifts of the Spirit" manuscript, pp. 8–11, for a more detailed discussion of this issue.

5. "A Record of the Organization and Proceedings of the Female Relief Society of Nauvoo," 18 Apr. 1842, LDS Church Archives, microfilm of original, Joseph Smith collection, hereafter cited as "Relief Society Minutes of Nauvoo."

6. Relief Society Minutes of Nauvoo, 28 Apr. 1842.

7. Mary Ellen Kimball, Journal, 2 Mar. 1856, Church Archives; emphasis added.

8. *Journal of Discourses Delivered by President Brigham Young, his Two Counselors, the Twelve and others.* Reported by G. D. Watt, J. V. Long and others, Liverpool and London, 1856, Vol. 13 (November 14, 1869), p. 155. Hereafter cited as *Journal of Discourses.*

9. Cache Valley Stake Relief Society Minute Book A, 1869–1881, 18 June 1868, LDS Church Archives.

10. Zina Diantha Huntington Smith Young, Diary, vol. 13, Aug.–Dec. 1881, LDS Church Archives.

11. *Woman's Exponent* 7 (1 Nov. 1878): 86.

12. *Journal of Discourses* 21 (8 Aug. 1880): 367–68.

13. Circular Letter, Salt Lake City, Utah, 6 Oct. 1880, LDS Church Archives.

14. *Woman's Exponent* 13 (15 Sept. 1884): 61.

15. Cache Valley Stake Relief Society Minute Book B, 11 Sept. 1886, 46–48, LDS Church Archives.

16. Wilford B. Woodruff to Emmeline B. Wells, editor, *Woman's Exponent*, 27 Apr. 1888, Correspondence of the First Presidency, LDS Church Archives.

17. *Woman's Exponent* 17 (15 Aug. 1889): 172.

18. *Young Woman's Journal* 4 (4 Jan. 1893): 176–77.

19. Ruth May Fox, diary, 8 Mar. 1896.

20. Louisa L. G. Richards to President Lorenzo Snow, 9 Apr. 1901, LDS Church Archives.

21. Relief Society Minutes of Nauvoo, 1901, LDS Church Archives.

22. Relief Society Minutes of Nauvoo, special meeting of officers of the General Board, 2 May 1901, vol. 1. 352, LDS Church Archives.

23. *Young Woman's Journal* 14 (8 Aug. 1903): 384.

24. James R. Clark, ed., *Messages of the First Presidency*, 5 vols. (Salt Lake City: Bookcraft, 1970), 316. The first question concerned washing and anointing:

Is it necessary for one or more sisters to be set apart for that purpose? . . . or should it be done under the direction of the Presidency of the Relief Society, or could any good sister officiate?

This seems to include three questions.

Firstly, our late President Sister Eliza R. Snow Smith said many times, "Any good sister who had received her endowments and was in good standing in the Church, might officiate in washing and anointing previous to confinement, if called upon, or requested to do so by the sister or sisters desiring the blessing: (but should not offer her services.)

Secondly, not necessarily under the direction of the Presidency of the Relief Society, although it is most likely whoever was called upon to render such services would be a member of the Relief Society in her own Ward. Some sisters are gifted in ministering and comforting with faith, and adaptability, who might not be chosen to preside or fill any official position in the Relief Society, then the sister herself who desires the blessing might have some choice as to whom she would prefer, and there are many little things might be taken into consideration, all cases are not alike, all circumstances are not the same, wisdom and the guidance of the Holy Spirit are things necessary in all such matters.

Thirdly, in reference to children in sickness, one could not always wait to consult the Presidency of the Relief Society; mothers, grandmothers, and often other relatives attend to a sick child both in administering and in the washing with pure water and anointing with the consecrated oil; but generally in neighborhoods, there are sisters who are specially adapted to minister to children, and who have in a large degree the gift of healing under the influence of the Holy Spirit, who are possessed of greater humility and have cultivated the fit, or whom the Lord has greatly blessed.

Second question: "Should the washing be sealed?" It is usual to do this in a few simple words, avoiding the terms used in the Temple, and instead of using the word "Seal" we would use the word "Confirm" in the spirit of invocation.

Third question: "Have the sisters a right to seal the washing and anoint, using no authority, but doing it in the name of Jesus Christ, or should men holding the Priesthood be called in?" The sister[s] have the privilege of laying their hands on the head of the one officiated for and confirming the anointing in the spirit of invocation, and in the name of Jesus Christ, not mentioning authority. The Lord has heard and answered the prayers of the sisters in these ministrations many times.

In suggestions made in reference to washing and anointing the sisters are always advised to kneel and offer prayer previous to officiating in any sacred duty.

25. Joseph F. Smith to Nephi Pratt, Dec. 18–21, 1908. Correspondence of the First Presidency, Reel 39, LDS Church Archives.
26. Relief Society Minutes of Nauvoo, 17 Dec. 1909, 136, vol. 3: 184.
27. Oakley [Idaho] 2nd Ward Relief Society Minutes, LDS Church Archives.
28. Maureen Ursenbach Beecher, Comments, n.d., 1–2.
29. Oakley [Idaho] 2nd Ward Relief Society Minutes, LDS Church Archives.
30. Lucile H. Ursenbach statement, 14 Aug. 1980. In possession of Maureen Ursenbach Beecher.
31. Cache Valley Stake Relief Society Minute Book B, 1881–1914, vol. 2, 5 Mar. 1910, 438–40, CR 1280, 14.1. Other testimonies borne that day included:

    Sister Moench felt that we had so much good said today. Said while she was very young she went out to wash and anoint the sic[k.] Said Sister Richards had given them a foundation to go by and had said to get the spirit of the Lord then they would do right. Related and experience in blessing a child who had been given up by the doc and it got well. Know that if we get the faith and the spirit of God with us we can bless as well as the Brethren....

    Pres. Hattie Hyde spoken of her experiences in Wyo. where the brethren had helped the sisters to bless and anoint the sick.

    Sister R. Moench said that Pres. Young had said that the sisters need not be set apart for this calling but if they can call in any good brethren to seal the anointing so much the better.

    Pres. Lucy S. Cardon said they use to in the Temple have the brethren seal the anointing but now they do not. Knows that one sister can bless another. We have that privilege but when we can get the brethren we should have them seal the blessing.
32. *Messages of the First Presidency*, 4: 314–15.

    To the Presidents of Stakes and Bishops of wards:

    Questions are frequently asked in regard to washing and anointing our sisters preparatory to their confinement. In a circular issued by the leading sisters of the Relief Society a number of questions on this matter have been answered and correct instructions given, but notwithstanding this having been done, we judge from the contents of letters received by us that there exists some uncertainty as to the proper persons to engage in this administration; we have therefore considered it necessary to answer some of these questions, and give such explanations as will place this matter in the right light. We quote some of these questions and give our answers:

    1. Is it necessary for one or more sisters to be set apart to wash and anoint the sick?
    2. Should it be done under the direction of the Relief Society?

Answer: Any good sister, full of faith in God and in the efficacy of prayer may officiate. It is therefore not necessary for anyone to be set apart for this purpose, or that it should be done exclusively under the direction of the Relief Society.

3. Must the sister officiating be a member of the Relief Society?

Answer: It is conceded that most of our sisters, qualified to perform this service and gifted with the spirit of healing and the power to inspire faith in the sick, belong to the Relief Society, but if the sick should desire to have some good sister who is not a member of the Relief Society administer to her, that sister had the right to so administer.

4. Have the sisters the right to administer to the sick children?

Answer: yes: they have the same right to administer to sick children as to adults, and may anoint and lay hands upon them in faith.

5. Should the administering and anointing be sealed?

Answer: It is proper for sisters to lay on hands, using a few simple words, avoiding the terms employed in the temple, and instead of using the word "seal" use the word "confirm."

6. Have the sisters a right to seal the washing and anointing, using no authority, but doing it in the name of Jesus Christ, or should men holding the priesthood be called in?

Answer: The sisters have the privilege of laying their hands on the head of the person for whom they are officiating, and confirming and anointing in the spirit of invocation. The Lord has heard and answered the prayers of sisters in these administrations many times. It should, however, always be remembered that the command of the Lord is to call in the elders to administer to the sick, and when they can be called in, they should be asked to anoint the sick or seal the anointing.

7. Are sisters who have not received their endowments competent to wash and anoint sisters previous to confinement?

Answer: It must always be borne in mind that this administering to the sick by the sisters is in no sense a temple ordinance, and no one is allowed to use the words learned in the temple in washing and anointing the sick. Sisters who have had their endowments have received instructions and blessings which tend to give them stronger faith and especially to qualify them to officiate in this sacred work, but there are good faithful sisters, who through circumstances have not received their endowments, and yet are full of faith and have had much success in ministering to the sick, who should not be forbidden to act, if desired to do so by our sisters.

In conclusion we have to say that in all sacred functions performed by our sisters there should be perfect harmony between them and the Bishop, who has the direction of all matters pertaining to the Church in his ward.

Your brethren,
Joseph F. Smith
Anthon H. Lund
Charles W. Penrose
First Presidency

33. Conference Report, 3 April 1921, 190–91.
34. Relief Society Minutes of Nauvoo (sixth meeting), 12 Apr. 1842.
35. For a more detailed discussion see Newell, "Gifts of the Spirit" manuscript, p. 36.
36. Conference Report, 5 Oct. 1928, 8–9.
37. Martha A. Hickman to Pres. Louise Y. Robison, 28 Nov. 1935, LDS Church Archives.
38. Louise Y. Robison, 5 Dec. 1935. Copy in possession of author.
39. Photocopy of holograph, courtesy Charlott Boden Erickson, LDS Church Archives.

Carol Cornwall Madsen (1930–), "Mormon Women and the Struggle for Definition: The Nineteenth-Century Church" (1981)

Just as Linda Wilcox reconstructed the doctrinal history of the Heavenly Mother and Linda King Newell recovered a lost tradition of Mormon women's giving healing blessings, another member of Salt Lake City's Wednesday lunch group, Carol Cornwall Madsen, investigated the expansive role the women of the early Relief Society had played in LDS Church governance. The mother of six children, Madsen came to the study of Mormon women's history after she returned to work in 1974, taking a job at the University of Utah's Women's Resource Center. There she found herself engaged in the burgeoning women's movement, hosting high-profile guests such as Gloria Steinem and attending a two-week intensive course in women's history with Joan Hoff Wilson, a pioneer in the field. "The more I learned and the more I had an association with some of the movers and shakers in this movement and the more I read, the more excited I became about rediscovering women's lives," Madsen recalls. She began graduate studies in history at the University of Utah in 1976, just as politics around the Equal Rights Amendment intensified. "The principle of equality between men and women in marriage and public life was very much an issue of personal interest to me. We, along with many others, were very surprised when the Church came out against the ERA because it had been so supportive of women's rights in the nineteenth century," Madsen remembers. "In time I came to terms with the feminist movement in my own life—what I could accept, and what I could reject—and be true to my own convictions." After speaking on a panel on women's history at the IWY convention in 1977, Madsen was invited by LDS Church historian Leonard Arrington to join Maureen Ursenbach Beecher and Jill Mulvay Derr as the first professional historians employed by the LDS Church Historical Department to work on women's history. Along with Beecher and Derr, Madsen decided that "it would be better and more could be accomplished if we worked within the institution to effect changes that might assist women in feeling more necessary within the structure of the Church." In this essay, Madsen reveals how necessary women's Relief Society leadership had truly been to the nineteenth-century Latter-day Saint movement. The subject of Relief Society leadership was both a timely and a tender one: under a bureaucratic initiative known as "Priesthood Correlation" during the 1960s and 1970s, all LDS Church programs and operations had been placed under the supervision of the Church's all-male priesthood hierarchy; the female leadership of the once-independent Relief Society lost the authority to develop and administer its own programs, finances, and publications. Madsen's research revealed a time when Relief Society leaders understood themselves as "priestesses" in an organization parallel and equal in influence and authority to the men's priesthood and with an equal share of leadership in the Latter-day Saint movement. After receiving her Ph.D. in 1985, Madsen joined the history faculty of Brigham Young University, where her decades-spanning career would produce dozens of articles and books, including an award-winning study of the life of nineteenth-century *Woman's Exponent* editor, Relief Society president, and suffragist Emmeline Wells.

Source

Madsen, Carol Cornwall. "Mormon Women and the Struggle for Definition: The Nineteenth-Century Church." *Dialogue, A Journal of Mormon Thought* 14.4 (1981): 40–47.

References and Further Reading

Madsen, Carol Cornwall. *An Advocate for Women: The Public Life of Emmeline B. Wells, 1870–1920*. Provo and Salt Lake City: Brigham Young University Press and Deseret Book, 2006.
Bench, Sheree Maxwell. "'True to My Own Convictions': A Conversation with Carol Cornwall Madsen." *Mormon Historical Studies* (Spring 2008): 87–117.

"MORMON WOMEN AND THE STRUGGLE FOR DEFINITION: THE NINETEENTH-CENTURY CHURCH"

I would like to concentrate on three aspects of the religious life of early Mormon women which I think helped them define and understand themselves and their place within both the theology and the institution of Mormonism. All had their beginnings in the Nauvoo period when women emerged as a visible, collective entity through the organization of the Relief Society. Most members today are familiar with what has become a symbol of that organization's beginning—Joseph giving the key *to* women, not in behalf of women, as we generally hear, and told them that knowledge and intelligence would flow down from that time forth. "This," he said, "would be the beginning of better days for this society."[1]

The organization of the Relief Society came about from the voluntary effort of women during the construction of the Nauvoo Temple. Sarah Kimball's suggestion that a female benevolent society be organized for this purpose, however, was met by Joseph's statement that he had something better for them.[2] From the beginning, Relief Society members perceived their organization as distinctive from the ladies aid and benevolent societies that were flourishing elsewhere. Formed "after the pattern of the priesthood," it had been "organized according to the laws of heaven," explained John Taylor, present at its inception.[3]

In the years that followed the re-establishment of the Relief Society in the Salt Lake Valley, its potential as a parallel force with the priesthood in building the kingdom blossomed. Eliza R. Snow, by appointment of Brigham Young, directed the affairs of the society throughout the territory, organizing and assisting the various units to meet the needs of the community which Brigham Young had outlined. But while the impetus for organization this time originated with the Prophet, the women planned, developed and implemented many of the specific economic, community, educational and religious programs that came to be their share of kingdom building. There was wide latitude in their stewardship.

With the exception of Emma Smith, Eliza R. Snow was unique among women leaders in the Church. She not only held the position of "Presidentess of all Mormon women's organizations," indeed of all Mormon women, she was also the wife of the living prophet. As Maureen Beecher has described, she was the "chief disseminator of the religion to the women of the Church," and conversely, we might add, their advocate with the Prophet.

The interconnection of priesthood and Relief Society as enunciated by the Prophet Joseph was continually reinforced by later church presidents. "Let male and female operate together in the one great common cause," John Taylor told a conference audience.[4] Wilford Woodruff confirmed this mutual labor: "The responsibilities of building up this kingdom rest alike upon the man and the woman."[5] Lorenzo Snow exhorted the sisters to take an interest in their societies for they were "of great importance. Without them," he repeated, "the Church could not be fully organized."[6] Presiding Bishop Edward Hunter expanded the words of Joseph to the sisters. "They have saved much suffering," he said, "and have been a great help to the bishops. They have the priesthood—a portion of the priesthood rests upon the sisters."[7]

It was in the temple experience that Mormon women of the early Church most fully defined themselves and their place in both the temporal and eternal kingdom. Here they learned their relationship to priesthood in very personal and tangible ways, particularly those who received all of the temple ordinances. Joseph recorded, before meeting with the Relief Society at its sixth meeting, that he was going to give a lecture to the sisters on the priesthood, showing them how they would come in possession of its gifts, privileges and blessings. Subsequent events indicate that he intended to prepare them, just as he had the brethren, to receive the fullness of the gospel, or the priesthood ordinances that were to be administered in the temple. Conscious that his time was limited, he introduced these ordinances to a selected group of men and later women before the completion of the Nauvoo Temple. When it was completed many of those who had received their endowment beforehand became the first temple officiators. "Woman," Emmeline B. Wells remembered, "was called upon to take her part in administering therein, officiating in the character of priestess."[8] This term was consistently applied to women who performed temple service. Eliza R. Snow, Zina D. H. Young and Bathsheba W. Smith, who served, each in her own time, simultaneously as general president of the Relief Society and as temple matron (using a contemporary term) were frequently referred to as Presiding High Priestesses.

Once again women and men were called to unite their efforts in another aspect—the most important one—of their religious life. "Our sisters should be prepared to take their position in Zion," John Taylor announced at a Relief Society conference. "They are really one with us, and when the brethren go into the temples to officiate for the males, the sisters will go for the females; we operate together for the good of the whole . . . all acting mutually, through the ordinances of the Gospel, as saviours upon Mount Zion."[9]

I believe it is impossible to overestimate the significance of temple work in the lives of early Mormon women. As both initiates and officiators they knew they were participating in the essential priesthood ordinances of the gospel in the same manner as their husbands, their fathers or their brothers. Moreover, they knew it was a universal work for both the living and the dead, and the appellation, "Saviours on Mount Zion" was not just a poetic phrase. Nor was it mere hyperbole in the words of welcome given by the Kanab Relief Society officers when Eliza R. Snow and Zina D. H. Young visited:

> We welcome sisters Eliza and Zina as our Elect Lady and her coun-
> selor, and as presidents of all the feminine portion of the human race,
> although comparatively few recognize their right to this authority. Yet,
> we know they have been set apart as leading priestesses of this dispen-
> sation. As such we honor them.[10]

Besides bringing women and men together to work as partners in performing priesthood ordinances, the temple also underscored their interdependence in the eternal plan. Marriage was an essential saving ordinance and through marriage women had access to priesthood. James E. Talmage, author of *House of the Lord*, explains:

> It is a precept of the Church that women of the Church share the
> authority of the priesthood with their husbands, actual or prospective;
> and therefore women, whether taking the endowment for themselves
> or for the dead, are not ordained to specific rank in the priesthood.
> Nevertheless, there is no grade, rank, or phase of the temple endow-
> ment to which women are not eligible on an equality with man.[11]

Lucy Meserve Smith, wife of apostle George A. Smith, was one who expressed very clearly this perception of shared priesthood. Writing of a particularly frightful experience in which she felt the tangible presence of evil spirits, she recalled that

> the holy spirit said to me they can do no harm where the name of Jesus
> is used with authority. I immediately rebuked them in [that name] and
> also by virtue of the Holy Priesthood conferred upon me in common
> with my companion in the Temple of our God.[12]

In a patriarchal blessing given to her at the death of her husband, Zina Y. Williams was also reminded of the particular power given to her in the Temple: "These blessings are yours, the blessings and the power according to the Holy Melchizedek Priesthood, you received in your endowments."[13]

While the debate went on around them concerning their precise relationship to priesthood, women went about with a knowledge that they did indeed have a claimable right, not just to its blessings but also to its gifts and privileges, as Joseph had promised. In their homes it was exercised jointly with their husbands, or alone as their share of the gift in their husband's absence, in behalf of their families and sometimes friends or co-workers. In their church activities it informed the authority delegated to them to officiate in their various callings. In the temple it was utilized directly by women as they administered the priesthood ordinances to other women.

Thus through the sealing ordinances of the temple, men and women became not only heirs to the blessings and privileges of priesthood but candidates for godhood, ultimately, according to Talmage, "administering in their respective stations, seeing and understanding alike, and cooperating to the full in the government of their family kingdom." Conscious of the inequities that unbalanced the relationships of men and women in this life, he added, "Then shall woman be recompensed in rich measure for all the injustice that womanhood has endured in mortality."[14]

So it was that from their membership in the Relief Society which they understood to be an essential part of church organization, they functioned alongside priesthood in implementing and supervising temporal concerns. More important, from their participation in spiritual affairs through the exercise of spiritual gifts and their share in the uses of priesthood, and especially from the promise of godhood which awaited the faithful man and woman only together, Mormon women felt themselves to be an integral, viable force within the kingdom.

Notes

1. Minutes of the Nauvoo Female Relief Society, 28 April 1842, typescript copy, LDS Church Archives, Salt Lake City, Utah, p. 32.
2. "Third Quarterly Conference, Relief Society, Salt Lake County," *Woman's Exponent* 7 (July 1, 1878): 18.
3. "A Record of the Organization, and Proceedings of The Female Relief Society of Nauvoo," March 17, 1842, typed manuscript, LDS Church History Library.
4. *Journal of Discourses* 19 (21 October 1877): 246.
5. "Relief Society, YLMIA, and Primary Reports," *Woman's Exponent* 9 (July 15, 1880): 31.
6. Box Elder Stake Relief Society Minutes, 1875–1884, December 10, 1876, manuscript LDS Church History Library.
7. "Grain Meeting," *Woman's Exponent* 6 (December 1, 1877): 102.
8. Emmeline B. Wells, "Pen Sketch of an Illustrious Woman [Eliza R. Snow]," *Woman's Exponent* 9 (October 15, 1880): 74.
9. "Relief Society Conference, Juab Stake," *Woman's Exponent* 8 (June 1, 1879): 2.
10. M. Elizabeth Little, "A Welcome," *Woman's Exponent* 9 (April 1, 1881): 165.

11. James E. Talmage, *The House of the Lord* (Salt Lake City: The Church of Jesus Christ of Latter-day Saints, 1912), 94.

12. Historical Record of Lucy M. Smith, manuscript, LDS Church History Library. (Record begins: "Salt Lake City June 12th 1889 Historical Sketches of My Great Grandfather.")

13. Zina Y. [Williams] Card Papers, L. Tom Perry Special Collections, Harold B. Lee Library, Brigham Young University, Provo, Utah.

14. "The Eternity of Sex," *Young Woman's Journal* 25 (October 1914): 600–604.

Laurel Thatcher Ulrich (1938–), "The Pink *Dialogue* and Beyond" (1981)

In 1981, Laurel Thatcher Ulrich, a member of the original circle of Boston-area Mormon feminists and a newly minted faculty member at the University of New Hampshire, looked back on the first decade of the contemporary Mormon feminism with a sense of well-earned satisfaction. In this warm and frank personal essay, she celebrates the achievements of the first decade of Mormon feminists in producing new books and periodicals, recovering essential dimensions of Mormon women's history, and building a national community of Mormon women committed to what Claudia Bushman had called the "dual platforms" of Mormonism and feminism. Ulrich acknowledges the immense pressures that Mormon feminists shouldered as they witnessed a church they loved mobilize its members against the Equal Rights Amendment and espouse a deeply conservative view of women's roles that would have disappointed and stunned the politically emboldened women of nineteenth-century Mormonism. She also speaks intimately about dynamics within the Mormon feminist movement, including moments of frustration, disagreement, conflict, and struggle—dynamics that were common to any grassroots social movement but that could be particularly unsettling to women steeped in an LDS culture that by the late twentieth century had grown deeply quietistic and conflict-averse. To be a Mormon feminist, Ulrich wrote, was "to care enough about the Church to want to see it better, to cherish the past without denying the future, to love and respect the brethren while recognizing their limitations, to be willing to speak when no one is listening." It would also mean careful nurturing of the relationships that bound Mormon feminists one to another, relationships that had sustained and would continue to sustain the movement and its members in difficult historical moments to come. Ulrich's essay is vital inasmuch as it glimpses the profound dailiness of the Mormon feminist movement and the domestic acts of care that Mormon feminists undertake to create time, space, and opportunity for themselves and others to reflect on their lives and tell their stories.

Source

Ulrich, Laurel Thatcher. "The Pink *Dialogue: A Journal of Mormon Thought* and Beyond," *Dialogue* 14.4 (1981): 28–39.

"THE PINK *DIALOGUE* AND BEYOND"

Sometime in June 1970, I invited a few friends to my house to chat about the then emerging women's movement. If I had known we were about to make history, I would have taken minutes or at least passed a roll around, but of course I didn't. All I have now to document that momentous gathering are memories. I remember Claudia Bushman sitting on a straight oak chair near my fireplace telling us about women's lives in the nineteenth century. Since she had just begun a doctoral program in history, she was our resident scholar. If we had a resident feminist, it was Judy Dushku, who came to that first meeting with a rhymed manifesto she had picked up at the university where she taught. We laughed at the poem's pungent satire, then pondered its attack on "living for others." "Isn't that what we are supposed to do?" someone said. Our potential for disagreement was obvious, yet on that bright morning we were too absorbed in the unfamiliar openness to care.

The talk streamed through the room like sunshine. None of us recognized that we were beginning a discussion that would continue for more than a decade. We only knew that it felt good to talk, and that we did not want to stop when it was time to go home.

Our group talked about Betty Friedan, Kate Millet, Rodney Turner and the latest Relief Society lessons; about birth control, working women, church politics and homosexuality; about things we knew well, like housework, and about things we knew not at all, like the relevance of feminism to working class women. In our most extravagant moments, we did not know whether to be angry at our mothers, at our husbands or at God. To our dismay we often found ourselves angry with each other. I do not wish to exaggerate our struggles. A certain amount of turmoil is probably characteristic of any group project, as most Mormons know. Yet in a church context, both our pain and our achievement were different. We had called *ourselves* to this task. Without a confirming priesthood blessing and without any clear historical precedent, we had taken upon ourselves a project which would neither build buildings nor win converts and which by its very nature would disturb the equilibrium of our lives.

In my manic moods, I like to remember that. If I could somehow figure out the exact date of our first meeting, I would propose it for historic recognition. A handsome brass plaque would look nice, set in the front lawn of my old house at 380 Dedham Street in Newton, somewhere between the peach tree and the birch. "Here," the inscription would read, "in this ordinary looking, gambrel-roofed house, the second generation of Mormon feminists was born." A feminist is a person who believes in equality between the sexes, who recognizes discrimination against women and who is willing to work to overcome it. A Mormon feminist believes that these principles are compatible not only with the gospel of Jesus Christ but with the mission of the Church of Jesus Christ of Latter-day Saints. I can speak with authority for only one member of the second generation of Mormon feminists—myself—yet I am quite serious when I say that *for me* that first meeting in my living room in Newton was historic. Although I had encountered "the problem with no name" long before Betty Friedan described it [in *The Feminine Mystique*], I was ambivalent about solutions. By 1970, I had begun to make small adjustments in my own life, but I still believed that my deepest conflicts were personal rather than general. If I were a better person, I reasoned, a more Christ-like and less-neurotic person, I would not find it so difficult to "live for others." Taking night classes was my strategy for keeping up my spirits so I could carry on the more important work at home. As my husband and I used to joke, "tuition is cheaper than a psychiatrist."

In the past few weeks, I have been rereading some of the correspondence I saved from the year we were working on the pink *Dialogue*. As in going back to an old journal, I have been amused, dismayed, embarrassed, and encouraged, recognizing my own shortcomings and at the same time discerning direction in what at the time seemed chaos. That meeting in Newton now seems like the beginning of a long journey outward from self-pity and self-condemnation. The year of talking helped. Seeing myself in others' reactions, I was able to objectify my problems. I remember the amusement on Judy Dushku's face during a meeting at Grethe Peterson's house when I confessed my embarrassment at coming home one day and finding my husband sitting at the sewing machine mending his pants. I also remember one intense meeting at Bonnie Horne's house when the whole group responded in an unbelieving chorus to my tearful proclamation that I would give up my children rather than my courses. Identifying my own worst fears helped me climb over them.

In 1971 few Mormon women were really prepared to speak. Before we could write with any depth about Tough Issues, we had to do a little more experimenting with our own lives. We also had to learn more about our own place in history. I will never forget the exhilaration of walking in late to one of the *Dialogue* meetings and hearing Claudia reading the story of Ellis Shipp from Leonard Arrington's newly submitted manuscript on women in church history. When she came to the fateful passage in which Ellis defies her husband to go back to medical school, the whole room cheered. "Yesterday you said that I should not go. I am going, going now!" With Ellis's words Leonard let the pioneer generation of Mormon feminists out of the closet, and there was no putting them back.

At the very moment Mormon women began to discover their lost history, they were swept up by history and thrust into the arena of politics by the Church's pronouncement on the ERA. Suddenly in 1978 Mormonism and feminism seemed incompatible. When Mormon history became a topic of conversation in corridors at the University of New Hampshire, when a local Unitarian Society invited me to speak then questioned me about IWY, when a country band refused to play at our ward square dance "because of your Church's attitude toward women," I knew that my adulthood as a Mormon feminist had begun.

In November of 1979, a professor in my department at UNH stopped me on the way to class one day to ask why I wasn't "out in Salt Lake City" defending my sister. I explained that excommunication was a local matter in the Mormon Church, that Sonia Johnson seemed to have run into some problems with her bishop, but that I was quite sure the Church would never let a woman be excommunicated for her political beliefs. At that point, I had scarcely heard of Sonia Johnson. I could no more imagine a bishop excommunicating a woman for supporting the ERA than I could imagine a ward organist flying a banner over stake conference proclaiming the support of Mother in Heaven. The next few weeks taught me a great deal about the Church and about myself. The Sunday after the excommunication a good friend and I found ourselves shouting at each other in the kitchen at Church. Why should we have to defend *either* Sonia or her bishop? Wasn't the bitterness in Virginia enough, without having it spread through the Church? I resented the excommunication because I resented what it taught me about the priesthood. The vision of that all-male council trying a woman's membership was more revealing than any of the rhetoric on either side.

In the shadow of such events I have gradually become aware of the immense contradictions within the Church as it struggles to stretch and grow with the times. That the Church of Jesus Christ of Latter-day Saints simultaneously enlarges and diminishes women should hardly be surprising since it was born and has grown to maturity in a larger society which does the same. In my opinion, the solution is neither to keep quiet nor to picket the tabernacle. To do either is to accept the very heresy we want to overcome—the misguided notion that the Church is somehow to be equated with the men at the top. We must relearn an old lesson from Sunday School—the Church rests upon the testimonies of its individual members. I resist teachings and practices which diminish women not only because I am a feminist but because I am a Mormon.

For me, learning to question the present structure of the priesthood has been a positive as well as a negative experience. With feelings of anger and betrayal has come a new sense of responsibility; with recognition of discrimination has come renewed conviction of the essential message of the gospel of Jesus Christ. I am convinced that an effective challenge to male dominance can only be built upon "principles of righteousness." Trusting the spirit of the priesthood in the Church, Mormon women must recognize the potential for priesthood in themselves.

"Now faith is the substance of things hoped for, the evidence of things not seen."[*] To care enough about the Church to want to see it better, to cherish the past without denying the future, to love and respect the brethren while recognizing their limitations, to be willing to speak when no one is listening—all of

---

[*] See Hebrews 11:1.

these require faith. Because I am not at all certain that the next decade will be any easier for Mormon women than the last, I offer these personal experiences as a kind of testimony. Ten years ago, in a small gathering in a living room in Newton, a few women began to talk to each other. They not only discovered the value of the personal voice, they learned the importance of accepting responsibility for their own perceptions. Risking conflict, they grew in their ability to serve. Opening themselves to others, they were unexpectedly strengthened in knowledge and in faith.

II

LIVED CONTRADICTIONS

MORMON FEMINISM IN THE 1980s

The national fight over the ERA put women's lives and choices at the center of a political battle—a fact that Mormon feminists experienced with particular intensity. LDS Church leaders and Mormon anti-ERA supporters had framed their opposition to the ERA as a defense of women's "traditional" roles and protections as wives, mothers, and daughters. But Mormon feminist historians remembered that Mormon women had always assumed a broad range of social and economic roles in the communities where they lived. In the nineteenth and early twentieth centuries, Mormon women had traveled East to study medicine and the arts and stepped out as vocal political advocates for women's suffrage and polygamy. Brigham Young had said:

> *We believe that women are useful, not only to sweep houses, wash dishes, make beds, and raise babies, but they should stand behind the counter, study law or physic, or become good bookkeepers and be able to do the business in any counting house, and all this to enlarge their sphere of usefulness for the benefit of society at large. In following these things, they but answer the design of their creation.*

A century later, LDS Church leaders delivered a very different message. LDS Church president Ezra Taft Benson's 1987 address "To the Mothers in Zion" called Mormon women to abandon this engagement in the broad public sphere and to focus on homemaking and childrearing. Encouraged by their leaders, Mormons seemed to feel a growing urgency to define themselves and their families against the norms of the wider "world," even as they continued to assimilate beyond the Rocky Mountain West and into American society. One of the most popular and widely circulated Mormon essays of the decade, "Patti Perfect," published in the feminist magazine Exponent II, *gently satirized the incredible pressures that Mormon women felt to center their identities around running their homes and raising families with impossible levels of efficiency and grace.*

117

The essays collected in this section document the personal and political pressure-laden contradictions that centered on Mormon women's life choices and the way Mormon feminists managed them. Nurtured by literary scholar and editor Mary Bradford and publications like Exponent II *and Salt Lake City–based* Network *magazine, Mormon women adopted the personal essay as an independent space where they could sort through the doctrinal and theological implications of their experiences with grace, wisdom, and humor. It was her reading of Elouise Bell's essay "The Meeting" (anthologized in this section), a humorous but revelatory commentary on profound gender inequality in weekly Mormon worship services, that moved Kelli Frame first to tears of painful recognition and then to feminist action. She helped found the openly feminist Mormon Women's Forum in Salt Lake City in 1988. Its original charter read:*

> *The Mormon Women's Forum invites all people to examine women's issues. We make no demands on any organization or system of belief, and we do not lobby for specific changes. In questioning the traditional interpretation of women and their roles, we endeavor to regain the history of yesterday's sisters and to explore the diversity of today's sisters in hope of securing a meaningful birthright for tomorrow's daughters.*

By writing and organizing, Mormon feminists created spaces where they could analyze how gendered Church teachings, practices, and policies impacted their lives. They grappled with Church policies that diminished the independence of women's organizations and restricted women's authority to lead and even pray in church meetings, and they talked in new and more expansive ways about the historic and future relationship between women and priesthood power.

Nadine McCombs Hansen (1947–), "Women and Priesthood" (1981)

During their first decade at work in the LDS archives, Mormon feminist historians realized that the early twentieth century's transformation of Mormonism from a renegade frontier sect into an American church with the consolidation of Church bureaucracy around an all-male priesthood chain of command, dimensions of Mormonism significant to women—including the doctrine of Heavenly Mother and the time-honored woman-centered forms of religious authority and spiritual practice—had been diminished or lost. What emerged in their place was a new emphasis by Church leaders on the importance of women's roles as homemakers, wives, and mothers. Pressure for LDS women to conform to these roles grew as the LDS Church argued its opposition to the Equal Rights Amendment as an effort to protect women against the complications that might stem from gender equality under the law. Nadine Hansen, a California-based mother of four finishing her bachelor's degree in economics, studied the Church's literature on the ERA but did not find its arguments credible. "I began to realize that behind the 'Equality yes, ERA no' rhetoric was a sentiment which said, 'Equality NO!'" she later recalled. Hansen became an outspoken member of Mormons for ERA after learning from Sonia Johnson that LDS Church leaders had used their ecclesiastical influence to solicit anti-ERA political contributions from wealthy Mormons in California. Her essay "Women and Priesthood" takes the case for equality one bold step further in arguing for the ordination of women to the LDS lay priesthood. Hansen sets Mormonism's view of gender and priesthood within the context of historical Judaism and Christianity, pointing out the biblical presence of Jewish and Christian women identified as "prophetesses" and "apostles." She also dismantles many of the biblical-based arguments commonly used to support the restriction of the LDS priesthood to men, and she asserts that the gender-equal exercise of priesthood would benefit the entire LDS faith—men and women alike. Three decades after she wrote this essay, Hansen would participate in the Ordain Women efforts at LDS General Conference in October 2013 and April 2014.

Source

Hansen, Nadine. "Women and Priesthood." *Dialogue: A Journal of Mormon Thought* 14.4 (1981): 48–57.

"WOMEN AND PRIESTHOOD"

"How do you feel about women holding the priesthood?" It is a question which has hardly been raised except in whispers among Mormons, let alone treated with enough respect to warrant serious consideration. When a non-LDS reporter asked President [Spencer W.] Kimball about the possibility of ordaining women, the reply was "impossible." Members of the Church generally regard this response as adequate and definitive. I perceive, however, dissatisfaction among Mormon women over the rigidly defined "role" church authorities consistently articulate for women. As we rethink our traditional place in the Church and society, we will almost inevitably kindle discussion of the ordination of women.

Although the question of ordaining women is a new one for Mormons, it is not so new to Christendom. Christian feminists are taking a new look at scripture, and have found support for women's ordination—support which has always been there, but which until recently was unnoticed.

The early Christian church had its beginnings in a culture that was deeply biased against women. Rabbinic teachings, developed during the post-exilic centuries when Judaism was fighting to maintain its cultural and religious identity, often emphasized the strictest interpretations of the Torah. Women were subordinate to their husbands, were not allowed to be witnesses in court, were denied education and were restricted in religious practices. Women at the time of Jesus were more restricted than were women in the Old Testament. Yet early Christianity saw a brief flowering of new opportunities for women as new religious patterns cut across the deepest class divisions of the society—race, condition of servitude and sex. Wrote Paul, "There is neither Jew nor Greek, there is neither bond nor free, there is neither male nor female: for ye are all one in Christ Jesus" (Gal. 3:28).

Some New Testament passages refer to women in terms which indicate that the women were ecclesiastical leaders, although this meaning has been obscured by the way the passages are translated into English. Phoebe of Romans 16:1–2 was a woman of considerable responsibility within her religious community. Junia of Romans 16:7 is believed by many scholars to refer to a woman apostle. Indeed a Roman Catholic task force of prominent biblical scholars recently concluded,

> An examination of the biblical evidence shows the following: that there is positive evidence in the NT that ministries were shared by various groups and that women did in fact exercise roles and functions later associated with priestly ministry; that the arguments against the admission of women to priestly ministry based on the praxis of Jesus and the apostles, disciplinary regulations, and the created order cannot be sustained. The conclusion we draw, then, is that the NT evidence, while not decisive by itself, points toward the admission of women to priestly ministry.[1]

It is not in the New Testament alone that we can find precedents for a broader religious participation for women. The Old Testament also tells us of women who rose to prominence, despite the obstacles they faced as women in a culture which restricted them in many serious ways. Deborah and Huldah were prophetesses (Judges 4, 2 Kings 22), but these women have rarely been held up as examples for LDS women to emulate. In fact, their existence as prophetesses is problematic to official Mormon commentators. The Bible Dictionary in the new Church-published Bible lists Deborah simply as "a famous woman who judged Israel . . ." with not a single word about her being a prophetess. Last year's Sunday School manual is even more judgmental. It expressly states, "Deborah is described as a 'prophetess' evidently because of her great righteousness and faith. However, she was not in any way a religious leader, for such is contrary to God's order and organization." The student is referred to Luke 2:36–38 and Acts 21:8–9, both of which tell of prophetesses who fit more neatly into Mormon notions about how women can be prophetesses.[2] Huldah, whose influential prophecies both proved correct *and* were twice accompanied by "Thus saith the Lord," was omitted completely in the new LDS Bible Dictionary![3] Even though the Bible tells us very plainly of these women's activities, they have still been overlooked and their prophetic ministries have been discounted. If this can occur at a time when it is becoming increasingly difficult to ignore women's contributions to the Kingdom of God, it should come as no surprise to us that only the most remarkable of women would find their way into ancient scriptures. One might wonder how many other accomplished women were omitted.

Probably the most commonly cited justifications for assigning a subordinate role to women (and therefore excluding them from priesthood) are found in the writings of Paul. Mormons have been highly selective in accepting and rejecting the teachings of Paul. On the one hand we have rejected his counsel on such matters as celibacy (I Cor. 7:8–9), on women speaking and teaching in church (I Cor. 14:34–35,1 Tim. 2:11–12), and on women wearing headcoverings while praying or prophesying (I Cor. 11:5). On the other hand, we have uncompromisingly accepted the idea of women's subordinate place in marriage (Eph. 5:22–24, 1 Cor. 11:3), and have extended this subordination to the Church as well. This inconsistency stems, I believe, from a far too literal application of the epistolary understanding of the stories of the creation and fall. That is, a few passages in the epistles attempt to justify women's subordination by explaining that Eve was created after Adam and for his benefit (I Tim. 2:13, I Cor. 11:7, 9), and that she was the first to "fall," (I Tim. 2:14) thereby causing all women to be required to be subordinate to their husbands. We have taken this reasoning literally but have applied it selectively, rejecting part of the resulting counsel as culturally motivated while accepting part of it as eternal truth. We therefore permit (in fact, encourage) women to speak and teach in church (culture now permits that). But in doing so, women must remain subordinate to men (eternal proper order).

A Pauline argument for the subordination of women to men—"Adam was not deceived, but the woman being deceived was in the transgression"—is problematic to Mormon theology, since Mormons view the fall as an event which was both necessary and desirable for the progress of Adam and Eve and the entire human family, while simultaneously viewing it as a transgression which merited punishment. The story contains a double message which is difficult to explain in any way consistent with other aspects of Mormon theology. If, as Paul claims, Eve was truly deceived and Adam was not, then why should Eve's punishment be greater than Adam's? Should not the punishment be greater for one who *knowingly* disobeys than for one who is "deceived"? If, on the other hand, Eve was *not* deceived, but rather fell intentionally as some Mormon leaders have claimed,[4] in order to bring about the necessary condition of mortality and knowledge of good and evil, then why is she punished more severely than Adam, who enters mortality only after she urges him to do so? Mormon writings and sermons are replete with accolades to our first parents for their willingness to "fall," yet Eve is placed in a subordinate position to Adam for being the first to do that which she was sent to earth to do. Moreover, Mormon belief holds that "men will be punished for their own sins and not for Adam's transgression"[5] yet *all* women are expected to give due submission to their husbands on account of Eve's transgression, an act over which no other woman has any control.

Paul's statements on the subject serve as effective arguments for maintaining the status quo, but they are not at the root of the role designations of subordination for women and superordination for men. The real root of this hierarchical ordering, it seems to me, is the Mormon concept of man's, and woman's, ultimate destiny. Under this concept, woman is subordinate to man because God is male and because only men can become like God. Although it has become fashionable to give verbal affirmation to the equality of the sexes, and even to the *eternal* equality of the sexes, the fact is that our present-day concepts of heaven and eternal progression grew out of a theology which did not encompass any such egalitarian belief. For example, Orson Pratt said, "The Father of our spirit is the head of His household, and His wives and children are required to yield the most perfect obedience to their great Head."[6] Today's church leaders have said little about our Heavenly Mother's relationship to Heavenly Father and have not, to my knowledge, indicated whether or not they would agree with Orson Pratt. But until we begin to see our ultimate destiny as a genuine equal partnership, we will likely find it impossible to believe that women and men are inherently equal, and we will persist in using Pauline discourses about women to buttress our view that men are divinely designated to be eternal leaders, while women are divinely designated to be eternal followers. In a circular pattern of thinking, our concept of the heavens could continue to prevent us from allowing women to be leaders on earth, while the lack of women leaders on earth continues to cause us to project our earth-view into the heavens.

There are undoubtedly many women who prefer to remain excluded. They feel they enjoy all the blessings of the priesthood, while being free from its responsibilities. But the rising expectations of women today are causing many of us to re-examine our feelings about the strict role assignments that have circumscribed us, compartmentalized us, and divided us, male and female. Filling important church offices is a great responsibility to be sure. But it is also a great opportunity for growth. Because women are denied priesthood, they are also denied this opportunity. In addition, they are denied the opportunity to be part of the ongoing decision-making process in our wards, our stakes, our Church. In everything from deciding who will fill church callings to deciding where and when to purchase property, women are regularly asked to sustain decisions which have been made by men, but they are given little opportunity to influence those decisions before they are made. Often these decisions have a very great impact on women, as is the case when undertakings involving large time or financial commitments are openly discussed in priesthood meeting, yet women are generally not consulted about them.

Many women felt dismayed by the loss of autonomy they experienced when the Relief Society was "correlated," losing its magazine and the opportunity to raise and manage its own funds. Yet even though women were the ones most affected by these changes, they were not permitted to make the decision about how the Relief Society would be structured. The decision was made for them. By men. Hierarchical decision-making might well continue to cause dismay and dissent if women filled all church leadership positions on an equal basis with men. But the chances of decisions being made which adversely affected women—such as the one a few years ago to deny women the opportunity to offer prayers in sacrament meeting—would be lessened, because women would be more likely than men, even well-meaning men, to be aware of how any given decision would affect other women. It is a simple matter of common experience.

Having an all-male priesthood affects our attitudes toward women and men much more deeply than we realize. Many people sincerely believe that granting priesthood to men while denying it to women in no way influences their egalitarian ideals. But would we still feel the same if instead of an all-male priesthood, we had an all-female priesthood? How would we feel if every leadership position (except those relating directly to men and children) were filled by a woman? If every significant problem had to be resolved by women? If every woman and every man who needed counseling from a spiritual leader had to be counseled by a woman? How would we feel if every member of the stake high council were a woman? If each month we received a message in sacrament meeting from a high councilwoman? If the presiding officer in all church meetings were a woman? If church courts were all held by women? How would we feel if we could ordain our twelve-year-old daughters, but not our sons? If each week our daughters blessed and passed the Sacrament? If our young women were encouraged to go on missions, and our young men permitted to go only if they were older than our young women? If in the mission field all zone and district leaders were young women, to whom slightly older young men had to report? If our brother missionaries could teach investigators but were denied the privilege of baptizing and confirming them? How would we feel if only mothers could bless, baptize and confirm their children? If men did most of the teaching of children, and women filled nearly all ward executive positions? If women addressed the annual men's general meeting of the Church, to instruct them in how to best fill their role as men? Would men in this situation still be so sure that in the Church, men and women are equal, even though the men have a different role?

Before June 1978, we all readily understood that the [LDS Church's] denial of priesthood to black men was a serious deprivation. Singling out one race of men for priesthood exclusion was easily recognized as injustice, and most of us were deeply gratified to see that injustice removed by revelation. But somehow it is much more difficult for many people to see denial of priesthood to women as a similar injustice. The revelation on behalf of black men apparently came in response to the heartfelt concern of church leaders for their brothers, a concern which moved them to "plead long and earnestly in behalf of these, our faithful brethren, spending many hours in the Upper Room of the Temple supplicating the Lord for divine guidance."[7] It was only after these "many hours" of prayer that the revelation came. I long for the day when similar empathy can be evoked on behalf of our faithful sisters.*

It is my hope that we will not become entrenched in an absolutist position which precludes the possibility of dialogue and change on this issue. I am reminded of the absoluteness of terms with which the policy of denial of priesthood to black men was defended, and I wonder, if we had not been so adamantly certain that the Negro doctrine could never change, might it have changed sooner than it did? What part do we, the membership, play in change? Does our readiness to accept change influence its timing?

Men and women alike rightly consider the priesthood to be a great gift from God, and the right to bear the priesthood to be a special honor, an honor which is denied to women. If the day comes—and I believe it will—when women and men alike will be bearers of both the blessings and burdens of the priesthood, the artificial barriers of dominance and submission, power and manipulation, which sometimes strain our male-female relationships will lessen, and we will all be freer to choose our own paths and roles. In Christian unity we will go forward together, with power to bless our own lives and the lives of others, and with opportunity for a fuller, richer spiritual life and participation for all the children of God.

Notes

1. The Task Force of the Executive Board of the Catholic Biblical Association of America, "Women and Priestly Ministry: The New Testament Evidence," *The Catholic Biblical Quarterly* 41 (1979): 612–13.
2. *Old Testament Part I—Gospel Doctrine Teachers Supplement* (Salt Lake City: Church of Jesus Christ of Latter-day Saints, 1980), 163. These prophetesses include Anna, an elderly woman at the time of Jesus' birth, whose prophecy was that of bearing her testimony about Jesus "to all them that looked for redemption in Jerusalem" (Luke 2:36–38). The Bible also identifies Miriam (the sister of Moses) as a prophetess. The Dictionary lists Miriam, but does not indicate that she was a prophetess.
3. The old Cambridge Bible Dictionary, on which the new one is based, did list Huldah, stating that she was "a prophetess in Jerusalem in the time of Josiah." Thus the omission is not accidental. Likewise in the case of Deborah, the old Dictionary listed her as a prophetess.
4. John A. Widtsoe, *Rational Theology as Taught by the Church of Jesus Christ of Latter-day Saints* (Salt Lake City: Deseret Book, 1965), 51. Widtsoe says, "The fall was a deliberate use of a law, by which Adam and Eve became mortal, and could beget mortal children. . . . The Bible account is, undoubtedly, only figurative."
5. Second Article of Faith.
6. From Orson Pratt, *The Seer* 1 (October 1853), 159.
7. D[octrine] & C[ovenants] Official Declaration 2.

* Theologian Janan Graham-Russell points out that the LDS Church's policies of racial segregation also excluded Mormon men and women of Black African descent from participation in LDS temple rites. She addresses the intersectional implications of this segregation for Black Mormon women and Mormon feminism in her essay in Part IV of this volume.

Mary Lythgoe Bradford (1930–), Selections from *Mormon Women Speak* (1982)

At a moment when the LDS Church's political commitment to the Equal Rights Amendment translated into a new retrenchment around women's roles as homemakers and mothers, Mary Lythgoe Bradford created opportunities for Mormon women to examine the more complicated truths of their lives. A Salt Lake City native, Bradford was the first in her family to attend college, enrolling at the University of Utah. She studied with Lowell Bennion (1908–1996), a Mormon educator, humanitarian, and lay theologian, and earned a master's degree in English with a thesis on Virginia Sorensen (1912–1991), a celebrated Mormon novelist whose books examined themes of individual conscience and community life in ways that engaged national and global audiences. Through her studies of Mormon literature and her work with the soft-spoken, pragmatic Bennion, Bradford developed a commitment to living a carefully examined Mormon faith and to the personal essay as a venue for theological and spiritual inquiry. This commitment was grounded in Bradford's own keeping of a diary, which she began at age thirteen. Essay writing was also for Bradford "a logical extension" of a "vital form" of Mormon expression—"the testimony." She promoted Mormon personal essays as the first woman editor of *Dialogue: A Journal of Mormon Thought* from 1978 to 1983, and in her 1982 collection *Mormon Women Speak,* she encouraged many never-before-published Mormon women writers to undertake deeply personal and yet public examinations of their lives as Mormon women. According to Bradford, it was the first ever collection of personal essays by Mormon women. For Reva Beth Russell, who originally wrote "A Purple Rose" for a *Dialogue* essay contest, the experience of working with Bradford to develop the essay for publication was pivotal: "I felt validated as an intelligent woman," she later said. Contributor Cherie Taylor Pedersen was also transformed by writing about gender and Mormonism. "I have found it necessary to re-examine the concepts pertaining to womanhood that I had once unthinkingly accepted." Two essays from that volume anthologized here glimpse among everyday Mormon women a quiet insistence on their own complicated truths and a nascent feminist consciousness.

Source

Bradford, Mary Lythgoe, ed. *Mormon Women Speak: A Collection of Essays.* Salt Lake City: Olympus Publishing, 1982.

References and Further Reading

Bradford, Mary Lythgoe. *Leaving Home: Personal Essays.* Salt Lake City: Signature Books, 1987.
Bradford, Mary Lythgoe. "I, Eye, Aye: A Personal Essay on Personal Essays." *Dialogue: A Journal of Mormon Thought* 11.2 (1978): 81–89.

Bradford, Mary Lythgoe. "Virginia Sorenson: A Saving Remnant." *Dialogue: A Journal of Mormon Thought* 4.3 (1969): 56–64.

REVA BETH RUSSELL (1948–), "A PURPLE ROSE" (1982)

A vivid memory of my youth is as a Mia-Maid at Rose Night: How tense I became when the sweet girls chose white or pink or red roses, with the appropriate moral values from the lesson manual; how irritated when they couldn't find a purple rose for me to add to the bouquet. I remember saying, "I choose this yellow rose because they couldn't find a purple rose. I choose a purple rose because it is unique, yet beautiful. It is unparalleled in its effort to excel in a field where it is so alone. I will be myself and think for myself."

In a field of lily white roses I've always felt like a purple one. I can visualize myself in the pre-existence complaining about the necessity of an appendix in a mortal body, or insisting that my heavenly name be spelled differently from the millions of others. To my non-Mormon friends I appear normal-Mormon. I teach a class of 13 and 14 year olds in Sunday School, attend Relief Society, direct ward plays, bake my own bread and love quilting. I sew the family's clothing, grow and bottle my own vegetables in the fall. I am very defensive about anything infringing on my night with my family and have even admitted that I would like another child.

To my normal-Mormon friends I appear almost apostate. I am president of the community women's organization that raised money for respectable causes such as the mentally retarded and the local hospital but has also raised money for "evil" projects such as sex education in the schools and birth control information. Last year I was chairwoman of the club's Las Vegas gambling night where we earned eleven thousand dollars at poker, craps, blackjack and roulette. I have said no to many ward requests—other than those to which I have committed myself through a specific calling. I have been chastised for missing an impromptu pre-planning Relief Society meeting when it conflicted with my long-standing commitment to play piano at a nursing home. (I wasn't "furthering the work of the Lord.") I have even refused to host Tupperware parties.

I have goals for myself as a person, wife, mother, community leader and church member, and so to keep my sanity, I have decided to choose exactly which directives I will obey. I choose to attend a city council meeting rather than work on my genealogy. I choose between limiting my family to three right now instead of becoming the raving maniac mother of four. I choose exactly how many items I can comfortably make for the ward bazaar to show my support while still allowing myself time to get my Christmas ready in a cheerful manner. I even posted some scriptures, I can honestly say I read them every day.

When I read stories out of the manuals, whether Primary, Relief Society, or Family Home Evening, the decisions always seem to be black and white.

Everything fits into place for the white rose in the lesson. Maybe because I am a purple rose all of the issues in my life are gray.

The Santa Fe community was recently involved in a heated controversy over sex education in the schools. I had previously taught sex education on a volunteer basis. I agreed with the sex education group who pointed out the documented ignorance of the youth in this area and how ignorance had and would lead to unwanted pregnancies.

But this same pro-sex education group shows films advising young people not to go to their parents for help. The anti-sex education group warns that sex education would only whet the appetites of the youth to learn more. I disagree with that argument but can see their reason for protesting the distribution of pamphlets advocating masturbation. During this controversy, several ladies in the ward wanted me to help drive sex education from the classroom.

The pro-sex education group wanted me to help keep the curriculum in the classroom. I felt in the middle, not being able to champion either side but able to see points of view, and pleading for a middle ground. Be it ERA [the political advocacy group], Common Cause or [the anti-abortion organization] Birthright, I am never at peace.

I don't fit the mold at home either. I hear that President [David O.] McKay and his wife never had a cross word. In a Sacrament Meeting a Seventies' president declares that his marriage is perfect—and I know mine isn't, and it would be wrong to pretend that my husband and I don't ever fight. I struggle with the fact that I can't be a perfect member of the Church and that all of my petals aren't perfect. I will often reach the boiling point and yell at my kids—after a Relief Society lesson on how to maintain a perfectly reverent mood in the home. (I even yell when non-member neighbors are out in their yards.) Maybe it's because I know I'm not perfect that I resent being called "Sister Russell." (The real reason, I suspect though, is that the identity represented by my first name and maiden name is lost.)*

Life challenges me to juggle my selfish goals. I insist on doing my best when I teach or conduct a meeting, and this means many hours of preparation. I also insist on the same quality time for my children. I love their active bodies. I love kissing the sleep from them. I love their refreshing outlook on the world: ("Everybody lived with Jesus before they were born, even murderers and robbers"). I love teaching them the love of Christ and listening to their simple prayers ("And bless Grandma Loveridge that when she is resurrected she won't have cancer again"). Amid the work, laundry, the constant prattle, special diets, and emergency room visits in the middle of the night, there is no greater thrill than a loud, off-key, but sincere rendition of" "Mother, I lo-o-v-e you-u. Mother I do-o-o." But my entire

---

* Russell refers to the Mormon custom of referring to adult members of the faith as "Brother [last name]" or "Sister [last name]."

seventy years or so on earth won't be spent chasing a little nude body down the hall to diaper it, or proudly taking pictures of the cutest kid at the school program or worrying about the teen out with the car. For me there are so many things to learn, to see, to experience and to master that I refuse to cloister myself in one role.

Somewhere I picked up the notion that I can do anything, and I thank my parents, teachers and husband for that priceless gift—it keeps the limits ever-changing and challenging.

I view myself as struggling, trying not to fall in a rut or mold. I would cringe if someone told me I look Mormon. I must admit that I don't feel as I expect a Mormon woman to feel, yet being Mormon is as much me as being a woman. Now and then I have resented being Mormon as much as I resent my monthly menstrual cycle, but I would not undergo a Mormonectomy any more than I would an unnecessary hysterectomy. Both together help make me.

CHERIE TAYLOR PEDERSEN, "EXPANDING THE VISION" (1982)

I grew up in a Mormon home in a part of the country where Mormons were an interesting oddity. My teenage years were spent in the company of friends who neither shared nor fully understood my beliefs, but far from envying my Utah cousins their proximity to church friends and activities, I congratulated myself on having the opportunity for a broader outlook on life than that of Mormons in more insulated communities. However, I became part of such a community when my application to a New England woman's college was turned down, and I applied instead to Brigham Young University.

I looked forward to my experience at a Mormon school in Utah. The prospect of being in an environment where my beliefs and way of life were accepted and understood seemed appealing. I had been different long enough. Ignoring jokes about BYU as the happy hunting ground for girls bent on snaring a returned missionary,* I flew west to seek an education. When I left Provo several years later with a diploma, a husband and two babies, I had indeed received an education; along with academics, I had learned what was expected of me as a Mormon woman. Conservative and a traditionalist by nature, I never thought to question the messages I received, both from listening to talks directed at young women and from observing the lives of older women around me.

---

*Beginning in the late 1960s, serving a term in full-time proselytizing missionary service became an expected rite of passage for Mormon men aged nineteen and older; marrying a "returned missionary" emerged in the same decades as a defining priority for young Mormon women.

I learned that the emphasis on marriage at BYU had not been exaggerated. Ten years down the road, I look back incredulously at the scope of some of the activities designed to facilitate that goal. Commonplace were such staples of dormitory life as candle passings (highly romantic engagement ceremonies) and Eternal Marriage Nights featuring hope chest items, bridal gowns and talks on preparing for marriage. Ads for wedding rings and invitations flourished in the student newspaper. Women spent study time making cookies and Christmas stockings and dinners for the men they hoped would take them to the temple and thence to some happily-ever-after wonderland.

The impetus behind these activities stemmed from a concept that taught young women to view their preparation for life largely in terms of preparation for marriage. Under that influence I, too, became so caught up in the quest that I seldom thought about the possibilities of any life outside the framework of marriage. Despite my parents' emphasis on education and personal development, I felt it imperative to graduate wearing not only cap and gown, but a wedding band as well.

My years at BYU, as well as experiences in other Mormon circles after I graduated, introduced me to what I perceived as the "ideal" Mormon woman. To this day I remember a talk given by a woman whom I admired, in which she sketched for us—an audience of BYU coeds—life as envisioned by a starry-eyed young bride aspiring to be little more than a good homemaker and soothing refuge for her husband. Her desire for intellectual development seemed to stem from a desire to be conversant about his interests rather than a need to focus upon her own. Blissfully they would coast through life while raising a large and righteous family. At nineteen, I thought this limited picture was beautiful.

Other images were held up for my inspection, reinforced by countless stories of heroic pioneer predecessors, strong women enduring the hardship and heartbreak of pioneer life without complaint. These were industrious women who became proficient in the many domestic skills necessary for the sustenance of their families, leaving a legacy of thrift and hard work to their daughters. These were spiritual women who relied on the Lord for support of their children and themselves after their husbands were sent away as missionaries to faraway lands.

As I looked around, it seemed that contemporary Mormon women were equally hard-working, capable people who not only oversaw large households with seeming equanimity, but who stocked cupboards with home-canned fruits and vegetables, made quilts and baked bread (always with an extra loaf for a neighbor), and supported husbands in time-consuming church positions. Any excess energy and creativity became channeled into callings in the various auxiliaries. Spare time for more self-serving pursuits seemed a luxury, not a right.

I know the prototype well because I became one. I sought to conform to a way of life I associated with obedience to principles of the gospel. My aims were admirable, but they created enormous pressure to reach a mythological perfection through what I perceived as selflessness. Wasn't that, after all, what the idealistic young bride of that BYU talk had in common with those invincible pioneer women and their equally impressive descendants?

After spending the first six years of our married life in school and a few lean years after that seeking to establish a foothold, my husband and I had finally "made it" in the sense that we were realizing some long-term goals. We had four bright, healthy children and a comfortable home.

After surviving the stress of our early years together, our marriage now seemed to be on solid ground. My husband's profession made our lives financially secure; we were both active in the Church—I as a teacher in Relief Society, he as a new bishop. I had everything I considered important in this life—and more.

But far from feeling the satisfaction I thought I should have felt, I was frequently depressed and filled with self-doubt. Rather than rejoicing in the home and children I had been taught to cherish, I found myself feeling more like a slave to their many demands. And although I was proud of my husband and his accomplishments, I began to yearn for my own in areas other than domestic. I tried to suppress these stirrings of discontent, certain that I had no "right" to such feelings. Watching other women cope with unhappy marriages, serious financial strain and poor health, how did I dare not be happy? I felt spoiled. I felt ungrateful. Worst of all, I felt that by having needs that seemed to conflict with family and church obligations I somehow fell short of the ideal Mormon womanhood had come to symbolize.

Against this internal discord beat the counterpoint of an ideology fostered by the women's movement: the clarion call to "be" someone, to accomplish in wider fields than those usually afforded to full-time wives and mothers.

Dangerous indeed for a woman bred on such maxims as, "No success can compensate for failure in the home," and "The hand that rocks the cradle rules the world." In an attempt to find a comfortable middle ground, I began to re-examine the concept of selflessness. Is it possible to be too selfless, I wondered? Assuming that selflessness can be placed opposite selfishness on a moral spectrum, is it possible that the one extreme is as harmful as the other? At what point does selfishness cease to be a vice? Subjective questions, these, requiring subjective answers. Neither the women's movement nor the Church is equipped to provide them. I decided that each woman must struggle to find her own answers and, because life is never static, answers that seemed satisfactory at one time must necessarily be discarded and new ones found to fit the changing circumstances of a woman's life. Increasingly, the persistent voices of the women's movement contributed to my thinking about that fragile balance between selfishness and selflessness. To many of its opponents the movement teaches selfishness and in some respects that may be a valid observation. However, it helped me realize that those abilities and needs which transcend accustomed roles are deserving also of opportunities for expression without the penalty of guilt.

I have sensed in the turmoil of change fostered by the women's movement a sisterhood nurtured in the sharing of feelings and experiences by women reaching out to one another for answers. We have within the structure of the Church a formal organization of women dedicated to such a sisterhood. It can only fulfill its purpose if its members feel free to reach out to one another without fear of censure. True concern transcends differences and becomes a support system of mutual respect.

MARY LYTHGOE BRADFORD (1930–), "ACROSS THE GENERATIONS" (1984)

In her own personal essays, Mary Bradford brought keen powers of perception, generous humanity, and quiet humor to bear on even controversial Mormon subjects. "I was convinced," she wrote, "that the doctrines and the beliefs of the church were strong enough to withstand analysis and discussion." In this 1984 essay, Bradford calls attention to and celebrates a cohort of older Mormon women who identified with the women's movement and were willing to honor their faith through analysis and discussion of its gender politics. The Provo, Utah–based Alice Louise Reynolds Forum met from 1978 to 1981 on the Brigham Young University campus, hosting candid discussions of sex discrimination, violence against women, racism in Utah and the Church, and the Equal Rights Amendment. In 1981, campus administrators revoked the group's permission to use the Alice Louise Reynolds room in the library, a room that Forum members had raised funds to create and furnish, because it planned to discuss the Equal Rights Amendment and feature perspectives from the National Organization for Women. Undeterred, the group continued to meet monthly, first in the Provo city library and then in the Provo Municipal Building; in 1984, it was renamed the "Algie Ballif Forum," in memory of founder Algie Eggertson Ballif (1896–1984), a two-term Utah legislator, cousin to the novelist Virginia Eggertson Sorenson (1912–1991) and the labor and consumer advocate Esther Eggertson Peterson (1906–1997). "We are having struggles," Ballif said during the Forum meeting Bradford attended in 1980, "and we don't want to give up those struggles. They are very valuable." We find in this essay a testimony to the resilience of Mormon women, their willingness to struggle, and the power of their faith to inspire acts of conscience, even at historical moments as overwhelmed by gender retrenchment as the ERA-dominated early 1980s.

Source

Bradford, Mary Lythgoe. "Across the Generations." *Exponent II* 11 (Fall 1984): 6.
Bradford, Mary Lythgoe. *Leaving Home: Personal Essays.* Salt Lake City: Signature Books, 1987.

References and Further Reading

Bentley, Amy L. "Comforting the Motherless Children: The Alice Louise Reynolds Women's Forum." *Dialogue: A Journal of Mormon Thought* 23.3 (1990): 39–61.

"ACROSS THE GENERATIONS"

I had to pinch myself. I was actually standing in the rose garden at the Roosevelt home in Hyde Park, New York, staring at Roosevelt faces—sons, grandchildren, great-grandchildren of [Franklin Delano Roosevelt] and Eleanor, my childhood heroes. Eleanor Roosevelt was the better half of the country, the woman who went where no one else dared to go. I did not think of her as strange or funny, the way some of my contemporaries did. She spoke for the oppressed in a quavery voice that I grew to believe was the voice of a saint.

"Everybody here is a Roosevelt but me," I told myself. I had been invited to this centennial celebration of Eleanor's birth as a guest of Esther Peterson, who was there as a speaker. Many years before, Esther Peterson had adopted Eleanor as mentor and model in her own dedication to service. Her experience in labor causes and women's rights led to paths already trod by Eleanor. They first met at White House receptions and again at Val-Kill, but it was Esther's work as assistant secretary of labor under President Kennedy that brought them together. Eleanor was chairman and Esther vice-chairman of the President's Commission on the Status of Women (1961–63). Eleanor had responded to the call with the words, "This will be the last big thing I do." Indeed, she died just before the report was published.

"The will of a woman is the strongest force in the world," she once said. Do today's women understand that the work of Eleanor and Esther paved the way for them? Esther is almost a generation younger than Eleanor, and I am almost a generation younger than Esther. I ask myself, "Does my generation have the strength that Esther's and Eleanor's had? And will my generation teach our children to appreciate the doors they opened for us?"

Certainly, we can continue to excavate the contributions of our pioneer mothers and we can celebrate contemporary foremothers like Algie Eggertsen Ballif, Esther's sister. In her own way, Algie was a symbol worthy of Eleanor. When I walked into the Eleanor wing of the Roosevelt Library at Hyde Park, my first thought was of Algie. A crystal sculpture dedicated to Eleanor is inscribed, "Instead of cursing the dark, she chose to light a candle." Algie's sight was almost gone when she died. When a stroke dimmed her lively mind, she laughed at the demons of darkness. That laughter, combined with unfailing energy for the causes of Mormon women, kept her active for eighty-eight years and posted her at the center of a group of women who bear some of the most distinguished names in Mormondom. Educated, talented, many of them in their seventies and eighties, they call themselves the Alice Reynolds Women's Forum. They meet to speak, to listen, and to engage in debate, usually in a room they funded themselves on the BYU campus.

In 1980, I met with the Alice Reynolds Forum in my role as editor of *Dialogue*. Nineteen women, two husbands, and two of my children gathered in a circle around Helen Candland Stark. Helen began by showing the group an egg timer, admonishing them to be brief, and stating the purpose, "to help Mary Bradford in her awesome task of speaking for the sisterhood of the church in the forthcoming women's issue of *Dialogue*." She asked that we all "speak our small truths." The women talked both of their frustrations with the church and their strong commitment to it. They described disappointed attempts to meet with church leaders and their sorrow at the excommunication of Sonia Johnson. They spoke of campaigns for public office and local reform movements they had sponsored. Single women, widowed and divorced women spoke of both acceptance and loneliness. Married women paid tribute to their husbands. All expressed love for the young of the church and the generation they hoped would be spared the need to fight old battles all over again.

Algie Ballif was the glowing fireside of the evening. She and another sister, Thelma Weight, described discussions in her parents' home where "we children were never hushed up. We heard things, and we listened and we asked questions. This has never left us." Algie thanked the group for their honesty, for their willingness to share their deepest feelings. She celebrated them for their diversity and went on to praise the "diversity in the human heart." "We are having struggles," Algie said, "and we don't want to give up those struggles. They are very valuable." At that moment I understood a little better the source of energy in the room. Algie, Thelma, Helen, and the others were survivors who were actually glad for the strength and opportunity that struggle brings. I felt inadequate in their presence. I asked myself, "Do they also serve who only sit and write?"

But Algie's praise of diversity gave me courage. If I, and others far more eloquent than I, persist in the difficult art of speaking and writing the truth, we may yet light a candle for our daughters—and our sons.

Margaret Merrill Toscano (1949–), "The Missing Rib: The Forgotten Place of Queens and Priestesses in the Establishment of Zion" (1985)

In the 1970s, Mormon feminist historians had discovered that during the lifetime of Joseph Smith, especially in the 1840s when Smith developed LDS temple rituals, Mormon women had understood themselves (with Smith's encouragement) as practitioners of a form of priesthood. Margaret Merrill Toscano, a thirty-six-year-old scholar of Greek and Latin and an instructor at Brigham

Young University, took the case one step further. In a paper first delivered in 1984, Toscano drew from both historical sources and her own training as a scholar of ancient myth and ritual to argue that, by virtue of their participation in temple rites, LDS women "can and do hold the priesthood." It was a landmark contribution to Mormon feminist thought, one that likely cost Toscano her position at Brigham Young University. Toscano argues that the "fullness of the priesthood" is available to both men and women through the temple endowment, that this "fullness" conveys to both men and women full access to the authority to perform religious ordinances, but that it also requires men and women to work together "to realize the fullness of gospel blessings." By redefining priesthood not as an administrative chain of command but as a "fullness" of power to be exercised cooperatively between men and women, Toscano urges a total rethinking of the meaning of priesthood in LDS life. In 1981, Nadine Hansen had argued that ordination of women was an inevitability, but Toscano expresses concern that simply demanding ordination to priesthood defined by a male chain of command would reinforce the corporate nature of the modern LDS Church. Here and elsewhere (as seen in "Put on Your Strength" in this volume) Toscano has argued for a radical restructuring and rethinking of the nature and function of priesthood in order to move away from hierarchical structures altogether. Men and women may have different orientations to priesthood power, she speculates, but Toscano rejects the idea of gender-divided "complementary" roles for men and women and asserts a more nuanced vision of a cooperative practice of priesthood that transforms and sanctifies priesthood holders—male and female—and the entire community of faith.

Source

Toscano, Margaret Merrill. "The Missing Rib: The Forgotten Place of Queens and Priestesses in the Establishment of Zion." *Sunstone* 10.7 (July 1985): 16–22.

References and Additional Reading

Toscano, Margaret Merrill. "'Are Boys More Important than Girls?': The Continuing Conflict of Gender Difference and Equality in Mormonism." *Sunstone* 146 (June 2007): 19–29.
Toscano, Margaret Merrill. "Is There a Place for Heavenly Mother in Mormon Theology?" *Sunstone* 133 (July 2004): 14–22.

"THE MISSING RIB: THE FORGOTTEN PLACE OF QUEENS AND PRIESTESSES IN THE ESTABLISHMENT OF ZION"

In Mormon theology, priesthood keys are essential to administer the ordinances of salvation and to organize and superintend the Church. For this reason, the restoration of the priesthood has long been viewed as one of the most important events in the establishment of the Church. Yet, though the Church commemorates the restoration of the Aaronic and Melchizedek priesthoods, little if anything is ever said about the restoration of the priesthood "by the hand of Elijah the prophet." For Joseph Smith, however, Elijah's mission was of the utmost importance to the Church, since Elijah restored the keys of the fulness [*sic*] of the priesthood.˙

Significantly, among Joseph's first revelations from Moroni, given in 1823, appears the pronouncement that it would be by Elijah, not John the Baptist or Peter, James, and John that the priesthood would be revealed (D&C 2). Though Elijah appeared in April of 1836, it was not until May 4, 1842, that Joseph began transmitting to other men the keys of this priesthood by means of the temple endowment. Later, Joseph organized these newly endowed members into a group most commonly referred to as "the quorum."

A year later, on the evening of September 28, 1843, Joseph Smith "was by common consent & unanimous voice chosen president of the Quorum & anointed & ordained to the highest order of the priesthood (& Companion—d[itt]o)."[1] Perhaps the most significant aspect of this important event is contained in the last two words of this report words which are added parenthetically: "(& Companion—d[itt]o)."

These words mean that Joseph's companion, Emma Smith, was also anointed and ordained to the highest order of the priesthood. She had, prior to this date, received her endowment from Joseph, making her the first woman to receive these ordinances; and she was the first woman to be admitted into the quorum. Thereafter, she was in charge of administering to other select women the endowment ordinances which not only transmit priesthood power and keys to those who receive them, but which are a necessary prerequisite to the bestowal upon both men and women of the fulness [*sic*] of the priesthood. It was Joseph's intent that all faithful women were to receive what Emma received when she was "anointed and ordained to the highest order of the priesthood" with her husband.[2] Women, then, can and do hold the priesthood. But this fact has been obscured and overlooked much in the same way that Emma's ordination was subordinated in the report just quoted.

In Joseph's view, women needed the priesthood as much as the men did because the priesthood was not merely a status or fraternity, but a requirement for full salvation. Unlike the modern Church, which tends to regard priesthood as a managerial system for the purpose of correlating and controlling the worldwide Church and as a means of insuring a homogeneous and cost-effective organization, Joseph saw priesthood as raw spiritual power. For him it was inextricably

---

˙Mormon belief holds that the Old Testament prophet Elijah appeared to Joseph Smith and Oliver Cowdery in the LDS temple at Kirtland, Ohio, in April 1836 to "restore" additional priesthood authority to conduct religious rites in LDS temples that could "seal" mortal family relationships to survive after death into the eternities. This "sealing" power is sometimes described as the "fullness" of the priesthood, as Toscano writes here.

entwined with God's spirit that permeates the universe. Priesthood is a necessary prerequisite to handling and controlling the powers of heaven.[3]

While Joseph taught that the reception of the gift of the Holy Ghost brings with it such spiritual gifts as revelations, visions, and tongues, he also taught that the reception of the fulness [sic] of the priesthood by a holy anointing brings similar but higher gifts: revelations of greater knowledge and wisdom, including the discernment of spirits, the reception of the ministry of angels, the voice of Jehovah, the visitation of the Father and the Son, and, finally, the power of an endless life.[4]

The anointing to the fulness [sic] of the priesthood is among the very last ordinances of salvation on a continuum that begins with faith in Jesus Christ and ends with the washing of the feet. The purpose of these ordinances is to sanctify an individual by giving to him or her one degree of spiritual power upon another until he or she is able to bear the full weight of God's glory and come into union with God himself and with other sanctified individuals.[5]

For Joseph, the main purpose of the keys restored by John the Baptist and Peter, James, and John was to administer the ordinances which would eventually allow men and women to be endowed and anointed kings and priests and queens and priestesses, so that they could have direct and personal contact with God. For Joseph, this was the whole point of religion. He stated, "this is why Abraham blessed his posterity: He wanted to bring them into the presence of God. . . . Moses sought to bring the children of Israel into the presence of God, through the power of the Priesthood, but he could not."[6]

Since contact with God is the essence of religion, then personal revelation is an indispensable ingredient of the religious life. For Joseph the "spirit of revelation" and the "priesthood" were very closely linked.[7] With the reception of the fulness [sic] of the priesthood, a man and woman receive the spirit, power, and calling of Elijah:

> Now for Elijah, the spirit power & calling of Elijah is that ye have power to hold the keys of the revelations ordinances, oricles powers & endowments of the fulness of the Melchezedek Priesthood & of the Kingdom of God on Earth & to receive, obtain & perform all the ordinances belonging to the Kingdom of God even unto the sealing of the hearts of the . . . fathers unto the children & the hearts of the children unto the fathers even those who are in heaven.[8]

No person can "attain to the Joint heirship with Jesus Christ with out being administered to by one having the same power & Authority of Melchisedec."[9] By receiving the keys of the fulness [sic] of the priesthood through the holy endowment and the second anointing, a man and woman make their calling and election sure and may receive the visitation of God the Son and be initiated by him into the presence of God the Father.[10]

Since in Joseph's view, this priesthood is essential for full salvation and for contact and union with God, it seems inconceivable that he could withhold it from women. And, in fact, he did not.

Joseph saw the offices of the priesthood* in the Church as necessary appendages to the fulness [*sic*] of the priesthood,[11] and male Church members were ordained to these offices to prepare them to receive their anointings. But Joseph did not ordain women to these offices. However, he did have a plan to prepare the female members of the Church for the fulness [*sic*] of the priesthood. The organization of the Female Relief Society of Nauvoo lay at the heart of this plan, which the Prophet unfolded in the discourses he gave to the Relief Society between March 17 and August 31, 1842.

In the first of these speeches, the Prophet directed the Relief Society women to follow the pattern of the priesthood quorums by establishing in their organization a presidency and other officers. When Emma Smith was elected president, Joseph explained that she was to teach the "female part of the community."[12] This remark constitutes an interpolation of Doctrine and Covenants 25, which actually told Emma she would be ordained "to expound the scriptures, and to exhort the church," not just its female members (D&C 25:7). Elsewhere, however, Joseph expanded women's sphere of influence by saying that, although their administrations should be confined to their close acquaints, their knowledge and preaching could "extend to all the world."[13] Joseph emphasized that Emma and women in general have the calling to learn, write, and teach by virtue of their having received the gift of the Holy Ghost.[14] Thus, women are not simply told to stay in the home and content themselves with "the things of the world."[15]

In Joseph's next speech, he advised the Relief Society to make a careful selection of its new members; for he saw the organization as a means to prepare women for the fulness [*sic*] of the priesthood—a necessary step in building Zion, which was to be patterned after the "ancient order of things." He said: "The society should move according to the ancient Priesthood, hence there should be a select society, separate from all the evils of the world, choice, virtuous and holy."[16] The term "ancient priesthood" refers to the priesthood of the Ancient of Days, Adam and Eve, the priesthood given to men and women jointly.[17] Hence, Joseph could tell the Relief Society that they should "move according to the ancient Priesthood," because they too would share in it. The Relief Society was clearly to be a school to prepare women for the holy order, just as the offices and quorums of the priesthood in the Church were organized to prepare men for the same purpose.

That the ancient order is connected with the building of Zion is indicated by Joseph's stated intention "to make of this society a kingdom of priests as in Enoch's day—as in Paul's day."[18] The original version of this statement was later

---

*"Offices" are ranks within the Aaronic and Melchizedek priesthood—deacons, teachers, priests, elders—that entail specific ritual powers and responsibilities.

edited so that the word "society" was changed to "Church" to read: "The Lord was going to make of the Church of Jesus Christ a kingdom of Priests." This was done perhaps because it seemed incredible that Joseph would have said that he intended to make Relief Society women into "priests."

But I don't believe that the original statement was in error. I think Joseph used the masculine form here in the same way Jesus did in the apocryphal Gospel of Thomas. In that text, Peter objects to the fact that Jesus seems always to be in the company of Mary. Jesus answers this criticism, declaring: "I myself shall lead her in order to make her male."[19] Jesus did not mean that he was going to change Mary's sex but that he was going to make her one with him, a fact he explained when he says: "When you make the two one, and when you make the inside like the outside and the outside like the inside, and the above like the below, and when you make the male and female one and the same, so that the male not be male nor the female female, then will you enter [the Kingdom]."[20] When a man and woman become one in God, the outer loses its identity as outer, and the inner is no longer inner because they have merged into one eternal entity. The female does not become a male, nor the male a female, but rather both become one. They both become a whole person, a holy person, a divine being, a "Man" of Holiness. The term *man* is used here in the same sense it was used in Genesis: it embraces both the male and the female counterparts. Thus, Joseph Smith, in applying the masculine term *priests* to the women of the Relief Society, was not merely making an oversight or indulging in male chauvinism; rather he was using a shorthand expression to refer to an ancient and complex spiritual teaching.

One month later, in his speech of April 28, 1842, Joseph directly addressed the question of woman's relationship to the priesthood by discussing the practice of women giving blessings. He observed that women have the right to administer to the sick because of the ordination and authority they receive by virtue of the gift of the Holy Ghost conferred by the laying on of hands. Joseph explained that the ability to cast out devils, speak in tongues, and heal the sick are given to all, "whether male or female," who believe and are baptized.[21] The fact that God honors the administration of women by healing the person blessed, said Joseph, shows that there is no harm in the practice. "It is no sin for any body to do it that has faith, or if the sick has faith to be heal'd by the administration."[22]

Joseph, however, did not leave the matter there. He added a second justification for women laying hands on the sick by implying that women would soon have an even greater right to administer in spiritual gifts than that given them by virtue of the gift of the Holy Ghost. This greater right was to consist of the priesthood which was to be conferred upon them in the temple. But because Joseph had premonitions of his death, he felt an urgency to begin the work of conferring this priesthood on women before the temple was completed: "He said as he had this opportunity, he was going to instruct the Society. . . . He spoke of delivering the keys to this society and to the Church—that according to his prayers God had appointed him elsewhere."[23] The keys that Joseph spoke of in this passage are those priesthood keys, revealed in the temple, by which the heavens are opened so that spiritual power and knowledge may be received and the source of revelations tested.

That Joseph intended women to receive the priesthood is further demonstrated by his statement found in the *History of the Church*:

> At two o' clock I met the members of the "Female Relief Society," and gave a lecture on the Priesthood, showing how the sisters would come in possession of the privileges blessings and gifts of the Priesthood, and that signs should follow them, such as healing the sick, casting out devils, &c., and that they might attain unto these blessings by a virtuous life, and conversation, and diligence in keeping all the commandments.[24]

In this and other discourses to the Relief Society, Joseph spoke at length on the subject of charity and showed its connection to the spiritual gifts and the priesthood. Joseph taught that charity as the pure love of Christ was the root of purity and the beginning of unity. If the kingdom of God was to be built, it would be founded on Christ's love. For this reason he warned the members of the Relief Society to avoid fault-finding and self-righteousness. Joseph observed that charity not only brings unity of feeling but is indispensable to achieving unity with God.

This is an important temple concept. By addressing charity, Joseph was, once again, preparing the women for the higher ordinances leading to the fulness [*sic*] of the priesthood. For Joseph connected charity or "perfect love" with the highest order of the priesthood and with the doctrine of making one's calling and election sure. He said: "Until we have perfect love we are liable to fall."[25]

Joseph was attempting to expand the view the women had of charity and their own priesthood destiny. For though they initially thought of the Relief Society as an organization dedicated to humanitarian service, Joseph Smith also saw it as a vehicle for building the City of God, where women could commune with Jesus face to face. He saw women functioning in a priestly role to save souls, not merely to administer to their temporal needs: "Away with self-righteousness. The best measure or principle to bring the poor to repentance is to administer to their wants—the Society is not only to relieve the poor but to save souls."[26] The "poor" to which Joseph referred are the "poor in spirit," who need the "bread of life," Jesus Christ.

But why couldn't the women have received the same preparation as the men, through the priesthood quorums already functioning in the Church? Why did Joseph create for women a route to the fulness [*sic*] of the priesthood that was different from that charted for the men? There are no clear answers to these questions nor to the question of whether or not this difference will always exist. However, there are a few statements that may help us to understand why women are not ordained to priesthood offices in the Church structure.

One such statement is Joseph's remark that a "woman has no right to found or organize a Church—God never sent them to do it."[27] This is related to another statement by Joseph: "The Kingdom of God was set upon the earth in all ages from the days of Adam to the present time whenever there was a man on earth who had authority to administer the ordinances of the Gospel."[28] Elsewhere we read that if there is but one king and priest left upon the earth he could reorganize the Church.[29]

In all of these statements, the common idea is that it must be a man who commences the work of the gospel through the administration of ordinances. Through their ecclesiastical offices, men are the ones who perform the ordinances of rebirth, which bring an individual into the family of Christ. In performing these initial ordinances men are, so to speak, like physicians who deliver the newborn babe into Christ's kingdom. Once a person is in the Church, however, he or she is nurtured by men and women equally; for both can teach and exhort, give blessings, prophesy, and receive revelation. In short, they both can enjoy all the gifts of the spirit on an equal footing for the edification of the whole body of Christ.

When a person is ready to receive the higher ordinances in the temple, it is again the man who initiates. At the outset of this dispensation, Emma Smith received her endowment from Joseph. However, once she had been anointed a queen and a priestess, she too could and did introduce other women into the mysteries of the holy endowment. So it appears that women can perform initiation rites under limited circumstances, for women anoint, wash, and convey the tokens of priesthood to other women. But, though it is the duty of the male priesthood holders to commence the work, it is important to observe that the last ordinances pertaining to the fulness [sic] of the priesthood cannot be administered by men; they must be administered by women.

The anointing to the fulness [sic] of the priesthood is divided into three parts, which do not necessarily take place in the order discussed here. The first part is an anointing administered by the head of the high priesthood, who anoints the man to be a king and priest to God and the woman to be a queen and priestess to her husband. The second part of this ordinance consists of the washing of feet, by which the king and priest is made clean every whit. The third part consists of certain ordinances conferred by the wife upon the husband in which she washes and anoints various parts of his body—last of all his feet. From the Heber C. Kimball account of this portion of the ceremony, the part performed by his wife Vilate, we learn that this ritual was a reenactment of the washing and anointing of the body of Jesus done by one of the Marys. Jesus, in the Gospel of John, is recorded as saying that Mary performed this ordinance "against the day of my burying" (John 12:7). Heber C. Kimball connects this ceremony with death by saying that the woman does this so that she might have claim upon her husband in the resurrection.[30] Although this statement may be interpreted to mean that the woman is dependent upon the man for her resurrection, it might also be interpreted to mean that the man must look to the woman for the ordinances which confer the power of endless life. In this view, the woman is the vehicle through which the man obtains power to come forth from the tomb, even as she is the vehicle by which he is brought forth from the womb. This brings to mind the myth of Osiris, whose resurrection was dependent upon the effort or work of Isis in the Egyptian ceremonies, where, incidentally, a woman had to be present at every "awakening."[31]

Thus, in God's plan men and women possess balanced responsibilities. For while males are intended to initiate, females are intended to complete and bring to fruition. This interdependence is perhaps best symbolized in the creation of a new human being: in the creative process, the woman is as vital as the man; both contribute life. The old cliché that men have the priesthood and women have motherhood is clearly inappropriate; it makes no sense. Women have motherhood, and men have fatherhood. Men have priesthood, and women have priesthood too. Motherhood and fatherhood have to do with creating physical life, with creating sons and daughters; priesthood has to do with spiritual motherhood and fatherhood, which concerns spiritual begetting, nurturing, and birth; it has to do with creating sons and daughters unto God.

Women, then, also have a priestly calling, a lifegiving calling, similar to the man's but not identical to it. Though there are some ordinances she cannot perform there are others that she may perform and there is at least one ordinance which she alone can perform. It is clear, however, that the male and female, in their priestly function, must act in union to realize the fulness [*sic*] of gospel blessings.

Without a proper apportionment of the spiritual contributions of both the male and female, there can be no birth, no enduring rebirth, no inner life, no continuing contact with God, no significant revelation, no balanced manifestation of the spiritual gifts, no mature counsel, no triumph over Satan, no equality in which all things are held in common. In short, there can be no city and kingdom of God. It is into the seamlesss cup of balanced and spiritually regenerated sexual union that God has promised to pour the fulness [*sic*] of his priesthood, which is the power of God.

In light of the fact that women have an important and coequal priestly function, it should not be surprising to learn that Joseph Smith allowed women some role in the governance of the Church in the months just prior to his martyrdom. In September of 1843, Joseph not only gave the women the endowment and the fulness [*sic*] of the priesthood, but he also included them in the quorum of the anointed, or the holy order. Although it has been argued that this quorum never functioned as a priesthood quorum in the Church and that it was simply the antecedent to an endowment congregation in today's temple practice,[32] there is evidence to the contrary.

If Joseph thought of the holy order merely as an endowment group why did he not treat it as an ephemeral body? Why did he meet with them regularly? Why did he continue to instruct them? Why was he chosen as president of the holy order if the quorum itself had no special significance? Why did he allow this quorum to partake of the sacrament and engage in other activities beyond instruction in the temple endowment? The quorum conducted prayer circles, not merely for the purpose of instructing the members in the details of the prayer circle, but for the purpose of addressing in prayer problems affecting the whole Church.

Though prayer meetings may not seem as important as administrative meetings to members of the modern Church, Joseph instilled in the minds of his followers the idea that the true order of prayer was the most effective means of bringing about change. Joseph did not have a managerial view, he had a sacral one. He believed (as perhaps did St. Thomas More) that a kingdom could be governed by prayer. For this reason, prayer was not just another private devotional; it was an act of spiritual administration, a way to call upon God to bring about needed changes and needed action.[33]

However, Joseph's vision of priesthood faded quickly after his death. And as it faded, so did the importance of the quorum, the place of women in it, and the role of women as priestesses in Zion. Ironically, though the Quorum of Apostles succeeded to Joseph's place because of their anointing to the fulness [sic] of the priesthood,[34] once they assumed leadership, they shifted the preeminent authority away from the quorum of the anointed. An apostolic dispensation quickly replaced the "dispensation of the fulness [sic] of the priesthood," a phrase used by Joseph Smith to the Relief Society.[35] Whether Brigham Young did this consciously because he believed that the time for Zion was not yet, or whether he did it because necessity simply dictated this course of action is not clear. It is apparent, however, that it was under the administration of Brigham Young that the anointed quorum and the concept of woman's role in the priesthood simultaneously received quick death blows.

Following the martyrdom of Joseph Smith, the quorum met less frequently. As more and more Church members were endowed, the quorum ceased its separate meetings altogether. With its discontinuance, women were no longer included in prayer circles, except at that point in the endowment ceremony when instruction on prayer circle is given.

Women's role in Joseph's system was further curtailed in 1844 when Brigham Young suspended the Relief Society organization. When the Prophet's successor reorganized the society on a churchwide basis in 1867, the focus of the organization was much more temporal than spiritual.

Thus, while Joseph's attitude toward the role of women as queens and priestesses and his view of the function and place of the anointed quorum were expansive and tended to widen women's spiritual horizon, those leaders coming after him were quick to delimit women's sphere of action in the Church with clear, bright lines. In order for women to take their rightful places as queens and priestesses, the Church must first accept the primacy of spiritual power over temporal power, the primacy of the unseen over the seen, the primacy of the sacral over the secular. If we women simply demand ordination to the ecclesiastical offices of the priesthood as a means of seizing power in the administrative structure, then we have missed the point of Joseph's vision and are striving for the wrong objective. We are fighting the wrong battle—the battle of the sexes, which is a struggle for power in this world, for the whip handle, for the number-one spot, for the management of the corporation.

But the priesthood does not bring with it the right to this kind of coercive power. This is "unrighteous dominion." True power—the power of the holy priesthood—is the power of God, the power of life, the power of divine love, the power that restores, unites, harmonizes, and balances extremes. The fulness [*sic*] of the priesthood is the power of eternal life, endless life, and endless lives. This is the power we are enjoined to seek. It does not come by male or female chauvinism or by militancy. It comes by waiting upon the Lord.

Ultimately, I suppose, my position on women's place in the priesthood, the Church, and the kingdom of God is not that of a political or social activist but that of a mystic. For though I believe that the Church will never be organized properly until women are acknowledged as joint holders of the holy priesthood and are brought into the leading councils of the Church, I feel even more strongly that to demand these things will only make matters worse and lead to greater disarray.

So what is my answer to the problem? Charity. Joseph Smith spoke prophetically when he told the Relief Society in every speech he ever gave to them that it was essential for them to have charity—not that brand of charity that manifests itself as petty demonstrations of humanitarian service, but the real thing: the pure and sacrificial love of Christ, that is not puffed up, that seeks not its own, that loves the truth, and that endures all things.

And what will happen if the women of the Church endure patiently the deprivation of their priesthood rights in charity? In Joseph's words, "God shall say to them, come up higher."[36] It is God, finally, who must bring this about. It is with His hands that Zion will be built. It is not in our hands anymore. "Man cannot steady the ark," said Joseph Smith, "my arm cannot do it—God must steady it."[37] And when at last these blessings come, they shall come *gloria solius Dei*—by the glory of God alone.

Notes

1. D. Michael Quinn, "Latter-day Saint Prayer Circles," *BYU Studies* (Fall 1978): 85.
2. See *Teachings of the Prophet Joseph Smith*, pp. 137, 226 [hereafter *TPJS*].
3. See D&C 121:36.
4. See *Words of Joseph Smith*, pp. 42, 245, 246, 253 [hereafter *WJS*].
5. See *WJS*, pp. 341, 350, 365–66.
6. See *WJS*, p. 9.
7. See *WJS*, pp. 212, 230.
8. *WJS*, p. 329.
9. *WJS*, p. 245.
10. See *WJS*, p. 330.

11. See *WJS*, p. 330.
12. *WJS*, p. 105.
13. See *WJS*, pp. 118–19.
14. *WJS*, pp. 105.
15. D&C 25:10.
16. *WJS*, p. 110.
17. See Moses 6:7; D&C 113:8; *TPJS*, p. 237.
18. *WJS*, p. 110.
19. James N. Robinson, ed., *Nag Hammadi Library*, p. 130 [hereafter *Nag Hammadi*].
20. *Nag Hammadi*, p. 121.
21. *WJS*, p. 115.
22. *WJS*, p. 116.
23. *WJS*, p. 116.
24. *HC*, 4:602.
25. *TPJS*, p. 9.
26. *WJS*, p. 124.
27. *TPJS*, p. 212.
28. *WJS*, p. 155.
29. cf. *TPJS*, pp. 271–72.
30. See "Strange Events" in the Heber C. Kimball Journal, Church Archives.
31. Hugh Nibley, *The Message of the Joseph Smith Papyri: An Egyptian Endowment*, pp. 148–51.
32. Quinn, "Prayer Circles," p. 89.
33. See *HC*, 5:45–46.
34. See Andrew Ehat, "Joseph Smith's Introduction of Temple Ordinances and the 1844 Succession Question," BYU M.A. Thesis, 119.
35. See *HC*, 5:140.
36. *WJS*, p. 116.
37. *WJS*, p. 121.

Linda Sillitoe (1948–2010), "an elegy in lower case (for president spencer w. kimball)" (1985)

Award-winning and Pulitzer Prize–nominated journalist Linda Sillitoe, a Utah-born Mormon and feminist in her own right, covered the LDS Church's anti-ERA campaign in Virginia, the founding of Mormons for ERA, and the excommunication of Sonia Johnson. But this did not deter the LDS Church-owned *Deseret News* from hiring her as a staff writer in the early 1980s. Sillitoe found quiet allies in the trenches. As the Equal Rights Amendment ratification struggle ground on, Sillitoe recalls, "Some kind but anonymous soul printed the [ERA-related] wire stories the newspaper did not run and dropped them on my typewriter." One night in the fall of 1985, with LDS Church president Spencer W. Kimball nearing death, Sillitoe found herself alone in the newsroom. Kimball was revered among Mormons as the LDS Church president who had received the revelation to end the Church's ban on priesthood ordination and temple worship for Black Mormons; he had also demonstrated special regard for indigenous Mormons in the Americas and the Pacific. But for Mormon feminists, his legacy would be complicated. "I remember sitting at my typewriter experiencing one emotion after another," Sillitoe later recalled. "During the years of the Equal Rights Amendment, a number of women had tried earnestly to reach President Kimball, believing he would support their cause if only he could hear their viewpoint. They were rebuffed by male secretaries. After Sonia's excommunication, I learned that President Kimball wept. I also knew that he was firmly against the Equal Rights Amendment. Whatever the reason, he would not hear women as he had loved Indians or prayed in behalf of black men. He would not act and no one more sympathetic waited in the wings. Now he was close to death." There in the *Deseret News* newsroom Sillitoe wrote the poem "an elegy in lower case (for president spencer w. kimball)." Her poem demonstrates both the deep affection and the aching disappointment that Mormon feminists could feel for LDS Church leaders.

Source

Sillitoe, Linda. "an elegy in lower case (for president spencer w. kimball)." *Crazy for Living.* Salt Lake City: Signature Books, 1993.

References and Further Reading

Sillitoe, Linda. "Church Politics and Sonia Johnson: The Central Conundrum." *Sunstone* 5.1 (January–February 1980): 35–42.
Sillitoe, Linda. "Fear and Anger in Virginia: The New Mormon Activists (Part 2)." *Utah Holiday* (April 1979): 9–12.
Sillitoe, Linda. "The New Mormon Activists: Fighting the ERA in Virginia." *Utah Holiday* (March 1979): 12–14.
Sillitoe, Linda. "Off the Record: Telling the Rest of the Truth." *Mormon Women's Forum Quarterly* 1.4 (Fall 1990): 1, 8–13. Rpt. *Sunstone* 14.6 (December 1990): 12–26.
Sillitoe, Linda, and Paul Swenson. "A Moral Issue." *Utah Holiday* (January 1980): 18–20, 22–34.

"an elegy in lower case (for president spencer w. kimball)"

i pay my respects by saying what's true
    in love and anger
you served us crumbs, you see, and we hungered
    for our own bowls
    of bread and milk
love your silvery chains, my sisters
    we did we do
for they are your redemption

oh it is not so simple says my brain
>   he let sisters too
gowned in white into those clean chambers

american brothers too are yoked unequally

but it is too late now for anything
but the lush oversimplification from my heart

in this lush room where we keep prophet ghosts
>   i want to fold you in
like a child too sleepy to trust in slumber

but say instead goodbye hopeflicker goodbye

for my brothers' sake i weep at your death
for my sisters i keep my seat as you pass

Laurel Thatcher Ulrich (1938–), "Lusterware" (1986)

Although Mormon culture placed great value on expressions of unequivocal certainty in faith, Mormon feminists knew that their allegiance to what Claudia Bushman had called the "dual platforms of Mormonism and feminism" brought moments of struggle and conflict as well as coherence and comfort. How to negotiate these complicated dimensions of religious experience within the context of the demanding everyday commitments of Mormonism has been an enduring theme for the writers of the Mormon feminist movement. Mary Bradford had urged Mormon women writers to adopt the personal essay as a form for the thoughtful exploration of faith. This essay by historian Laurel Thatcher Ulrich exemplifies the powers of the form. In a voice that is simultaneously vulnerable and wise, Ulrich describes her own process of sorting out the lasting truths and beauties of Mormonism from its ordinary troubles and disappointments: this very process, "this uneasy dialogue," she asserts, is a completely valid form of faith. Just as Mormon feminist poet Claire Whitaker had urged her Mormon sisters in the 1970s to be more honest and open about their flaws and worries, just as Algie Ballif and the Mormon feminists of the Alice Louise Reynolds forum vowed to embrace their struggles, Ulrich takes up the Mormon feminist commitment to fearless and discerning truth-seeking—a commitment true to the roots of the Mormon tradition.

Source

Ulrich, Laurel Thatcher. "Lusterware." In *A Thoughtful Faith*, ed. Phillip Barlow. Centerville, UT: Canon Press, 1986.

"LUSTERWARE"

I have been thinking lately about an Emily Dickinson poem I first heard twenty-five years ago in an American literature class at the University of Utah. I remember feeling intrigued and somewhat troubled as the professor read the poem since he was reported to be a lapsed Mormon. "Was that how it felt to lose faith?" I thought.

> It dropped so low—in my Regard—
> I heard it hit the Ground—
> And go to pieces on the Stones
> At bottom of my Mind—
> Yet blamed the Fate that flung it—less
> Than I denounced Myself,
> For entertaining Plated Wares
> Upon my Silver Shelf.

Since then I have lost faith in many things, among them Olympia typewriters, *New York Times* book reviews, and texturized vegetable protein; and yes, like most Latter-day Saints I have had to reconsider some of my deepest religious beliefs. I have always been a somewhat skeptical person. I can remember raising my arm in Beehive class in the Sugar City Ward and telling my teacher that regardless of what she said I did not think that polygamy was sent by God. That kind of behavior may have had something to do with the palm reading I received from another teacher at an MIA gypsy party. She traced the lines on my upturned hand and told me my "head" line was longer and better developed than my "heart" line. For a while I worried about that.

As I have grown older, I have become less fearful of those "stones at the bottom of my mind." In fact, I am convinced that a willingness to admit disbelief is often essential to spiritual growth. All of us meet challenges to our faith—persons who fail to measure up, doctrines that refuse to settle comfortably into our minds, books that contain troubling ideas or disorienting information. The temptation is strong to "Blame the fate that flung it" or to ignore the crash as it hits the ground, pretending that nothing has changed. Neither technique is very useful. Though a few people seem to have been blessed with foam rubber rather than stones at the bottom of their minds (may they rest in peace), sooner or later most of us are forced to confront our shattered beliefs.

I find Emily Dickinson's little poem helpful. Some things fall off the shelf because they did not belong there in the first place; they were "Plated Wares" rather than genuine silver. At first I didn't fully grasp the image. The only "Plated Wares" I knew anything about were made by [American silversmiths] Oneida or Wm. Rogers. Although less valuable than sterling, that sort of silverplate hardly falls to pieces when dropped. Then I learned about lusterware, the most popular

"Plated Wares" of Emily Dickinson's time. In the late eighteenth century, British manufacturers developed a technique for decorating ceramic ware with a gold or platinum film. In one variety, a platinum luster was applied to the entire surface of the object to produce what contemporaries called "poor man's silver." Shiny, inexpensive, and easy to get, it was also fragile, as breakable as any other piece of pottery or china. Only a gullible or very inexperienced person would mistake it for true silver.

All of us have lusterware as well as silver on that shelf we keep at the top of our minds. A lusterware Joseph Smith, for instance, is unfailingly young, handsome, and spiritually radiant; unschooled but never superstitious, persecuted but never vengeful, human but never mistaken. A lusterware image fulfills our need for an ideal without demanding a great deal from us. There are lusterware missions and marriages, lusterware friendships, lusterware histories, and yes, lusterware visions of ourselves. Most of these will be tested at some point on the stones at the bottom of our minds.

A number of years ago I read a letter from a young woman who had recently discovered some lusterware on her own shelf. "I used to think of the Church as one-hundred percent true," she wrote. "But now I realize it is probably ten percent human and only ninety percent divine." I gasped, wanting to write back immediately, "If you find any earthly institution that is ten percent divine, embrace it with all your heart!" Actually ten percent is probably too high an estimate.

Jesus spoke of grains of salt and bits of leaven, and He told His disciples that "the kingdom of heaven is like unto treasure hid in a field; the which when a man hath found, he hideth, and for joy thereof goeth and selleth all that he hath, and buyeth that field" (Matthew 13:44). Thus a small speck of divinity—the salt in the earth, the leaven in the lump of dough, the treasure hidden in the field—gives value and life to the whole. Now the question is, where in the Church of Jesus Christ of Latter-day Saints do we go to find the leaven? To the bishop? To the prophet? To the lesson manuals? Do we find it in Relief Society? In sacrament meeting? And if we fail to discover it in any of these places shall we declare the lump worthless? Jesus' answer was clear. The leaven must be found in one's own heart or not at all: ". . . the kingdom of God is within you" (Luke 17:21).

Many years ago a blunt bishop countered one of my earnest complaints with a statement I have never forgotten: "The Church is a good place to practice the Christian virtue of forgiveness, mercy, and love unfeigned." That was a revelation to me. The Church was not a place that exemplified Christian virtues so much as a place that required them. I suppose I had always thought of it as a nice cushion, a source of warmth and comfort if ever things got tough (which they seldom had in my life). It hadn't occurred to me that the Church could make things tough.

Eliza R. Snow expressed it this way in a hymn that seems to be missing from the new book:

Think not when you gather to Zion,
Your troubles and trials are through,
That nothing but comfort and pleasure
Are waiting in Zion for you:
No, no, 'tis designed as a furnace,
All substance, all textures to try,
To burn all the "wood, hay, and stubble,"
The gold from the dross purify.

Probably the hymn deserved to be dropped from the book. The third stanza suggests that the author, like more than one Relief Society president since, had made too many welfare visits and had listened to too many sad stories. Her charity failing, she told the complainers in her ward to shape up and solve their own problems:

Think not when you gather to Zion,
The Saints here have nothing to do
But to look to your personal welfare,
And always be comforting you.

In the Church, as in our own families, we have the worst and the best of times.

A young missionary on a lonely bus ride somewhere in Bolivia thinks he is equal to what lies ahead. He can endure hard work, strange food, and a confusing dialect. But nothing in the Mission Training Center has prepared him for the filthiness of the apartment, for the cynicism of his first companion, or for the parakeet who lives, with all its droppings, under the other man's bed.

A young bride, ready to enter the temple, feels herself spiritually prepared. By choosing a simple white gown useable later as a temple dress she has already shown her preference for religious commitment over fantasy.* She has discussed the covenants with her stake president and she feels she understands them. Yet sitting in the endowment room in ritual clothing no one had thought to show her, saying words she does not understand, she turns to her mother in dismay. "Am I supposed to enjoy this?" she says.

An elders quorum president, pleased that his firm has won the contract for the ward remodeling project, prepares for the hard work ahead. He knows the job will be demanding. He expects some tension between his responsibilities as project manager and his commitment to the Church, but he is ready to consecrate his

---

*Marriages between observant members of the LDS Church are performed within LDS temples. Temple marriages promise to "seal" spouse to spouse for the eternities; they exclude many customary wedding elements such as bridesmaids, processions, and so forth.

time and talents for the upbuilding of the Kingdom. What he doesn't expect is the anger and the humiliation that follow his year-long encounter with the Church bureaucracy. "I wonder how far up this sort of thing goes?" he asks, and contemplates leaving the Church.

A middle-aged woman reads deeply in the scriptures, sharing her insights with friends individually and in a small study group. She feels secure in her quest for greater light and truth until she begins to examine certain troubling episodes in Church history. The discrepancy between the official accounts and the new accounts distresses her. Has she been lied to? And if in one issue, why not many? Confiding her doubts to her friends, she feels them back away.

"And the rain descended, and the floods came, and the winds blew, and beat upon that house; and it fell not: for it was founded upon a rock" (Matthew 7:24–25). What rock can secure us against such storms? Occasionally some gentle soul, perhaps as puzzled as my Beehive teacher by my outspoken ways, will ask, "What keeps you in the Church?" "My skepticism," I answer, only half in jest. Over the years I have noticed that Saints with doubts often outlast "true believers." But of course the answer is inadequate. I don't stay in the Church because of what I don't know, but because of what I do.

The Church I believe in is not an ascending hierarchy of the holy. It is millions of ordinary people calling one another "brother" and "sister" and trying to make it true. Not so long ago I had one of those terrible-wonderful experiences that I have been talking about. It started in an innocuous way, then built to a genuine crisis, a classic Liahona-Iron Rod* conflict between me and my bishop. After a week of sleepless nights I went into his office feeling threatened and fragile. What followed was an astonishingly open and healing discussion, a small miracle. As I told a friend later, "If we hadn't been Mormons, we would have embraced." Our opinions didn't change much; our attitudes toward one another did. I give him credit for having the humility to listen, and I give myself credit for trusting him enough to say what I really felt. The leaven in our lump was a common reaching for the Spirit.

I am not always comfortable in my ward. There are weeks when I wonder if I can sit through another Relief Society lesson delivered straight from the manual

---

*In the Book of Mormon, in 1 Nephi 8, a prophet named Lehi dreams of the search for God as a walk on an obstacle-laden path; an "iron rod" running alongside the path serves as a trustworthy guide. In 1 Nephi 16, the "liahona" is a compass given by God to Lehi and his family to guide their travels through the wilderness. It functions according to the "faith and diligence" (1 Nephi 16: 28) of those who use it. After a talk delivered by historian Richard Poll at a Sunday "sacrament meeting" in Palo Alto, California, in 1967 and later published in *Dialogue: A Journal of Mormon Thought*, the "liahona" and the "iron rod" have become within the context of contemporary Mormonism symbols for two different approaches to living the faith: "iron rod" Mormonism indicates a more rigid, obedience-focused approach to living the faith, while "liahona" Mormonism represents a still faithful but more seeking and intuitive approach. See Richard D. Poll, "What the Church Means to People Like Me," *Dialogue: A Journal of Mormon Thought* 2.4 (1967): 107–17.

or endure another meandering discussion in Gospel Doctrine class. Yet there are also moments when, surprised by my own silence, I am able to hear what a speaker only half says. Several months ago as I was bracing myself for a Fast and Testimony meeting, a member of the bishopric approached me and asked if I would give the closing prayer. I said, "Yes," feeling like a hypocrite, yet at the same time silently accepting some responsibility for the success of the meeting. Were the testimonies really better? When I stood to pray I was moved to the point of tears.

For me the issue is not whether The Church of Jesus Christ of Latter-day Saints is the One True Church Upon the Face of the Earth. That sounds to me like a particularly Zoramite brand of lusterware:

> Now the place was called by them Rameumptom, which, being interpreted, is the holy stand. Now, from this stand they did offer up, every man, the self-same prayer. . . . We thank thee, O God, for we are a chosen people unto thee, while others shall perish. (Alma 31:22, 28)

The really crucial issue for me is that the Spirit of Christ is alive in the Church, and that it continues to touch and redeem the lives of the individual members. The young man survived his mission, returning with a stronger, more sober sense of what it meant to serve. The bride returned to the temple and enjoyed it more. The elders quorum president, though still struggling with his anger, knows it is his problem to face and to solve. The middle-aged woman grew through her loss of faith into a richer, deeper spirituality.

As I study the scriptures very few contemporary problems seem new. I wonder how men in tune with the divine can appear to be so complacent and self-righteous in their dealings with women. Then I read Luke's account of the visit of the angel to the women at the tomb on the first day of the week: "It was Mary Magdalene, and Joanna, and Mary the mother of James, and other women that were with them, which told these things unto the apostles. And their words seemed to them as idle tales, and they believed them not" (Luke 24: 10–11). I wonder how a church purportedly devoted to eternal values can invest so much energy in issues that strike me as unimportant. Then I read the nineteenth chapter of Leviticus and find the second greatest commandment, "Thou shalt love thy neighbour as thyself," side by side with a sober command that "neither a garment mingled of linen and woolen come upon thee" (Leviticus 19:18–19). Every dispensation has had its silver and its lusterware. God speaks to His children, as Moroni taught us, in our own language, and in our own narrow and culture-bound condition. To me that is a cause for joy rather than cynicism. I love Joseph Smith's ecstatic recital in Doctrine and Covenants 128:

> Now, what do we hear in the gospel which we have received? A voice of gladness! a voice of mercy from heaven; and a voice of truth out of the earth. . . .

A voice of the Lord in the wilderness of Fayette, Seneca county. . . .

The voice of Michael on the banks of the Susquehanna. . . .

The voice of Peter, James, and John in the wilderness between Harmony, Susquehanna county, and Colesville, Broome county. . . .

And again, the voice of God in the chamber of old Father [Peter] Whitmer, in Fayette, Seneca county, and at sundry times, and in divers places through all the travels and tribulations of this Church of Jesus Christ of Latter-day Saints!* (D&C 128:19–21)

Joseph's litany of homely place names, his insistence that the voice of God could indeed be heard on the banks of an ordinary American river or in the chamber of a common farmer, gives his message an audacity and a power that cannot be ignored. For me Joseph Smith's witness that the divine can strike through the immediate is more important than any of the particulars enshrined in the church he established. If other people want to reduce D&C 128 to a data processing program for handling family group sheets, that's fine. I am far more interested in that "whole and complete and perfect union, and welding together of dispensations" that Joseph wrote about.

Two or three years ago I attended a small unofficial women's conference in Nauvoo[, Illinois]. The ostensible purpose was to celebrate the founding of the Relief Society, but the real agenda was to come to terms with the position of women in the contemporary Church. The participants came from many places, a few of us known to each other, many of us strangers, the only common bond being some connection with the three organizers, all of whom remained maddeningly opaque as to their motives. I cannot describe what happened to me during those three days. Let me just say that after emptying myself of any hope for peace and change in the Church I heard the voice of the Lord on the banks of the Mississippi River. It was a voice of gladness, telling me that the gospel had indeed been restored. It was a voice of truth, assuring me that my concerns were just, that much was still amiss in the Church. It was a voice of mercy, giving me the courage to continue my uneasy dialogue between doubt and faith. I am not talking here about a literal voice but about an infusion of the Spirit, a kind of Pentecost that for a moment dissolved the boundaries between heaven and earth and between present and past. I felt as though I were re-experiencing the events the early Saints had described.

I am not a mystical person. In ordinary decisions in my family I am far more likely to call for a vote than a prayer, and when other people proclaim their "spiritual experiences" I am generally cautious. But I would gladly sift through a great trough of meal for even a little bit of that leaven.†

---

*Joseph Smith here names a number of sites in New York and Pennsylvania important to the founding of the LDS Church.

† See Matthew 13:33 and Luke 13:20–21.

The temptations of skepticism are real. Sweeping up the lusterware, we some-times forget to polish and cherish the silver, not knowing that the power of dis-cernment is one of the gifts of the Spirit, that the ability to discover counterfeit wares also gives us the power to recognize the genuine.

Judith Rasmussen Dushku (1942–), "The Day of the Lambs and the Lions" (1987)

Early Latter-day Saints had gathered into their own communities and crossed the plains to Utah in the hopes of building Zion, a religious utopia defined by equal-ity, charity, and purity of purpose. Even after outmigration from Utah, assimila-tion, and globalization of the faith in the twentieth century (which meant that most Mormons no longer lived in majority-Mormon communities), LDS people continue to think of the Church and their local congregations as units of Zion and to feel a sense of responsibility to ensuring that in these spaces goodness and righteousness prevail. In this essay, Judith Dushku, one of the founders of Boston's Mormon feminist circle and *Exponent II*, makes a feminist plea for the betterment of Zion. Dushku addresses spousal abuse in LDS communities and calls for the eradication of "inequity" between men and women and all forms of "condescension, manipulation, and belittlement," using the lyrics from a beloved LDS hymn, "The Spirit of God like a Fire Is Burning" (1836) by W. W. Phelps. See also Dushku's essay "Feminists" anthologized in Part I of this volume.

Source

Dushku, Judith. "The Day of the Lambs and the Lions." *Exponent II* 13.3 (1987): 2.

"THE DAY OF THE LAMBS AND THE LIONS"

"How blessed the day when the lamb and the lion/shall lie down together without any ire." [In these lines from the hymn "The Spirit of God like a Fire Is Burning,"] W. W. Phelps really did distill what seems to me the very essence of what I imag-ine and hope eternal life in the presence of God to be. The idea of there being a time and place where all of us might dwell together "without any ire," touches me to the core. Perhaps because there seems no end to "ire" in life; imagining any-thing more than a moment without it is sweet. When I try to put some meat on this vision, to fill it out a bit, I imagine a situation where there is no coercion, no fear, no exercising of unrighteous dominion by anyone over anyone else! What a sight! This is juxtaposed to what I've decided in my effort to summarize the ugli-ness of the world as I have experienced it is the key to most evil and cruelty: the controlling of one by another. The deadening effect that being controlled has on the coerced both in body and in spirits the core of sin. The use of power by one to harm, to cause pain to another, especially one less powerful, is always ugly, and I hate it. Whether it is the use of a heat sensitive napalm on bodies of fleeing peasants in the mountains of Guatemala (such inequality of power is what makes that scene especially ugly), or the use of the loathing look of an unkind parent to manipulate a child to a certain behavior, I recoil.

Not long ago a handsome husband walked into the congenial foyer of our church after meetings and stared harshly at his energetic and radiant wife. "We are waiting in the parking lot," he snarled. You would have thought that he had struck her. A look of terror overtook her face, and she struggled to pack her things out to the car, apologizing over and over to him for forgetting her promise to meet him at the car after Relief Society. She stuttered excuses to all of us for behaving so irresponsibly. She then tried to cover for him by explaining that her husband was really very good to her. "He lets me take the car alone on Wednesdays. He even babysits for me one night a week." I felt sick. Everyone laughed and tried to ignore the ugliness of this spouse abuse. The idea of one person using the superior power that society's habit had bestowed on him to frighten another, whom he claimed to love and honor, was abhorrent to me. It might as well have been a wrestling match between a heavyweight and a bantam. It was unfair, and the inequity of it made it so ugly.

Inequity is dangerous because it allows for dominance and use of unrighteous force. It is the source of much of the "ire" that must disappear before the lamb and the lion can lie down together in peace and harmony, mutual respect and love. I suspect that I will have to wait until the day when Jesus descends with His chariot of fire for this ire to be gone. But when asked for my dream for the future, I could not help but hope that some progress will be made towards this end on this old earth. Surely the unrighteous exercising of power and dominion can diminish a bit, at least in the Church, where we struggle to perfect ourselves to some degree. I try not to be naive and idealistic, but it isn't too much to expect that the Kingdom lead the world away from abuse and inequity, is it?

I am hard on the Saints, I know. I expect more of us. I want so badly for all forms of condescension, manipulation, and belittlement to have no place in this community. And yet I see it often and in so many relationships. Mostly, it seems to me to persist between men and women in many different settings. And while I try to "move on" to other battles and other issues, all it takes is for one man to diminish one woman to trigger my sadness and make me sing for the blessed day when the lamb and the lion shall lie together in peace.

Violet Tew Kimball (1932–), "Wife #3" (1987)

Although Mormon feminists embraced their polygamy-practicing pro-suffrage foremothers (see, for example, Judith Dushku's 1976 essay anthologized in Part I of this volume), polygamy itself continued to be a sensitive and controversial subject for Mormon women. The LDS Church had ceased to perform plural marriages of living partners in 1890, but the doctrine of polygamy, received as a revelation by Joseph Smith and canonized in LDS scripture Doctrine and Covenants 132, has never been renounced and remains a part of Mormon theology. To this day, LDS Church policy still permits a living man to be married or "sealed" to multiple wives for the eternities—for example, a widower or divorcee may be sealed to a second wife—but it does not permit the sealing of one living woman to multiple husbands for the eternities. In this poem, Violet Tew Kimball, a grassroots historian who would later hike the Mormon pioneer trails and write about Mormon pioneer history for children, delves into the complicated feelings surrounding polygamy. Her poem "Wife #3" is written from the perspective of Emmeline B. Wells, editor of the *Woman's Exponent*, a nationally known advocate for women's suffrage, president of the Relief Society from 1910 to 1921, and a plural wife of Daniel Wells (1814–1891). Its epigraph comes from Wells's diary for October 1, 1874:

> O if my husband could only love me even a little and not seem so perfectly indifferent to an [*sic*] sensation of that kind, he cannot know the craving of my nature, he is surrounded with love on every side, and I am cast out[.] O My poor aching heart where shall it rest its burden, only on the Lord, only to Him can I look every other avenue seems closed against me. . . . I have no one to go to for comfort or shelter no strong arm to lean upon no bosom bared for me, no protection or comfort in my husband.

Historian Carol Cornwall Madsen (see her essay anthologized in Part I of this volume) notes that on the same day that Wells penned this diary entry, she published a very differently toned reflection on marriage in the *Woman's Exponent* under her pen name Blanche Beechwood:

> Is there then nothing worth living for, but to be petted, humored and caressed, by a man? That is all very well as far as it goes, but that man is the only thing in existence worth living for I fail to see. All honor and reverence to good men; but they and their attentions are not the only sources of happiness on the earth, and need not fill up every thought of woman. And when men see that women can exist without their being constantly at hand, that they can learn to be self-reliant or depend upon each other for more or less happiness, it will perhaps take a little of the conceit out of some of them.

The contradiction between Wells's public bravery and her private sorrow reflects the deeply conflicted feelings many Mormon women harbor about polygamy. Kimball's poem also interrogates the idea that a Mother in Heaven would countenance the practice of plural marriage.

Source

Kimball, Violet Tew. "Wife #3." *Exponent II* 13.3 (Spring 1987): 6.

References and Further Reading

Madsen, Carol Cornwall. "Emmeline B. Wells: Romantic Rebel." In *Supporting Saints: Life Stories of Nineteenth-Century Mormons*, ed. Donald Q. Cannon and David J. Whittaker (Provo, UT: Brigham Young University, Religious Studies Center, 1985), 305–41.

Kimball, Violet Tew. *Stories of Young Pioneers in Their Own Words.* Missoula, MT: Mountain Press, 2000.

"WIFE #3"

"I have no one to go to for comfort or shelter . . ." Emmeline B. Wells

Someone else calls you husband.
Father is also one of your titles.
Some bind by law
some by love.

I would not want to
usurp rights or privileges
of the others,
or impinge on your measured time.
I have learned to stand alone.

But sometimes . . .
sometimes when cold,
sickness and sorrow
sap my spirit and strength
and I yearn for unproffered comfort,
I feel betrayed.

Would it be a sin
if my load were lifted?
Would nature be wounded
if I could have this craving stilled,
and the love and desire I feel
be returned?

Mother
I cannot believe
this burden was imposed
by Your decree.

Carol Lynn Pearson (1939–), "Walk in the Pink Moccasins" (1988)

As the *Exponent II*'s classic "Patti Perfect" essay showed, humor offered an excellent resource for coping with the pressures inflicted by contemporary Mormonism's idealization of stay-at-home-motherhood. In this essay, Carol Lynn Pearson uses the humorous device of symbolic gender role reversal to push back against the pressure of talks like Ezra Taft Benson's "To the Mothers in Zion" (1987), which purported to honor motherhood but instead highlighted profound asymmetry in the contemporary LDS Church's view of the status, purpose, and authority of men and women. American feminist writers like Gloria Steinem had relied on symbolic gender role reversal in essays like the classic "If Men Could Menstruate" (1978) to make visible and challenge power asymmetries accepted as natural and inevitable. By writing the script for an imaginary Mormon church meeting in which an all-female hierarchy speaks on behalf of a female god to instruct men in their divine purpose, Carol Lynn Pearson makes visible and challenges the unequal power dynamics enacted in every Mormon meeting where leaders from the Church's all-male hierarchy relied upon male-authored scriptures to instruct women on how a male God expected them to live. Pearson first delivered "Walk in the Pink Moccasins" as a talk at a gathering of the Mormon Women's Forum, a Mormon feminist organization founded in 1988 in Salt Lake City to promote "open and honest discussion of women's issues within the context of Mormonism."

Source

Pearson, Carol Lynn. "Walk in the Pink Moccasins." *Sunstone* 137 (May 2005): 21.

"WALK IN THE PINK MOCCASINS"

Men cannot possibly know what it is like to be a female child in a Motherless house unless they are shocked into glimpsing what it would be like to be a male child in a Fatherless house. I have had for years a kind of Walter Mitty daydream in which I teach them. I become one of the Presiding Sisters, speaking to the "boys of comparable age."

My dear young brethren, it is such a delight to be able to speak to you today. Your faces and your clothing look so clean and fresh. I know that our Mother in Heaven is pleased as she looks down on you this day. And I want, first of all, to convey to you the fact that our Mother loves you. I am persuaded that She loves you just as much as she loves her daughters, and I hope you can believe that.

And what a marvelous plan She has laid out for you! What a glorious role you are called to fill! How you must have rejoiced in spirit as She created the earth and placed there her crowning creation, Eve, the first and perfect woman. But of course our Mother could see that Eve was not complete, that she needed a worthy helpmeet to assist her in the great work she was called to do. And so this is where you come in, dear brethren. A rib from Eve's own body was fashioned into the body of Adam, and he was given her as a friend and helpmeet. What a glorious and noble calling! So important was he to Eve, and so important the commandment her Mother had given, that even when Adam sinned because he was deceived, Eve knowingly sinned with him so they could remain together.

And over the centuries, how you must have rejoiced as the plan unfolded further—through the great Matriarchs, Sarah, Rebekah, Rachel—as our Mother's holy prophetesses continued to reveal her word to us, as woman after woman was sent to do important work, making us all better people so that we could bless the lives of our husbands and children.

Keep yourselves clean and pure, dear brethren, that one day one of our Mother's choice daughters might look with favor upon you, claim you as her own, and give to you the glorious privilege of serving as her helpmeet, adding glory unto her as she adds glory unto the Mother.

And do not listen to the voices that cry out to you from the world. We are living in dark and evil times. Satan herself desires you. Do not listen to the voices that tell you you are suppressed, that entice you to a thing called full personhood and freedom. The role of man has always been made clear by God Herself. The place he occupies in our Mother's plan is not in question—it is now, always has been, and always will be to stand by the side of woman, assisting her in the great work she has been given to do.

It is true that new doors are opening for man to contribute in many fields besides his primary one, and we are glad when a man shows talents and abilities in a wider range of service. We encourage this. We are proud of the achievements of our fine young men.

And as the light of our Mother grows brighter in this world, we learn even more of the glorious truths concerning manhood, that it is intended indeed to be a partnership with woman. In fact, one of the truths of our age, and I believe with all my heart this is a truth even though it is not official and we don't want to talk about it and the words were written by a man—somewhere we've a Father there! Imagine! Somewhere we've a Father there!

In my daydream, when the dust of the shock settles, the men nod their heads and say, "I see," and they are never quite the same again.

Elouise Bell (1935–), "The Meeting" and "When Nice Ain't So Nice" (1990)

Elouise Bell recalls that her student Kathleen Flake—who served on the Utah International Women's Year committee and would become a distinguished scholar of religion and law—once reflected on Mormon feminist struggle: "Elouise, there's the carrot and the stick. There are a lot of sticks being wielded out there now. But because you use humor as your carrot, as your mode of choice, you can get across some points that can't be made with the stick." In these two essays, Elouise Bell, like Carol Lynn Pearson, opted for a humorous approach to feminist consciousness-raising. In "The Meeting," which circulated among Mormon feminists in typescript long before its publication, Bell follows Pearson in using symbolic role reversal to reveal the deep gender imbalance in Sunday meetings. "When Nice Ain't So Nice" begins as a light-hearted reflection on Mormon cultural pressure to be "nice"—a pressure that weighs more heavily on women—and evolves into a profound meditation on what niceness costs, destroys, and hides. "Sonia Johnson didn't break the rules in the Church handbook so much as the unspoken taboos. She wasn't nice. She did not conform. She didn't obey. She laundered the Church's dirty linen in public," Linda Sillitoe observed in 1990. Bell's essay crystallizes "niceness" as a Mormon feminist issue. Both "The Meeting" and "When Nice Ain't So Nice" originally appeared in Bell's regular column for *Network* magazine, which was launched in April 1978 as a resource for the working women of Utah and continued through 1989.

Source

Bell, Elouise. *Only When I Laugh*. Salt Lake City: Signature Books, 1990.

"THE MEETING"

Scene: Inside a large, conventional meeting house. There is the usual pre-meeting hubbub. Women are busily conferring with one another over agenda and announcements; at the door, two women are shaking hands with members of the congregation as they enter, trying diligently to call each entrant by her name.

The men are hurriedly urging children into pews, settling quarrels and trying to arrange seating so that the least mayhem will ensue. Some of the men do a better job than others at juggling their paraphernalia: in addition to diaper bags and bottles of apple juice or milk, most have "quiet books," small toys, and some have rather large and cumbersome Primary materials to hang onto and keep track of.

Three or four younger men are radiantly absorbed in small bundles wrapped in fancy crocheted afghans; their fuzzy-headed infants are all dressed in special finery for the occasion, and the seats immediately around them are filled with smiling, wet-eyed grandfathers, uncles, brothers; and over the heads of the crowds, we can see visiting teachers nodding their assurance that they will be ready when the moment presents itself.

Presently, a confident, comfortable-looking woman in her late forties takes her seat on the stand. She is almost immediately flanked by two others: a slender, dark-suited woman of about thirty who keeps whispering last-minute information to the woman in the center; and a woman of perhaps sixty who appears totally unflappable, as if, having engineered reconstruction after the Flood and supervised logistics during the Exodus, she is scarcely about to be intimidated by anything the present moment might demand of her.

Behind them, on the second row, sit four men of varying ages, each in black trousers, white shirt, and black tie. The youngest of the three women, whose name is Abbot, steps to the pulpit. She smiles silently at the buzzing congregation for a few moments, and as the crowd quiets, we hear a tiny voice call out boldly, "That's MOMMY!" Abbot smiles benignly at the child, while the father, seated in the second pew, blushes, puts a hand gently over the child's mouth, and shakes his head hopelessly at his neighbor.

ABBOT: Sisters and brothers, it's time to begin. We welcome you all here, members and visitors and friends, and hope your time with us will be pleasant. Now I'm afraid we have a large number of announcements today, but they are all important, so we ask for your attention.

To begin with, Brother Hales of the elders group has asked me to tell you that our lovely brethren are collecting empty one-quart oil cans, to be used by the group in making special Christmas projects. They are going to construct Christmas tree stands, candle molds and toys from these used oil cans, I'm told. Elder Hales has placed a large carton outside the south entrance and would appreciate it if you'd all deposit your empty oil cans there, and in so doing contribute to this worthwhile project.

Next, we want to remind you of the Education Week program early next month. Four of our members will be participating, and I'm sure we'll all want to attend and take advantage of this special opportunity. Sister Lorraine Larson will be giving a lecture on "Eschatology and Ether in the Perspective of the Book of Revelation." Sister Ellen Hemming is speaking on "The Gnostic Scrolls and Our Concept of Spirit Translation." Brother LeRuth Davis will have a workshop titled "Twenty Tips for Keeping a Tidy Garage," and Brother Terry Joe Jones will repeat last year's popular series on "Being a More Masculine You."

Brother Allen informs me that the quorum is having a special fireside this next Sunday evening with two important guest speakers. Sister Amanda Ridgely Knight will discuss "The Role of Man: Where Does He Fit in the Eternal Plan?" And Sister Alice Young Taylor will lecture on "Three Important Men from Church History."

Next weekend is a big one for the younger teens in our congregation: the Beehive class is going to kayak down the Green River, under the direction of Sister Lynn Harrison. And as I understand it, the deacons will be here at home, helping to fold and stamp the ward newsletter.

In the Young Men's meeting tonight, the boys will have something special to look forward to—a panel of Laurels from the stake will discuss "What We Look for in Boys We Date." Here's your big chance, boys!

Now finally clipped to your programs you see a proposal—and I stress that that is all it is so far—for a method of handling our financial commitments for this next year. This is of vital importance to *every member*. I stress that. We want *every one of you* to go home, gather your husbands and children around you, examine this proposal, and decide if you can give us your sustaining vote on it.

(At this point, the third woman on the stand, whose name is Chaplin, gets up and whispers briefly to the speaker.)

ABBOT: Sister Chaplin reminds me that the basketball team will be practicing this week in preparation for the stake playoffs Saturday. Practice will be every afternoon this week from 4 until 6. Coach Tanner has asked that every player get there right at four, or a little before, if she can. Young women, we want you to know how proud we are of you! In the same vein, the boys' basketball team has also been doing nicely; if I'm not mistaken, they are leading the region and also have a game sometime this next month. Practice for the boys' team will be over in the old stake house from 5 to 6:30 a.m. this next week. Any boy having a basketball is asked to bring it, since we're a little short on equipment for the boys' team.

Well, I think that's all of the announcements. We will open the meeting by singing on page 102, after which Brother Donny Dee Williams will give the invocation.

The chorister steps to his stand and leads the congregation in the following song:

> We are cooking, daily cooking
> Food that strengthens, food that fills,
> Casseroles that feed the starving,
> Wheat from ever-turning mills.
> Wheat that's grown and ground and garnished,
> Wheat that's fiber-rich and pure,
> Wheat for woman, to sustain her,
> As she labors strong and sure.

After the prayer, Abbot returns to the pulpit.

ABBOT: I am happy to report that our numbers are growing: we have had six babies born this last month alone! I'll just mention each one, and you can congratulate the happy parents after service.

Sister Jean Hammond and her husband Dale have a new little girl, to be named Rachel Sariah Hammond. Sister and Brother Ellen Taylor, a girl to be named Ellen Fielding Taylor, Jr. Sister and Brother Margaret Jones, a girl to be named Elizabeth Eleanor Jones. As you know, this baby is Sister and Brother Jones' sixth, but the very first girl they've managed to have, and I just want to share with you what Margaret said this past week. Someone who didn't know the family asked her how many children she had. "Six," she said, "and they're all girls but five!"

Now in case you think we've forgotten the opposite sex, Sister and Brother Anne Henderson are welcoming a little boy to their home; he's to be named LeWinky Henderson. Gale and Jimmy Jenson also have a new boy, to be named Tippy Tom Jenson; and Meredith and Billy Joe Gordon have a son whom they have named Fortitude Oak Gordon.

Well, our congratulations to all the families and their new members.

Right now, it's time for a special number from our Singing Fathers. They will announce their own selection.

(*The four men dressed in black trousers come to the front of the stand, cluster together, place their arms on each other's shoulders, and set themselves for singing. At this point, one man whispers to another, who steps forward.*)

> QUARTET MEMBER: We will sing "O My Mother."
> O my Mother, Thou that dwellest in the high and glorious place,
> When shall I regain Thy presence, and again behold Thy face?
> In Thy holy habitation, did my spirit once reside?
> In my first primeval childhood, was I nurtured near Thy side?
> For a wise and glorious purpose Thou has placed me here on Earth,
> And withheld the recollection of my former friends and birth,
> Yet ofttimes a secret something whispered, "You're a stranger here,"
> And I felt that I had wandered from a more exalted sphere.
> I had learned to call Thee Mother, through Thy Spirit from on high,
> But until the key of knowledge was restored, I knew not why.
> In the heavens are parents single? No, the thought makes reason stare.
> Truth is reason. Truth eternal tells me I've two parents there.
> When I leave this frail existence, when I lay this mortal by,
> Mother, Father, may I meet You in Your royal courts on high?
> Then, at length, when I've completed all You sent me forth to do,
> With Your mutual approbation let me come and dwell with You.*

After the song, Abbot returns to the pulpit.

ABBOT: Thank you very much, brothers, for that special number. Now our speaker today, sisters and brothers, is a returned missionary from our congregation, Sister Eve Wentworth. Sister Wentworth filled a highly successful mission to Japan, was made a district supervisor after she had been out only twelve months, and in due time became Second Counselor to President Marileo Yashimoto of the Nagoya Japan Mission. I happened to meet President and Brother Yashimoto at conference last month, and she told me there wasn't a missionary in their mission

---

* Bell here presents a reversal of "O My Father" (1845), a hymn by Eliza R. Snow that presents Mormonism's best-known and most enduring articulation of belief in a Heavenly Mother.

who had been a finer example of dedication and leadership than Sister Wentworth. We're happy today to hear from Sister Eve F. Wentworth.

(In the interests of saving space and avoiding repetition, we here give, instead of Sister Wentworth's complete speech, a copy of the ward clerk's notes thereon.)

SPEAKER: Sister Eve F. Wentworth, recently returned missionary.

Summary of remarks: Missionary work—the central calling of House of Israel. Reason Israel was chosen of God. Greatest thing we can do to bless world in anguish. All worthy women to shoulder this responsibility. Mission also the making of character. Boys must help young women prepare for calling. Must never tempt young women or cause them to fall. Tight pants, dangers of. Bare chests an abomination before Lord. Boys don't understand female nature, how easily ignited. Must set example. Not to be cause for some young woman's unworthiness to serve mission. Use time when women are on missions to improve selves, prepare for marriage, prepare to be companion to returned missionary, conduit whereby spirits of women are sent to earth. Can be learning skills—gardening, yard work, home repair, etc. Young women to be serious about missions—cosmic in scope. Eternal consequences. Work affects ages yet unborn, fate of nations. Prepare well. Study scriptures in depth; learn languages; social skills. Avoid getting serious abt. boys prior to call. Boys—charming distractions. Then recounted her own experiences from mission—healing sick, rebuking spirits, receiving revelation abt. impending catastrophe, directing district missionaries out of danger. Value of gentlemen missionaries. Did much good, worked right along with sisters. Need more of right kind of brother missionaries in field. Closed with testimony of work.

Closing song: "Come All Ye Daughters of God."

Closing prayer: Sister Hannah Ruth Williams

"WHEN NICE AIN'T SO NICE"

The problem with Nice isn't that it's sometimes wimpy; the problem is that Nice can be dangerous. C. S. Lewis praises courage as the virtue that protects all other virtues. That is, it is courage which enables us to be truthful when speaking the truth may be risky; it is courage that backs up loyalty when loyalty is unpopular; it is certainly courage which makes patriotism meaningful in times of danger. By the same logic, I believe it is niceness which can corrupt all the other virtues. Niceness edits the truth, dilutes loyalty, makes a caricature of patriotism. It hobbles Justice, short-circuits Honor, and counterfeits Mercy, Compassion, and Love.

As I look around the neighborhood, the campus, the community, and the church, I see the way nice people act when they disagree: sentimentally or deviously towards those we encounter face to face, and hostilely towards those we don't know. For thirty years I have been upset and puzzled by the fiercely hostile tone of many Letters to the Editor of BYU's student newspaper. These letters are not merely impassioned, not just full of youthful vigor and sass, not purely angry. They are hostile and mean-spirited. Whether discussing red tape in the Administration Building, parking on campus, or pricing in the Bookstore, the letters drip with innuendo, invective and scripture-laden scourging. All this from neatly dressed, smiling youths who hold doors open for each other and walk clear across campus to turn in stray Number Two pencils to the Lost-and-Found depository.

Nice takes other tolls. According to an article in the *Deseret News*, 11 October 1989, pharmaceutical houses have hard data showing that Utahns (with a national reputation as your generic nice people) use huge quantities of tranquilizers and anti-depressants, far more per capita than the populations of other states. Depression of course has many causes, but repressed anger is among the foremost. Anger is punished and prohibited from childhood in cultures that teach the poisonous pedagogy and preach the creed of niceness. I fantasize about what life in Happy Valley might be like if the lid of niceness were eased off the pressure cooker of emotions.

If the cultural mandate to be Nice has driven men's darker sides into hiding, what can we say about women, who aren't even supposed to *have* dark sides? Passive aggression is one of the milder manifestations of Niceness, seen in the woman who wouldn't say no to anyone, but who will repeatedly keep you waiting an hour, or "accidentally" smash the fender on your borrowed car, or "forget" an important responsibility she promised to manage. More deadly is the Nice Lady who never raises her voice, never utters the slightest profanity, but whose devastating words and emotional abuse leave permanent scars as disfiguring to the soul as any physical battering is to the body.

You've heard of the Nicene Creed, the Christian confession of faith first adopted in 325? Now hear the Nice Creed:

> We believe in being Nice,
> in speaking softly at all times, even when loud objection may be more logical;
> in saying nothing in response to minor inconveniences such as being jostled on a bus, or relegated to a back seat, or not being allowed to ride at all, or being run over by the bus;
> and in saying even the most appalling things in soft, non-committal tones, even, if worst comes to the worst, in whispers.
> We guard against silence as against speaking out, for in silence is Thought born;
> therefore, we cultivate and foster small talk, which says naught yet smothers silence.
> We believe that pleasantries are better than truths, friendliness better than honor, jocularity better than Justice.

We believe that neatness is the end of logic and cleanliness the epitome of order.

And we most devoutly believe in seeing nothing that is disconcerting or unpleasant.

We believe in turning the other head, closing the other eye, stopping the other ear, and biting the other tongue.

Etymology often uncovers hidden truths. The word "nice" can be traced back through Middle English to mean strange, lazy, foolish; through Old French to mean stupid or foolish; to the Latin "nescius," meaning ignorant, not knowing. Bear in mind that George Orwell insisted most ignorance is intentional, and you understand the serious danger of niceness: deliberate, lazy not knowing. Not wanting to know, not willing to know, not about to know.

Know what? Why, anything. Anything at all. Not to take one nibble from one piece of fruit of the Tree of Knowledge of Good and Evil, but to remain, instead, Nice. Not to know about History, except for a few pretty branches used as decoration. So much of History is not nice at all. For one thing, those who refuse to ignore history are destined to think about it. Certainly not to know about Poverty. Distinctly not nice. Nice people do not want homeless shelters in their neighborhoods, or their town, if it comes to that; they don't want group homes or halfway houses or soup kitchens; in fact, they are nervous about public benches on the streets unless they are built with dividers to prevent reclining; nice people don't sleep on benches, after all. Not to know about Death, but to confine him to curtained cubicles in isolated "units" of hospitals and nursing homes. Death is unequivocally not nice.

Nice flies under false colors, wants the reputation of the gentle dove without the wisdom of the wise serpent. It is the Great Imposter, having none of the power of Virtue but seeking the influence thereof. Nice is neither kind, nor compassionate, neither good nor full of good cheer, neither hot nor cold. But, being puffed up in its own vanity, it is considerably more dangerous than luke-warmth.

Nice, in short, ain't so nice.

Sonja Farnsworth (1947–), "Mormonism's Odd Couple: The Priesthood-Motherhood Connection" (1991)

Throughout the 1970s and 1980s, LDS Church leaders placed a growing emphasis on motherhood as the essentially defining spiritual responsibility of women, and they relied on this idea as a premise for opposition to women's institutional leadership and priesthood ordination and to the Equal Rights Amendment. Mormon feminists responded to the pressure that Church leaders' idealization of motherhood brought to bear on Mormon women—those whose lives did not fit the prescribed model, including working mothers, single mothers, childless women, and unmarried or divorced women, as well as those who acknowledged the everyday disappointments and vulnerabilities of motherhood, or yearned for broader venues in which to express themselves and explore their potential. In this essay, Sonja Farnsworth argues that the exaltation of motherhood in Mormon rhetoric was not rooted in Mormon doctrine or scripture. She traces its rise to the 1950s and documents its sources in secular American culture rather than the Mormon faith. The oft-heard explanation for the exclusion of women from the lay priesthood and Church decision-making was (and continues to be) that "[m]en have priesthood; women have motherhood." "What does the coupling of motherhood with priesthood really mean for the contemporary church?" Farnsworth asked. "It means that the 'plain and precious truth' of motherhood as a simple but authentic partnership with fathers has been buried in the perennial rhetoric about a partnership with God, which is revived whenever traditional views of women are challenged. While this rhetoric seems to protect female needs, in reality it has protected male authority and denied women what is properly theirs. This rhetoric points to church leaders seemingly unaware that they have been influenced by 'the philosophies of men mingled with scripture.'"

Source

Farnsworth, Sonja. "Mormonism's Odd Couple: The Priesthood-Motherhood Connection." *Mormon Women's Forum Newsletter* 2.1 (March 1991): 1, 6–11.

"MORMONISM'S ODD COUPLE: THE PRIESTHOOD-MOTHERHOOD CONNECTION"

"Women have motherhood and men have priesthood," or so the saying goes. Increasingly during the past fifteen years some have identified the confusing mismatch in this arrangement, the fact that like apples and oranges, the two roles form an "odd couple," whose union lacks the symmetry of partnerships like motherhood and fatherhood; motherhood and priesthood are different categories, how can they claim the clear partnership embodied in these naturally occurring couples? The church's answer is that motherhood is priesthood's equivalency because it is equally divine in purpose and function. In his 1989 talk, "A Tribute to Women," Boyd K. Packer cited the "separate natures of man and woman," describing the female role in exclusively maternal terms. "The limitation of priesthood to men," he added, "is a tribute to the incomparable place of women in the plan of salvation.... Men and women have complementary, not competing responsibilities."[1] His use of the word "complementary," however, is perplexing, for motherhood's natural complement is not priesthood but fatherhood. Moreover, if to be complementary means to mutually supply another's lack, then the natural complement to the word priest is priestess. LDS doctrine supports this construction because a man cannot achieve godhood without being sealed to a wife, and in the temple ceremony this "wife" is a priestess, not a mother. Where in fact does this priestess fit? Why has the more obvious partnership of priest and priestess been overshadowed in LDS rhetoric by a holy alliance of motherhood and priesthood? How did such an "odd couple" get together?

A survey of Mormon writings indicates that motherhood and priesthood were first officially linked in the 1954 revision of Apostle John A. Widtsoe's book *Priesthood and Church Government*. Speaking to the issue of male-female equality, the book stated that "the man who . . . feels he is better than his wife because he holds the Priesthood . . . has failed to comprehend the meaning . . . of priesthood . . . because woman has her gift of equal magnitude—motherhood . . . motherhood is an eternal part of the priesthood."[2] This reference to motherhood as something equal in magnitude to priesthood seems to be the first written source of many LDS statements on motherhood and its exalted partnership with God. Contemporary LDS rhetoric on motherhood bears its imprint, arguing that motherhood is what women have *instead* of priesthood.

LDS motherhood rhetoric generally appears whenever the church senses a challenge to separate sex-roles. An example is the previously cited talk, "A Tribute to Women," in which Apostle Boyd K. Packer denounced the notion that LDS women have legitimate rights to priesthood ordination. It makes four standard arguments: first, that motherhood is woman's divine and exclusive role; second, that the safety of the world depends on the enforcement of separate sex-roles; third, that evil influences are blurring these separate spheres; and fourth, that women are superior to men. For Latter-day Saints, Elder Packer's words are "scripture." However, there is evidence that the ideas they express exactly match those of the secular world. Church leadership has been heavily influenced by secular notions of womanhood and these have obscured the expanded vision of women as queens and priestesses revealed by Joseph Smith.

[Elder Packer argues] that women not only should not but must not have the priesthood, since the survival of the world depends upon the separation of duties for men and women:

> The well-being of the mother, the child, the family, the Church . . . of all humanity rests upon protecting [motherhood]. . . . [Its] obligations are never-ending. The addition of such duties as would attend ordination to the priesthood would constitute an interruption to, perhaps an avoidance of, that crucial contribution which only a mother can provide.[3]

Secular motherhood rhetoric also commonly turns to the theory of separate spheres as a rationale for excluding women from traditionally male domains. A survey of philosophical ideas reveals the roots of the theory of separate spheres. Plato may have allowed for female participation in the public sphere, but Aristotle's view of women as mere incubators for male sperm took precedence. Even in recent history thinkers have interpreted women's role as one of monolithic maternity. For example, eighteenth-century theorist John Locke said that women's reproductive function made them unfit to govern.[4] Jean-Jacques Rousseau imagined an ideal society in which the female was "mother" and the male was citizen.[5] Nineteenth-century England added much to the idea that women were primarily mothers. Victorians portrayed mothers as untouched by something so vulgar as sexual desire. Husbands were to be viewed, as if they were "children of larger growth." This purified motherly element was to be "the salvation of the world."[6] In the 1880s biologist Patrick Geddes contributed his combination of social theory and scientific discovery. Looking through a microscope he observed sperm flagellating wildly around a passive ovum. This, he claimed, verified the temperamental differences between the sexes, for nothing could alter something determined at the lowest form of life. He was successful in promoting a theory that since women are the moral superior of men, they must raise the children or society would never progress to a higher level.[7] Repeatedly nineteenth-century rhetoric assumed that women were extensions of their reproductive functions and thus belonged to a special category.[8]

Today few Latter-day Saints challenge the partnership of motherhood and priesthood, although the Standard Works [of scripture] say virtually nothing about it. On the other hand the temple ceremony refers to women not as mothers but as priestesses. In addition LDS scholars have found much evidence that Joseph Smith viewed women as priestesses and have shed considerable light on the relentless process that distanced women from their rights to this title and participation in the rituals of healing and other gifts of the spirit.[9] In creating the female Relief Society, Joseph Smith organized it to be self-directing, saying it should "move according to the ancient priesthood" and adding that he would "make of this society a kingdom of priests."[10] Joseph's statements made no connection between this priesthood and motherhood. The effect of his words expanded women's views of their spiritual and ecclesiastical power. Their documented participation in the rituals of prophesying, healing, and blessing the sick emphasized their priestly duties in a very real way. However, after Joseph died his generous descriptions of what women had were replaced by frequent references to what they did not have. The result appears to have been a complete reversal of his intentions.

For example, in the 1850s Brigham Young said that "women can never hold the priesthood apart from their husbands."[11] Although phrased in negative form, this statement clearly expressed the belief that women held the priesthood, albeit "with their husbands." In the 1880s John Taylor built upon the negative approach, saying "it is not the calling of these sisters to hold the priesthood, only in connection with their husbands." This statement diminished the link by suggesting that male priesthood was a "calling" while female priesthood was not. Then in 1907 Joseph F. Smith severed the association completely. "A wife does not hold the priesthood with her husband," he asserted," but she enjoys the benefits thereof with him."[12] Thus were women gradually detached from any genuine sense of priesthood.

Surely this situation begged for some sort of reconciliation—a way of explaining women's divine role which would confirm the church's exclusion of women from the priesthood and still not deny the role of priestess revealed in the temple ceremony. The merger of motherhood and priesthood into a team of separate but equal partners satisfied both these needs. One can easily see how the church, needing something to replace the fast-fading vision of its emancipated spiritual female, mistook this conveniently submissive impostor for its own. Thus Mormonism found a way of excluding the priestess while *seeming* to include her, and women were neatly released from the embarrassing business of defining their own connection to priesthood. Ironically "mother" would now do that for them and then give birth to Mormonism's oppressively domestic and popularly conceived model of womanhood known as "Molly Mormon" and "Patti Perfect."*

So what does the coupling of motherhood with priesthood really mean for the contemporary church? It means that the "plain and precious truth" of motherhood as a simple but authentic partnership with fathers has been buried in the perennial rhetoric about a partnership with God, which is revived whenever traditional views of women are challenged. While this rhetoric seems to protect female needs, in reality it has protected male authority and denied women what is properly theirs. This rhetoric points to church leaders seemingly unaware that they have been influenced by "the philosophies of men mingled with scripture." The theory of "separate spheres" is secular not sacred.

It is sadly ironic that even as feminism has alerted us to women's equality with men, the expanded vision of womanhood revealed by Joseph Smith has been resisted and diminished by his own followers. Mormon women, despite their rich tradition of the priestess, have lost much through the teaching that motherhood and priesthood are a sacred marriage of complementary spiritual roles. There will be much to gain if Mormons realize that this union is really a "secular" marriage, a "marriage of convenience," and that motherhood and priesthood are an "odd couple" nurturing a passel of illegitimate theological ideas.

Notes

1. Boyd K. Packer, "Tribute to Woman," *Ensign* 19 (July 1989): 74.
2. John A. Widtsoe, *Priesthood and Church Government*, rev. ed. (Salt Lake City: Deseret Book Co., 1954), 38–39.
3. Boyd K. Packer, in *Ensign* 18 (July 1988): 74.
4. Kathleen Bennion Barrett, "Still Pending: Legal Justice for Women," in *Women of Wisdom and Knowledge* (Salt Lake City: Deseret Book Company, 1989), 252.

*For a Mormon feminist critique of this model of womanhood, see the gently satirical essay "Patti Perfect," *Exponent II* 10.2 (Winter 1984): 13.

5. Martha Vicinus, *Suffer and Be Still: Women in the Victorian Age* (Bloomington: Indiana University Press, 1973), 120.

6. Sheila M. Rothman, *Woman's Proper Place: A History of Ideals and Practices, 1870 to the Present* (New York: Basic Books, 1978), 43.

7. Ibid.

8. Barrett, 252.

9. Linda King Newell, "The Historical Relationship of Mormon Women and the Priesthood," *Dialogue: A Journal of Mormon Thought* 18 (Fall 1985).

10. "Nauvoo Relief Society Minutes," *The Words of Joseph Smith*, eds. Andrew F. Ehat and Lyndon W. Cook (Provo, UT: BYU Religious Studies Center, 1980), 110.

11. Newell, "Women and Priesthood," 23.

12. Ibid., 26.

III

Defining Moments

Mormon Feminism in the 1990s

The 1990s witnessed the emergence of a critical mass of Mormon feminists—from faculty members at Church-owned Brigham Young University to independent scholars and activists—who pushed the movement toward new frontiers in consciousness, theology, and action. Theologians like the sisters Janice Allred and Margaret Toscano found resources in Mormon history and doctrine to tell a powerful new story about the little-discussed but deeply held LDS belief in a Heavenly Mother, as well as about the powers of priesthood that Church founder Joseph Smith intended to convey to LDS women through the organization of the Relief Society and Mormon temple ceremonies. At the same time, Mormon feminists such as environmentalist activist and writer Terry Tempest Williams and literary critic and educator Cecilia Konchar Farr modeled a publicly vocal activist stance on issues of general feminist concern like reproductive rights, breast cancer, domestic violence, rape, and sexual abuse, as well as on conservation and anti-war issues. Mormon feminist conversation and activism, it seemed, had rebounded from the defeats of the Equal Rights Amendment era and had assumed new vigor, reach, and influence, especially among younger Mormon women.

But backlash followed. Intense pressure and official sanctions were brought to bear on feminist faculty members at Brigham Young University and on Mormon feminist writers, scholars, and activists more generally, a development closely chronicled by Mormon feminist historian Lavina Fielding Anderson. The pressure reached a new level of intensity in the years 1993–2000, when Konchar Farr was fired by Brigham Young University and Anderson, Toscano, and Allred were among several feminist and progressive scholars and activists targeted by high-ranking Church officials for excommunication. Also in 1995, the First Presidency and Quorum of the Twelve Apostles of the LDS Church released "The Family: A Proclamation to the World," a statement that declared the sanctity of family relationships while also asserting that familiar nineteenth- and twentieth-century European-American gender roles—men as leaders and providers; women as mothers and nurturers—were divinely appointed and eternal. All of these events, but most especially the excommunications, had profound, *far-reaching, and deeply personal impacts on Mormon feminists. Still, the landmark writings of Mormon feminist scholars and historians had revealed that, despite and beyond contemporary institutional politics and pressures, Mormon history, scripture, and theology offered rich resources for those who would believe, as the Book of Mormon teaches, that "all are alike unto God—male and female, bond and free, black and white." Mormon feminists grappled with the threat of church discipline and with feelings of pressure, grief, anger, and fear in different ways. Some disaffiliated or discontinued their activity in the LDS Church, while others stayed. Some silenced themselves on feminist issues so as to preserve their employment at Church-owned universities and their Church membership, and still others took their feminist commitments underground, gathering for retreats and conferences and on Internet mailing lists and discussion groups they hoped would be "safe spaces" during this difficult decade.*

Cecilia Konchar Farr (1958–), "I Am a Mormon, and I Am for Choice" (1992)

Born in Pittsburgh, Pennsylvania, Cecilia Konchar Farr converted to Mormonism with her mother at the age of eight. During the 1980s, Konchar Farr worked as a journalist in the American Rust Belt, witnessing the human despair caused by steel mill and coal mine closures; she also lost her sister to an untimely alcohol-related death. Both experiences moved Konchar Farr to commit to a lifetime of activism. "Never again would I stand idly by and watch a woman's life fritter away into hopelessness," she later recalled. Farr came to Brigham Young University to begin her graduate studies in English in 1985 and under the direction of Professor Gloria Cronin became the first BYU student to write a thesis from a feminist perspective. After obtaining her Ph.D., she was hired in 1990 by Brigham Young University to teach feminist literature and theory. Her hire came at a moment of increased flexibility on the usually conservative campus and heightened feminist visibility nationwide. BYU students had founded VOICE, a campus feminist group in 1988, and Konchar Farr's arrival helped galvanize the group to activism. During the early 1990s, VOICE organized Provo, Utah's first "Take Back the Night" demonstrations, campus speak-outs and teach-ins on violence against women, a drive to found a campus women's resource center, and, after a female student was attacked in broad daylight in a wooded area at the southern edge of campus, a mock campus "curfew" on men. In November 1991, flyers bearing a BYU seal appeared around campus announcing that "men will no longer be allowed to walk alone or in all-male groups from 10 p.m. until 6 a.m." The mock curfew, which received national press attention, used the classic feminist device of symbolic gender role reversal (see examples in Carol Lynn Pearson's "Walk in the Pink Moccasins" anthologized in Part II of this volume) to reveal the injustice in well-intentioned advice by campus leaders that women should limit their hours and movement on campus and always be accompanied by male escorts; if men were the assailants, VOICE asked, why shouldn't they be expected to limit their mobility as well? During these years, Konchar Farr herself assumed a public role writing and speaking on feminist issues, taking pains always to specify that she neither represented Brigham Young University nor sought to change the LDS Church. What she wanted, as a Mormon and a feminist activist, Konchar Farr explained, was to change the world for the better. After the Utah legislature passed especially stringent anti-abortion legislation in 1991, Konchar Farr agreed to speak at a pro-choice rally in Salt Lake City in January 1992. This speech ignited a campus controversy over faculty activism. BYU administrators pressured Konchar Farr to stop speaking and writing for the public; they also clamped down on other progressive faculty and withdrew a speaking invitation to Mormon feminist and historian Laurel Thatcher Ulrich, who had received the Pulitzer Prize for her 1991 book *A Midwife's Tale: The Life of Martha Ballard, Based on Her Diary, 1785–1812*. In 1993, Konchar Farr was fired from Brigham Young University. This speech played a signal role in her termination, an event viewed nationwide as a serious infringement on academic freedom and as further evidence of the LDS Church's opposition to the women's movement.

Source

Farr, Cecilia Konchar. "I Am Mormon, and I Am for Choice." Unpublished manuscript, January 1992.

References and Further Reading

Waterman, Bryan, and Brian Kagel. *The Lord's University: Freedom and Authority at BYU.* Salt Lake City: Signature Books, 1998.

"I AM MORMON, AND I AM FOR CHOICE"

I come to you today not as a representative of BYU, though I am a professor there, not as a representative of the LDS church, though I am a faithful and believing Mormon. This afternoon I hope to represent the many Mormons I know who are anti-abortion and pro-choice.

There are many of us, though most are silent because we are afraid. Our brothers and sisters in the church have staked out a political ground on this issue and constructed a false consensus on a shaky foundation of imagined unanimity. They've made us think we don't belong, and that we have no right to speak. But Mormons are a diverse group. Many of us are feminists; we speak for the rights of women, and we speak for choice.

I support what the First Presidency of the LDS Church has said about how terrible abortion is, how painful an option, how regrettable a decision. This is a moral issue so difficult and so sensitive that it is pulling our country apart. But it is also a political issue.

Think about what we say when we allow government to intervene in our private lives. If we allow government the right to say when we can't have an abortion, do we also allow it the right to dictate when we must have one? This is not the business of legislation. In the tradition of Utah pioneer politics, we say "Hands Off!" We demand the right to make our own moral decisions without the interference of government.

And we say this loudly and clearly as women. Because, as [feminist legal theorist] Catherine MacKinnon has said "the abortion choice should be available and must be women's." Whether or not the embryo is a life, whether or not the act of abortion itself is immoral become secondary questions because as MacKinnon asks, "Why should not women make life or death decisions?" And I add, why should not women in our religious community make theological decisions? The same women that Mormon men trust to bear and rear their children—can't we make moral decisions?

An anti-choice stand is not a political position that Mormons can fall into line behind like little toy soldiers. Not if we respect women and value women's lives. Not if we cherish our right to live according to our own consciences and to practice our religion in our own homes unhindered by government interference. This is not a question on which we can be silent any longer. I hope many of you out there will join me in saying, loud and clear to our legislators and leaders: Listen to me. I am Mormon, and I am for choice.

Carol Lynn Pearson (1939–), *Mother Wove the Morning* (1992)

Why did a religion that celebrated motherhood stigmatize discussion of God the Mother, whose doctrinal reality Mormon leaders had affirmed from the movement's first decades? Carol Lynn Pearson explored these questions in her 1980 poem "A Motherless House" (anthologized in Part I of this volume) and resumed her creative search for God the Mother after losing her husband to AIDS-related causes in 1984, an experience she documented in her memoir *Goodbye, I Love You: The Story of a Wife, Her Homosexual Husband, and a Love Honored for Time and All Eternity* (1986). *Mother Wove the Morning* features sixteen characters, historical and imagined, from Paleolithic women to Egyptian priestesses and Israelite matriarchs, from early Christian Gnostics to Emma Smith and American suffragette Elizabeth Cady Stanton. Pearson debuted the one-woman play at her local community theater in Walnut Creek, California, in 1989; over the next few years, she performed it more than 300 times across the country and around the world, including a performance at Brigham Young University in 1991 as campus feminist activism was cresting. Published in 1992, *Mother Wove the Morning* reflects the growing boldness and activism of Mormon feminism in the 1990s. Just as Cecilia Konchar Farr had spoken from a Mormon feminist standpoint to join Mormon women with national feminist priorities like reproductive rights, Pearson connected the Mormon search for the Heavenly Mother, initiated by early feminists like Linda Wilcox and Lisa Hawkins Bolin (anthologized in Part I of this volume), to a broader search for the divine feminine that united women from many religious traditions in the 1990s.

Source

Pearson, Carol Lynn. *Mother Wove the Morning.* Walnut Creek: Pearson Press, 1992.

References and Further Reading

Pearson, Carol Lynn. *Goodbye, I Love You: The Story of a Wife, Her Homosexual Husband, and a Love Honored for Time and All Eternity.* New York: Random House, 1987.

EXCERPTS FROM *MOTHER WOVE THE MORNING*

When I was young, I wrote a poem about living in a Motherless house, where kindest patriarchal care does not ease the pain, where I bury my face in something soft as a breast, where I am a child, crying for my Mother in the night.

But you see, in my heart I know that the Creator that brought us here is in some wonderful way both Father and Mother—that perhaps, in the beginning, on that primordial day, Mother wove the morning and Father made the evening, joyfully, together. Why, then, did I grow up feeling that my world was a Motherless house? On December 10th, 1963, and I know because I checked my diary, I ran through the rain by myself to the Jerusalem museum. And I stood there open-mouthed as the museum director pointed out certain artifacts as showing the transition from worship of the female to worship of the male. I was dumb-founded. The Goddess—under glass.

One more story. On Mother's Day of 1982—yes, I do keep a very good diary—after I finished the breakfast in bed that my children brought me, I told the four of them I wanted them to sit with me for a little and talk about God.

Aaron groaned. Emily punched him. "Aaron, it's *Mother's Day!*"
"Okay, Emily," I said, "you first. I want you to close your eyes and tell me what you see when you think of God."
"Okay. Well, then—I see a man—he's pretty old—he's dressed in a long robe, and he has a very stern expression on his face."
"Do you like him?"
"I—I don't think he likes me. I know he's supposed to love me, but he's telling me that if I'm not good when the millennium comes, I'll get burnt to a crisp."

I felt my heart break. Fourteen years old.

And even if she had found her picture of God warm and inviting, which I know God surely to be, there he was—totally male. And there she was—the other—as I had been, the other. And as so many millions of women had been.

I began to think about all those women. Did they know anything I didn't know? Oh, I wanted to find them, to see through their eyes. So I went out searching. I walked backward in time. I walked through their villages and courtyards and homes and dungeons, crying out, "Where is my Mother? Nobody can tell me you can have a Father without a Mother. Did she abandon us on the doorstep without even a note?"

And as quiet as ghosts, some of my sisters appeared, and they began to speak to me. And the things they told me have turned my life upside down. Or, I think, right side up. And I know that you would be just as interested as I was, and so they and I sat down and put together this play for you.

RACHEL AND THE TERAPHIM

Who told you I have them? Is this what you seek, the teraphim, the little images of the gods and goddesses I have taken? You seek them too, like my father Laban seeks them? Listen. He shouts now in the tent of the maidservants. "Where are the teraphim?" he shouts. "Where are my gods and goddesses?" Oh, listen to him shout! And if he finds them with me, I will pay with my life!

But he will not find them. See? I place myself on the camel cushion, my skirts like so, and under my skirts I hide the teraphim, the little images I have taken. Oh, you are saying, that is too easy, her father will find them.

Oh, no! No. You wait and see.

You think I am a robber? I steal because they are mine and my right to hold them has been stolen from me, as right after right has been stolen from me. But these—these I steal back again—to help me remember.

In the days of Sarah, grandmother to my husband Jacob and wife to Abraham, the ways of the mothers still prevailed. Sarah was a priestess, a prophetess of power, the mother, the Matriarch, and she knew the old ways, the ancient order in which the mothers were honored and all the people blessed. But the new ways came, the customs that honored the fathers and exacted obedience to them.

We have stories of wandering nomads that came on horses with their thrusting weapons of bronze in their hands to kill and take slaves. Theirs was a god of war and mountain, a male without a female, and with them the peace of the mothers vanished from the earth—woman became property—cities had walls.

Oh, I remember Sarah, and I bless her name! But the names of the mothers are being erased—as if written by a finger on the desert floor before a wind—and my seed, I fear, will not know the name of my mother; or the name of the Goddess of

Mesopotamia, for whom I was named Rachel, "Mother of the Holy Lamb." I leave the land of the Goddess to go to the land of the patriarchs. But I carry with me, hidden here beneath my skirts, her memory and her hope.

Do you hear him? Now he is in the tent of my sister Leah. "Where are my teraphim?" Shhhhh! My father, you know, has traveled a seven days' journey to find us, for we left without his knowledge when he had gone to shear his sheep. And this morning I listened from my tent as he said to my husband Jacob, "Why have you stolen my gods?" And Jacob said, and he spoke truly, "I have not stolen your gods. Come in and search. And if you find them with any one of us, that person shall not live!"

It is true. My husband Jacob, who cried and kissed me on the first day we met, who loves me and worked fourteen years to obtain me—he will see that I am killed if the teraphim are found.

So. You may think it strange. For the sacred images I would risk my life? There is more to life, you know, than breath. A life that has given up its meaning is not a life. A life that has given up its power is not a life. These little goddesses and gods I hide beneath my skirt—mine by the matrilineal prerogative—are my meaning and my power, and without them what good would my life be to me? But my life will be spared, and I will tell you why. In a moment my father will come to my tent to search and I will say to him, "Father, forgive me that I cannot rise before you, for the period of women is upon me." And my father will not come near to me, for if he were to touch me he would be unclean and accursed!

(Laughs) The ancient ways of the mothers—the curse of the woman—will save my life!

EMMA SMITH: THE MORMON FIRST LADY

You will not find another shawl like this in all the city of Nauvoo[, Illinois]. Joseph gave it to me. It is beautiful, isn't it? I wore it last month when I went to St. Louis, but mostly I just take it out to look at.

Oh, they stare at me in St. Louis, I can tell you, and not for my shawl. "Look," they whisper, "There goes Mrs. Smith, the wife of Joe, the Mormon Prophet. Why do you suppose she stays with him?"

How many women are his wives now? Oh, you would like to know, wouldn't you? Eleven that I know of, and more you can be certain.

But Joseph loves me! And no other woman in Nauvoo has a shawl like this.

Don't bother turning away your eyes. "Poor, degraded, mindless Mormon woman," you are saying.

No! You don't understand. The gospel that Joseph restored is for the women as well as the men, and already we have made such strides that some of the brethren complain. Joseph ordained and set apart many women to lay on hands, anoint with oil, heal the sick. He tells us that we, like Miriam and Deborah, may have the gift of prophecy receive revelation for ourselves, become queens and priestesses. No one can say that the poor, Mormon women are downtrodden.

Well, it is true that after we had ground up our china to make the plaster for the Kirtland temple shine, after we had woven the veils, we were not invited in—until some time after the brethren. We are *always* after the brethren. And, yes, I have sometimes had my fill of Brigham pointing out that women were made to be led and directed and to submit cheerfully, for we have not the degree of light and intelligence that our husbands have. But, I say all in good time, and for now let us count our blessings.

Joseph has even taught—we don't speak much of this, for it would be another stone for our enemies to cast against us, and I ask you to be careful where you tell it—Joseph has even taught that in the heavens there is not only a Heavenly Father, there's a Heavenly Mother, as well. "How could there be a Father?" he asks, "If there were not also a Mother, as divine as he?"

And he tells us that we might someday become—like them! Imagine! In some eternity I might become a Goddess!

You are judging him harshly. Yes, you are. "How can a man who so exalts women," you are saying, "subject his own wife, whom he claims to love, and the wives of his followers, who are good and tender-hearted women, to the monstrous evil of polygamy? How can he claim this comes of God?" That is what you are saying, isn't it? But no, you are wrong. I have said that too, but I was wrong. I was listening to Satan, who seeks to destroy me! If you knew Joseph you would know why I love him as much as any woman has ever loved a man. I disobeyed my father and eloped with him. No better man, save Jesus, ever walked this earth. Joseph is forever giving away his boots, coming home again barefoot. He is a very-loving man. No, that is not it! God commanded it that righteous seed. . . .

I was a stumbling block to the whole Church! Joseph told me—God told me in a revelation to Joseph, "Let mine handmaid, Emma Smith, receive all those that have been given unto my servant Joseph. And if she will not abide this command-ment, she shall be destroyed, saith the Lord, your God."

Oh, I fought! But I did not want to be destroyed! So I agreed. I chose the two Partridge sisters, Emily and Eliza, whom I had taken in before as my daugh-ters. I instructed them in the beautiful principle of patriarchal marriage. I stood and watched as Judge Adams, a high priest in the Church, married them to my husband.

But no other woman in Nauvoo has a shawl . . . !

How did Sarah do it? She gave Hagar to Abraham. Did she love him? How does the Muslim woman do it today? Millions of them.

Oh, I think sometimes of the wife of God the Father, that Mother Joseph has told us of: Well, if what Joseph teaches is true, that as we are now, God once was and as God is now we may become, then—then God our Father must have numer-ous wives, more even than Joseph!

I would like to speak to the Father's first wife! She must not have been so rebellious as I. And I would say to her, "How did you do it?"

Susan Elizabeth Howe (1949–), "The Blessing" (1992)

In 1847, early Mormon leader Eliza R. Snow gave Mormonism its most definitive and best-known articulation of the doctrinal reality of a Heavenly Mother in her hymn "O My Father." "In the heavens are parents single? / No the thought makes reason stare," Snow wrote. "Truth is reason, truth eternal / Tells me I've a mother there." Almost one hundred and fifty years later, the Utah-born poet and Brigham Young University professor Susan Elizabeth Howe followed Snow in using hymnody to make real the experience of female divinity. Howe, who received her Ph.D. in 1989 from the University of Denver, wrote the play *A Dream for Katy: A Celebration of Early Mormon Women* to be performed at the Brigham Young University Women's Conference in 1992. The play centers on a young, ambitious, and visionary woman named Katy who wrestles with the question of how to be "a Mormon woman in the twenty-first century." Significant Mormon women of the nineteenth century, including Ellis Shipp, Eliza R. Snow, and Emmeline Wells, come to Katy's aid. Concluding the play is a sung poem entitled "The Blessing"—set to the tune of the well-loved Mormon hymn "If You Could Hie to Kolob" (1842) by W. W. Phelps—in which a chorus of prominent nineteenth-century Mormon women and her own deceased mother offer a blessing of wisdom, courage, strength, and discernment to Katy. Just as "If You Could Hie to Kolob" captured the cosmological expansiveness of Mormon theology in the nineteenth century, "The Blessing" explores and enacts an expansive sense of women's spiritual authority and power: "There is no end to glory; / There is no end to love; / There is no end to being; / We will join the gods above." As Mormon feminist historians like Linda King Newell had shown, the tradition of Mormon women's giving healing blessings by the laying on of hands had been lost in the early twentieth century (see Newell's essay "A Gift Given, a Gift Taken" in Part I of this volume.) Rather than mourn the absence of opportunities for women to bless their daughters within the ritual contexts of Mormonism, Howe uses literature to make such blessings a living reality.

Source

Howe, Susan Elizabeth. "The Blessing." *Mormon Women's Forum Quarterly* 5.2 (July 1994): 12.

References and Further Reading

Howe, Susan Elizabeth. *A Dream for Katy: A Celebration of Early Mormon Women* (1992).
Howe, Susan Elizabeth. *Salt*. Salt Lake City: Signature Books, 2013.

Howe, Susan Elizabeth. *Stone Spirits*. Provo, UT: Redd Center for Western Studies, 1997.
Howe, Susan Elizabeth, and Sheree Maxwell Bench, eds. *Discoveries: Two Centuries of Poems by Mormon Women*. Provo, UT: BYU Studies Press, 2004.

"THE BLESSING"

In the power of the spirit
We your mothers on this day
Give to you our sacred blessing
To guide you on your way.
Dear blessed, noble daughter
Of great vision, love and soul,
The world, so sad and broken
Needs your gifts to make it whole.

Emulate Christ's loving service
Every moment of your life;
Hold his countenance before you
Through each day of joy and strife.
There is honor in your mission;
There is glory in your youth.
Seek the best in all your labors
That your life may shine with truth.

Many lives will be discouraged;
Many faithful hearts will fail;
Many turn from joy to pleasure,
Many hopes grow old and stale.
In such times of loss and sorrow
When the world would bring you low,
Think on this great love we bear you;
We are here to help you know

There is no end to virtue;
There is no end to might;
There is no end to wisdom;
There is no end to light.
There is no end to glory;
There is no end to love;
There is no end to being;
We will know them all above;
There is no end to glory;
There is no end to love;
There is no end to being;
We will join the gods above.

Margaret Merrill Toscano (1949–), "Put on Your Strength, O Daughters Of Zion: Claiming Priesthood and Knowing the Mother" (1992)

In 1992, Mormon feminist theologian Maxine Hanks published *Women and Authority: Re-emerging Mormon Feminism*, a landmark 460-page volume that marked the arrival of a critical mass and an emboldened maturity in Mormon feminism. Featuring the voices of more than 150 Mormon women, *Women and Authority* reprinted classic essays on Mormon feminist topics like Heavenly Mother and priesthood by Linda Wilcox, Sonja Farnsworth, and Linda King Newell (see their essays anthologized in this volume), primary source excerpts from more than a century of Mormon feminist history, as well as new essays by leading voices in Mormon feminism. In her contribution to Hanks's anthology, Margaret Toscano builds on her own prior theological studies and on the work of Mormon feminist historians like Linda King Newell and D. Michael Quinn in recovering from historical documents a sense of what LDS temple "endowment" rites and the Relief Society meant to Joseph Smith and early Mormon women: the vesting of Mormon women with priesthood power. Toscano advances this line of inquiry by exploring practical, social, ethical, cultural, and institutional barriers to making women's exercise of priesthood and greater knowledge of Heavenly Mother a reality. She also draws from ancient scripture studies and speculative theology to offer new suggestions for envisioning a Heavenly Mother and female deity—as she and her husband Paul Toscano did in their co-authored book *Strangers in Paradox: Explorations in Mormon Theology* (1990). Toscano offers steps both pragmatic and visionary that LDS men and women might take to realize the feminist potential of Mormon theology, encouraging her brothers and sisters to "put on their strength" now. Both she and her husband Paul Toscano became targets of the same LDS Church effort to discipline less orthodox scholars and authors whose writings pushed at or beyond the boundaries of current Church doctrine. Like D. Michael Quinn, Paul Toscano was summoned to an LDS Church disciplinary court and was excommunicated in September 1993; Margaret would be excommunicated in September 2000.

Source

Toscano, Margaret Merrill. "Put on Your Strength, O Daughters of Zion: Claiming Priesthood and Knowing the Mother," in *Women and Authority: Re-emerging Mormon Feminism*, ed. Maxine Hanks, 411–435. Salt Lake City: Signature Books, 1993.

References and Additional Reading

Toscano, Margaret Merrill, and Paul Toscano. *Strangers in Paradox: Explorations in Mormon Theology*. Salt Lake City: Signature Books, 1990.
Toscano, Margaret Merrill. "Is There a Place for Heavenly Mother in Mormon Theology?" *Sunstone* 133 (July 2004): 14–22.

Toscano, Margaret Merrill. "'Are Boys More Important Than Girls?': The Continuing Conflict of Gender Difference and Equality in Mormonism." *Sunstone* 146 (June 2007): 19–29.

"PUT ON YOUR STRENGTH, O DAUGHTERS OF ZION: CLAIMING PRIESTHOOD AND KNOWING THE MOTHER"

If Women Have Priesthood, Why Can't They Use It?

The statements of Joseph Smith along with the structure and content of the temple endowment confirm that every endowed Mormon woman holds the priesthood. Many Mormon women have not acknowledged the temple endowment as the source of their priesthood for various reasons. The most common are: (1) many are not aware of this fact; (2) some women see priesthood as a male privilege, contrary to female nature; (3) some women do not want to be part of the hierarchical structure; and (4) some women do not want to receive priesthood through men or in the name of Melchizedek.

Priesthood Through Men

Some Mormon women argue that if women accept the priesthood from men, they are acquiescing to patriarchal authority, implying that a woman's power is derived from and therefore is inferior to a man's. While female subordination in the temple endowment only adds to this concern, this dilemma is not avoided by rejecting the endowment and seeking instead the ecclesiastical priesthood, since this too is male-controlled. The question is: How can women become equal members of the church priesthood order when they must receive permission to function within that order from men?

In my view the resolution of this problem requires us to reevaluate what was for women one of the most important events in the history of the LDS church. On 28 April 1842 at a meeting of the Female Relief Society of Nauvoo, Joseph Smith "spoke of delivering the keys to this society and to the Church."[1] This was a reference to the keys of the priesthood communicated through the temple endowment. When Joseph passed on these keys, women received a priesthood that originated not with him or any other man but with God. As with men, women's priesthood is derived from the divine source. Though all priesthood is one, it has differing orders and manifestations. The manifestation of the priesthood may be different in women than in men, and women are undoubtedly entitled to their own priesthood orders and offices. It was perhaps with this in mind that Joseph Smith stated that he would make of the Relief Society "a kingdom of priestesses" and that the church itself was not complete without a temple in which the priesthood could be revealed to all Latter-day Saints, women and men alike.

Though Joseph Smith transmitted these important keys, he was merely a conduit of the power, not the source. He gave us gifts which had been given to him by

God to hold in trust for us. As members of the church community we have all been given gifts which are to be used for the benefit of others. None of us is entirely independent. Even Jesus relied on others. He received power for the resurrection by means of a holy anointing conferred on him by Mary. Yet we would not say that because Jesus received this ordinance from a woman that he was therefore inferior or subordinate to her; he collaborated with her. On the Mount of Transfiguration, Jesus received keys from Moses and Elias, and yet Jesus was Lord of heaven and earth before and after that event.* In his teachings Joseph Smith makes frequent reference to the giving back and forth of keys among many male priesthood figures. It may be then that the frequent transmittal of keys among angels and divinities bespeaks the existence among these personages not of a rigid hierarchy but rather of a fluid community.

Joseph Smith's act of delivering keys to women need not be seen in hierarchical terms as an act of subordination but as an act of liberation—for "keys" in Mormon theology are the "right of presidency, the directing, controlling, governing power."[2] It is significant that Joseph did not presume to define women nor their priesthood offices. He seemed to recognize those privileges as belonging to them and to those women who would come after them. He took the responsibility for defining the male part of priesthood. And he also introduced a model for men and women to hold priesthood in joint-tenancy in the Holy Order. But he left it to women to find for themselves what God wanted for them.

The women in Joseph's day began to do this in a limited way. They accepted the keys that Joseph conveyed to them, acted independently, and did not ask permission to give blessings and minister to each other. The Relief Society functioned as a self-governing women's organization in many ways until this century. But even in today's priesthood-correlated church, the keys of priesthood given to women have never been taken away. They continue to be bestowed on women in the temple. They are waiting to be used.

It is undoubtedly true that in spite of the liberating statements of Joseph Smith to the Relief Society which imply self-governance, he still saw that body as subordinate to the male order. Joseph, like all of us, was a product of his society. While his teachings may fall short of the full equality that many of us desire today, nonetheless they are an important doctrinal foundation which gives historical precedence for women's right to priesthood. Perhaps Joseph went as far as he could for his day, and perhaps it is for our day to establish the importance of the equality of men and women.

Some feel that women should declare their own priesthood separate from the male order. It is doubtful, however, that many Mormon women would accept the validity of a self-declaration of priesthood unconnected to the restoration or conferral of authority by heavenly messengers. The priesthood of women must come

---

*Toscano here invokes an LDS interpretation of the scriptures at Matthew 17:1–9.

from God in a way that does not sever them from the church. The reception of priesthood in the temple endowment affirms the divine source of women's right to the priesthood in a church context. This is not to reject the idea that women can receive private revelations about their callings. The Book of Mormon reinforces two mechanisms of priesthood transmittal: the holy calling that comes directly from God to an individual and the ordination mediated through an earthly priesthood structure (Alma 13). Ideally one should have both the personal calling and the ordination. This distinction emphasizes the fact that priesthood power and spiritual authority are not derived from an earthly source, but the acceptance into a priestly order and the scope to act within a community do depend on human acknowledgement.

Women do not need permission from men to use their priestly power in private ways such as giving blessings or exercising other spiritual gifts. But in order for women to use priesthood in visible ways in the larger religious community, there must be acceptance by the community of their priestly calling. Many Mormon women have gifts of leadership. To confine their priestly role to the private sphere deprives the larger church community of their spiritual gifts. This underscores the need for women to be ordained to offices and accepted into the ecclesiastical priesthood. Within the church structure, women cannot function as fully as men unless they are part of the priesthood order.

Women in the Hierarchy

Some Mormon women want nothing to do with the hierarchical priesthood system that operates the modern church. They see priesthood leadership as power-centered and corruptible. Some women emphasize the private and devotional aspects of worship and claim that these are not stressed enough in the church. Certainly this is true; the spiritual dimension of priesthood should be primary. But I see difficulties if women reject or abandon the organizational dimensions of priesthood. Community is an inevitable component of the religious life. Even in strictly democratic groups, power structures usually emerge. Often by ignoring or denying the reality of authority and leadership, a climate for the abuse of power may inadvertently be fostered. However, if authority is addressed openly and checks and balances established, abuses can be minimized. Women will not eliminate authoritarianism and unrighteous dominion by denying themselves the institutional dimensions of priesthood or by discarding priesthood altogether. In either case authority structures will exist as long as there is an institution.

Certain checks and balances against the abuse of authority are inherent in the priesthood system. These are not often enough discussed. Doctrine and Covenants 121 refers to the "rights" and the "powers" of the priesthood. The power of the priesthood is the power of God attended by the gifts of prophecy, revelation, knowledge, wisdom, and healing. This power comes without ordination or church authorization to those who seek and desire it. The rights of the priesthood come through ordination approved through official church channels. Both the power and the rights of the priesthood can be abused. A spiritual person can use his or her gifts for self-aggrandizement just as an ordained person holding church office can exercise authority unrighteously. Nevertheless, we need both forms of authority in the church, for the rights of the priesthood bring order and the power of the priesthood brings life. Each of these two concepts of priesthood acts as a check against the abuse of power by the other. If priesthood is seen only as spiritual power, then leadership can be claimed only by those who can demonstrate spiritual gifts. Control then moves into the hands of a few spiritually elite. Ordaining everyone in the community to priesthood and considering each voice as important with an equal vote, regardless of individual gifts, promotes equality and a democratic community. On the other hand if priesthood is only a matter of ordination, the idea develops that office means spiritual competence, which leads to spiritual deadness. But when spiritual power and knowledge are accorded equal status with priesthood or ecclesiastical office, then power is rightly balanced, spirituality is fostered, and content is placed on an equal footing with form.

Another check against the abuse of power is the vote of the general assembly made up of all members (or a representative body of all members) of the church. This body can exercise a veto power on church leaders.[3] Unfortunately, the "sustaining vote" in the church today is a mere formality that may not express the wishes and spiritual insights of members. Because we stress obedience to authority and emphasize the tradition that revelation comes only through the general authorities, we have lost sight of the "sustaining vote" as a check on authoritarianism. With this loss we have also lost the vision of a general assembly of priestesses and priests who can receive the mind and will of the Lord. These and other checks and balances must be revitalized to mitigate misuse of priesthood authority.

Some Mormon women reject priesthood because they fear power since they do not want to misuse it and become abusive themselves. However, even power and aggressiveness have their positive side. Power in its most basic form is the ability to think, to act and order resources. Even power over other people is not always undesirable. We all have power whether we recognize it or not: parents have power over children, teachers over pupils, friends over each other. In all of these relationships, power is used. For good people to eschew all power is for them to invite a monopoly of power by the power-hungry or evil-minded. Also by failing to admit our power, we may become more susceptible to misusing or manipulating it. To have power is to have the ability to make mistakes. Yet the church should not be denied female leadership because some women wish to avoid making the same mistakes they have accused men of making. Women, like men, do and will abuse power. However, if both men and women share authority jointly, take equal responsibility for the welfare and governance of the church, and respect the power and limitations of each other, corruption will become less likely.

Male Privilege

Many Mormon women reject priesthood because they equate it with maleness and feel that to exercise priesthood would be contrary to their nature as women. This is an understandable objection since our scriptural and church models for priesthood are almost always men. Many Mormon women would feel strange or afraid to say the word priestess aloud. Perhaps if women could see other women using the priesthood and acting in leadership roles, then they would not connect it with maleness. When I first read about Eliza R. Snow, Bathsheba Smith, and other early Mormon women acting as priestesses, it made the notion of women and priesthood more acceptable to me. We need more female role models, and we need to emphasize the heroines we have in our scriptures and history.

We must also address the male-centered priesthood language in church practice, literature, and scriptures.

Naming Women's Priesthood

In the religious sphere how do we include female discourse? Should there be separate terms to emphasize differences or should there be neutral terms to show commonality? Or should we employ both simultaneously? For example, should we refer to the power of God held by women as priesthood or priestesshood? And what about priesthood offices? We already have feminine forms for some terms: prophetess for prophet, priestess for priest, matriarch for patriarch, deaconess for deacon, presidentess for president (although president may sound better for both). The title "teacher" can also be applied to men and women alike. But what about elder? Perhaps the word matron could serve as a counterpart to elder. They share the same archaic quality; they both carry connotations of age and wisdom. Moreover, the word is connected to the matron or chief female temple worker as well as being related to the title "Matronit" used in the Jewish mystical tradition to refer to a goddess figure.

And what about the priestly orders: Levitical, Aaronic, Patriarchal, Melchizedek, Enoch? Should they be used or should women be members of orders named after women of similar spiritual stature? If so, whose names should be used? Perhaps we can identify female equivalents for these orders. For example, Miriam, the sister of Moses and Aaron, may be an appropriate name to designate the women's lesser priesthood order: hence, the Miriamic priesthood. Sarah could serve as the model for the matriarchal priesthood as Abraham serves as a model for the patriarchal. The word Melchizedek could continue to serve as the name of the high priesthood for both men and women because it is not really a man's name but an ancient title derived from two Hebrew roots: *melek* meaning "king" or "queen," and *zedek* meaning "righteousness." Thus Melchizedek can mean either "queen of righteousness" or "king of righteousness." Women may still dislike the term because it has been associated for such a long time with men. It would be a shame though to lose a term that can mean "queen of righteousness" as well as "king of righteousness" and that can symbolize the union of male and female in the greater priesthood.

Such changes in terminology would emphasize women as priestess models. Elizabeth and Mary were counterparts to John the Baptist or forerunners, Eliases,[*] who came to prepare the way of the Lord. Mary Magdalene was a counterpart to Elijah, holding the sealing power and anointing Jesus for his resurrection from the dead, even as Elijah anointed the widow's son at Sereptah [1 Kings 17: 7–16]. Eve served as a counterpart to Jesus himself: she acted to bring about mortal life as he acted to bring about eternal life. Emphasis could be placed on spiritual and scriptural heroines, such as Pharaoh's daughter and her ladies in waiting who saved and raised Moses. Young Mormon women could be taught more about Esther, Ruth, Naomi, Huldah, Deborah, Junia, Phoebe, and others who filled prophetic and priestly roles.

Because the temple is the source of priesthood for women, females should play more prominent roles in the endowment ceremony. Now the only female role is that of Eve, but others could be introduced by revelation. Joseph Smith indicated that the term "Elohim" refers to a council of Gods; thus, female deities could be included. Peter, James, and John could be joined by Mary, Martha, and Mary Magdalene. If the attention of church leaders and members were directed to such women, they would become the subject of study, and perhaps their doings and sayings would become a more familiar part of Mormon literature.

Transformation of Priesthood Structure and Holy Order

Is it possible to include women in the priesthood structure without creating a separate priesthood for each gender or forcing women into traditional male priesthood roles? Male and female priesthoods should certainly not be two separate churches. Besides such separation does not promote equality, since separate but equal is never really equal. And such an arrangement is inimical to community. After all the principal purpose of priesthood is to unite, to heal, to atone (to make at one). On the other hand becoming one should not obliterate the distinction between male and female or abolish the concepts of sisterhood and brotherhood, which are now reinforced through the female Relief Society organization and the male priesthood quorums.

The temple ceremony may serve as a useful model because it incorporates both separation and union of females and males as well as of individuals and communities. The endowment constitutes an individual, spiritual journey that ends in the presence of God, which represents Zion, the community of saints—the unity of men and women (the church) and a united priestly order (the Holy Order of

[*]Elias is often used in the Bible as a version of the name Elijah; Toscano uses the term "Elias" here in the sense given by Matthew 17:12–13.

God). In the temple men and women strive individually and together to attain this blessed state.

Women and men need structures that will allow them to work separately and together, to be independent and interdependent, to maintain their individual identities, while simultaneously being interlinked. On a practical level this concept could be used to define church offices such as ward bishop, stake president, and even church president as joint offices held by a man and a woman or a married couple working as co-holders of the office, each with her or his own vote.[4] Single members could also serve in these offices alone or with a counterpart of the opposite sex. Practical benefits could be seen in personal interviews, where females from age twelve could be interviewed by a female bishop or female stake president instead of a male. Using male/female partnerships is a way to reconstitute the offices of the church to reflect the equality of male and female in the priesthood, to prevent rivalry between the sexes, and to further the spiritual well-being of the church.

What I am advocating is not simply an incorporation of women into a male system. I am calling for a transformation of the entire Mormon priesthood system. I am asking for the acceptance of the fullness of the priesthood and the Holy Order of God, in which female and male priesthood holders work together as equals. Including women in the priesthood structure would recenter the church and cause us to see everything in a new light. It would require us to rethink the meaning and essence of priesthood, to recognize the spiritual foundation upon which priesthood rests, to see the connection between the gospel that promises us spiritual rebirth and the priesthood that promises us spiritual maturation, and to understand priesthood as the necessary expression of the divine will that gives life and light to all things. Such a transformation would compel us to restructure our language, our perceptions of history, our expectations of the future, and our appreciation of the meaning of male and female. And in time such a change would move us away from restricted and outmoded models of priesthood hierarchy toward the establishment of a genuine religious community governed by a true lay priesthood, the body of Christ, a kingdom of priestesses and priests, with equal right to know and speak in the name of the Godhead, in whose image we are made, male and female.

Notes

1. Andrew F. Ehat and Lyndon W. Cook, eds., *The Words of Joseph Smith* (Provo, UT: Religious Studies Center, Brigham Young University, 1980), 116.
2. Bruce R. McConkie, *Mormon Doctrine* (Salt Lake City: Bookcraft, 1966), 377.
3. See Margaret Merrill Toscano and Paul James Toscano, *Strangers in Paradox: Explorations in Mormon Theology* (Salt Lake City: Signature Books, 1990), 150.
4. In Newell, "Gifts of the Spirit: Women's Share," in Maureen Ursenbach Beecher and Lavina Fielding Anderson, eds., *Sisters in Spirit: Mormon Women in Historical and Cultural Perspective* (Urbana: University of Illinois Press, 1987). Also, the *Young Women's Journal* reported in 1896 that "the Seventy's wife bears the priesthood of the Seventy in connection with her husband, and shares in its responsibilities" (7:398).

Lavina Fielding Anderson (1944–), "The LDS Intellectual Community and Church Leadership: A Contemporary Chronology" (1992)

In July 1992, Margaret and Paul Toscano, Lavina Fielding Anderson, Janice Merrill Allred, and others founded the Mormon Alliance, a grassroots organization that sought to document instances of what it termed "ecclesiastical abuse" or "spiritual abuse" in the LDS Church and to promote better understanding among members and leaders of the potentially abusive aspects of ecclesiastical relationships. "Ecclesiastical abuse occurs when a Church officer, acting in his official capacity and using the weight of his (less frequently her) office, coerces compliance, imposes his personal opinions as Church doctrine or policy, or resorts to such power plays as threats, intimidation, and punishment to insure that his views prevail in a conflict of opinions. The suggestion is always that the member has weak faith, or inadequate testimony, and lacks commitment to the Church," Anderson and Allred explained. "Spiritual abuse occurs when a member, through the actions of another, is made to feel limited or lacking in free agency, diminished in value in the eyes of God, unworthy to pray, unworthy or incapable of receiving answers to prayer, outside the influence of Christ's atonement, and excluded from the Savior's love and grace." Its organizers founded the Alliance after noting a pattern of heavy-handed LDS Church institutional interactions with members whose perspectives were viewed as unorthodox or who addressed in their writing or scholarship matters considered sensitive by the Church. At an August 1992 conference, Lavina Fielding Anderson presented an extensive chronology documenting what she later described as an "increasingly unhealthy relationship between the Church and its intellectuals and feminists"; at that same conference, news broke that the LDS Church maintained a "Strengthening the Members" committee to monitor such members, including keeping files of their writings. In the year that followed, Anderson tracked what seemed to be an escalation in acts of discipline and intimidation, including institutional and public reprisals against BYU faculty members Cecilia Konchar Farr and Martha Sonntag Bradley (see Konchar Farr's essays anthologized in this volume) and statements from high-ranking Church leaders declaring feminists, gays and lesbians, and intellectuals as "dangers" to the Church. She spoke out by publishing a chronicle of anti-feminist intimidation in the December 1992 *Mormon Women's Forum Quarterly* and a long article documenting instances of "spiritual" or "ecclesiastical abuse" in *Dialogue: A Journal of Mormon Thought*. In September 1993, Anderson herself was called into a disciplinary court and excommunicated. The conclusion to her chronology, reprinted here, urges a feminist intervention to correct what she described as a "power differential" in the "hierarchical" LDS Church structure that was harmful to the well-being of Church members and the Mormon community.

Sources

Anderson, Lavina Fielding. "The LDS Intellectual Community and Church Leadership: A Contemporary Chronology." *Dialogue: A Journal of Mormon Thought* 26.1 (1993): 7–64.

References and Further Reading

Anderson, Lavina Fielding, and Janice Merrill Allred. *Case Reports of the Mormon Alliance.* Vols. 1–3. Salt Lake City: Mormon Alliance, 1996–1997.

Anderson, Lavina Fielding, and Armand L. Mauss. "The Church and Its Scholars: Ten Years After: Two Perspectives." *Sunstone* 128 (July 2003): 13–23.

"THE LDS INTELLECTUAL COMMUNITY AND CHURCH LEADERSHIP: A CONTEMPORARY CHRONOLOGY"

First, we must speak up. We must stop keeping "bad" secrets when our church acts in an abusive way. We must share our stories and our pain. When we feel isolated, judged, and rejected, it is easy to give up, to allow ourselves to become marginalized, and to accept the devaluation as accurate. If we silence ourselves or allow others to silence us, we will deny the validity of our experience, undermine the foundations of authenticity in our personal spirituality, and impoverish our collective life as a faith community. During the 1970s and 1980s I was an observer and occasionally a co-worker as a handful of modern women scholars discovered Mormon women's history. They did it from the documents. No living tradition had survived of the spiritual gifts and powers of Mormon women, of how they saw themselves, of their vision for women of the church and the world. By failing to perpetuate the past as a living tradition, the women and men who were its guardians had erased it. I cannot adequately express how much this hurt me. I learned for myself that silence and self-censorship are terrible wrongs. Reducing the diversity of voices in a community to a single, official voice erases us. We must join in the on-going dialogue between individual and community out of necessity and also out of love.

Second, we must protest injustice, unrighteousness, and wrong. I pay my church the compliment of thinking that it espouses the ideals of justice and fairness. I am confused when leaders confiscate temple recommends of members who publicly praise the church's actions. Blacklists, secret files, and intimidation violate my American sense of fair play and my legal expectation of due process. They violate the ideal that truth is best served by an open interchange, that disagreement can be both courteous and clarifying, and that differences are not automatically dangerous. Most importantly I am dismayed when the organization that teaches me to honor the truth and to act with integrity seems to violate those very principles in its behavior. I am bewildered and grieved when my church talks honorably from one script and acts ignobly from another. Some of the incidents I have mentioned make me cry out with James: "My brethren, these things ought not so to be" (James 3:10).

Third, we must defend each other. Some official actions are obvious attempts to marginalize and punish intellectuals and feminists. Although some intellectuals and feminists may well be bitter, those I know personally are not trying to undermine the faith of others, do not hate the church, and are not cynical about their personal faith. To the extent that there is anti-intellectualism and anti-feminism in the church's response, it is unfair. Also unfair are any malice and irresponsibility in the activities of intellectuals and feminists. We need to provide honest feedback to each other, as well as express caring and concern for each other. If I am saying excessive, irresponsible things, I need to know it. And I will hear it most clearly from my friends. We must sustain and support individuals who are experiencing ecclesiastical harassment. Such support will help prevent overreactions and speed the healing process in the survivor. Supportive observers may also help prevent some ecclesiastical abuse.

Fourth, we must protest, expose, and work against an internal espionage system that creates and maintains secret files on members of the church. If there were some attempt to maintain a full and complete record—including the record of church service, the lives influenced for good, and the individual's spiritual strength—I might feel differently. I might also feel differently if individuals had access to their files. But they are secretly maintained and seem to be exclusively accusatory in their content. I find such an activity unworthy in every way of the Church of Jesus Christ.

Fifth, we must be more assertive in dealing with our leaders. I have had good experiences with my stake president. But I am repelled by reports of puppet interviews, where a stake president or bishop is ordered to interview and/or punish a member on information secretly supplied by ecclesiastical superiors. Such a procedure does not uphold the ideal of confidentiality. Rather it violates the trust that should exist between member and leader, and we should say so. Furthermore the stake president, not the offended general authority, is required to deal with the offender. This process short-circuits the scriptural injunction of face-to-face confrontation, including "reproving betimes with sharpness, when moved upon by the Holy Ghost; and then showing forth afterwards an increase of love" (D&C 121:43). Perhaps more importantly such a system isolates and insulates leaders from members. These leaders create hostile stereotypes of members who are "evil" and "deserve" to be punished and excluded. Similarly members judge and stereotype faceless and voiceless general authorities who are known to them only through punitive intermediaries. Both behaviors are equally damaging.

Sixth, we need to support, encourage, and sustain ecclesiastical leaders who also value honesty, integrity, and nurturing. Michael Quinn's stake president is one heartening example. In March 1992 David Knowlton movingly told a large audience at Sunstone in Washington, D.C., how, after repeated abrasive encounters with his stake president, he went to his bishop who listened, asked him how he felt, and gave him a blessing. David reported that he could not stop weeping during this interview, which did much to heal his wounds.

And seventh, we must seek humility as a prerequisite for a more loving, a less fearful, community. The apostle Paul queried, "Am I therefore become your enemy, because I tell you the truth?" (Gal. 4:16) My prayers for the church's ecclesiastical officers have never been more sincere than during the past few months, even when my sorrow and anguish have been most intense.

I consider myself to be simultaneously a loyal Latter-day Saint, an intellectual, and a feminist. My identity involves all three elements. I cannot truncate my life by excising one or more elements in a misguided search for simplicity. In Nauvoo, black convert Cathy Stokes changed my life forever by telling me, "When I went to the temple, I consecrated all of me. That included my blackness. If the Lord can use it, it's his." She set me on the road to realizing that the Lord wanted all of me, even the parts that the church did not want and could not use. With the utmost reverence I declare that I have tried to make a full consecration.

White Roses: Statement (1993)

In September 1993, tensions between the LDS Church and Mormon feminists and intellectuals peaked with the excommunications or disfellowshipments of six Mormons who had written or spoken out about issues considered sensitive by Church leaders. Among those excommunicated were Mormon feminists Lavina Fielding Anderson, Maxine Hanks, and Lynne Kanavel Whitesides, president of the Mormon Women's Forum. Paul Toscano and Michael Quinn, both of whom had written about Mormon theology and history from feminist perspectives, were also excommunicated. Also in September 1993, Margaret Toscano received a letter from LDS Church officials instructing her that if she continued to speak or publish her writings on Mormon history and doctrine, she, too, would be brought into a disciplinary court. In this difficult moment, some Mormon feminists walked away from the Church or resigned their membership. Others who were fearful of facing a similar fate and its potentially devastating consequences—excommunication could bring loss of family and friends and even employment with the LDS Church or a Church-owned university like BYU—resolved to go silent. Many mourned the climate of fear, anger, and suspicion gripping the faith they loved. In response to the purge of scholars and feminists, Brigham Young University professor and feminist literary scholar Gail Turley Houston conceived of a gesture of mercy, healing, and peace. Houston helped organize Mormon feminists and progressives in 118 cities around the world to contribute to the purchase of one thousand white roses to be delivered to LDS Church headquarters in downtown Salt Lake City between the morning and afternoon Saturday sessions of the Church's semi-annual General Conference. Shirley Paxman of Provo, Utah, and Irene Bates, both long associated with Mormon feminist forums like the Alice Louise Reynolds and Algie Ballif Forums, read the following statement and delivered the flowers to the Church's Presiding Bishop. Houston was fired from Brigham Young University in 1996 for speaking her feminist beliefs in public.

Source

"White Roses Statement." *Mormon Women's Forum Quarterly* 4.4 (December 1993): 7.

"WHITE ROSES STATEMENT"

In the spirit of peace, we Latter-day Saints from around the world send these thousand white roses to the General Authorities who have been called to serve Jesus Christ and the members of his church. We entreat you to accept these flowers as a symbol of our devotion to Christ's Gospel of love, mercy, faith and hope. The roses symbolize our support both of the Church and of the members who have recently had disciplinary action taken against them. Therefore, in the spirit of peace, we make this appeal: let the fear and reprisals end. Though the times are challenging and difficult, we find hope in the belief that we can face such challenges with dignity and grace with the belief that God cherishes diversity, that He loves all his children, and that He does not seek to exclude any who love him from membership in his Church.

Laurel Thatcher Ulrich (1938–), "Border Crossings" (1994)

Mormon feminist pioneer Laurel Thatcher Ulrich responded to the excommunications of 1993 with a powerful reassertion of Mormon feminist identity. Press coverage of the excommunications tended to sensationalize the plight of Mormon feminists and to caricature the Mormon faith as flatly patriarchal; meanwhile, some members of the LDS Church seized on the excommunications as a premise for questioning the authenticity of Mormons with feminist convictions. As a rejoinder to Mormons and non-Mormons who insisted that Mormon feminism was an impossibility or an "oxymoron," Ulrich boldly claims for Mormon feminists the right to define their identity on their own terms. Mormon feminism, according to Ulrich, is a complex and multiple identity, capable of dynamism, independence, and resilience.

Source

Ulrich, Laurel Thatcher. "Border Crossings." *Dialogue: A Journal of Mormon Thought* 27.2 (1994): 1–7.

"BORDER CROSSINGS"

It happened again as I was walking through the New Hampshire woods with a woman I knew only slightly. We had been chatting amiably when the words "Mormon feminist" escaped my mouth. From the expression on her face, I knew exactly what she was going to say.

"Mormon feminist! That sounds like an oxymoron!"

I bristled, though I didn't mean to, annoyed at having to explain myself once again.

Yes, I am an active, believing Mormon. I was baptized at the age of eight, graduated from seminary, and married in the Salt Lake temple. For thirty-five years I have tried to remain true to my temple covenants, including the one about consecrating my time and talents to the church. I have taught early morning seminary, written road shows, edited the stake newsletter, and picked apples, plums, peaches, and pears at the stake welfare farm. With my husband, I recently completed my third stint as Gospel Doctrine teacher in our ward.

And, yes, I am a feminist. I deplore teachings, policies, or attitudes that deny women their full stature as human beings, and I have tried to act on that conviction in my personal and professional life. I have written two books and more than a dozen articles in women's history. I give money to the day care coalition in my town and the women's political caucus in my state. I helped draft my university's non-sexist language policy.

I am quite aware that some people consider these commitments incompatible. A couple of years ago, a member of the Women's Commission at my university, learning that I was Mormon, said in astonishment, "I am surprised your church hasn't thrown you out long ago." "Thrown me out!" I gasped. "I'm a pillar of my congregation." The very same day I was queried by an LDS acquaintance I had not seen for several years. Hearing about my awards for feminist scholarship, she asked earnestly, "Do you go to church? Do you bear your testimony?" I groaned and told her, tongue in cheek, that I was an agnostic Gospel Doctrine teacher.

I am not an oxyMormon. I am a Mormon. And a feminist. As a daughter of God, I claim the right to all my gifts. As a Mormon, I embrace ideals of equality and a critique of power that also shaped early feminism. Yet my commitment to the Church of Jesus Christ pushes me beyond a mere concern for "rights." As a feminist I know that structures matter, that formal authority makes a difference in the way people think as well as behave, that institutional arrangements can lock in prejudice, yet I also know that legal protection is hollow without spiritual transformation and that the right spirit can transform a seemingly repressive system. I have tasted equal worship in the Church of Jesus Christ of Latter-day Saints. Unfortunately, I have also observed the smug condescension of men who believe they have been called as lord and tutor. Against such behavior I assert both my Mormonism and feminism.

To claim multiple identities is to assert the insufficiency of any one label, including Mormonism. According to my Compact Oxford English Dictionary, an oxymoron is not simply a self-contradictory expression like "freezing heat" or "swampy desert." It is a rhetorical figure in which contradictory or incongruous terms are intentionally joined in order to complicate or enlarge meaning. Although in current usage the word is "often loosely or erroneously used as if merely a contradiction in terms," a true oxymoron is "an expression in its superficial or literal meaning self-contradictory or absurd, but involving a point." The phrase "Mormon feminist" can work that way. Those who assume Mormonism is inherently hostile to women or, conversely, that feminism undermines faith, sniff at the phrase. But when confronted with a real person claiming to be both things at once, they are forced to reconsider their assumptions. Feminism may be larger than they imagined and Mormonism more flexible.

When anxious church leaders denounce feminists they compound the distortion. Each group reduces the other to its own worst nightmare, and the war is on. In such a climate it is tempting to run for shelter, saying less about feminism among Mormons and less about Mormonism everywhere else. But a silence based on fear is no solution. As long as the issues are there, unacknowledged and unresolved, the anger and hostility will remain. I think it is better to gently but consistently tell the truth. I am a Mormon and a feminist.

A few years ago I attended an invitational conference in U.S. women's history. The organizers, fully committed to diversity, had gone out of their way to include women from large and small colleges, from every part of the United States, and from many minority groups. When one scholar expressed surprise that no one from BYU had been invited, a well-known nineteenth-century historian responded, "Oh, we don't want them!" Orthodoxy feels the same wherever it is found. Certainly there is a need for boundaries, for rigorous defense of ideas and ideals that matter, but defenders of every faith too often violate their own ideals in the very act of defending them. The gospel of Jesus Christ teaches us that light falls across borders, that the sun in its revolutions brightens both sides of a wall, spilling through the spaces in our fences. Mormon intellectuals should not forget that Jesus gathered his disciples from among sinners, publicans, and pharisees, even zealous pharisees like Paul, a man who knew what it meant to live in a multi-cultural world. To the saints at Ephesus, Paul wrote: "For he is our peace, who hath made both one, and hath broken down the middle wall of partition between us" (Eph. 2:14).

I do not apologize for what I am—an intellectual who reveres the scriptures; a Sunbeam teacher who would sooner write than eat; a transplanted westerner at home in the east. I can no more deny my religious identity than I can divest myself of my Thatcher freckles or my Rocky Mountain accent. Nor would I discard my feminist values. The women's movement has refreshed my life like the "sea change" that sometimes hits my town in those steamy, grey days so common on the east coast in mid-summer. At such moments a blue, almost Western, sky breaks through the haze.

Janice Merrill Allred (1947–), Excerpts from "Toward a Mormon Theology of God the Mother" (1994)

Janice Merrill Allred was born in Mesa, Arizona, to a family with deep roots in the Mormon movement; she is the sister of the scholar and theologian Margaret Merrill Toscano (see her essays anthologized in this volume). In 1991, Allred began a systematic theological study of Mother in Heaven. Earlier Mormon feminist writers had engaged the subject through historical research or imaginative writing, but Allred assumed a rigorously theological approach to Heavenly Mother's contradictory place in Mormon doctrine. On the one hand, Joseph Smith had revealed that God was a married couple—a coequal and coeternal Father and Mother, but LDS Church teachings consistently presented the Godhead as three distinct male-gendered beings. "Toward a Mormon Theology of God the Mother" seeks to reconcile this seeming paradox. In 1992, while pregnant with her ninth child and as tensions between the LDS Church and Mormon feminists and intellectuals were deepening, Allred deliberated whether or not to present a version of this essay at the Sunstone Symposium, a forum for discussion of Mormon belief, thought, and experience. "I knew that I was taking a risk by choosing to write about God the Mother," Allred later wrote. "[LDS Church] President Gordon B. Hinckley had given an address to the Regional Representatives in April 1991, warning them to beware of 'small beginnings of apostasy.' Prayers to Mother in Heaven were cited as an example. I knew of several women who had been released from callings and chastised just for *talking* about the Heavenly Mother. However, the theology of God the Mother was a topic I very much wanted to write about. If female and male are equal, then God must also be female. I do not believe in a godhead that does not include God the Mother." She resolved to deliver her paper at the Sunstone Symposium in August 1992. In November 1992, she was called into a meeting with a local Church leader who had been instructed by LDS Church officials in Salt Lake City to monitor her. Allred continued under close scrutiny for the next eighteen months, meeting regularly with ecclesiastical leaders who pressured her not to publish her writings. Her essay "Toward a Mormon Theology of God the Mother" appeared in *Dialogue: A Journal of Mormon Thought* in 1994. Allred was excommunicated in 1995.

Source

Allred, Janice Merrill. "Toward a Mormon Theology of God the Mother." *Dialogue: A Journal of Mormon Thought* 27.2 (1994): 15–39. Republished in Janice Allred, *God the Mother and Other Theological Essays* (Salt Lake City: Signature Books, 1997): 42–68.

References and Further Reading

Allred, Janice Merrill. "My Controversy with the Church." *Mormon Women's Forum: An LDS Feminist Quarterly* 6.1 (Spring 1995): 1–16.
Allred, Janice Merrill. "White Bird Flying: My Struggle for a More Loving, Tolerant, and Egalitarian Church," in *Case Reports of the Mormon Alliance*, vol. 2, ed. Lavina Fielding Anderson and Janice Merrill Allred, 117–323. Salt Lake City: Mormon Alliance, 1996.

EXCERPTS FROM "TOWARD A MORMON THEOLOGY OF GOD THE MOTHER"

"What kind of a being is God?" inquired Joseph Smith. "I will tell you & hear it O Earth! God who sits in yonder heavens is a man like yourselves.... It is the first principle to know that we may converse with him and that he was once a man like us, and the Father was on an earth like us."[1] He also said, "If men do not comprehend the character of God they do not comprehend themselves."[2] Today Mormon women say, "If I do not comprehend the character of God the Mother, I cannot comprehend myself." They ask, "What kind of a being is she?" From Mormon theology there is one thing we can conclude: she is a woman like us; she has a woman's body. Without it she could not be our mother.

Feminist theologians have demonstrated the need for the feminine principle in our concept of deity. They have argued that picturing God as male leads to valuing masculine attributes, values, and experience over feminine ones and contributes to the oppression of women. The symbol of the Goddess is necessary, they say, to affirm the goodness of the feminine, to enable women to claim their female power, and to acknowledge the goodness of the female body. Ironically, the vast majority of them do not believe that the Goddess possesses a real female body.

It would seem that Mormons who have believed for over a hundred years in the real existence of the Goddess, the Mother in Heaven, should be far ahead of other Christians in developing a theology of God the Mother. However, our belief in her as a real person puts us at a disadvantage. If the Goddess is merely a symbol of deity, as the male God is also a symbol, then certainly God can be pictured as either male or female with equal validity. Joseph Smith, after asking what kind of a being God is, asked his congregation, "Have any of you seen or heard him or communed with him?"[3]

For Mormon theology this is a very important question. God must reveal himself or we have no knowledge of him. Must we then wait for a revelation of the Mother before we have any knowledge of her? The answer is both "Yes" and "No." We must be aware of the possibility of idolatry, of creating her in our own image, of making her into what we conceive the perfect woman should be, of using our images of her to control or manipulate others. On the other hand, we should also recognize the importance of our own seeking after God. Comprehending ourselves is as vital to comprehending God as comprehending God is essential to comprehending ourselves. Our own experiences, our loneliness, our communion with others, our sorrows, our joys, our sins, our striving for righteousness, our demand for justice, our finding forgiveness, our reaching out to God for knowledge and comfort are all experiences with the divine. And we should not assume that there has been no revelation of the Mother or that waiting for her to reveal herself need be entirely passive.

In this essay I attempt to reinterpret the Mormon concept of the Godhead. This interpretation is based on three convictions. I believe that God the Mother is equal to God the Father in divinity, power, and perfection. I believe that God, both Father and Mother, is deeply involved in our mortality and immortality. I also believe that God the Father has revealed himself in the person of Jesus Christ. Although he is male, for me he is an adequate model. He modeled many roles for us—father, mother, teacher, friend, son, lover, servant, lord—and also many attributes. If he were the only God, he would be enough. But there is another god and she has a woman's body like mine. I want to know her, not simply as a model, but as a person. That she is God as well as woman is as important for men as it is for women as it affirms the equality of male and female and of masculine and feminine attributes and values. At the same time I must add that I am in no way whatsoever attempting an official reinterpretation of LDS doctrine; that prerogative rests solely with the leaders of the church. I am interested simply in offering a possibly new understanding and appreciation of the Mother based on my own reading and personal reflection.

The doctrine of the Godhead presently taught by the Latter-day Saint church is that the Godhead consists of three distinct individuals or personages. These personages are God the Father, his son Jesus Christ, and the Holy Ghost. Each of these individuals has a particular mission in relation to humanity; God the Father is the father of all the spirits of mortal beings. He is the ultimate source of all power and knowledge, and the other two members of the Godhead are subordinate to him. Jesus Christ is the Son of the Father; he is the first born of the spirit children of God and the only begotten of the Father in the flesh. This enabled him to become the Redeemer and Savior of humankind. Because of his death and resurrection everyone will be resurrected, and through his atonement all who repent and believe in him will be forgiven of their sins and receive eternal life. Jesus represents the Father and acts as his agent. The Holy Ghost, unlike the Father and the Son who possess bodies of flesh and bone, is a personage of spirit. He is one of the spirit children of God the Father and has the mission of revealing truth and testifying of the Father and the Son. He is also called the Comforter because he gives peace, hope, and comfort.

Although Mormons believe that we have a Heavenly Mother, she is not included in the Godhead. Does this mean that she is not also God? Does this mean that she has no mission to perform in relation to our mortal probation, that her role is restricted to giving birth to our spirits and nurturing us in our premortal lives? I find such conclusions unacceptable. God the Mother must be equal to God the

Father; she must play an equally active role in bringing to pass the immortality and eternal life of man and woman.

The Book of Mormon tells us of revelations given to a few which the prophets were not permitted to write or which they were commanded to seal up until a later time, and the Doctrine and Covenants speaks of knowledge "that has not been revealed since the world was until now; a time to come in the which nothing shall be withheld, whether there be one God or many gods, they shall be manifest" (121:26, 28). One God that has not been manifest is the Mother. Surely this is a promise that she will be revealed. Also the fact that she is not directly revealed in the scriptures does not necessarily lead to the conclusion that the scriptures have nothing to say about her. Indeed, new revelations always demand a reinterpretation of scripture and permit us to see things and understand things in ways we previously could not.

The Mother in the Godhead

We now look for the Mother. She is present in the scriptures, but she is hidden; even as we do not see light in a room but see the room and all things in it by the light which is present, so is she in the scriptures.

Nephi explains why Jesus was baptized: to obey the Father in keeping his commandments and to set an example for us. "And he said unto the children of men, Follow thou me" (2 Ne. 31:10). In Doctrine and Covenants 132:6 the Lord reveals a "new and everlasting covenant . . . [which] was instituted for the fulness of my glory; and he that receiveth a fulness thereof must and shall abide the law." The new and everlasting covenant is the covenant of eternal marriage. As we have seen, those who inherit celestial glory receive a fullness of God's glory and are called gods. According to the revelation on eternal marriage, those who do not marry by the new and everlasting covenant and are not sealed by the Holy Spirit of Promise "cannot be enlarged, but remain separately and singly, without exaltation, in their saved condition, to all eternity; and from henceforth are not gods," but those who do marry by the new and everlasting covenant and are sealed by the Holy Spirit of Promise "shall. . . be gods, because they have all power." If the Lord requires us to keep the law of celestial marriage to become gods, then Jesus himself must certainly keep it. The laws he institutes are to make us like him. In the celestial glory all are equal; therefore the daughters of God are equal to the sons of God and God the Mother is equal to God the Father in power, might, and dominion.

If the gods are divine couples, then we can assume that God himself is also a divine couple, that God the Father, as a being of spirit and body, is eternally joined to God the Mother, also a being of spirit and body. "The Father" then must also mean "the Mother" as "sons of God" certainly includes "daughters of God."

This suggests another way of interpreting the Godhead. The Father is the divine couple, Father and Mother, each possessing a spirit and a glorified body.

They must together be the source of light or spirit which permeates all things. If the name "the Father" refers to the union of the two personages who together are God, then perhaps the other two names in the Godhead refer to them separately. As we have seen, "the Son" refers to the flesh, so the Lord or Jehovah, as the embodied God, is the Son. But the name "the Son," as Abinadi points out, more specifically points to his mission as the Redeemer, to his taking on himself a mortal body to redeem us from sin. Perhaps, then, the Holy Ghost is the name of the Mother which refers to her work among us in mortality.

One objection that has been made to the suggestion that the Holy Ghost is the Mother is that the Holy Ghost is a personage of spirit but the Mother must have an immortal, glorified body as the Father does. Indeed, this same objection is likely to be raised against the idea that Jesus is God the Father. If Jesus is God the Father, it will be argued, then he must have had an immortal, physical body before he took on himself a mortal body. But many Mormons will object that the scriptures teach that the resurrected body and spirit are inseparably connected, so Jesus must have been a personage of spirit before he became a mortal man and thus he could not have been God the Father. However, given the teachings of Joseph Smith about the importance of the body—that all beings with bodies have power over those who do not, that it was necessary for us to obtain bodies to become like God—it is impossible that Jesus, the Lord God, the Creator of heaven and earth, the Holy One of Israel could have been what he was and have done all he did without a body. Although a resurrected person is not subject to death in the sense that his body and spirit will separate without his will or control, it may be that he has the power to separate his body and spirit if he so desires.

If it was possible for the Lord to lay down his immortal body to take on mortal flesh, then surely it is also possible for the Mother to lay down her immortal body to become the Holy Ghost.

The scriptures refer to the Holy Ghost, the Holy Spirit, the Spirit, the Spirit of God, the Spirit of the Lord, the Spirit of Christ, the Comforter, and the Spirit of truth. Two possible meanings that we have ascertained for these names are the personal spirit of Jesus Christ and the substance or power that emanates from God and pervades all things in differing degrees. The scriptures do not make it clear whether the Holy Ghost is an individual being or a power. However, there are several passages which declare that the Father, Son, and the Holy Ghost are one God. How are we to interpret this? The official doctrine of the LDS church at this time is, as has been pointed out, that they are three distinct individuals. I have tried to show from the scriptures that the Son is one individual, who is also called the Lord, God, and our Redeemer, and that the name "the Father," when it refers to one individual, refers to the same person who is Jesus Christ. The Holy Ghost could also be interpreted as the power of God, since Jesus refers to himself as the Spirit of truth and the names "my Spirit," "Spirit of the Lord," "Spirit of God," etc., are actually used more frequently than and often synonymously with the Holy

Ghost. Thus the names "Father," "Son," and "Holy Ghost" could all refer to one individual God, but I would argue that this interpretation would also require us to recognize God as Mother, Daughter, and Holy Ghost.

There are, however, reasons to believe that there is an individual being, a god distinct from Jesus Christ, called the Holy Ghost who has a special mission to perform among humans. Nephi taught his people that the words of Christ are given by the power of the Holy Ghost. "I said unto you that after ye had received the Holy Ghost ye could speak with the tongue of angels. . . . Angels speak by the power of the Holy Ghost; wherefore they speak the words of Christ" (2 Ne. 32:2–3). The connection between angels and the Holy Ghost is interesting. Angels are messengers of God who are seen as well as heard; whoever is ministered to by an angel knows he has seen and heard a being distinct and different from himself. The Holy Ghost, however, speaks to the mind and heart (D&C 8:2). It is sometimes difficult to distinguish her voice from our own inner voice. The reason she is not clearly pointed out as an individual in the scriptures is because she does not often manifest herself as an individual distinct from ourselves. It is also possible that there are many spirits working with the Holy Ghost to perform her work.

Jesus, during the Last Supper, spoke of two distinct comforters; one he called the Holy Ghost and the Spirit of Truth, the other he also called the Spirit of truth. Joseph Smith taught that the Second Comforter was Jesus Christ himself.[4] He also taught that the Holy Ghost is a personage of spirit who is also God who also has a distinct mission to perform for us even as the Son atoned for our sins.[5]

Everlasting covenant was made between three personages before the organization of this earth, and relates to their dispensation of things to men on the earth; these personages, according to Abraham's record, are called God the first, the Creator; God the Second, the Redeemer; and God the Third, the witness or Testator.[6]

But numerous scriptures testify that the being who would become Jesus Christ created the earth. And in Moses 6:8–9 we read, "In the day that God created man, in the likeness of God made he him; in the image of his own body, male and female, created he them." If God created male and female in the image of his own body then God the Creator must be the Divine Couple, a Man with a male body and a Woman with a female body. If God the Creator is the Divine Couple and God the Redeemer is the male part of the Divine Couple, then it is reasonable to conclude that God the Witness or Testator is the female part of God the Creator.

God himself came down among the children of men to redeem his people. He sacrificed his immortal body and took on himself a mortal body to become one of us and suffer the pains and sorrows of mortality. He sacrificed his mortal body so that he might conquer death and bring about the resurrection of all humanity and he suffered the pains of all our sins so that we might be redeemed.

God herself came down among the children of women to succor her children. She sacrificed her immortal body to be with us; she remains a spirit so that she can always be with us to enlighten, to comfort, to strengthen, to feel what we feel, to suffer with us in all our sins, in our loneliness and pain, and to encircle us in the arms of her love. She bears witness of Christ and leads us to him, teaching us of their will so that we might partake of eternal life in their kingdom.

Prophecies of the Revelation of the Mother

We find the Mother in the scriptures, then, wherever they speak of the Holy Ghost, but of course they do not identify the Holy Ghost as our Mother. When will she be revealed? Do the scriptures prophesy of her revelation?

Joseph Smith taught that in the last days many things would be revealed. The purpose of this is to bring about a whole and complete and perfect union. In order to do this, lost and hidden things from past ages will be revealed as well as things which never have been revealed (D&C 128:18). The Lord told Joseph Smith, "God shall give unto you knowledge by his Holy Spirit, yea, by the unspeakable gift of the Holy Ghost, that has not been revealed since the world was until now" (121:26). The clause "that has not been revealed since the world was until now" is usually considered to modify "knowledge." However, it could also modify "the Holy Ghost," yielding "The Holy Ghost has not been revealed since the world was until now," that is, in the last days. However, whether this interpretation is admitted the Lord says that there is "a time to come in the which nothing shall be withheld, whether there be one God or many, they shall be manifest" (v. 28). So the Holy Ghost, either as one with God or one of many gods, will be revealed in the last days. Therefore we should look for prophecies of her revelation among the prophecies of the last days. We should not expect to find any plain prophecies. Prophecies of the future are usually metaphoric, allusive, and suggestive rather than plain and since the Mother herself is hidden in the scriptures, we can expect that prophecies concerning her appearance will be even more hidden.

Worshipping the Mother

For Mormons the question of whether we should worship the Mother has focused mainly on whether we should pray to her.* Those who think we should not pray to her point out that Jesus commanded us to pray to the Father in his name and conclude that the only acceptable form of prayer is to address God as

---

*In April 1991, Gordon B. Hinckley, then a member of the First Presidency and later LDS Church president, responded to growing feminist-generated interest in the doctrine of Heavenly Mother by telling regional Church authorities that praying to Heavenly Mother constituted "the small beginnings of apostasy." In September 1991, at a churchwide women's meeting, he said, "In light of the instruction we have received from the Lord Himself, I regard it as inappropriate for anyone in the Church to pray to our Mother in Heaven. . . . The fact that we do not pray to our Mother in Heaven in no way belittles or denigrates her . . . none of us can add to or diminish the glory of her of whom we have no revealed knowledge." See "Daughters of God," *Ensign* (November 1991).

Heavenly Father and end the prayer in the name of Jesus Christ. I have tried to show that Jesus is the Father whom we worship. In Doctrine and Covenants 93, which clearly teaches that the Son is the Father, the Lord says, "I give unto you these sayings that you may understand and know how to worship, and know what you worship, that you may come unto the Father in my name." This means that Jesus Christ is the name of the Father which we should use when we pray to him and worship him. He has other names but we should call him Jesus Christ because that is the name through which we are saved. "Behold, Jesus Christ is the name which is given of the Father, and there is none other name given whereby man can be saved" (D&C 18:23). If the words are changed around a little this reads, "Behold, Jesus Christ is the name of the Father which is given." Mormons usually interpret this verse to mean that Jesus Christ is the name given by the Father, which is also a true interpretation, but it obscures the more fundamental one.

If we are to pray to Jesus, the question arises, "To whom did Jesus pray?" As a mortal man he prayed to the Father and as God among the Nephites he also prayed to the Father. But I have shown that the Father, the Man of Holiness, is Jesus Christ. Surely Jesus did not pray to himself. Perhaps the Father whom Jesus prayed to was the same being who on several occasions introduced Jesus as "My Beloved Son." Who was this? The voice is described in 3 Nephi 11:3.

> . . . and it was not a harsh voice, neither was it a loud voice; nevertheless, and notwithstanding it being a small voice it did pierce them that did hear it to the center, insomuch that there was no part of their frame that it did not cause to quake; yea, it did pierce them that did hear it to the very soul, and did cause their hearts to burn.

This description has several points in common with descriptions given of the voice of the Holy Ghost. It was a small voice but it pierced those who heard it to the center and it caused their hearts to burn. I believe that this being who bears witness of Jesus Christ is his Beloved, the Woman of Holiness, who is now the Holy Ghost. She calls him, "My Beloved, who is the Son."

Should we pray to the Mother? Although we are not commanded to pray to her, we are commanded to pray with her. "He that asketh in the Spirit asketh according to the will of God" (D&C 46:30). And when we pray, we invoke her presence (19:38). And our prayers are answered through her. Understanding this, we certainly may address her directly in our prayers. However, prayer, unlike ritual, does not require a form given by God in order to be efficacious. In its most fundamental sense prayer is a reaching out for God. The deepest longings of our hearts, our strivings for goodness, our hearts broken by our sins and failures, the pains of our humanity, our hope for love, and finally our deepest desires to know God are all prayers to him and her.

Jesus taught us to pray to the Father, not to set up barriers between us and God, but to remove them. God is your Father, he taught us. You need not be afraid to approach him because he loves you. You are fathers yourselves, he reminded us; you know that you respond to your children's pleas. "How much more will your Father which is in heaven give good things to them that ask him?" (Matt. 7:11) She is our Mother, a Mother who knows our needs before we can express them, a Mother who is here before we call out to her.

Which of you mothers, if your child cries out in the night, will not hear her cries and go to her and put your arms around her and comfort her? If you, then, being weak, know how to comfort your children, how much more does our Mother in Heaven comfort us when we stand in need of comfort?

Or which of you mothers, if your child is confused or has a problem, will not give him counsel? If you, then, lacking knowledge of the future, know how to counsel your children, how much more does our Heavenly Mother guide us when we ask to know what we should do?

Or which of you mothers, if your child asks you a question, will send him away? If you, then, being ignorant of many things, know how to enlighten your children, how much more does our Mother in Heaven give truth to those who seek it?

Or which of you mothers does not know that your children need you to be with them? If you, then, being selfish, will sacrifice to be with your children, how much more is our Mother, not in heaven, but here with us?

Notes

1. Andrew F. Ehat and Lyndon W. Cook, eds., *The Words of Joseph Smith* (Provo, UT: BYU Religious Studies Center, 1980), 344.
2. Ibid., 340.
3. Ibid., 344.
4. Ibid., 4–5.
5. Ibid., 64.
6. Joseph Fielding Smith, comp., *Teachings of the Prophet Joseph Smith* (Salt Lake City: Deseret Book Co., 1968), 190.

Lynn Matthews Anderson (1956–), Excerpts from "Toward a Feminist Interpretation of Latter-Day Saint Scripture" (1994)

In this essay, Lynn Matthews Anderson, a lay scholar of Mormonism, addresses the situation of women in Latter-day Saint scriptures, the Book of Mormon and the Doctrine and Covenants. When Anderson turned twelve, she went to the bishop of her southern California ward and demanded that he make her a deacon. In 1990, now a BYU graduate, returned missionary, and mother of three, Anderson created one of the earliest Mormon feminist Internet mailing lists: "Electronic

Latter-day Women's Caucus, plus men," or ELWC+. In addition to maintaining this crucial Internet site for discussion of LDS women's issues, Anderson was making a close study of the Book of Mormon in order to develop an easy-to-read edition of the scripture for her children. Her study led her to confront women's near total absence from Mormonism's signature sacred text. This absence should "startle, discomfort, and inspire Latter-day Saints—especially our leaders—to ask questions both about the role of women in the church 'back then' and especially about their role now." As she seeks to develop a specifically Mormon frame of reference, she acknowledges feminist theologians from the Jewish and Catholic faith traditions who have also addressed the absence or exclusion of women from sacred texts. Anderson exemplifies an initiative among Mormon feminists in the 1990s to join broader conversations among feminists of faith and thus to represent Mormon experience, scripture, and theology as deserving of rigorous study and respectful consideration.

Source

Anderson, Lynn Matthews. "Toward a Feminist Interpretation of Latter-day Saint Scripture." *Dialogue: A Journal of Mormon Thought* 27.2 (1994): 185–203. Copyright 1994–2015 by Lynn Matthews Anderson.

References and Further Reading

Anderson, Lynn Matthews. *Easy-to-Read Book of Mormon: A Learning Companion*. Apple Valley, MN: Estes Book, 1995.

"TOWARD A FEMINIST INTERPRETATION OF LATTER-DAY SAINT SCRIPTURE"

Females scarcely figure or matter in our sacred books. While this is true for the Bible, it is even more true for [LDS scriptural texts] the Book of Mormon, Doctrine and Covenants, and Pearl of Great Price. Writing of the effects of women's invisibility in Torah, noted Jewish feminist theologian Judith Plaskow observed, "The silence of women reverberates through the tradition, distorting the shape of narrative and skewing the content of the law."[1] Similarly, Latter-day Saints' ignorance of and indifference to the content of our own scriptures vis-à-vis women distorts our own sacred narratives, skews the content and language of our doctrine, and short-circuits the revelatory process by promoting the erroneous belief that all answers to contemporary questions about women's place and role in Christ's church can be found in the standard works.

Women in Latter-Day Scripture: Impoverished Inheritance

Judith Plaskow argues for the need to document and acknowledge the full extent of women's invisibility and marginality in Jewish scripture because, in her words, "if we refuse to recognize the painful truth about the extent of women's invisibility, we can never move forward."[2] Perhaps it has been too painful for Latter-day Saints to acknowledge the way women are overlooked or portrayed in our scriptures.

Compared to the Bible, which mentions nearly 200 women by name, references to women in latter-day scripture are sparse. Out of the three latter-day books of scripture, only fourteen women are named: six in the Book of Mormon—three biblical figures (Eve, Sarah, and Mary), along with Sariah, Abish, and the harlot Isabel; five in the Doctrine and Covenants—Emma Smith, Vienna Jacques, Sarah, Hagar, and Eve. Surprisingly, the Pearl of Great Price contains the greatest number of named women (ten). Whereas the Bible directly quotes scores of women (both named and unnamed), only three individual Book of Mormon women are quoted (Sariah, Lamoni's consort, and wicked King Jared's daughter), along with one group of women (the daughters of Ishmael). No women's words are recorded in the Doctrine and Covenants; and in the Pearl of Great Price only Eve is quoted.

Although there are a handful of latter-day scriptures to which Mormon feminists can point as markers of the right relation of women and men to one another and to God (e.g., 2 Ne. 26:33; Mosiah 5:7, 27:25; Ether 3:14), such can scarcely lessen the shock of such female-denigrating phrases as "the whore of all the earth" (1 Ne. 14:10, 11; D&C 29:21, cf. D&C 86:3), "the mother of abominations" (1 Ne. 14:9,10, 13, 16; D&C 88:94, cf. D&C 88:05), and "the mother of harlots" (1 Ne. 13:34, 14:16) as metaphors for human (usually male) sinfulness. Nor can such entirely mitigate the overall impression of our scriptures' negative portrayal of women, particularly in "the keystone of our religion"—the Book of Mormon. Women are frequently portrayed there as mere chattel—lumped together with flocks, herds, and other possessions (Mosiah 22:2, 8; Alma 2:25, 3:2, 7:27, 58:12; 3 Ne. 3:13; see also Mosiah 2:5, 11:12). Book of Mormon women are commodities to be used as gifts or bribes (Alma 17:24, Ether 8:10–12); their sexuality is used to protect men (Mosiah 19:13–14); they become the wives of their kidnappers (20:3–5, 23:33). Nephite women are not only taken prisoner (Alma 58:30–31, 60:17), they are evidently helpless to prevent their own starvation (53:7). Women's minds as well as their feelings are "delicate" (Jacob 2:7,9), and their emotionality is a threat to the survival of the community (Mosiah 21:9–12). Even individual women notable enough to receive positive mention are nevertheless also portrayed in negative ways: emotionally weak (Abish, in Alma 19:28); incapable of coherent communication (Lamoni's queen, in v. 30); complaining and faithless (Sariah, in 1 Ne. 5:1–3).

There are scarcely any accounts of women acting in anything other than tightly-defined or constrained circumstances, with the possible exceptions of Morianton's maidservant, who nonetheless responds as a victim of male brutality (Alma 50:30–31), and evil King Jared's prodigiously evil Jaredite daughter (Ether 8:7–12, 17)—who, incidentally, seems to be the only literate woman in the Book of Mormon. What is more important, however, is that women's infrequent appearances in latter-day sacred narrative serve only to facilitate the telling of male stories. To paraphrase Judith Plaskow, women in these male texts are not subjects or molders of their own experiences but objects of male purposes, designs, and desires. They may be vividly characterized, but their presence does not negate their silence. If they are central to plot, the plots are not about them.[3] Even the account of Lamoni's unnamed queen (Mosiah 18:43–19:30)—arguably the most powerful story involving a Book of Mormon woman—is a supporting, secondary scene in the much larger story of the sons of Mosiah's proselyting success among the Lamanites (Alma 17–26).

Of particular significance, however, is the fact that women are not intended as the audience for God's word in either ancient or modern times. To illustrate, women are peripherally addressed (in other words, are acknowledged as being present) in only three out of two dozen or so major discourses or doctrinal expositions in the Book of Mormon, all of which are clearly addressed to men and often provably only to men. (Even the resurrected Jesus directs his words to men in the mixed-gender multitude, as in "Pray in your families, that your wives and your children may be blessed" [3 Ne. 18:21].) Without exception, every word intended for readers in modern times who "shall receive these things" (Moro. 10:3–5) is directed only to men: the writers, redactors, and even the translator of the Book of Mormon assumed a solely male audience for its salvific message.

One might expect to find things more even-handed in our most modern book of scripture, the Doctrine and Covenants. Yet disappointingly, it is the worst of our scriptures where women are concerned. There are no women's voices or stories therein, and fewer than 4 percent of its verses pertain explicitly to women or use "female" language (in other words, use specifically female nouns or pronouns). Of this 4 percent, only one-third directly or indirectly addresses women or contains doctrine or counsel specifically applicable to women. The other two-thirds is made up of references to women as objects or as metaphorical images, the most prominent of which is the female personification of Zion, which accounts for 28 percent of all female language in the Doctrine and Covenants. With the exception of section 25, in which God directly speaks to Emma Smith through Joseph, only one portion of one other revelation (section 128, a canonized letter from Joseph Smith) directly addresses women.[4]

Androcentric language and masculine focus in virtually all the revelations create barriers to understanding women's place in our doctrine and theology. For example, although women are mentioned as "begotten . . . daughters unto God" on the myriad created worlds (76:24), what does it mean that the vision of the celestial kingdom and criteria for entrance (76:50–70) are described in solely male terms? Those inheriting celestial glory are called "priests and kings" (v. 56), "priests . . . after the order of Melchizedek" (v. 57), and "gods, even the sons of God" (v. 58). If women are to share in "all things . . . present or things to come" (v. 59), or to "dwell in the presence of God . . . forever" (v. 62), and if our "bodies [will be] celestial," and our "glory [will be] that of the sun" (v. 70), no mention is made of these facts. In revelation after revelation women are completely unaccounted for—in the premortal existence, in this life, in the hereafter.

Another example of women's exclusion from larger theological considerations is in Doctrine and Covenants 84. In what ways can this section be applied to women? What can a woman infer about herself and her standing before God when she reads verses 33–38?:

> For whoso is faithful unto the obtaining these two priesthoods of which I have spoken, and the magnifying their calling, are sanctified by the Spirit unto the renewing of their bodies. They become the sons of Moses and of Aaron and the seed of Abraham, and the church and kingdom, and the elect of God.
>
> And also all they who receive this priesthood receive me, saith the Lord; for he that receiveth my servants receiveth me; And he that receiveth me receiveth my Father; and he that receiveth my Father receiveth my Father's kingdom; therefore all that my Father hath shall be given unto him.

Will women's bodies be sanctified unto renewal? Can women become daughters of Moses and Aaron, are women counted as Abraham's seed? (And what of Sarah and the other prophets' wives? Who are their children?) Are women part of "the church and kingdom, and the elect of God"? If women receive the Lord's servants by accepting the gospel and by being baptized and confirmed as members of Christ's church, are they eligible to receive all that the Father has, including priesthood? (Or will women receive what the Mother has, and if that is the case, what does the Mother have?) Might the "wo" pronounced on "all those who come not unto this priesthood" (v. 42) include the sisters of the church? (And if the temple endowment serves to induct women into the priesthood, as some have suggested,[5] why aren't Mormon women aware of this "induction"?)

Most sobering is to ponder the implications of Official Declaration 2, received and canonized in 1978: it is addressed only to general and local priesthood officers, beginning with the salutation "Dear Brethren." This letter's content is also male-oriented; while it mentions that from that point on, every worthy male can be ordained to the priesthood, "and enjoy with his loved ones . . . the blessings of the temple" (presumably some of the "loved ones" are female), women are not part of this momentous event—neither as audience nor subject, even though this announcement also paved the way for all worthy adult women of all races to attend the temple. Thus even toward the end of the twentieth century, one must ask: Why are women, who make up the majority of the adult membership of the church, still situated at the nether end of "revelatory channels"?

Theological Implications of Exclusion

Some people, on being told of the dearth of things female in our scriptures, respond with indifference or a defensive "so what?"—the latter generally accompanied by the protestation that, regardless of the language, regardless of the erroneous assumption of audience, "obviously" women are now included and "of course" scriptures apply to women today. But previously there has been little detailed textual examination relative to women and the Book of Mormon, the Doctrine and Covenants, and the Pearl of Great Price, which makes the topic of women in latter-day scripture vulnerable to misinterpretation and manipulation. In a religion that adheres to a literalistic concept of dispensationalism—that is, that God has repeatedly revealed a set body of saving knowledge to human beings through prophets—it is only natural as individuals and as an institution to approach both biblical and latter-day scripture with the expectation of finding certain themes therein. Thus all too often what we glean from the scriptures is more a reflection of the assumptions we bring with us than what the texts themselves actually say. When we ignore the facts of women's historical exclusion in all walks of life—religious, economic, or political—we easily fall into the trap of projecting women's current status onto the reality of the past.

A feminist re-reading and reinterpretation of latter-day texts should startle, discomfort, and inspire Latter-day Saints—especially our leaders—to ask questions both about the role of women in the church "back then" and especially about their role now. The importance of this issue cannot be overemphasized: If our theology and doctrine are based on texts exclusive of women in the past, how can we find answers there to questions which concern or include women today? The facts of women's exclusion in the Book of Mormon and Doctrine and Covenants carry with them important implications, not the least of which is the idea that a theology based on exclusion must be recast when those who were once excluded become included.

The evidence of women's theological irrelevancy in scripture attests to the need for analyzing our reasons for now including them as well as for reexamining the rationale for that inclusion. If we now recognize that women were excluded previously because of past cultural biases, how can we know, short of revelation, that we are not also acting today on the basis of our own biases in continuing to exclude women from certain aspects of church membership? Although answers to certain questions, such as the need for women to be baptized, are explicit in the Doctrine and Covenants (20:72–74), the Doctrine and Covenants does not give explicit answers to the proper relationship of women to priesthood authority and church governance, nor to what is becoming an even more urgent issue: the proper worship of God the Mother as well as God the Father.[6] Specific knowledge about these "new" issues cannot be found in our scriptures: the questions themselves, in the context of the times and cultures of origin (including the nineteenth century), were not comprehended, much less formulated. Indeed, such issues have only begun to be understood in our own day, and the vast majority of questions defining these issues have yet to be officially acknowledged, much less thoughtfully explored.

In sum, that there is so little pertaining to women in our scriptures indicates not that what little we have is somehow sufficient on which to base policy and practice, but that there needs to be more. Given the apparent attitude among some current LDS leaders that "if God wants things to be different, he will let us know," it seems likely that we will continue to trade our birthright of revelation for a pottage of culturally contaminated tradition.[7] Until such new revelation is sought for, however, I believe it is the task of Mormon feminism to recover and reconstruct women's stories wherever possible, as well as to develop and promulgate new ways of evaluating and interpreting the scriptures.

Recovering Women's Stories

Over the past two decades Jewish and Christian feminist theologians have made significant contributions to textual reconstructions to recover women's untold stories in sacred writ. Textual reconstruction involves exegetical study—a critical examination of the original texts on which a given translation is based—as well as the incorporation of secular data to create a context for interpretative analysis. While Mormon feminists find their task more formidable because of the dearth of textual references to women and at least where the Book of Mormon is concerned the absence of original text material and corroborating historiographical and archaeological evidence, it is nevertheless possible to use correlative material from Old Testament studies to expand our understanding of women's position in portions of the Pearl of Great Price and the Book of Mormon—particularly if we treat the latter as a society shaped by the Law of Moses.

Another kind of challenge awaits LDS feminists in approaching the Doctrine and Covenants, which differs significantly from other scriptures in that it contains little narrative history but instead records God's direct words to Joseph Smith, often in response to Joseph's or other men's questions or concerns. Still, during the past twenty or so years there has been an upsurge of interest in the stories of early LDS women, some of whom kept diaries and journals. While one cannot extrapolate from these sources and put words into God's mouth, it is nonetheless possible to explore in greater depth the impact of these androcentric revelations in the lives of women who were admittedly only "auxiliary" thereto. For nearly every man called by revelation to serve a mission in the early days of the church, for example, there was a wife left behind to grapple with the vicissitudes of supporting a family in difficult circumstances. God's help to these women deserves to be recognized as equally essential to the growth and progress of the church as the better-publicized stories of God's help to their missionary-husbands.

Establishing a Mormon Feminist Interpretive Framework

We cannot ignore the foundational texts of our religion; nor can we afford to dismiss those things in them we find unsettling or distasteful. But unless we are willing to worship a God who is sexist, partial, and misogynist, we cannot ascribe all that is found in our scriptures to deity. Rather, we need to develop an interpretive framework that permits us to distinguish between timeless truths and human influences. In short, although we as Mormons, and more particularly we as Mormon feminists, are decades behind colleagues in other faiths in recognizing the need for developing a feminist interpretive approach to scripture, we can begin to make amends by building on the work of non-LDS feminists in approaching scriptural interpretation faithfully yet critically—reevaluating texts that appear out of harmony with the life and mission of Jesus and highlighting previously overlooked, undervalued, or misunderstood texts in which God affirms the equal worth of women and men.

While I believe part of this critical reevaluation necessitates a shift in our assumptions about scriptural authority, Latter-day Saints are theoretically in a strong position to make such a shift. For one thing, our scriptures attest to the notion of human error and weakness intermingling with timeless truth: the Eighth Article of Faith says that we believe the Bible is the word of God "as far as it is translated correctly" (with the clear implication that not all of it reflects God's will); Moroni's preface to the Book of Mormon speaks of the possibility of faults which are "the mistakes of men"; but most important is what this scripture tells us: God works with people "in their weakness, after the manner of their language, that they might come to understanding" (D&C 1:24; see also 2 Ne. 31:3). In other words, God speaks to people within rather than outside of their particular cultural context, and such contexts have everything to do with the perception of women's stories and experiences as worthy for inclusion in sacred writ.

Our own belief about the relative authority of scripture makes it possible for us to use some, if not all, of the tools being developed by Judeo-Christian feminists to reinterpret biblical texts. One such tool is what Elisabeth Schussler Fiorenza calls "a hermeneutics of suspicion." This "hermeneutics of suspicion . . . takes as its starting point the assumption that biblical texts and their interpretations are androcentric and serve patriarchal functions" and "questions the underlying presuppositions, androcentric models, and unarticulated interests of contemporary biblical interpretation."[8] This tool, I believe, can be applied to latter-day scripture and its tradition-based contemporary interpretation whether one attempts to find the applicability to women of an exclusive, androcentric text such as Alma 13; or to reconcile the unchristian elements of coercive polygyny with the expansive elements of eternal marriage relationships in Doctrine and Covenants 132; or to make sense of the negative characterization of Lamech's wives as lacking compassion when examined in the context of the fuller narrative of Moses 5:43–55.

Despite the fact that our texts are steeped in patriarchal language and imagery, I believe the tools of feminist theology can enable us to use latter-day scripture to overcome the sin of patriarchy in three ways: contextually, interpretively, and thematically. By contextually, I mean that latter-day scripture provides evidence to show that the structures of patriarchy, both ancient and modern, deny the full humanity of women. This denial establishes the unreliability of uncritically using patriarchal prooftexts as a means of authoritatively answering questions relevant to contemporary gender issues. By interpretively, I mean that despite the patriarchal context and androcentric language of our scriptures, modern prophets have interpreted the doctrines found in many specific texts as binding on, applying to, and inclusive of women. Such texts in and of themselves testify to the need for serious reconsideration of current attitudes, practices, popular "theology," and doctrinal interpretation concerning the status of women in God's church. By thematically, I mean that latter-day scriptures, taken as a whole, contain recurrent ideas and motifs, two of which, however dimly or differently understood by their writers and redactors (or even by their translator), point to: first, that the parameters of the salvation offered through Christ's atonement are universal, crossing lines of gender, race, and class; and second, that equality in a society is a correct measure of its righteousness—when the people are righteous, they treat one another as equals; when they fall into unrighteousness, there is great inequality both temporally and spiritually.[9]

Using a dual basis of agency and charity for reinterpreting those texts used historically to justify oppression of women also enables LDS feminists to question larger assumptions imposed by millennia of patriarchal influence. This telestial influence continues to make itself felt even in the restored church, as our adherence to rigid sex-role stereotypes and increasing emphasis on "channels" and "protocol" shows. Those with an authoritarian bent will likely view reducing the gospel to its foundational elements as dangerous: doing so ultimately returns individual salvation to a place of primacy in the church, as well as restores an important key in discerning between human opinion and divine revelation. These two criteria hold in abeyance any assignation of divinity to human pronouncements, policies, and programs which uphold rather than destroy inequality, sex-role stereotyping, and other dehumanizing aspects of sexism; and, further, such criteria empower the Saints to break away from the ever-growing weight of patriarchal tradition which increasingly insists on enforced conformity rather than freely-chosen unity, on loyalty to persons and offices rather than to principle, and on assumptions of infallibility and inspiration even when those holding positions of authority do not ascribe their utterances, programs, or policies to God's inspiration.

Notes

1. Judith Plaskow, *Standing Again at Sinai: Judaism from a Feminist Perspective* (San Francisco: Harper Collins, 1990), 9ff.
2. Plaskow, 8–9.
3. Plaskow, 2–3.
4. Yet after the initial welcome burst of inclusivity—"And now, my dearly beloved brethren and sisters" (v. 15)—Joseph writes only to men, as in verse 22: "Brethren, shall we not go forward in so great a cause?" and verse 25: "Brethren, I have many things to say to you on the subject." Portions of sections 90 and 132 indirectly address specific individual women—in other words, God speaks directly to Joseph Smith about specific women, as in "it is my will that my handmaid Vienna Jacques should receive money" (90:28) and "if she [Emma Smith] will not abide this commandment, she shall destroyed" (132:54). A handful of other verses deal with women in relation to church law (most of which are found in section 42).
5. See D. Michael Quinn, "Mormon Women Have Had the Priesthood since 1843," in Maxine Hanks, ed. *Women and Authority: Re-emerging Mormon Feminism* (Salt Lake City: Signature Books, 1992), 365–409.
6. In two separate instances in 1991 President Gordon B. Hinckley counseled first with regional representatives and then with women of the church about not praying to Mother in Heaven. President Hinckley cited several examples of Jesus praying to the Father, including the Lord's Prayer, and then said, "But, search as I have, I find nowhere in the Standard Works an account where Jesus prayed other than to His Father in Heaven or where He instructed the people to pray other than to His Father in Heaven ... The fact that we do not pray to our Mother in Heaven in no way belittles or denigrates her. None of us knows anything about her" ("Report of the 1991 Women's Broadcast," *Ensign* 21 [Nov. 1991].) The appeal to "argument from silence" rather than stating that the counsel represents God's will on the subject has troubled a number of Latter-day Saints (see, for example, the letters to the editor section in several issues of *Mormon Women's Forum* following publication of President Hinckley's statement in the *Ensign*). Interestingly, President Hinckley referred to Jesus' instruction in 3 Nephi 18:21 that his hearers should "pray ... unto the Father ... that your wives and your children may be blessed," apparently without noting the gender referent that excludes women and children from this counsel.
7. For example, while President Hinckley admitted to the possibility of change with regard to women and priesthood at the 1985 Women's Conference, his remarks seemed to indicate a desire for God to take the initiative, thereby marking a departure from what Mormons are taught is the pattern of revelation—that God bestows greater light and knowledge on those who pray, study, ponder, and ask (Lynn Matthews Anderson, "The Mormon Church and the Second Sex," 10, Oct. 1992, privately circulated; see also Gordon B. Hinckley, "Ten Gifts from the Lord," *Ensign* 15 [Nov. 1985]: 86: "[A] few Latter-day Saint women are asking why they are not entitled to hold the priesthood. To that I can say that only the Lord, through revelation, could alter that situation. He has not done so, so it is profitless for us to speculate and worry about it").
8. Elisabeth Schussler Fiorenza, *Bread Not Stone: The Challenge of Feminist Biblical Interpretation* (Boston: Beacon Press, 1984), 15ff. Hermeneutics is the critical analysis and/or development of interpretive methodology.
9. I am not suggesting that equality and respect for others ever eliminated gender discrimination even during periods of greatest righteousness, as in the City of Enoch or during the 200 years following Christ's visit to the Nephites. To propose such, especially for the latter situation, would be problematic, since women of the first generation (to say nothing of men) would have been completely unprepared psychologically, culturally, and otherwise for such equality. See my "Nephite women & patriarchy," 30 Nov. 1992, electronic essay, Mormon-L archives, Brigham Young University, Provo, Utah.

Cecilia Konchar Farr (1958–), "Dancing Through the Doctrine: Observations on Religion and Feminism" (1995)

Even as she faced reprisals from Brigham Young University for her public feminist advocacy, Cecilia Konchar Farr continued to work, write, and speak out from the intersections of her Mormon faith and her feminism. Earlier Mormon feminists had pledged to demonstrate the coherence of what Claudia Bushman described as the "dual platforms" of Mormonism and feminism. In this essay, Konchar Farr addresses the tensions between them. She calls on the broader feminist movement to re-examine its secular biases, to respect the historic role religion has played and continues to play in progressive political movements, and to enact its commitment to diversity by making space for feminists of faith. At the same time, she calls on Mormon feminists to step beyond their insularity and to be more welcoming of diverse perspectives and approaches within the Mormon feminist movement. Her acknowledgment of tensions within Mormon feminism recalls Laurel Thatcher Ulrich's frank assessments in her 1981 essay "The Pink *Dialogue* and Beyond" (anthologized in Part I of this volume) and marks out a path for the movement's future growth—especially its need to include women of color.

Source

Konchar Farr, Cecilia. "Dancing Through the Doctrine: Observations on Religion and Feminism." *Dialogue: A Journal of Mormon Thought* 28.3 (1995): 1–12.

"DANCING THROUGH THE DOCTRINE: OBSERVATIONS ON RELIGION AND FEMINISM"

I generally call myself a radical feminist, meaning that I imagine huge changes, not just reformative or cosmetic changes, are going to be necessary to alter women's oppressed situation in our world. We need to strip our institutions down to the bare structures, then see if they need rebuilding or renovation. I believe differences come even among religious feminists and, in my experience, Mormon feminists when we examine how to approach these patriarchal structures—the father's house, in Audre Lorde's terms.* Do we attack them with the father's tools? With our own? Should we build our own houses across the street? Or do we reject the

---

*Konchar Farr here references the essay "The Master's Tools Will Never Dismantle the Master's House" (1984), a critique of the exclusion of women of color and lesbians in the mainstream feminist movement, by the Black feminist lesbian writer, theorist, and activist Audre Lorde (1934–1992). Lorde asserts that racism and homophobia are tools of patriarchal oppression and should have no place within feminism that seeks to dismantle patriarchal structures of oppression.

imperialist constructions that deface that earth and go off to live in canyons and deserts? A question that I hear often from many of my (as we say in Mormonism) gentile friends [is], "Why do you stay in such a male-dominated religion?" I am often tempted to ask them, admittedly begging the question, which institutions they associate with are not dominated by men—their banks, their government, their schools or factories or hospitals? I stay because Mormonism means something to me at the deepest levels of my being. So I find myself, in my own religious odyssey, sitting in a structure I have deconstructed, but that I admire still. I stare at the clouds through the open beams where the ceiling once was and admire the beams without wishing for the ceiling.

Recently some feminist thinkers, Gloria Steinem among them, have called for a return to consciousness-raising groups as a way of bringing feminism back to local relevance and back into the everyday lives of women. Feminist thinkers, mostly in the Academy, have turned our movement into a theory, they argue, to the detriment of the movement. This nostalgic place, where feminism was about the "liberation" of individual women rather than the complex, interwoven systems and institutions of oppression, is, I think, where Mormon feminism has remained.

In the spring of 1993 I attended my first Mormon feminist retreat, Pilgrimage, with several graduate students and English teachers—all women in our twenties or early thirties—who had met together once a week for nearly a year to study feminist theory. A combination consciousness raising/support/study group, we had spent part of winter semester studying Mormon feminism. We began to outline a Mormon feminism from our roots in feminist theory and cultural criticism, a feminism based only partly on our own experiences. This feminism, we decided, was not so much a reaction to disillusionment or mistreatment as it was an enactment of our theory and our theology. At Pilgrimage our feminist thinking was set against the backdrop of the longstanding tradition of Mormon feminism which surrounded us there. Aside from a group of women we admire and respect, here is what we saw at Pilgrimage:

- A feminism based on individual liberation, where meetings consisted mainly of entertainment, affirmation, and sharing stories of awakenings and abuses.
- A homogeneous feminism that seemed, for the most part, comfortable in its familiar surroundings.
- An insular feminism that based its desires for change almost solely on getting male leaders to understand women in the church.
- A non-theoretical feminism, whose major premise was that women should no longer be silent.
- An apolitical feminism that saw most of the women resisting a pull into a mild protest campaign, led by some of the more activist members of the group, which involved wearing small white ribbons on their lapels at church.

It was a feminism in the wilderness or focused on reform, and a feminism that highlighted all of the imperfections of our smaller group—our homogeneity, our middle-class consciousness, our insularity. It was also a feminism quite different from the Mormon feminism we had been developing hopefully together in some of the following ways: One member of our group worked on the rape crisis hotline in Provo. She, like many activist feminists, talked to rape victims, sometimes several a week, took them to the hospital and the police station. She insisted that we always keep broad social and cultural change on our agenda. Another woman, actually an undergraduate, but certainly not your average undergraduate, studied Hispanic literatures. She never let us forget that white women are not the center of the world—that we aren't even a majority of women in many parts of America. She inspired us to read the theorist/novelist/poet Gloria Anzaldúa together. Another had just finished teaching for a year in inner-city schools in Boston and had, she told us, altered her approach to life at a very basic level to accommodate what she learned there. Together we confided and theorized and negotiated. And we demonstrated, organized, and gave political speeches.

In short, though our discussions were, like consciousness-raising groups, local and personal, they were also theoretical and global, always with immense political and cultural pretensions. We, in other words, are determined not so much to change the church as to change the world, because when we change the world the church will follow. Instead of locating ourselves in the church, we located the church in ourselves—and ourselves in the world. As one member of our group wrote to me recently, "I am more interested in connecting Mormon women with mainstream women's movements and concerns in academics, politics, and in the political world." Most of us agree that religious institutions resist change and close most doors to revolution. (The case of Galileo is instructive here.) However, sometimes they open a skylight to revelation, and therein lies hope for changing the church. We approach this hope on its own philosophical ground: We pray for change. But in the meantime there's a lot to be done, and we feminists must be about our Mother's business. We need to be much more anxiously engaged beyond the boundaries of our religious congregations and our individual souls. Barring revelation over which we have no tangible control in the strictly established patriarchal hierarchies of contemporary religion (imagine Joan of Arc in Salt Lake or Vatican City today), these broader activities are the only way to change the church.

For me this means returning to my basic faith in Mormon doctrine for renewal and spiritual strength as I work to change the world, because, in all honesty, it is in that doctrine that created me as a moral being that I discover the passion for social and political activism.

Lynn Matthews Anderson (1956–), "I Have an Answer: Questions to Gospel Answers" (1996)

Unsettling questions about the invisibility of women in LDS scripture and the lack of women's participation in LDS Church leadership and decision-making raised by Mormon feminists have historically been met by LDS Church leaders and more conservative Mormons with reassertions of the certainty and unchangeability of current Church policies. During the 1990s, the *Mormon Women's Forum Quarterly* introduced a column entitled "I Have an Answer: Questions to Gospel Answers," an ironic send-up of the "I Have a Question: Answers to Gospel Questions" column in the LDS Church-owned *Ensign* magazines. Using the feminist form of the symbolic gender role reversal (see, for example, Carol Lynn Pearson's "Walk in the Pink Moccasins" or Elouise Bell's "The Meeting" anthologized in Part II of this volume), the *MWFQ* "I Have an Answer" column celebrated the power of asking questions in a Mormon culture that valued its own sense of having all the answers to life's difficulties. In 1996, Lynn Matthews Anderson used the "I Have an Answer" column to poke holes in the assertion often used by LDS Church authorities to explain anti-equality and anti-feminist stances: the assertion that differences between the sexes were fixed, essential, and fundamental. In 1995, the LDS Church had released a statement entitled "The Family: A Proclamation to the World," which declared that biological differences between men and women reflected definitive and eternal differences in the souls and God-appointed roles of men and women—a major innovation in LDS theology that many feminists immediately questioned or rejected.

Source

Anderson, Lynn Matthews. "I Have an Answer: Questions to Gospel Answers." *Mormon Women's Forum Quarterly* 7.1–2 (Spring–Summer 1996): 19.

"I HAVE AN ANSWER: QUESTIONS TO GOSPEL ANSWERS"

ANSWER: "There are basic things that a man needs that a woman does not need. There are things that a man feels that a woman never does feel. There are basic things that a woman needs that a man never needs, and there are things that a woman feels that a man never feels, nor should he. These differences make women, in basic needs, literally opposite from men."—BOYD K. PACKER, "The Equal Rights Amendment," *The Ensign*, March 1977.

QUESTIONS: Are women and men members of the same species? If so, how can one sex's basic needs be somehow "literally opposite" from the other's? What are the things that women feel that men shouldn't feel? (Menstrual cramps?) What happens if a man feels something he supposedly "shouldn't" feel? Does that turn him into a fake man? What if a woman feels something that she's "never" supposed to feel? And how will women and men know if what they're feeling is something they're not supposed to feel?

President Packer continued, "A man, for instance, needs to feel protective, and yes, dominant, if you will, in leading his family. A woman needs to feel protected, in the bearing of children and in the nurturing of them . . ."

Which men "need" to feel dominant? (Avoid them!) Why does a man "need" to feel dominant? Isn't domination antithetical to true leadership and a characteristic of the "natural man" that King Benjamin says is an enemy to God (Mosiah 3:19)?

How is the protection a woman supposedly craves any different from the need for security and safety common to both sexes? Is motherhood somehow more under attack than meaningful fatherhood? Ironically, LDS men spend less quality time with their children than non-LDS men; it seems that fatherhood, not motherhood, is more in need of protection among the saints. Don't men need to feel protected in the nurturing of their children? Certainly men who choose to spend time in non-traditional ways—as full-time fathers, for example—seem to need protection from the verbal attacks and sanctions from right-wing traditionalists!

President Packer: "When God created male and female, He gave each important differences in physical attributes, in emotional composition, in family responsibility."

With the exception of gross biological distinctions, is there not an enormous amount of overlap between the sexes—emotionally, spiritually, intellectually? Where in scripture has God made the kinds of role assignments alluded to? Moses 5:1 indicates that Eve worked alongside Adam; Moses 5:3 indicates that their male and female offspring "began . . . to till the land, and to tend flocks, and they also begat sons and daughters." There does not seem to be quite the division of labor between parenthood and "earning a living" as modern-day rhetoric insists upon. (And, in fact, this division is largely a 19th century middle-class innovation, not at all a "timeless" or "divinely-mandated" requirement.)

Is it any wonder that women are kept from equal privileges and access to decision-making power when so many men believe in a definition of "true womanhood" that all too frequently diverges from adult human behavior?

Finally, and most importantly, does God relate to us as members of categories or as individuals? Why then do we base practice and policy on frequently erroneous stereotypes and generalities rather than on respect for individual needs and capacities, regardless of sex? Why does so much of current Church practice seem heavily invested in such simplistic categorization? Does God truly place order above what is needful to help each of us progress as individuals? And why would order be in any way threatened by allowing individual women and men the opportunity to fulfill the measure of their creation? Should we continue to mindlessly follow the traditions of the fathers, even when they are demonstrably harmful to ourselves and others?

Carol Lynn Wright Pearson (1939–), "Could Feminism Have Saved the Nephites?" (1996)

In this essay, Carol Lynn Pearson extends Lynn Matthews Anderson's reflections on the absence of women in LDS scripture by investigating the spiritual consequences of the exclusion of women from leadership and authority. The Book of Mormon made virtually no references to the influence of women or to women leaders among the Nephites, the civilization whose rise and catastrophic fall it chronicled. Was it possible, Pearson wonders in this essay, that the Nephites' exclusion of women contributed to their demise and destruction? Moreover, what were the spiritual consequences for Mormon men and women of centering their faith around a text in which women were mentioned far less frequently than they were mentioned in the Bible? Pearson closes by discussing positive steps that Mormons can take to moderate the harmful impacts of women's absence from the scriptural canon.

Source

Pearson, Carol Lynn. "Could Feminism Have Saved the Nephites?" *Sunstone* 19.1 (March 1996): 32–40.

"COULD FEMINISM HAVE SAVED THE NEPHITES?"

I believe that the Book of Mormon is indeed a book written for our day, that it contains many powerful lessons that can greatly benefit us. I propose that there is a lesson in this book that we have not really examined, one that is profoundly important. I propose that a society that negates femaleness will likely be a society that is militaristic—or that a society that is militaristic will likely be a society that negates femaleness; whichever the cause and whichever the effect, the result will be disaster. Historically, patriarchy and militarism are blood brothers, and the operative word is "blood." Technically, patriarchy is "the rule of the fathers." As it translates into experience, it is the view that male is primary and central and female is secondary and auxiliary—that God is male and there is no complementary female divine. Resultantly, the "masculine" is idealized and worshipped, and the "feminine" is diminished, marginalized, and abused.

Let us examine these two phenomena—militarism in the Book of Mormon and the accompanying bias against and negative portrayal of women. According to *Warfare in the Book of Mormon*, approximately one hundred separate instances of armed conflict exist in the Book of Mormon record.[1] Hugh Nibley estimates that the book devotes approximately one-third of its content directly or indirectly to military matters.[2] Scenes of bloodshed and almost unbelievable violence stain the pages of the book. In just one battle, the Nephites slay 12,532 Amlicites, and the Amlicites slay 6,562 Nephites. Nephi cuts off the head of Laban [1 Nephi 4: 17–18]; Ammon cuts off the arms of the enemies of King Lamoni [Alma 17: 36–38]. The book's violence is unforgettable.

Evidently less obvious to some is the parallel absence and/or negative portrayal of women in the Book of Mormon. A few years ago, I read the book specifically to focus on what it says about women, circling in red every female reference. And as I did, it became more and more clear why I had always felt like an unwelcome visitor as I entered Nephite society, a stranger in a strange land indeed. The valuable things I have gleaned from the Book of Mormon have been bought at the expense of putting my femaleness aside and ignoring what is said of it. And while I am more than my femaleness, my femaleness is a profound and highly valued part of me, and to have to put it away when I pick up the book violates my spirit.

When I encounter the occasional statement that would appear inviting to women, I stare at it as at an anachronism: "He inciteth them all to come unto him and partake of his goodness; and he denieth none that come unto him, black and white, bond and free, male and female . . . , and all are alike unto God, both Jew and Gentile" (2 Ne. 26:33). Or, "And now, he imparteth his word by angels unto men, yea, not only men but women also" (Alma 32:23).

Where are the stories to demonstrate this expansive doctrine? In the account we have been given, a huge division exists between male and female, a clear devaluing of the female. Angels do not visit women. Do we have here preaching without the practice? Was there something going on that did not make its way into the record? All we know is what appears in the book's pages, and what appears does not invite women or honor femaleness.

Only two instances in the entire 522 pages provide evidence that women are being specifically addressed along with men. Lehi speaks to and blesses both the sons and the daughters of his sons Laman and Lemuel: "Behold, my sons and my daughters . . . I would that ye should give ear unto my words" (2 Ne. 4:3). That is the first and nearly the last time in the book that I, as a woman, feel specifically invited to the party. Thereafter, I have to invite myself until the very end of the book, where I read, "O ye fair sons and daughters, ye fathers and mothers, ye husbands and wives, ye fair ones, how is it that ye could have fallen!" (Morm. 6: 19).

Sometimes the exclusion of women seems particularly surprising. For instance, during King Benjamin's beautiful address in Mosiah 2, women are obviously physically present: "They pitched their tents round about, every man according to his family, consisting of his wife, and his sons, and his daughters, and their sons, and their daughters" (v. 5). Then King Benjamin speaks from his tower: "My brethren, all ye that have assembled yourselves together. . . . Yet, my brethren. . . . And now, I say unto you, my brethren. . . . O, all ye old men, and also ye young men, and you little children who can understand my words. . . ." (v. 9, 15, 20, 36, 40). One instance indicates that the listeners shall become the sons and the daughters of Christ, but every salutation is to only "my brethren."

This is the case throughout the book. King Mosiah sends "a written word" to the people: "Behold, O ye my people, or my brethren, for I esteem you as such. . . ." (Mosiah 29:5). We have come to assume that the good teachings in the book apply to both sexes, and yet there is room for us to quip: "Men are that they might have joy, and women are that they might provide it."

Nowhere in the book do we find the phrase, "My brethren and my sisters," or anything comparable to it. I am an outsider overhearing something important that is going on in another room. "Arise, my sons, and be men! . . . Awake, my sons!" Did Nephite women feel similarly ignored? Certainly, if only on a subconscious level. The general overhaul of school textbooks in the last couple of decades brought with it substantial evidence of what happens to the self-image of girls (and other groups) when they are excluded from the teaching material. Psychologists tell us that for one's mental health, being ignored is worse than being beaten.

If women are not spoken to in the Book of Mormon, they are spoken of. Occasionally. Except for references to the biblical women Eve, Mary, and Sarah, there are three women mentioned by name in the Book of Mormon: Sariah, wife of Lehi [1 Nephi 5:1–8, 8:14–16, 18: 19]; Abish, the Lamanitish woman in the story of Ammon and King Lamoni [Alma 19:16]; and Isabel, the harlot [Alma 39:3]. This starkly contrasts with the presence of women in the Bible. One hundred eighty-eight women are mentioned by name in the Bible, compared to three in the Book of Mormon. Indeed, two books of the Bible—Esther and Ruth—are named after women.

Numerous biblical women can serve as spiritual role models for women today: Huldah was a prophetess [2 Chronicles 34:22, 2 Kings 22:14]; Deborah was a prophetess [Judges 4:4]; Miriam was a prophetess [Exodus 15:20]. Not one woman in the Book of Mormon appears to have her own connection to the heavens. Sariah does not receive anything like the visionary experience that Lehi has. Nephi receives the vision of the Tree of Life after his father, but Sariah does not. Abish, who performs one of the few strong deeds by a woman in the book, had converted to the Lord because of a remarkable vision her father had had years before, not a vision of her own. Lamoni's queen is another spiritually dependent woman: she does not receive from God but from her husband's servants the knowledge that Ammon is a prophet. And she says to Ammon, who asks if she believes, "I have had no witness save thy word . . . nevertheless I believe . . ." (Alma 19:9).

I venture to guess that the only story about women in the Book of Mormon most of us have heard used in a Church talk is the mothers of the stripling warriors who instilled faith into their sons. (See Alma 56:47.)

Predictably, the huge majority of the references to women are to the nameless, faceless "our women" or "our wives" clearly listed with the Nephite men's possessions:

> And now, may the peace of God rest upon you, and upon your houses and lands, and upon your flocks and your herds, and all that you possess, your women and your children . . . (Alma 7:27)

> Our women did bear children in the wilderness . . . our women did give plenty of suck for their children. . . . (1 Ne. 17:1, 2)

> I, Nephi, did take my family, and also Zoram and his family, and Sam, mine elder brother and his family, and Jacob and Joseph, my younger brethren, and also my sisters. . . . (2 Ne. 5:6)

What? Nephi had sisters? Finally, after reaching the promised land and telling numerous stories about his brothers, Nephi mentions he has sisters? They are not spoken of before or after.

> And I did cause that the women should spin, and toil, and work, and work all manner of fine linen, yea, and cloth of every kind, that we might clothe our nakedness. . . . (Mosiah 10:5)

> And now the design of the Nephites was to support their lands, and their houses, and their wives, and their children. . . . (Alma 43:9)

> And it came to pass that he rent his coat; and he took a piece thereof, and wrote upon it—In memory of our God, our religion, and freedom, and our peace, our wives, and our children. . . . (Alma 46:12)

> Behold their women did toil and spin, and did make all manner of cloth, of fine-twined linen and cloth of every kind, to clothe their nakedness. (Hel: 6:13)

The strong anti-female statement made by Nephi society, however, comes not only from the lack of meaningful stories about individual women in the Book of Mormon but also from female imagery applied to things rather than people. Of course, the Mother of all negative female images in the Book of Mormon is—have you guessed it?—the great and abominable church, the mother of abominations, the mother of harlots, the whore of all the earth. I wonder if we appreciate what this really means. The males who lived in Book of Mormon times—and the males who read the book today—have as major symbols for their maleness: God the Father, Jesus Christ, the Holy Ghost, and all the prophets. And the females who lived in Book of Mormon times—and the females who read the book today—have as a major symbol for their femaleness; the great and abominable church, the whore of all the earth.

The low status of women in Nephite culture was predictably coupled with abuse of women. To be sure, Nephite men suffered enormously—being sent off to kill and be killed is a terrible fate. But it is a general rule that in every culture women receive an additional level of abuse because of their gender.

Various parts of the Nephite record refer to women being beaten (see Alma 50:30), having their tender hearts broken because of the faithlessness of their polygamous husbands (Jacob 2:23–35), being stolen as wives (Mosiah 20:5), being required to defend those who stole them (Mosiah 23:33), being taken prisoners (Alma 54:3), being offered as sacrifices (Morm. 4:21), being burned to death (Alma 14:8), being raped, being tortured to death and then having their flesh devoured by men, and being fed on the flesh of their husbands with only a little water (Moro. 9:8–10).

Besides contributing to the obvious abuses of women in the narrative, the anti-female bias evident among the Nephites may have been one of the numerous causes of their downfall, for the reasons presented in the first part of this discussion. We are told that after the visit of Christ there were approximately two hundred years of peace, when the people were as one. Who knows what softening of hierarchical status there was then in terms of class, race, gender? The only explanation of the end of that idyllic period is that the people began to be lifted up in pride, wearing costly apparel and no longer having their goods in common. They began to be divided into classes. One can only speculate how those divisions related to gender.

None of the prophets in the Book of Mormon suggest that the low status and negative portrayal of women is a characteristic of their fallen society, but they do suggest that their imperfections were many: The next to final prophet, Mormon, wrote: "Give thanks unto God that he hath made manifest unto you our imperfections, that ye may learn to be more wise than we have been" (Morm. 9:31).

"That ye may learn to be more wise than we have been." I have been taught all my life that the Book of Mormon gives us voices from the dust preserved that we may learn the lessons of this fallen people. Let me state again: A society that marginalizes its women and creates negative images of femaleness is a society that will not succeed, and indeed is a society that may very well destroy itself through war.

In a way, it is useless to ask the question, "Could feminism have saved the Nephites?," though it so intrigues me. What if? What if the Nephite women and the Lamanite women—like the great women of Aristophanes' Lysistrata—had said to their warriors, "I'm sorry, I will not share your bed until you find a better way than all this warring nonsense."

What if a woman had walked from her tent to the foot of the tower and said, "King Benjamin! I'm here too! Speak to me!—or approached King Mosiah or any of the other prophets and said, "Wait! What about me? What about the women?"

What if a committee of women from the Zarahemla Toiling and Spinning Society had approached the leadership and said, "Dear Brethren: We are weary of toiling and spinning and making all manner of cloth and watching you kill each other. We wish to weave the fabric of a new society. We would like to sit in your councils and help figure out how to save the world for our children's children!"

What if a few Nephite women had stood up in their Sunday class and said, "Brethren, I object to my femaleness being rendered in terms of the great and abominable church. Brethren, you tell me of the Father and the Son; where is my Mother?"

What if one or more of the Nephite prophets had said to himself, "There's something wrong with this picture. We are seeing things through only one eye. Why don't we open the other eye and invite the women to participate in our decision-making, in our political life, and in our spiritual life? Perhaps they have something to contribute more important than all manner of fine cloth."

What if? What if? But whatever female voices, or sympathetic male voices, may have ever spoken, they are long, long lost to the dust, and what they said, or wished they could have said, or might have said if they had had the awareness and the power, we will never know.

We have the awareness. And the power. Our voices are not yet lost to the dust. We can speak. And we must. It is time to say—on behalf of our Nephite sisters and brothers—on behalf of ourselves and our posterity—let us learn to be more wise than they have been.

I suggest three ways to be more wise.

First, I suggest that we teach the Book of Mormon in an expanded context, that we teach these stories with an acknowledgement of what they say about women and a clear statement that the message about women is not the message God wants us to have. And, in fact, that the Nephite view of women may have been one of the many things that led to their downfall. In the hundreds of talks and lessons on the Book of Mormon I have listened to in sacrament meeting, Relief Society, Primary, seminary, firesides, stake and general conferences—from men and women alike—I have never once heard the Book of Mormon approached with a sensitivity to what it says about my femaleness. Occasionally there has been a jest about the lack of women in the book, but never has there been a serious acknowledgment of what this means to all of us.

Because what it means is profoundly important, we cannot afford to ignore it. The messages that go into our spirits and our psyches as we study this book and absorb the positive images of the male and the absent or negative images of the female affect our lives, our self-images, our images of the opposite sex, our relationships to God, and our relationships to one another.

Second—and I argue with myself about this, because in a way it might muddy the clarity of one reason this was indeed a fallen people, but I suggest we examine it—it may be possible to correct some of the problem. For example, "the great and abominable church, the mother of harlots, the whore of all the earth": does it need to be female? The Church has a history of responding to demonstrated need and to voiced offense. The great and abominable church used to be characterized as the Catholic Church, but the later editions of [Bruce R.] McConkie's *Mormon Doctrine* show the change from that because we do not want to offend Catholics.

But how happy I will be when finally we make some adjustment in our language because we do not want to offend women.

The third thing I suggest—whatever we do about the past, making alterations or changing the context—is that we realize that the present is the point of greatest power; that now, this moment, we create new and powerful images of women and femaleness, that we create new volumes of history and indeed new scripture that will fill our minds and our hearts with positive female pictures, pictures of women serving as full and honored partners in our religious life. Patriarchy can be transformed into partnership, hastening our journey to Zion. And in that happy land, the beautiful daughters of Zion will dance and the beautiful sons of Zion will dance, and we will sing together a new song, and great will be the joy of it.

Notes

1. Stephen D. Ricks and William J. Hamblin, *Warfare in the Book of Mormon* (Salt Lake City: Deseret Book Co. and Foundation for Ancient Research and Mormon Studies, 1990), 5.
2. Stephen Ricks and William Hamblin, *Warfare*, 483.

IV

Resurgence

Mormon Feminism in the Early 2000s

In October 2003, Salt Lake Tribune journalist Peggy Fletcher Stack asked, "Where have all the Mormon feminists gone?" The difficult events of the 1990s, it seemed, had so discouraged Mormon feminists that the future of the movement was in question. But the advent of the Internet created new spaces where Mormon men and women with questions about faith and gender could find one another, form communities, dialogue, share resources, and learn, often with the protective cover of anonymous online identities. Blogs like Feminist Mormon Housewives, The Exponent log (an online venue supported by Exponent II), and Zelophehad's Daughters talked openly about how sex and gender roles impacted the day-to-day lives of Mormons, Mormon theology, and the practice of the Mormon faith, including temple worship, polygamy, Heavenly Mother, and the teaching of chastity and modesty to young people. Mormon feminist bloggers fearlessly plunged into sensitive topics in highly accessible online venues that welcomed community comment and participation. Their personal and humorous tone recalled the work of Mary Bradford and other early Mormon feminist editors in nurturing the personal essay as a key genre for Mormon feminist expression and theory. The blogs also attracted a range of participants, from deeply observant and involved LDS Church members to lapsed and former members who continued to identify as Mormons, and gained international media attention.

From the blogs came a resurgence in Mormon feminist organizing and action. Mormon feminists played key roles in efforts to document and oppose the LDS Church's fight against marriage equality. Younger feminists also organized high-visibility actions such as the international Wear Pants to Church Day in December 2012. Many have openly called for changes to Church policies that limit the participation of Mormon women in decision-making, while others have reopened the conversation about women and priesthood ordination. Spearheaded by Kate Kelly, veteran Mormon feminists including Lorie Winder Stromberg, Margaret Toscano, Nadine Hansen, and Chelsea Shields Strayer joined newer Mormon feminists like Hannah Wheelwright to launch the Ordain Women campaign in March 2013. Guided by the wisdom and experience of these seasoned women's rights activists and fueled by the passion and organizing of

Kelly, the group pushed for a more publicly accountable continuation of the conversation of women's ordination. Ordain Women's website published profiles of Mormon men and women who supported women's priesthood ordination. In October 2013, the group organized women seeking ordination to ask to be admitted to the traditionally men's-only "Priesthood" session of the LDS Church's General Conference. Photographs of the event—with hundreds of Sunday-dressed LDS women patiently waiting to enter a Church meeting but being turned away, one by one, by male LDS Church officials—attracted national media attention. The Ordain Women effort also sparked intense discussion in Mormon communities worldwide, raised the profile of the ordination question, and generated significant momentum for equality-supportive changes in LDS Church policy and practice that would have been considered "too radical" just a few years before. But Ordain Women's direct public approach to the ordination question also generated a backlash, and in June 2014, one of Ordain Women's founders, Kate Kelly, was excommunicated by the LDS Church.

While Kelly's excommunication has been deeply felt among Mormon feminists and their allies, there is no sign that it has discouraged or diminished the energy of the Mormon feminist movement. Key questions centering on priesthood for women, women's role in temple rites, the doctrinal persistence of polygamy, the absence of Heavenly Mother from Mormon worship and practice, and the enfranchisement of women's voices in day-to-day LDS Church decision-making have yet to be addressed by LDS Church leaders and continue to generate powerful discussion at the Mormon grassroots. These questions have been added to in recent years by concerns raised by Mormon women of color about doctrinal and cultural racism and the historic subjugation, tokenization, abuse, or marginalization of indigenous peoples within the LDS Church. Mormon feminists of color have challenged white Mormon feminists to examine and recenter the movement's agenda around issues like domestic violence, poverty, racism, and colonialism that impact Mormon women worldwide, especially in the Global South, where the faith is growing most quickly. As the Mormon feminist movement enters its fifth decade, it continues to offer the Mormon people an opportunity to examine our faith—its historical complexity, its human shortcomings, and its transcendent potential—as we continue to move toward the historic and scriptural ideal of building a Zion free from inequality and domination in all its forms.

Joanna Brooks (1971–), "Where Have All the Mormon Feminists Gone" (2003)

As a Brigham Young University student in the late 1980s and early 1990s, Joanna Brooks studied with Cecilia Konchar Farr, participated in teach-ins, speak-outs, and "Take Back the Night" marches sponsored by the campus organization VOICE, and then witnessed in the spring of 1993 institutional reprisals against feminist faculty and in the fall of 1993 church discipline of feminist intellectuals and activists like Lavina Fielding Anderson, Maxine Hanks, and Lynne Kanavel Whitesides.

As she would remember in her 2012 memoir *The Book of Mormon Girl*, this institutional backlash was understood by younger Mormon feminists as a clear message that the LDS Church had no place for them. In an October 2003 article entitled "Where Have All the Mormon Feminists Gone," journalist Peggy Fletcher Stack noted the sharp drop in Mormon feminist activity and quoted Claudia Bushman as saying that Mormon feminism is "dead or dying within our generation." Brooks answered Stack's question differently in this unpublished poem, drawing imagery from Mormon history—an 1838 Missouri militia attack on the Mormon settlement at Haun's Mill—to mark the flight of younger Mormon feminists but to affirm their survival, their strength, and the potential for the movement's resurgence.

Source

Brooks, Joanna. "Where Have All the Mormon Feminists Gone." Unpublished manuscript (2003).

References and Further Reading

Brooks, Joanna. *The Book of Mormon Girl: A Memoir of an American Faith.* New York: Free Press/ Simon & Schuster, 2012.

Stack, Peggy Fletcher. "Where Have All the Mormon Feminists Gone?" *Salt Lake Tribune* (October 4, 2003).

"WHERE HAVE ALL THE MORMON FEMINISTS GONE"

> The mob came for our writers first,
> for holy books written in milk, blood, tears.
>
> We gathered pages from the dusty streets
> and ran for the cornfields.
>
> Some of us are still lying face down in the fields,
> our damp bodies covering revelations.
>
> Some of us are still hiding in the poplar swamps,
> shivering in wet clothes, mud in our throats.
>
> Some of us vowed not to let them finish their job.
> We set out in dissolving boots, singing, seeking our next vision.

Lorie Winder Stromberg (1952–), "Power Hungry" (2004)

Some Mormon feminists reacted to institutional backlash by retreating or going silent. Lorie Winder Stromberg opted for a less deferential approach. "I've spent too many years on the defensive," she wrote in the classic Mormon feminist essay

"Power Hungry." Stromberg had served on the advisory boards of *Sunstone* magazine, *Dialogue: A Journal of Mormon Thought*, and *Exponent II*, and had been editor of the *Mormon Women's Forum Quarterly* throughout the 1990s, guiding the
decade's most important Mormon feminist publication. An advocate of women's
ordination, Stromberg challenged the presumption that it was unseemly for
Mormon women to seek a greater role in church leadership and broader opportunities to exercise spiritual authority. Her frank and unapologetic approach to
Mormon feminist issues suggested that careful appeals to male LDS Church leaders were not the only path to change. Change would come when Mormon women
overcame their reluctance to claim spiritual authority for themselves.

Source

Stromberg, Lorie Winder. "Power Hungry." *Sunstone* 135 (December 2004): 60–61.

"POWER HUNGRY"

Power is perceived as devouring and dominating. This is why feminists are deri-
sively accused of being power hungry, as if wanting power were necessarily a bad
thing. And it is, if power is seen only as coercive and controlling. But I've spent
too many years on the defensive. It's time I owned the term. Perhaps I am power
hungry. And my question is: Why aren't we all?

*If by power hungry you mean I desire the ability not only to accept responsibili-
ties in the institutional Church but also to be part of defining those responsibilities,
then, yes, I'm power hungry.* Over the years, many Church leaders have asserted
that we should be talking more about taking responsibility than exercising or
demanding rights.[1] But for women, this privileging of responsibility over rights
is problematic. Mormon women seem to have plenty of delegated responsibilities. What is lacking is their right within the organization to oversee and establish
their responsibilities. Responsibility devoid of rights is servitude.

I'm weary of the false dichotomies set up for women in the Church. Former
Relief Society General President Barbara B. Smith and Elder Russell M. Nelson
of the Quorum of the Twelve have both suggested that Mormon women ought
to choose integrity over visibility, charity over charisma.[2] What is wrong with
having both integrity *and* visibility, both charity *and* charisma? Members of the
Church's male hierarchy don't have to make such choices, so why should women?

*If by power hungry you mean I believe women must have a voice in the Church, then,
yes, I'm power hungry.* In a 1993 BYU Women's Conference panel discussion on
working with women, several male panelists admitted that they had never been
forced to take women seriously until they became colleagues.[3] While the panelists'
experiences were from secular settings, the question and answer period exploded
with faithful, mainstream Mormon women wondering how they could get their
Church leaders to listen to them. It was obvious to me, and I said so during this
session, that women in the Church will never have a voice until, as in the secular

arena, they are seen as colleagues—in this case, spiritual colleagues—within the power structure of the Church. How else will women truly be heard?

If by power hungry you mean I believe that women should not only be represented but should also be an integral part of every major decision-making body of the Church, then, yes, I'm power hungry. I've often said that I'm passionately ambivalent about priesthood. I'm not fond of hierarchies and am leery of structures that promote them because they are almost always abusive. However, having power within an institution is preferable to institutional powerlessness, particularly if we are able as women to bring to the center of our religious community the consciousness of what it is like on the margins.

Positional power in the Church is granted primarily to those who hold the priesthood. This is particularly true above the local level. While a charismatic woman might have significant influence on a ward or perhaps even a stake level, beyond that point, positional power for women evaporates. Since, for the most part, we as a Church no longer recognize charismatic power—only positional power—is it possible for women to have equal status to men in the Church without being ordained to the priesthood?

Perhaps recognizing the inequity inherent in an all-male priesthood, Bruce Hafen tried to minimize its importance. In his keynote address, "Women, Feminism, and the Blessings of the Priesthood," given at the 1985 BYU Women's Conference, Hafen listed several of the blessings that were available to both men and women in the Church. As if it were a mere trifle, he added, "The one category of blessing in which the role of women is not the same as that of men holding the priesthood is that of administering the gospel and *governing all things*" (my emphasis). As I read this, I wondered, how could Hafen deliver this line with a straight face, and perhaps more disturbing, how could an audience of women listen to it in silence?

If by power hungry you mean I would welcome a heightened ability to bless the lives of others, then, yes, I'm power hungry. Aside from its administrative function, if priesthood is merely a sort of temporal permission to tap spiritual resources already available to the faithful, then it is superfluous. If, however, priesthood truly is a real, bestowed power that can enhance our ability to bring comfort and peace and joy into the world, then, yes, I'm power hungry and unambivalently so. Who would not righteously want such a power?

Finally, if by power hungry you mean I want the ability to participate in a model of power based on partnership rather than patriarchy, based on empowerment rather than domination, then, yes, I'm power hungry. Christ came to overthrow traditional models of power, which were based on dominance, coercion, and control.[4] In their place, Jesus offered a model in which power is used to empower. Power used to dominate, coerce, or control will always burn itself out; only power used to empower is everlasting.

By now I've given sufficient weight to the word *power* in the term "power hungry." Alas, I've neglected the word *hungry*. Just as by power, I do not mean domination or coercion, but rather voice and influence and empowerment, so by hungry I do not mean gluttony. Rather, I'm talking about sustenance. I'm talking about a soul deep yearning for a life-sustaining, sacramental meal to which all are invited.

Notes

1. See Gordon B. Hinckley, "Ten Gifts from the Lord," Relief Society General Women's Meeting, 28 September 1985, published in *Ensign*, November 1985, 86; Patricia T. Holland, "A Woman's Perspective on the Priesthood," *Tambuli*, 6, no. 5 (June 1982): 21; Russell M. Nelson, "Woman—of Infinite Worth," *Ensign*, November 1989, 20.
2. Nelson, "Woman," 20; Barbara B. Smith, "The Legacy Remembered and Renewed," Relief Society General Women's Meeting, 27 March 1982.
3. "Relating to the Other: Building Bridges, Working Together," panel discussion with Kate Kirkham, Todd Britsch, Olani Durrant, Mack Lawrence, and Steven C. Walker, BYU Women's Conference, 29 April 1993.
4. Scott Bartchy, "Jesus, Power, and Gender Roles," Sunstone Symposium, 18 August 1994 (tape SL94–190).

Chieko Nishimura Okazaki (1926–2011), "There Is Always a Struggle" (2005)

Chieko Nishimura Okazaki grew up in Hawaii, the daughter of Buddhist Japanese-American farmworkers. She joined the LDS Church in Hawaii in 1941. A professional educator, Okazaki was appointed in 1962 to the global board of the Church's Young Women's Mutual Improvement Association, becoming the first person of color to serve in a global LDS Church capacity. She was called in 1990 to serve in the General Relief Society Presidency as one of the top three officers of the LDS Church's global women's organization. Okazaki was beloved for her warmth and energy as well as her candor and courage in speaking to difficult issues like sexual abuse and racism within LDS contexts. In this 2005 interview with Mormon historian Greg Prince, Okazaki describes her experience delivering a landmark address on sexual abuse in Portland, Oregon, in 1992; her remarks were released in an audiotape edition by LDS Church-owned Deseret Book in 1993. Okazaki also offers a rare inside perspective on the role of women in LDS Church decision-making, and affirms—just as Mormon feminist Algie Ballif had—the spiritual value of growth through struggle.

Source

Okazaki, Chieko, and Greg Prince. "'There Is Always a Struggle': An Interview with Chieko Okazaki." *Dialogue: A Journal of Mormon Thought* 45.1 (2012): 112–40.

References and Further Reading

Okazaki, Chieko. *Aloha!* Salt Lake City: Deseret Book, 1995.

Okazaki, Chieko. *Healing from Sexual Abuse.* Audiotape. Salt Lake City: Deseret Book, 1993. (Transcript available at http://www.ldswomenofgod.com/blog/wp-content/uploads/2010/01/Healing-from-Sexual-Abuse.pdf.)

Okazaki, Chieko. *Lighten Up!* Salt Lake City: Deseret Book, 1993.

"THERE IS ALWAYS A STRUGGLE"

Chieko Okazaki: Every time I'm invited to speak at a women's conference, I talk to the stake Relief Society president and ask, "Tell me your sisters' needs. What would you like me to talk about?" This time, the Relief Society president said, "Sexual abuse." I said, "Say that again?" "Sexual abuse." I said, "Is there anything else?" She said, "I hate to say this, but I wish you could speak about sexual abuse." I said I would and then I prayed and prayed. I had worked with some people who had this problem in their past to deal with, but I certainly wasn't an expert. And when I got there, that place was just packed!

Greg Prince: Did they know, in advance, that was what you were going to speak on?

CO: No, they didn't. No one knew except the stake Relief Society president and the stake president and the Regional Representative.

GP: So they all signed off on it in advance?

CO: Yes. The other board member I went with was doing a light-hearted, encouraging talk. I whispered to the stake Relief Society president, "I don't think I can speak after that." She said, "You're going to." So I thought, "Well, here I go." I started, and I gave a little bit of humor in the beginning. Then I got into it. There was silence. You could hear a pin drop. And then you could hear sniffles, people crying. There was a woman in the front row who just burst into tears and cried through the rest of the talk. All through the audience there were tears coming down. I thought, "Oh, what have I done?" But I went right on. After the meeting—it was 8:30 when we were through—until 10:00 there was a line of people who wanted to talk to me. At the end was a man. I thought, "Oh, don't tell me I'm going to talk to a man about being sexually abused." I knew it happened to boys as well, but I just wasn't prepared for it. He said, "I'm a bishop." He thanked me for being brave enough to give this talk. He said, "I have worked with ninety women. It got to the point where I could not say no to these women for therapy. The stake president and the Regional Representative stopped me from using Church funds, so I used my own money so these women could get therapy." Ninety! When inactive women heard that he was helping abuse victims, they had hope and wanted to talk to him. It's awful, when you think about it.

GP: All the women who were in line to talk to you, what was the message they were giving you?

CO: They were saying, "Thank you so much for opening this up. Thank you so much that I don't need to hide by myself, and worry and be concerned about me being the person who was wrong and that I did something really bad." They just recognized that somebody finally had opened this topic up and that now the Church would know that it's a problem that it's okay to talk about and that they were okay.

GP: So part of the secret of your success is that you've been willing to tackle hard topics that nobody else has. Any other secrets?

CO: I don't know if it's a secret, but I'm very honest when I talk to the women, especially about the gospel. For example, I was in another state where I had a speaking assignment, and there was a luncheon before. I was seated next to a mother and daughter. The daughter was inactive, but she'd come to this luncheon with her mother, who had told me how worried she was about her daughter and the choices she was making. I knew we didn't have much time, so I didn't beat around the bush. I said, "You know, you are blessed that you have been born in the Church. What a blessing it is that your mother is still very staunch in doing the things that she knows that she ought to do. But she is not making you do the same things, because she respects your agency. But that means you have to make a choice. Your choice is whether to leave the Church or to be in the Church. So, I'm just going to tell you that you should really study the gospel, get back into the scriptures and read them, and then God will tell you what your choice should be." Then I said, "You know, I have to make a lot of choices in life, too; but I'm glad it isn't whether I should leave the Church or not. That's a choice I made when I joined the Church." But when I was having this conversation with the daughter, I couldn't help thinking that I'd had moments when I thought, "Why should I belong to this Church when I'm not accepted? But it must be for a reason that I'm here." I gradually learned that part of that reason was so people would learn how to accept people who are not of their color. . . .

CO: I was the education counselor, so I worked with one of the men on the curriculum committee. We wanted to change the manual so that it brought up modern-day problems that women have to face and focus on how to implement some of the gospel doctrines and principles in dealing with the problem. I had written a general outline, and the Relief Society presidency approved it. So I talked about it to a man on the Curriculum Committee. He went to his boss, and the boss said, "We don't need a new manual for the Relief Society." "Why don't we need a new manual?" "We already are writing a manual for them." So he came back and told me that a new manual was already being prepared. I asked what it was, and he said, "Well, it's the manual on Harold B. Lee." It was the first one in that series of teachings of the Church presidents. I asked, "Why are they writing a manual for us on Harold B. Lee?" He didn't know.

I told the presidency, so we went and asked the Curriculum Committee, "What is this all about?" They said, "Well, we're already almost finished with the first book." We said, "You're almost finished with the first book, and you didn't tell us that you were doing this? Why is this is the first time we have heard about it? Chieko has been writing an outline in relation to what women need." So I asked, "Who is writing this manual?" It turned out to be five men, and the Melchizedek Priesthood quorums and Relief Society would have the same lessons. I asked, "Why aren't the women included in this?" Then they sort of got the point and called three women to the committee. I just thought, "Where are we, anyway, in this entire thing?" It was such a shock! I said, "How did this come about?" "Well, President Hinckley thought that many of the people who live outside the United States don't have the privilege of having any doctrinal books in their homes. He thinks we should have a manual where we have the prophets speak about their doctrines, so they would at least have a doctrinal book in their home." That's a good idea. "He decided maybe this would be a good thing to have for the priesthood and the Relief Society." "Well, why wasn't it discussed with us, too?"

We asked one time if we could be on the building committee and the temple committee, because sometimes we think, "Why did they build it this way?"—because it doesn't work very well for the women's needs. And we wanted to be on the temple committee, because there are many things that affect women in the temple. But we were never allowed to be a part of those committees. I think we could help a great deal, but you have to have leaders in the Church who are willing to make that possible.

GP: Do you see that as perhaps coming from beneath? That as you have new generations of women who are the wives of bishops and stake presidents, and who are ward and stake Relief Society and Young Women leaders, that they are going to grasp the reins a little bit stronger than their predecessors?

CO: I have to say that, in my sixty-four years in the Church, I sometimes see a little bit of a change that the women themselves prompt, but most of the time, I haven't seen women who would make that change possible. Wherever I go, I think that they already know their place. Maybe they'd be able to be more open if there were open-minded bishops or stake presidents who would listen to some of the feelings and the ideas of the women. But when women get the message that their job is to be supportive and just agree with the decisions of the bishop, they become clams.

GP: Should the Relief Society president sit in on bishopric meetings?

CO: It would be a great idea. They are in the council meetings, but in many council meetings the person who is in charge is the only one who is talking. I'm on several community boards, and sometimes I'm the only woman there or one of two or three women. If I got the message that I was supposed to just sit there and listen to the men, I'd quit that board. I'd say, "What am I here for?" I speak up a lot in all of these board meetings.

In contrast, in 1995 when "The Family: A Proclamation to the World" was written, the Relief Society presidency was asked to come to a meeting. We did, and they read this proclamation. It was all finished. The only question was whether they should present it at the priesthood meeting or at the Relief Society meeting. It didn't matter to me where it was presented. What I wanted to know was, "How come we weren't consulted?"

GP: You didn't even know it was in the works?

CO: No. They just asked us which meeting to present it in, and we said, "Whatever President Hinckley decides is fine with us." He decided to do it at the Relief Society meeting. The apostle who was our liaison said, "Isn't it wonderful that he made the choice to present it at the Relief Society meeting?" Well, that was fine, but as I read it I thought that we could have made a few changes in it.

Sometimes I think they get so busy that they forget that we are there. It's different from the time when Belle Spafford was president of the Relief Society. She was her own boss, as I read her life. And so was Florence Jacobsen. There's a great deal of difference now.

GP: Don't forget LaVern Parmley.

CO: Yes. "The Big Three," I call them. Boy, they were staunch and strong women!

GP: And it didn't bother David O. McKay one bit.

CO: No! It did not. Sister Spafford was on international and national women's committees. Mormon women were out there! But gradually, things were taken away from Belle Spafford. I remember when the U.N. sponsored a women's international meeting in Beijing. Elaine asked if we could attend, and we were denied. We couldn't go.

GP: Do you see change coming?

CO: There's change in society. Women are now presidents of companies and presidents of countries—

GP: But it's still in transition.

CO: Oh, yes, it's in transition. I guess it's a cultural thing. You know, when we went on our mission, the members would see Ed and me working together, and I would conduct the programs and assignments that I had, and the brethren were taken aback when they saw that. But in the three years we were there, we saw a lot of change about how husbands and wives worked together. Many Japanese women told me how much they appreciated the example that Ed and I were to them.

GP: And not because you were pushing an agenda, but because that's what you were.

CO: That's exactly right. And, you know, we need to talk about this to the young women.

GP: And let them know that it's okay for them to speak in an honest voice.

CO: It seems to me like Christ loved the women. I think he really included them in many areas where Jewish society excluded them. He didn't mind breaking those rules.

GP: So where do we need to go to get women in the Church where He wants them to be?

CO: I think women should continue really immersing themselves in the scriptures and praying so that they know what Christ really thinks. I think that women feel that they need to know every law and every principle of the gospel, and have to live it, so that they can be more perfect. They're hard on themselves because they're not already perfect. Whenever I speak, I try to share this principle with them: "I'm not perfect, but I try to live the principle as best I can. When I see that I can improve, I try to do that."

In one of my books is the talk I gave about the principle of *kigatsuku*. *Ki* means "within your soul." When you get to the point where you can see things and do them without being told, that means it's part of your soul, and you will be doing fine. When my mom used to teach me, she would say, "Oh, I'm looking for a *kigatsuku* girl." I'd see her sweeping the floor, so I'd run and get the dustpan. I was just a little girl then. She would say, "Oh, that was a *kigatsuku* girl." She would be washing clothes and she would say, "I'm looking for a *kigatsuku* girl." I'd look to see: "Oh, I need to rinse the clothes and hang them." We had to put our wood in the Japanese bath, and she would say, "I'm looking for a *kigatsuku* girl," and I'd look to see if she had enough wood. If she didn't, I'd go and get the wood.

But it got to the point where she didn't need to tell me anymore. I'd see things and I'd do it on my own. Being *kigatsuku* was part of my soul. I still have that within me. I see something, and I think it needs to be done, and I just go and do it. It becomes part of me, and this is how she taught me. She never lectured me and said, "This is the principle and you must do this." Instead, she taught me by doing it herself.

My mother taught me another principle: *on*. It meant that you felt gratitude and recognized your obligation to someone who had helped you. My greatest *on* in life is to my mother. She turned ninety-eight this year. She never lectured me, but she never stopped teaching me. I remember once when I was just a little girl and did something wrong. She took me by the hand and we walked into the bedroom and sat on the floor in front of the mirror, so that I could see both her and me. She told me that life is hard and that we learn by experience. She said, "I'm going to tell you some of the experiences I have had, ever since I was a little girl." Her life had been very hard. I just cried the whole time she talked to me. I had always loved her, but that love developed new depths as she talked. I realized then that all of us have to go through struggles to become the kind of person that we want to be.

She had a brilliant mind. Her mother died when she was in the sixth grade, and
she left school to take care of the younger children in the family. But she studied on her own. She could read papers and books in Japanese, which I can't
do. Once she said to me, "I'm getting to the point where the books are so hard
to read that I need a dictionary." So I sent her a dictionary. She taught me,
"No matter what you do, there is always a struggle. But when you pass that
struggle, you have reached a new level of perfection in your life."

I look at my work in the Church the same way. I'm going to struggle. I have
struggled. Christ struggled. When He died, He was struggling the most. Yet
He is going to come in His perfection when He comes back the second time,
and we can, too.

Kynthia Taylor (1977–), "The Trouble with Chicken Patriarchy" (2007)

The rise of Internet blogging reinvigorated Mormon feminism. Blogs gave
Mormon feminists the power to reach larger audiences in an immediate, interac-
tive format, and the public anonymity of the blog format—many early Mormon
feminist bloggers and commenters used pseudonyms or screen names—also
allowed Mormon feminists to maintain their privacy while publicly and candidly
exploring critical dimensions of faith and gender issues, offering a sense of protection from potential Church reprisals. In January 2006, *Zelophehad's Daughters*
joined the Mormon "bloggernacle," the constellation of Mormon-themed blogs
named after the historic Mormon Tabernacle in downtown Salt Lake City.
Launched by the seven siblings—six sisters, one brother—of the Taylor family of
Orem, Utah, *Zelophehad's Daughters* drew its name from a story from Numbers
27 wherein the daughters of a recently deceased man named Zelophehad ask
Moses to allow them to inherit their father's property, even though biblical law
mandated that only sons could stand to inherit it. With several of the Taylor siblings studying for advanced degrees in subjects ranging from theology to statis-
tics, ZD aimed "to contribute an academic angle on Mormon feminism," recalls
blogger Sheila Taylor. In this classic essay, blogger Kynthia Taylor (also known
as Kiskilili, a screen name chosen in tribute to an Akkadian demoness) critiques
Mormon gender theology as a "doctrinal hodge-podge" lacking systematic coherence and rigor. Mormonism's lack of systematic theology—a consequence in
part of its lay clergy—empowers LDS Church leaders to embrace rhetorically
contradictory positions: for example, stating in "The Family: A Proclamation to
the World" (1995) both that men and women are "equal partners" *and* that men
by "divine design" "preside" over their households. This "chicken patriarchy," as
Kiskilili names it, allows Mormons to publicly espouse egalitarian sentiments

without instituting gender equality in the Church's liturgy, policy, and practice. With the emergence of the feminist bloggernacle and the adoption of the more compact, vernacular, and accessible form of the blog post, the project of Mormon feminist theology shifted from reclaiming the potential energies of the past to naming and critiquing the contradictions and shortcomings of contemporary LDS doctrine on gender.

Source

Taylor, Kynthia. "The Trouble with Chicken Patriarchy." *Zelophehad's Daughters* (November 30, 2007). http://zelophehadsdaughters.com/2007/11/30/the-trouble-w ith-chicken-patriarchy/.

"THE TROUBLE WITH CHICKEN PATRIARCHY"

When it comes to patriarchy, the Church is all over the map. Husbands preside, but husbands and wives are equal partners. Boyd K. Packer has said, "While the husband, the father, has responsibility to provide worthy and inspired leadership, his wife is neither behind him nor ahead of him but at his side."* The two are "equally yoked" side by side, but the husband "provides leadership," implying that the wife supplies the "followership"—not from a position behind him, but rather at his side: perhaps they are meant to walk sidewise? (This all sounds more awkward than a three-legged race.)

Some rejoice in this doctrinal hodge-podge, reasoning that any of the Church's various positions on what patriarchy involves can be selected and advocated for as the "official" stance with a reasonable stamp of approval from the magisterium. Statements can be pulled willy-nilly from a wide array of publications to form the cornerstones to individuals' idiosyncratic conceptions of, and attempts to implement, what the Church teaches about gender and marriage. The trouble, though, is that the Church does not acknowledge its many faces of patriarchy, preaching as though its doctrine on the matter is uniform, unambiguous, immutable, and universally incumbent on its members.

Today, a certain wanderlust regarding what patriarchy entails has infected most of the Church's discourse on gender, which bops around between the two poles of patriarchy and egalitarianism without any clear destination. In the past, the waters were less muddied: husbands were granted divine authority over their wives, who were required to submit to their righteous leadership—an objectionable stance, perhaps, but not an inconsistent one. In the present, the Church has adopted a new stance but without giving up its old one: now wives not only submit, but they are also equal partners. (It's unclear what this is supposed to look like on the ground—sort of like when dictators hold "democratic" elections they mysteriously win?)

---

* See Boyd K. Packer, "The Relief Society," *Ensign* 28 (May 1998): 73.

This rather mind-boggling situation, in which the Church simultaneously embraces most of the spectrum on gender roles from traditionalist positions to egalitarianism, is not simply soft patriarchy, although a recent tendency to soften patriarchal language is one important ingredient in the mix. Neither is it traditional patriarchy, nor egalitarianism. Chicken Patriarchy never allows itself to be pinned down to a single perspective; chameleonlike, it alters its attitude from day to day and sometimes even from sentence to sentence, too chicken to stand up for what it believes. By refusing to settle down in any one place on the map, Chicken Patriarchs can embrace egalitarianism and still continue to uphold time-honored traditions of male authority.

Unfortunately, Chicken Patriarchy lacks the moral backbone to repudiate unequivocal occasions of patriarchy still observable in our scripture, ritual and organizational structure. It can never exorcise the more-or-less dead ghosts and occasional live demons of women's subordination or expected subordination because it fails to take a consistent stand, emitting as it does a storm of mixed signals. In the spirit of Elijah, I wonder: How long halt ye between two opinions?* If patriarchy be appropriate, follow it; but if egalitarianism, follow it.

If patriarchy is God's will, why not stand up and take the flak for advocating values that have been taught from Adam to Paul, from Joseph Smith through most of his heirs, from the temple to the pulpit? If it's not, why continue to cling to patriarchal language and women's ritual submission to men?

"What Women Know" (2007)

At the LDS Church's General Conference in October 2007, General Relief Society President Julie Beck gave an address entitled "Mothers Who Know," defining Mormon women's faithfulness in terms of their accomplishments as mothers and homemakers. Beck's address, which recalled LDS Church President Ezra Taft Benson's generation-defining February 1987 "To the Mothers in Zion" speech, struck a deep chord among veteran Mormon feminists due to its exclusionary focus on stay-at-home mothers, its narrow definition of women's spiritual accomplishment in terms of housekeeping and the production of religiosity in children, and its guilt-inducing perfectionist overtones. It soon became the subject of intense debate and reaction on Internet mailing lists and networks. "I remember feeling so sad and excluded hearing President Beck's talk, then getting angry and wanting to reclaim my place at the table, then excitedly sharing all these feelings and thoughts on feminist Internet lists," remembers Becky Reid Linford. "It galvanized me into doing something for the first time ever." Mormon feminists were able to utilize the powers of the Internet to creative an immediate,

---

*See 1 Kings 18: 21.

collective, and participatory response to Beck's talk. Led by Cheryl McGuire, Marnie Leavitt, Doe Daughtrey, Kay Gaisford, Paula Goodfellow, and Pauli Smith, the "What Women Know" collective—which included participants and former participants in *Exponent II*, Mormons for ERA, Mormon Women's Forum, and VOICE at BYU—authored a statement emphasizing the diversity of Mormon women's lives at home and in the workplace, the importance of shared responsibility and egalitarian families, and the danger of assessing a woman's spirituality based on the condition of her home or the religious choices of her children. The document was published on the Internet on November 15, 2007. Within seven days, hundreds of women and men had added their signatures. Speaking out in a way that could be perceived as criticism of Church leaders is considered taboo among many Mormons; for this reason, some "What Women Know" signers had to overcome private fears of reprisals from ecclesiastical leaders—the emotional legacy of the excommunications of the 1990s—and disapproval from Mormon family members, friends, and fellow congregants. But the experience of claiming a space in which they could publicly and collectively speak their truths about their lives as Mormon women proved transformative for the women who crafted and signed "What Women Know." Their effort marked the beginnings of a new form of collective Internet-based Mormon feminist activism.

Source

"What Women Know" (November 15, 2007), http://whatwomenknow.org.

"WHAT WOMEN KNOW"

In October 2007, Julie B. Beck, president of the Latter-day Saint women's organization the Relief Society, gave a speech in the semiannual worldwide General Conference titled "Mothers Who Know." Beck's focus on LDS families, and more particularly on the role and influence of mothers, is a subject close to our hearts. Who are we? We are women who differ in age, income, race/ethnicity, and marital status. Many of us are mothers, some with exceptionally large families. Some of us are grandmothers and great-grandmothers many times over. Some are young mothers, with infants and elementary-age children. Others of us—for reasons of biology, opportunity, or choice—do not have children. Some of us have never married. Some of us are single because of divorce, widowhood, choice, or limited opportunity. A few of us have been with the same partner more than 50 years. We all work—paid or unpaid, both inside and outside our homes. We share many decades of church service among us. In fact, our LDS background is our common denominator. Several ideas within the body of President Beck's talk conflict with our inspiration and experience. We are authors of our own lives, and this is the story we know to be true:

What Women Know

Fathers as well as mothers, men as well as women, are called to nurture. Nurturing is not confined to mothering or housekeeping, but is a universal attribute that communicates patience, peacefulness, and care.

Individuals and relationships flourish when we are able to share not only our strengths but also our mutual imperfections and needs. It is difficult to be compassionate with ourselves and others when we internalize injunctions to perform (e.g., "the highest-performing sister missionary," "the best homemaker in the world," "the most patient and loving mother"). Motherhood and sisterhood cannot be reduced to the performance of narrowly-prescribed tasks, but emerge from who we know ourselves to be.

Cleanliness depends upon access to resources and has more to do with priorities than purity of heart. We do not place the additional burden of "outward appearances" on our sisters who are hauling fuel and water long distances; who are struggling with poverty, isolation, or ill health; or who choose values that take precedence over orderly living quarters and polished looks.

Housework is something that grownups do and that children learn by example and instruction. Unfortunately, women and girls still perform the bulk of the world's low-paid and unpaid labor, including housework—often at the expense of their own education, leadership, creativity, health, and well-being. Men and boys who share care-work and household responsibilities make it possible for all family members to live happier, more fulfilling lives.

We reverence the responsibility to choose how, when, and whether we become parents. Many of us have adoptive and foster children and grandchildren from diverse ethnicities and cultures. We have given birth to children who range widely on every dimension—from personality, appearance, and sexual identity to physical, social, and mental ability. No matter what their differences, we care for them all.

Effective parenting is a learned behavior, and, as parents, we learn and grow with each child. Children come with their own gifts, challenges, and freedom of choice. We reject teachings that encourage women to shoulder ultimate responsibility for every aspect of child-rearing and family life, and to take on shame and guilt when things do not go according to plan.

The choice to have children does not rule out other avenues of influence and power. By valuing ourselves as lifelong achievers, apart from our roles as mothers, friends, partners, sisters, aunts, and grandmothers, we stand for creativity, public service, competence, and growth. We take joy in the collective contributions we make in the fields of government, medicine, academia, law, journalism, human services, business, art, health care advocacy, music, technology, child development, and science.

When it comes to employment, most women prefer the luxury of choice to the limitations of necessity. Women-friendly policies such as flex-time and comparable pay for women and men, access to health care, family leave for births and care-work, and affordable, high-quality childcare give all of us—single or partnered, impoverished or privileged—greater choice in how to support ourselves and our families.

We work because we want to; because we need to; and because we have no other choice. We know that "children are more important than possessions, position, and prestige." Some of us have been thrust into the position of sole economic support of our children through desertion, divorce, domestic violence, or death. Indeed, too many of us have learned that we are just one fully-employed male away from poverty.

Men are our fathers, sons, brothers, partners, lovers, and friends. Many of them also struggle within a system that equates leadership with hierarchy and domination. We distrust separate-but-equal rhetoric; anyone who is regularly reminded that she is "equally important" is probably not. Partnership is illusory without equal decision-making power.

We have discovered that healthy relationships are equitable relationships. A relationship that is balanced in terms of economic and emotional power is safer and more resilient than a relationship in which one partner holds most or all of the power. Women with active support networks and marketable skills have greater options, not only in relationships, but in life.

We claim the life-affirming powers of spirit and wisdom, and reject the glorification of violence in all its forms. We are filled with unutterable sadness by the Book of Mormon story of more than 2,000 young soldiers whose mothers teach them that faith in God will preserve them in battles in which they kill other mothers' children.* This is not a success story. It is a story of the failure of human relationships and the horrors of war. In a world that has grown increasingly violent, we believe that one of the most important passages in LDS scripture is D&C 98:16: "Therefore, renounce war and proclaim peace. . . ."

Our roles as mothers, sisters, daughters, partners, and friends are just a few of the many parts we will play in the course of our lives. We may influence hundreds, perhaps thousands of lives. But we are not our roles. We are created in the image of the divine—people of worth in our own right, in our choices, in our individuality, and in our belief that the life story we are ultimately responsible for is our own.

---

* Beck opened her talk by referencing the Book of Mormon story of two thousand young men or "stripling warriors" who are sent by their families into a devastating battle (Alma 53–57). Whereas this story is commonly glorified in LDS culture, "Women Who Know" here present the sacrifice of two thousand young men as a tragic loss.

Lisa Butterworth (1974–), "13 Articles of Healthy Chastity" (2010)

Just as in the 1980s Mary Bradford had encouraged Mormon women to adopt the personal essay as a venue for coming to terms with their questions about faith and gender, blogs allowed Mormon feminists to process their complex subjective experiences within and feelings about the faith with immediacy and emotional range. No one mastered this immediate, grassroots, and vernacular approach to Mormon feminism better than Lisa Butterworth. Born and raised in rural Castle Dale, Utah, Butterworth was a stay-at-home mother of three, Sunday School teacher, and Democrat, living in Boise, Idaho, who found herself feeling frustrated and desperately isolated as 2004 election-year political rhetoric escalated all around her. After Google-searching the words "Mormon" and "liberal," Butterworth discovered that the civil, thoughtful conversation about faith and politics she could not find in her congregation or home community was happening in the nascent bloggernacle. In August 2004, hungry for blog content that addressed issues of concern to progressive Mormon women, she launched "Feminist Mormon Housewives," with an original tagline "Angry Activists with Diapers to Change" that would later transition to "A Safe Place to Be Feminist and Faithful." Butterworth assembled a team of bloggers and moderators who addressed issues from theology and politics to gender dynamics in Mormon culture and the triumphs and indignities of motherhood, an acknowledgment both of the actual lives of many of the blog's writers and readers as well as the faith's historic emphasis on motherhood. Within a few years, Feminist Mormon Housewives had developed a loyal following of thousands of readers, won attention from the national media, and infused Mormon feminism with new and transformative energy for a new generation. In this 2010 essay, Butterworth offered a thorough and incisive critique of the way sexual morality had been taught to young Mormon women in the Church's official curriculum. She then offers an alternative set of ideas—"13 Articles" modeled on the "13 Articles of Faith" written by Joseph Smith as a summary of LDS doctrine in 1842—for conveying LDS Church standards of chastity in ways that affirmed fundamental Mormon doctrines about sexuality as a divine component of human nature and the agency, dignity, and authority of both women and men in making sexual choices.

Source

Butterworth, Lisa. "13 Articles of Healthy Chastity." *Feminist Mormon Housewives* (November 3, 2010). www.feministmormonhousewives.org/2010/11/13-articles-of-healthy-chastity/.

References and Further Reading

McKay, Tracy. "Perverting Modesty." *By Common Consent* (July 9, 2011). http://bycommon-consent.com/2011/07/09/perverting-modesty/.

"13 ARTICLES OF HEALTHY CHASTITY"

1. Overhaul the Y[oung] W[omen's] manuals, specifically emphasize chastity, virtue, and modesty as positive powerful choices, and affirm the sacred nature of our bodies and our respect for God.
2. Remove the defensive fear-based vignettes, change emphasis from "one-slip-n-you're-toast" to the healing power of the Atonement.
3. Ask youth leaders/teachers specifically to avoid object lessons that demean our divine nature or compare young women to objects (wilted flowers, tainted food, chewed up gum, battered wood, cabbages or licked cake).
4. Stop talking about modesty as anything other than a sign of self respect. Make boys guardians of their own virtue; girls have no stewardship over boys' thoughts or actions.
5. Ask teachers not to have activities emphasizing outward appearance (like make overs and fashion shows) because teaching girls they must always be "modestly hot" in order to attract a husband is still teaching the false illusory power of attracting male attention with our bodies.
6. Root out references to the myth of male weakness. Emphasize that men can control themselves.
7. Include nuance in discussions about sex thoughts, sex discussions, sexual desire, and porn. Our Young Women will think about sex, they will see porn, they will feel desire; they need to talk about sex with reliable adults; they need tools, not blanket prohibitions and condemnation.
8. Include lessons on physical abuse, sexual abuse, emotional abuse, and unrighteous dominion.
9. Empower girls to listen to personal revelation.
10. Emphasize that girls who are raped and abused are not responsible for their abuse. That there is no loss of chastity or virtue.
11. Train bishops on what date/acquaintance rape looks like. On my small blog alone, I can think of dozens of women who were called to repentance after being raped.
12. Encourage parents to have ongoing explicit age-appropriate discussions with their children about sex. It is vital that we lift the veil of silence and discomfort. Many Mormon parents are naively worried that they will give their children ideas, or somehow corrupt them with facts. The fact is that children are surrounded by sex, lots of bad information, and tons of sexually explicit materials. But it is a proven fact that the more reliable factual knowledge kids have about sex, the more they talk to their parents about sex, the less likely they are to engage in it. It may be too much to ask, but I dream of a day when the church provides parents with age appropriate manuals for a comprehensive factual approach to sex-education that uses words like penis and vagina and sex.

13. I am going to introduce my final and perhaps most pressing suggestion with another comment from F[eminist] M[ormon] H[ousewives] by AJ:

> Sexual abuse in my childhood had spurred in me an odd fascination with sex, leading to experimentation with masturbation and pornography. These issues were never addressed directly in Y[oung] W[omen's]. Everything I knew about the church's stance on these issues came from reading the priesthood session talks in the conference *Ensigns*. I felt such deep shame—not only was I a sinner, I was sinning in a way only boys were supposed to sin.
>
> Talking to bishops was awkward at best, harmful at worst. I was asked such inappropriate questions as "Did you orgasm?" and was even manipulated and seduced into a physical relationship with one of my bishops. More often the issues I faced when trying to confess these transgressions was embarrassment—more on the part of the bishop than myself.
>
> These men intended to help me would turn bright red and stutter that I should just stop these behaviors. They were too embarrassed to provide real support.
>
> Now, I think bishops are in general very good men trying hard to do God's work. But I was very, very deeply hurt by the actions of some of the bishops I worked with as a teen.
>
> The amount of pain and confusion caused by the bishop who developed a physically romantic relationship with me is immeasurable and ongoing. I believe he was essentially a good man who just made some very, very bad mistakes. He's received his punishment and forgiveness and he continues to takes steps to ensure that he never hurts anyone that way again.
>
> But after what I endured at his hands I feel it is absolutely 100% inappropriate for YW to be taught that they must discuss sexual transgressions with an untrained older man in order to obtain the Lord's forgiveness. I won't pass on that teaching to my daughters, and you can bet I'll never be turning to a priesthood leader for counsel regarding my sexuality again.

AJ's life unfortunately encapsulates all the problems that exist in the current system of women confessing to men. Even in the best case scenario, it is deeply inorganic, brutally awkward, and let's be frank: it's just plain old creepy. Young women should not be locked in a small office with a middle aged man who has not been trained in any way to counsel young people about sex, and then asked explicit questions about their sex lives. Even if he is the most spiritual kindly man in the world, the situation is just wrong. And when he is not that man, when he is a weaker man, the situation is ripe for abuse, and it is abused, far too frequently.

I can see two possible solutions to this problem. The first is to require that young women have a parent or YW leader present in her interviews with the bishop. I still see this as an imperfect solution, because while it does protect her, it also intrudes further on her privacy.

My preferred solution would be to turn the stewardship of women's sexuality over to women. Just as in the temple there are certain settings where it is inappropriate for a man to interact with women and in those situations women are given stewardship, so too is it inappropriate for men to be taking sexual confessions from women and to be asking sexually explicit questions of women. Relief Society presidents and Young Women's presidents could be given this stewardship as part of their calling, to exercise those keys in a limited way, just as matrons do in the temple.

We Mormons have a well-deserved reputation as some of the most innocent and uptight people on the planet, which is ironic considering our beliefs about sex and marriage. Unlike many other faiths, we believe that sex should be enjoyed and even celebrated between a wife and her husband. Given that Mormonism is a religion of embodied parent Gods, and we believe our bodies are a sacred gift and that sex may just be an eternal part of our celestial existence, I think we need to look at this problem with profound seriousness and make the changes necessary for Mormon women to feel empowered by their positive sex choices and celebrate their bodies as divine sexual beings.

Joanna Brooks (1971–), "Invocation / Benediction" (2010)

Throughout the late twentieth century, the LDS Church had pursued a program of "correlation," consolidating formerly independent auxiliaries under one hierarchical, male-headed chain of command and developing tightly coordinated and closely monitored channels for communicating with members. A sense of univocality, uniformity, and control characterized LDS Church manuals and publications and often Sunday meetings as well. But the rise in the 2000s of the Mormon bloggernacle provided venues for the articulation of an unprecedentedly broad range of individual perspectives, concerns, and experiences within the Mormon faith. On blogs and in their lived faith, Mormon feminists lead this movement toward a more open and accepting Mormonism. In this poem, Joanna Brooks uses an image from traditional Mormon women's handcraft, the quilt, to imagine a Mormonism broader than the institutional LDS Church, a faith welcoming to Mormons at all points on the orthodoxy spectrum, and accepting of the kinds of lived contradictions Mormon feminists have learned to live with as they negotiate what Claudia Bushman called the "dual platforms" of Mormonism and feminism. Hers is a hopeful rejoinder to the logic of excommunication—correlation's pushing out of members who didn't fit the orthodox mold—that had haunted Mormon feminists and progressives since the 1970s.

Source

Brooks, Joanna. "Invocation/Benediction." *Exponent II* 50.5 (December 2010): 18.

References and Further Reading

Brooks, Joanna. *The Book of Mormon Girl: A Memoir of an American Faith.* New York: Free Press/ Simon & Schuster, 2012.

"INVOCATION / BENEDICTION"

Father, Mother, help me piece together the contradictions of my life:
White cotton, red satin, brown polka dot; torn Sunday dress, Navajo rug,
  frayed baby blanket.
Make me insistent on every lonely shred, willing to sacrifice no one.
Where there is no pattern, God, give me courage to organize a fearsome
  beauty.
Where there is unraveling, let me draw broad blanket stitches of sturdy
  blue yarn.
Mother, Father, give me vision.
Give me strength to work hours past my daughters' bedtime.
Give me an incandescent all-night garage
with a quorum of thimble-thumbed grandmothers sitting on borrowed
  folding chairs.
We will gather all the lost scraps and stitch them together:
A quilt big enough to warm all our generations:
all the lost, found, rich, poor, good, bad, in, out, old, new, country, city,
  dusty, shiny ones;
A quilt big enough to cover all the alfalfa fields in the Great Basin.
Bigger. We are piecing together a quilt with no edges.
God, make me brave enough to love my people.
How wonderful it is to have a people to love.

Valerie Hudson Cassler (1958–), "The Two Trees" (2010)

"I am a Mormon because I am a feminist," wrote Valerie Hudson Cassler, an award-winning professor of foreign policy and expert in issues of gender and global security. Cassler, who was raised Catholic, converted to Mormonism in 1971 when she was thirteen years old, and she found in Mormon theology a deeply liberating alternative to traditional Judeo-Christian teachings that blamed Eve (and women after her) for the fall from the innocence of the Garden of Eden into a mortal world of sin and suffering. Mormon theology, by contrast, taught that without the experience of embodied mortality the souls of humankind could never learn and progress to become like their Heavenly Father and Heavenly Mother, and it celebrated Eve's decision to eat the fruit of the "tree of the knowledge of good and evil" (see Genesis 2:17) as a courageous and necessary choice. This view on gender, Cassler argues, makes Mormonism "the strongest, most progressive force for women in the world today." In December 2010, Hudson presented an extended commentary on the gender-progressive dimensions of Mormon theology and liturgy at a Mormon apologetics conference. (Apologetics is a mode of theology dedicated to the rational defense of a religious tradition.) Her influential essay "The Two Trees" draws from LDS scripture and temple liturgy to answer criticisms of gender inequality in Mormonism. Cassler presents a view of men and women as having different but complementary roles in God's plan for the growth and salvation of humankind. As mothers, women bring humankind into mortality and help direct each soul toward the good, Hudson asserts, an act symbolically reflected in Eve's choice to eat the fruit of the first tree—the "tree of the knowledge of good and evil" (see Genesis 2:17). Men administer the sacred rites such as baptism and LDS temple ceremonies that make it possible to return to the presence of God, an act symbolically represented as access to the second tree—the "tree of life" (see Alma 42:2–6 in the Book of Mormon). Some feminists have characterized perspectives connecting spirituality to gendered embodiment as biological essentialism. But Cassler and other religious feminists reject this characterization and assert that human biology is not the essential source of spirituality but rather a reflection or an expression of larger spiritual truths. Views like Cassler's have proved to be powerfully resonant among religious-identified women who are not only comfortable with symbolism but who also view symbols as the bearers of essential spiritual truths with power to reshape human reality. In some respects, Cassler's "The Two Trees" participates in a specifically Mormon feminist tradition of thought that traces back to Margaret Toscano's 1985 essay "The Missing Rib" (anthologized in Part II of this volume), wherein Toscano argued that men and women share priesthood power but may exercise that power differently. Both Toscano and Cassler seek to acknowledge gender difference while laying claim to equality. Whereas Toscano suggests that the egalitarian promise of Mormon theology should spur a greater regard for women's co-equal authority in contemporary LDS Church liturgy and practices, Cassler conveys a confidence that Mormon doctrine is already egalitarian and could reshape Mormon culture if understood correctly.

Source

Cassler, Valerie Hudson. "The Two Trees." Foundation for Apologetic Information and Research Convention, Sandy, Utah, August 5–6, 2010. http://www.fairmormon.org/perspectives/fair-conferences/2010-fair-conference/2010-the-two-trees.

References and Further Reading

Cassler, Valerie Hudson. "I Am a Mormon Because I Am a Feminist." *Mormon Scholars Testify* (September 2010). http://mormonscholarstestify.org/1718/valerie-hudson-cassler.

"THE TWO TREES"

I didn't join the Church because I was a feminist, but I stay in the Church because I am a feminist. And what I'd like to do to begin my talk is to review the main points of LDS doctrine that make this a revolutionary religion from a feminine perspective.

The Restored Gospel teaches me that the term "God" means an exalted woman and an exalted man married in the new and everlasting covenant (and we also get that from D[octrine] & C[ovenants] 132). We are taught that there is no God without men and women loving each other as equals. Heavenly Father is not an old bachelor. In fact, the one who's an old bachelor is Satan. This is revolutionary.

Second, the Restored Gospel teaches me that you will have your male or female body forever. It is not a curse, but a great gift and a blessing that you had to prove yourself worthy to have. Women in the audience, your breasts, your womb, your ovaries, are not cursings, sisters, they are blessings. And the Restored Gospel also teaches me that I will be married forever, and that I will have children forever, and that that life of being a woman married to my sweetheart and having children forever is the life that will bring me the fullest joy.

Another thing that I am taught is that men and women are equals before the Lord and before each other. Now, don't use the fallen world's sense of the term "equal"—"equal" does not mean identical. Let's face it, there are no two men who are identical, and yet they stand as equals before each other and before the Lord. Can we imagine an understanding of equality that means that a man and woman can be equals before the Lord and before each other? That is the vision of equality that the Restored Gospel teaches me.

I believe that we cannot fully understand this incredible doctrine of ours unless we go back to the story of the Garden of Eden. I believe and I hope to show today that the Restored Gospel completely alters the conventional story of the Garden of Eden. Let me just mention three points before we really get into it in detail.

Number one: the LDS do not believe that the Fall was a great tragedy. Rather, we believe that the Fall was foreordained, that it was for our progression, and that in that perspective, the Fall was a blessing.

Number two: the LDS do not believe that Eve sinned in partaking of the fruit of the First Tree, the tree of the knowledge of good and evil.

And number three, because we do not believe Eve sinned, we also do not believe that Eve was punished for her role in partaking of the fruit, but rather rewarded.

So, what we need to do now is to go back to that old story. We know that there is realm that is bounded by a chasm between all that is good and all that is evil. And in that holy realm, we know that we have Heavenly Parents, that we have a Father and we have a Mother, and that they are more than just symbolically our father and mother in some kind of literary sense, but that we are literally their children.

And we know that when God's children reached what I like to think of as teen-agerhood, it was apparent that the kids needed to go out and progress, and begin to understand what their Parents understood and value what their Parents value.

And so as we know a Plan was proposed, a plan of separation, a plan of full agency. Now we know we had some agency in the premortal existence, or there couldn't have been a War in heaven. There were choices to be made even in heaven, but we didn't have a full agency. There needed to be a separation for that. There had to be a progression; we had to understand the difference, as you know, between virtue and vice, pleasure and pain, all of these things, this knowledge we had to acquire.

So a Plan was presented, and as we know, one plan was championed by Christ and another was championed by Satan. And it is said that a third of the children of God did not choose the Plan of Jesus.

Let's talk a little about the rest of us, because I'm assuming all of us here are not part of that third, but rather the two-thirds who decided to go with this plan. And we know that the Plan had something to do with the setup of the Garden of Eden. That is, the Plan was to be a "round," if you will, and that the plan would take us from our heavenly home and if we walked that path well, the plan would bring us back to our heavenly home, now much more like our Heavenly Parents, with much more knowledge, a fuller agency, a desire to choose the right, with so much more than we ever could have acquired if we had stayed in heaven with a pale or dilute version of agency.

I think it's important to think about the fact that we have two trees and we have two people. Two trees, and a man and a woman. Why was Eve created second? Could it be that Eve was created second to demonstrate Adam's helplessness before the First Tree? Could it be—two people, two trees—that Eve was fore-ordained to partake first of the fruit of the First Tree?

To answer that question, we must ask ourselves what partaking of the fruit of the tree of the knowledge of good and evil means in a spiritual sense. It means to enter into mortality with a mortal body, to enter into full agency, and to have awakened within us the light of Christ that will serve us so well as we pass the veil. It is through women that souls journey to mortality and gain their agency, and in general it is through the nurturing of women, their nurturing love of their children, that the light of Christ is awakened within each soul. And I would include in that list of souls Jesus the Christ. Even Christ our Lord was escorted to mortality and veiled in flesh through the gift of a woman, fed at his mother's breast, awakened to all that is good and sweet in the world. Women escort every soul through the veil to mortal life and full agency. I believe that when we think about it—two people, two trees—that what we're really thinking about is two stewardships. And that the fruit of the First Tree symbolizes the gift that women give to every soul that chose the plan of Christ. It symbolizes the role and power of women in the Great Plan of Happiness. It was not, in this view, right or proper for Adam to partake first of the fruit of the First Tree. It was not his role to give the gift of the fruit of the First Tree to others. It is interesting to think that even Adam, who was created before Eve, entered into full mortality and full agency by accepting the gift of the First Tree from the hand of a woman. In a sense, Adam himself was born of Eve.

In the Great Plan of Happiness, who hearkened first to whom?[*] Adam hearkened first to Eve. Adam received the gift of the First Tree from the hand of a woman. Do men still hearken today? Many do, and I would daresay that probably all of the men in this audience have or will, that is, in addition to being born of your mothers, you also accept marriage and family as dear to your heart, and part of your vision of the happy life. You covenant to be the equal partner of your sweetheart, to be faithful and true to her, and to help bring children into the world with her, and to raise them. I think it's quite possible that en route to the First Tree there was also a covenanting, where the sons of God covenanted to hearken to the daughters of God in their apprenticeship to Heavenly Mother, and that Adam's partaking of the fruit from the hand of his wife, Eve, was his fulfillment of that covenant.

We believe that Adam will give the gift of the fruit of the Second Tree to the children of God, those who are worthy to receive it, just as Eve and her daughters give the fruit of the First Tree in the Garden of Eden to all who are worthy to partake of it. And that fruit of the Second Tree, as we know, are the ordinances of salvation and exaltation. Just as the veil into this life is guarded by the women, the daughters of God, so the veil that brings us home, is administered and guarded over by the sons of God. And those that have accepted the gift of the Second Tree from the hands of the sons of God will pass through that veil and back to that celestial place where they can be with their Parents once more.

We know that Eve, just as Adam hearkened to Eve, then Eve is asked by God to hearken to Adam in accepting the fruit of the Second Tree. We would be remiss if

---

[*] Cassler here references a vow made by women during LDS temple ceremonies to "hearken" to their husbands. In LDS temple liturgy, men do not make a complementary vow to "hearken" to their wives, a fact cited by some Mormon feminists as an instance of fundamental inequality; see Elizabeth Hammond's essay "The Mormon Priestess," anthologized in this volume.

we did not see that there were two hearkenings, two gifts given, two gifts received. Without either one, the Plan would not exist. It is a plan of equal partnership between men and women; a plan of joyous cooperation.

I love the Restored Gospel's vision of these things, because it gives me great joy then to consider the restoration of the priesthood. The restoration of the priesthood of God not only restores right relations between man and God; it restores right relations between men and women. Priesthood is not some extra given to men and denied women. Priesthood is a man's apprenticeship to become a heavenly father, and I believe that women have their own apprenticeship to become like their heavenly mother. The ordinances—and they are ordinances—of body and of agency—pregnancy, childbirth, lactation—the spiritual ordinances of the First Tree are not less powerful or spiritual than the ordinances of the Second Tree. Women have their own godly power. And a truism that holds fairly across the board is that those religions that despise the body tend to be those religions that devalue women.

Where love and equality between men and women do not exist, you cannot live the Gospel. You might as well start anew. God can always send angels and call prophets and uncover gold plates and whatever is necessary to restore the kingdom on earth. But that bedrock must be there. That means that gender equality is not some "politically correct" ideal to the Latter-day Saints. No, relationships of gender equality are the bricks of Zion, without which you cannot build Zion, because gender equality is how Heavenly Mother and Heavenly Father live.

Chelsea Shields Strayer (1981–), "Dear Mom" (2011)

A critical response to viewpoints like Valerie Hudson Cassler's celebrating the female-positivity of Mormonism came from Mormon feminists who observed how very little Mormon scripture and liturgy could offer in celebration of or information about the Heavenly Mother. Born in Provo, Utah, and raised in what she describes as a "very traditional" Mormon family—her father taught for the LDS Church Educational System, and her mother was a stay-at-home mother to eight children—Chelsea Shields Strayer is a bio-cultural anthropologist, mother, regular contributor to *The Exponent* blog (founded in 2006), and the president of the relaunched Mormons for ERA. In this essay, Strayer demonstrates that, despite decades of Mormon feminist efforts to explore the doctrinal reality of Heavenly Mother—see, for example, the essays by Linda Wilcox and Margaret Toscano (1992) in this volume—and to voice their hunger to know more—as did poets Lisa Hawkins Bolin, Margaret Rampton Munk, and Carol Lynn Pearson, those who sought to know God the Mother found themselves largely bereft. In an afterword to this post on *The Exponent* blog, Strayer explained, "I used to blame

church patriarchy for the absence of Heavenly Mother in LDS doctrine and rhetoric. Then I realized that I am treating her exactly like I don't want to be treated: as
silent support staff for the real work of men. If I treat her like a God, like someone
with power, position, and priesthood, then new feelings emerge. I feel angry. I
feel sad. I feel abandoned and confused."

Source

Strayer, Chelsea Shields. "Dear Mom." *The Exponent* (October 26, 2011). *http://www.the-exponent.com/dear-mom/*.

References and Additional Resources

Taylor, Sheila. "Why I Don't Want to Believe in Heavenly Mother." *Zelophehad's Daughters* (November 7, 2007). http://zelophehadsdaughters.com/2007/11/07/why-i-don't-want-to-believe-in-heavenly-mother/.

"DEAR MOM"

Dear Mom,

It was hard growing up without you. I love Dad and he was really good at a
lot of stuff, but it wasn't the same as having a mother. I knew you were out there
somewhere, but I couldn't talk to you. I couldn't get advice. I couldn't see what
I was going to look like when I got older, or what a lady is *really* like. I only knew
what Dad said they were like and I never seemed to relate much to his flawless
descriptions of selfless, compassionate, spiritual women. I mean I like all of those
qualities. I want to be like that, but I also have another side. A tough, adventurous,
foul-mouthed, chase the boys, win the competition, ask a lot of questions, pity no
fools, side. In fact, I've always imagined you with a little smirk leaning over the
kitchen doorway secretly encouraging this *other* side while you dispassionately
say, "Now child, behave."

But that is all there is. My imagination. Because I don't really know anything about you. I don't know what you do or who you are. I don't know if
you are powerful and strong or submissive and meek. I don't even know if you
remember or even care about me. All Dad will say is that you exist and that I'm
not supposed to talk about you. I don't know what that means. My brothers say
it is because you are so fragile that if we talked about you and said something
mean it would be bad. That used to make sense to me. I just accepted it as nor-
mal. I mean I didn't know any different. But I just had my first baby. A daughter. She's the greatest thing in my whole life. When she laughs it feels like my
heart is skydiving, when she cries it feels like my heart is breaking. I would do
anything for this child. I have given up large parts of my body, my career, my
love life, my time, energy, and self for this little girl. And I would do it again.
Over and over.

But I would never abandon her. I would never leave her. I would never willingly choose to end communication with her. Or ignore her during her difficult moments—the times when she is begging for a mom.

It was hard growing up without you. I needed a mom to teach me about boys, sex, modesty, my body, heartbreak, hormones, friendships, love, death, and life. I needed a mom to help me through my pregnancy, labor, birth, nursing, and all the sleepless nights and hair pulling days. No matter how thoughtful Dad was he could never come close to understanding this stuff. He could never understand what it feels like to belong to a family where the women are silent and the men make decisions. Where femininity is a caricature of personhood. Where no matter where I go, what I do, or who I talk to I am a girl first and a person second.

I'm a mother now. What used to suffice now stings. I don't care any longer what excuses people have made for you. You should have been here. You should have cared. You should have helped me in my difficult moments and taught me how to be a sister, daughter, mother, friend, aunt, cousin, wife, grandma, and woman. You should have helped me with the things that Dad and brothers didn't understand. You should not have abandoned me. I will never do that to my daughter. I will do anything it takes to keep her safe, to protect her, to support her, to encourage her, to help her, to teach her, to love her. Anything. There are no excuses that satisfy my heart of why you are absent from my life.

Sincerely,

Your Heavenly Daughter

Meghan Raynes (1983–), "Now I Have the Power" (2011–2012)

In March 2010, Jessica Oberan Steed, a community health advocate, and mother of three living in Mesa, Arizona, gathered a circle of fellow Mormon feminists—Meghan Raynes, Chelsea Shields Strayer, Susan Christiansen, Emily Clyde Curtis, Tresa Edmunds, Jenne Alderks, Stephanie Snyder, Elisabeth Calvert Smith, Kaimipono Wenger, and Caroline Kline—all veterans of the Mormon feminist bloggernacle who shared a commitment to taking action to advancing gender equality within the LDS Church. "It was after years of listening and being heard through blogs and in social groups that I decided to organize a group to move into the realm of advocacy," Steed wrote in March 2010 at *The Exponent* blog. "As an insular group of self-identifying Mormon women, we can talk, listen, validate, and talk some more, but until we recognize and take steps to make our voices heard by more church members, including those who can effect change, then nothing will change." Together, the women founded the activist-minded LDS Women Advocating Voice and Equality (LDS WAVE), which developed a series of "calls to action," including letter-writing campaigns to LDS Church leaders. LDS WAVE founding member Meghan Raynes, a social worker, former women's shelter director, anti-domestic-violence activist, and mother living in Denver, Colorado, writes about this shift in Mormon feminism from reflection to action and from Internet discourse to on-the-ground advocacy. Mormon feminist historians had reclaimed the history of Mormon women giving blessings, but here Raynes writes of a world where Mormon women are once again beginning to bless one another by the laying on of hands and outlines a vision for Mormon women to act with a greater sense of their authority. Her essay recalls the spirit of Margaret Toscano's "Put on Your Strength O Daughters of Zion" (1993), which urged LDS women to take the knowledge of the more expansive history of Mormon women's spiritual authority recovered by Mormon feminist historians and implement it within their personal, family, and congregational lives. Having survived the excommunications and anti-feminist reprisals of the 1990s and having reached a new generation of younger Mormon women, Mormon feminism—as Raynes envisioned it—appeared ready to do just that, reversing the pattern of Mormon women's asking for permission to use their power noted by Linda King Newell in her classic essay "A Gift Given, a Gift Taken" (anthologized in Part I of this volume).

Source

Raynes, Meghan. "Now I Have the Power." *The Exponent* (November 6, 2011). http://www.the-exponent.com/now-i-have-the-power/.

"NOW I HAVE THE POWER"

Several days ago I was at a park with my children. There was nothing particularly interesting about this park except for two older boys at one corner play-fighting. I don't like my children to watch or engage in violent behavior so I tried to keep their attention on the other side of the park. But we kept hearing snippets from their dialogue: "I have the power." "Ha ha, I just took your power." "You can't take it because I'm invincible." "I have your power, I have your power." "No. I have THE POWER."

My daughter, Sylvia, became more and more distracted by their exchange and before I could stop her, marched over to the two boys. Sylvia stared at them intently and then proclaimed, "Now I have the Power." She snatched at the air in front of their faces as if, in this one single gesture, all of their power and the power of the universe would be instantly transferred to her. The look on their faces was priceless because, at least momentarily, my three-year-old daughter had taken the power.

I was stunned but also delighted and so proud that this spirited little girl is my daughter. Sylvia is in that beautiful time before the forces of the world try to convince her she is smaller than she actually is. But along with my pride there was also a twinge of sadness and a jaded feeling of "if only it was that easy."

But what if it is?

As I've reflected on this experience over the past couple of days I've come to think that maybe Sylvia is on to something. In her little brain Sylvia knew that these boys would never just come over and bestow power upon her. No, she had to take what she felt was rightfully hers to have.

I wonder if this isn't analogous to the situation that we Mormon women find ourselves in? The issue of women and the priesthood has been talked to death but one thing is for sure, the male leaders of our church aren't going to walk over any time soon and bestow the priesthood upon us just because we ask nicely.

But the Power of God is available to us all. We as women have every right to declare, "I have the Power." To be clear, I am not talking about the institutional power that comes in the form of priesthood. I don't believe it would do women any good to all of the sudden start to perform living ordinances just because we declare we have the power to do so. But I believe the scriptures are very clear that we are all—man, woman, child—endowed with the ability to access God's power and utilize it for the good of our sisters and brothers. So many of us sit on the sidelines blaming our inaction on powerlessness and a lack of authority. This is a great lie that has been perpetrated and the fact that so many sisters feel as if they have no right or ability to be a conduit of God's love and power is to the detriment of us all.

Two years ago I received a blessing. I have been the fortunate recipient of many blessings in my life and while they have all been meaningful, this one was special. I had been suffering for some months from a major depressive episode and was in a very dark place. While I was never in immediate danger, I longed for and sometimes considered a permanent end to my suffering. It was during that time that I left my home to meet with some old friends. I had become adept at hiding just how serious my situation was; nobody in my family or ward knew and even my husband was unaware of the extent of my depression. Though I had my brave face on these women knew intuitively that I was in trouble.

Towards the end of our time together my dear friend asked if she and the other women could give me a blessing. I stalled at first, not wanting to admit that I needed help and also a little afraid of going down that path, but I was so tired and so desperate that in the end I agreed.

It was like so many of the priesthood blessings I have received from my husband and father; a kitchen chair was pulled into the middle of the room and the women gathered around me except that they placed their hands all over my body. A pair on my head, another on my shoulders, some on my arms and my hands, thighs and feet. The feeling was amazing: warmth and connection emanating from those hands and coursing through my body. And then she spoke. She did not use priesthood parlance but the more informal rhetoric of love, friendship and intimacy. My friend spoke of the things that she loved about me, how she knew I was in pain and blessed me that I would be able to escape it. Then another woman spoke, sharing her thoughts and hopes for me. And another, telling me that God knew me and had a special work for me to do. Each woman in that circle spoke, some blessing me some just expressing love. And I wept, tears of sadness and gratitude. When they were done my body felt alive again. After months of feeling only numb the energy in my body was overwhelming but also exquisite.

This blessing was my life raft. I was drowning and these women used the power of God in every sense of what that means to save me. Within two weeks my depression had lifted and has yet to return. I made it through an unexpected pregnancy and the start of my graduate program without any relapse at all. I was healed. This is nothing short of a miracle, and it was all because these wonderful women stood up against every thing they were ever taught about authority and power and rejected it. Instead they saw a sister in need of comfort and said, "I have the power to help her."

Utilizing the power of God requires faith, confidence and a willingness to serve the children of God. What a tragedy that we are losing out on the unique blessings women can provide if only they were encouraged to fully access the power of God. It's time to stop waiting for that encouragement; it's not coming. Now is the time to reach out and grab the power that God has for us.

Neylan McBaine (1977–), "To Do the Business of the Church: A Cooperative Paradigm for Examining Gendered Participation Within Church Organizational Structure" (2012)

Like the women of LDS WAVE, Neylan McBaine—a New York City–born and raised mother of three daughters, founder of the Mormon Women Project, a website that publishes and gives voice to the life stories from diverse Mormon women around the world, and a strategic marketing professional who had worked on the LDS Church's successful "I'm a Mormon" campaign to diversify and humanize the Mormon image—hoped to present ideas that could shift mainstream understanding of women's roles and expand leadership opportunities for all women in the LDS Church. In this August 2, 2012, address, McBaine carefully frames gender as an issue of critical importance to all who care about the future of the LDS Church. Speaking to an audience of mostly moderate and conservative LDS people, she provides a sensitive, thoughtful clarification of the feelings motivating feminist concern and advocacy, and she argues that the secular metrics of equality used to evaluate the status of women in the LDS Church are not in line with the way Mormon theology conceives of gender, with men and women having essentially different but complementary roles. McBaine thus picks up the vision of gender difference and complementarity argued by Margaret Toscano and Valerie

Hudson Cassler and advances it decisively into the practical realm of LDS Church administration and policy.

Source

McBaine, Neylan. "To Do the Business of the Church: A Cooperative Paradigm for Examining Gendered Participation Within Church Organizational Structure." Foundation for Apologetics Information and Research Convention (August 2, 2012). http://www.fairmormon.org/perspectives/fair-conferences/2012-fair-conference/2012-to-do-the-business-of-the-church-a-cooperative-paradigm.

References and Further Reading

McBaine, Neylan. *Women at Church: Magnifying LDS Women's Local Impact*. Salt Lake City: Kofford Books, 2014.

"TO DO THE BUSINESS OF THE CHURCH: A COOPERATIVE PARADIGM FOR EXAMINING GENDERED PARTICIPATION WITHIN CHURCH ORGANIZATIONAL STRUCTURE"

Part I: The Crisis

There is a tremendous amount of pain among our women regarding how they can or cannot contribute to the governance of our ecclesiastical organization and we need to pay attention to that pain. In 2011, a comprehensive survey of over 3000 people who had lost their belief in the gospel revealed that 47 percent of those respondents cited women's issues as a "significant" reason for their loss of faith.[1] The percentage of women who cited this specific issue as being the primary reason for their loss of faith was higher, at 63 percent. Additionally, 70 percent of single women who have lost their faith ranked women's issues as significant. Lest we think that these people who are losing their faith are an aberration or a fringe annoyance, in November of 2011, Elder Marlin Jensen confirmed that church members are "leaving in droves" and that "since Kirtland,"[2] the Church has not seen the exodus which we are now experiencing. Women's role in church governance is a primary reason many people are telling themselves it is okay to leave, and at the very least we should be distraught that this issue opens the door to the way out.

Part II: The Pain is Real

Allow me to tell you about my personal history as a further jumping off point for this discussion. I was born and raised in New York City as the only child of an eventually single, professional mother. I attended an all-girls school for twelve years, which, ironically, has made me appreciate the importance of gender-segregated experiences and responsibilities as an adult. From the example of my mother and other exceptional women, I gained an intuitive understanding of the gospel as empowerment; it was the means by which energy and productivity blossomed in each of these influential women.

The relationship of women to the church didn't strike me as a crisis until I moved to San Francisco and served in a Relief Society presidency there under a phenomenal woman and mentor. However, immediately after she was released from her calling she and her husband and their three children had their names removed from the church records, citing her inability to reconcile her role as a woman in the Church. Since that experience, traumatic for both me, personally, and for our whole ward, I have tried to reflect into what causes pain so deep that a woman will distance herself permanently from her culture, her family, even her entire worldview, to be free from that pain.

Unfortunately, denying this pain or belittling it is an all too common occurrence among both our men and our women. Consider this statement from a man in a metropolitan area bishopric: "I don't think that ambition or 'personal growth' of a woman in [the sphere of church governance] has any place in the church and that it is really a disguised form of pride. I'm wary of how impassioned female leaders could . . . play a role in that individual's path towards apostasy."[3]

When my 8-year-old daughter asks me why she'll never be able to pass the sacrament, is she being "prideful"? At work, I make decisions for men and male executives pay me to consult for them on business decisions in which I have expertise, yet as a member of my ward's primary presidency I have to get approval from my bishop to join Junior and Senior primary opening exercises. Am I on the path to apostasy because I wonder why this is so? With the broad sweep of the word "pride," the bishopric member quoted above instantly devalues the pain in my own daughter's sincere question or the requirement that I suspend my work experience when I interact with male leaders at church.

How can we help more in our community find peace in a middle ground, where the pain is acknowledged and we provide doctrinally sound tools and behavioral guidelines for addressing that pain?

Part III: Identifying the Sources of Pain

As we start that exercise, allow yourself for a moment to step into the shoes of someone who struggles with finding her place. Consider, for instance, the narratives that define the rights of passage of our youth and the source of this bitterness may become illuminated.

So many of our narratives about our youth involve those moments when a dad ordains his son to the Aaronic priesthood, and then the first Sunday the son gets to pass the sacrament, or bless the sacrament, or go home teaching or collect fast offerings or become an Eagle Scout or get a mission call. . . . These are times of spiritual outpourings and parental pride, the joy of eternal progression made tangible through the bodily actions taken on by that worthy son. It's not often a mother describes a similarly gripping scene when her daughter graduates from Mia Maids to Laurels.

To illustrate this point even further, there is a narrative that all LDS mothers of young daughters do share. It is the narrative of breaking the news to a young daughter that she will never be able to pass the sacrament, be the bishop, or become the prophet.

Consider this reflection by the mother of a six-year-old:

> The other day I overheard a conversation between my six-year-old daughter and my mother-in-law. They had been talking about how her older brother would become a deacon later this year. My daughter said enthusiastically, "When I turn twelve, I'm going to pass the sacrament too!" You should understand that one of this child's favorite Sunday rituals has been taking the sacrament tray from the administering deacon and distributing it to the rest of the family; when she returns the tray to the deacon and sits back down, she has a big smile on her face and it's clear that she feels she's done something very grown-up and important. So imagine her disappointment when her grandmother informed her that passing the sacrament is a job only for boys. Crestfallen, and with that childish sense of entitlement, my daughter asked, "But what do I get when I turn twelve?" . . . It made me very sad. My question is not what my daughter "gets" when she turns twelve, but what will be asked of her? What messages will she get about her role in the church? On the one hand we want to impress upon young men what a privilege and honor it is to [act in these sacred responsibilities], while on the other hand we insist to our young women (and women of all ages) that it's really no big deal. Seriously, ladies, you don't want [to have to do this stuff]. You shouldn't want [to have to]. Nothing but trouble, that priesthood! And yet, very important. Without it our church would be nothing. Worse than nothing, a fraud. But at the same time, you aren't missing out on anything. Trust us![4]

We require that our women suspend their understanding of social equality as it is currently represented in our modern society. This is consistent with our belief that we should be "in the world" but not "of" it, but we members should not flippantly dismiss how difficult this can be in actual practice for a woman whose role in worldly society has changed so swiftly and dramatically over the past hundred years.

Desiring to be used, engaged, recognized and appreciated for our public contributions is not, for most women, about the glory of public praise or being in the spotlight. It's not about wanting to eradicate the divine differences between women and men. It is simply about a basic human need in every person—man or woman—to be told, "You are needed. You matter. You have a purpose. Your opinions matter. Not just at home behind closed doors, not just with your children, as essential as those influences are, but also in the broadest context of the Lord's kingdom."

Part IV: The Cooperative Paradigm

Let's look at one common narrative we share when confronted about our system of gender segregation in this contemporary world. When confronted with an intentionally inflammatory accusation like "gender discrimination," we instinctively default to defensive claims that our women are actually just the same as our men because they speak in church, go to school, and get to feel the Spirit the same way. In an effort to bridge our own experience with the experience of our external audience, we rely on comparisons to hierarchical power structures of fallen world institutions: governments, corporations, and universities in which men and women ideally work side by side to advance to opportunities available to both genders. We talk in terms of opportunity, advancement, visibility, of hierarchical power, which are hallmarks of advanced worldly institutions, in America at least. If you'd like further proof of this tendency, go read through some of the answers members have given on Mormon.org to the question, "Why don't women hold the Priesthood?" and note how many times those answers cite the fact that our women speak in Sacrament meeting or run the Primary.

But leading an auxiliary organization that has influence over a subset of the population is not the same as leading the entire organization. When the outside world looks at our structure and sees men ecclesiastically responsible for even the highest ranked women in our organization, the media perceives our claims as being false advertising and we lose our credibility to tell our own story. It then becomes someone else's job to "uncover" the truth for us, leading down a path of exposes and betrayals.

Is there gender discrimination in the Church? If discrimination means separation according to gender, yes. If it means delineation of opportunities based solely on gender, yes. Many argue that different opportunities based on gender is unfair, adverse, and/or abusive by definition. The Church does not satisfy secular gender-related egalitarian ideals, period; and our institutional behavior fits that definition of gender discrimination in several inescapable ways. We shrink away from accurately representing how we work, thinking it condemns us as a church. And in the eyes of the world it might. But the Church does not, and should not, operate according to secular concepts of power, status, and if we attempt to justify ourselves in this paradigm we will not only fail, but betray our own ideals.

I suggest we argue it is true that Mormon women do not hold an equal number of global leadership positions as men, but that is not because they are of lesser value. It is because we believe we are working in an eternal paradigm in which roles and responsibilities are divided up cooperatively rather than hierarchically. Mormonism is a lay church so the members are the ministers, and this is a completely different organizational structure than traditional Christian priesthood or ministry, which is defined as an exclusive or trained clergy. Thus, when we talk about our ministerial structure to the outside world, we are starting from very different foundational understandings of what ecclesiastical ministry means. [In] our organization's cooperative structure of service, no one person is paid for his or her ministry or deemed of greater value than another and where each brings unique resources to his or her responsibilities.

One of beauties of the cooperative paradigm over the hierarchical paradigm is that the cooperative paradigm more accurately incorporates both ecclesiastical and sacerdotal definitions of priesthood, which seems to be understood generally throughout the church as being much more gendered than a close reading of scripture suggests. For example, let us return to the organizational language of the Doctrine and Covenants. Section 84 states: "And again, the offices of elder and bishop are necessary appendages belonging unto the high priesthood. And again, the offices of teacher and deacon are necessary appendages belonging to the lesser priesthood" (84:29–30; see also 107:5). Pay attention to that word "appendages." An appendage is "a thing that is added or attached to something larger or more important." Are not the offices of elder or bishop or teacher or deacon appendages to the priesthood, and not the priesthood itself? Are these so different from the female organizations, which we routinely call "auxiliaries"?

Part V: The Internal Shift

Maxine Hanks, one of the "September Six" who was excommunicated from the Church in September 1993 [and] was personally invited by church leadership to be rebaptized as a member of the Church, says, "I don't think gender tensions in Mormonism are due to inequality in the religion, but due to invisibility of that equality. The equality is embedded, inherent in Mormon theology, history, texts, structures. Gender equality is built into the blueprints of Mormonism, but obscured in the elaborations. . . . The inherent gender equality in Mormonism just needs to be seen by extracting it from other distracting elements and contexts."

What kinds of initiatives could we take as church members to excavate this gender equality that we currently not doing? How can we put into practice our desires to see this cooperative community become more of our practiced reality? In essence, while we are reining in our external claims, we need simultaneously to be broadening the practice of egalitarian ideals in our behavior so that with these opposite pulls we can have both internal and external meet harmoniously in the middle. I ask each man and woman in the audience today: What are you doing to excavate the power of the women in your ward and make their contributions more visible?

Women: We women need to do a better job of claiming the power and direct access that comes from being a child of God and realizing that power in the choices we make in our own lives. Ours is not a gospel of limitation; it is a gospel of empowerment to get the education we want, pursue our dreams, work in partnerships with spouses and friends to raise families, contribute to our com-munities as our talents dictate, and seek out answers to our deepest questions without intermediaries.

Men: In your ecclesiastical roles, many of you have frequent opportunity to make choices regarding how to use the talents and insights of the women in your ward. What can we do in our homes? I've been impressed with many of the things my husband has done to include our three daughters in his own servant leader-ship. For example, my husband takes our oldest daughter with him when he deliv-ers the sacrament to homebound ward members. I've seen my daughter carefully holding the trays on her lap in the car as they go off together.

As a mother, my language and attitude can make a difference with my daughter as she asks the hard questions about why she can't pass the sacrament or receive the priesthood authority. The time will come when she and I will study the cooperative paradigm together, or the Two Trees theory, or when she will work for a testimony of gender division for herself. But in the meantime, when my daughter asked me why only boys passed the sacrament, I answered her, "Esme, who really hands you the bread and water every week?" She thought, and said, "Well, actually you do." It's me, her mother. Inevitably, I'm the one sitting next to her. Or maybe it's her sister. Maybe it's her dad, but whoever it is, whatever gender that person is, whether she's related to them or has never seen them before, by them handing that tray to her, she is joining her family and her ward community in gaining equal access to the cleansing power of the Atonement. This will not always be a satisfactory answer for her, but while she is young and before we study more doctrinally rich answers, I hope I am modeling for her an example of finding power in my own sphere of responsibility.

Notes

1. Mormon Research Foundation, "Understanding Mormon Disbelief." Survey. March 2012.
2. Peter Henderson and Kristina Cooks, "Mormons Besieged by the Modern Age," Reuters, January 31, 2012. http://www.reuters.com/article/2012/01/31/us-mormonchurch-idUSTRE80T1CM20120131.
3. Personal correspondence.
4. Rebecca J, "My Feelings about Not Holding the Priesthood," *By Common Consent*, May 30, 2012. http://bycommonconsent.com/2012/05/30/my-feelings-about-not-holding-the-priesthood-part-two-of-a-million-parts/.

What Women Know Collective, "All Are Alike unto God" (2012)

In September 2012, the same collective of veteran feminists that produced the "What Women Know" petition published a sequel entitled "All Are Alike unto God," taking its name from the Book of Mormon scripture 2 Nephi 26:33, which promised that "all are alike unto God, black and white, bond and free, male and female." Authored by former *Mormon Women's Forum Quarterly* editor Lorie Winder Stromberg (see her essay "Power Hungry" anthologized in this volume) with contributions from Mary Ellen Robertson, Marnie Leavitt, and Lori LeVar Pierce, the petition identified twenty-two "simple steps" that could be taken (without changing the male-only priesthood ordination policy) to advance gender equality within LDS congregations. More than a thousand rank-and-file LDS Church members quickly signed the online petition, and within just two years of its launch, several of the petition's recommended changes—including lowering the age for female missionary service and inviting women to pray in General Conference—found their way into LDS Church policy and practice.

Source

"All Are Alike unto God." http://whatwomenknow.org/all_are_alike/.

"ALL ARE ALIKE UNTO GOD"

As Mormon women, we call upon the First Presidency, Quorum of the Twelve Apostles, and Relief Society General Presidency of the Church of Jesus Christ of Latter-day Saints to thoughtfully consider and earnestly pray about the full integration of women into the decision-making structure of the Church and the question of women's ordination.

In the interim, we join many others in suggesting some simple changes in institutional policy that will foster a more equitable religious community:

- Encourage partnership in marriage and eliminate the idea that husbands preside over their wives.
- Create parity in the Young Women and Young Men organizations through equivalent budgets, educational programs (leadership, career, and spiritual training,) and activities (sports, service, and outdoor events).
- Balance the stories and images of boys and men in church publications, talks, and other media with stories and images of girls and women.
- Invite women in Church leadership positions to speak and pray during General Conference in numbers equal to the participation of men.
- Encourage leaders to use gender-inclusive language whenever possible.
- Recognize that girls and boys, women and men are equally responsible for appropriate sexual behavior, and avoid reducing morality to sexuality, and modesty to a preoccupation with women's and girls' clothing.
- Instruct bishops to refrain from asking Church members probing questions about sexual practices and experiences.
- Call women to perform pastoral counseling, particularly for women and girls who have been sexually abused.

- Choose a General Relief Society Presidency and General Board that reflect the diversity of viewpoint and circumstance in the Church, and establish frequent meetings between the First Presidency and the General Relief Society Presidency.
- Include the Stake Relief Society President in Stake Presidency meetings, and appoint women to meet with the High Council.
- Delegate more expansive supervisory authority to the Stake and Ward Relief Society, Young Women, and Primary presidencies, including approval of personnel, programs, and activities.
- Include women among stake and ward leaders who hear evidence and offer judgment in Church disciplinary councils.
- Include the local Relief Society president in all bishopric meetings, and rotate the planning of Sacrament services among the Relief Society president and members of the bishopric.
- Examine all Church positions to determine whether they can be filled without regard to gender.
- Appoint women as presidents of Church universities and heads of administrative departments.
- Expand hiring practices in the Seminaries and Institutes of Religion and within the religion departments at Church universities to provide women the same placement, advancement, and tenure opportunities as men.
- Call young women as well as young men to serve missions at the same age and for the same length of time, and afford women the same opportunity as men to function as district leaders, zone leaders, and assistants to the president.
- Lift the prohibition on women's participation in the blessing of their children.
- Change temple marriage policies so that men and women have equal opportunity to be sealed to their second spouses after they are widowed or divorced.
- Consider further wording changes to temple ceremonies and ordinances such that both men and women make the same covenants and enjoy the same promises.
- Recognize women as witnesses for baptisms and marriage sealings.
- Restore the former institutionally accepted practice of women giving blessings of healing and comfort.

Kate Kelly (1980–), "Equality Is Not a Feeling" (2013)

Mormon feminist activism crossed a new threshold on March 17, 2013, with the launch of OrdainWomen.org, a website featuring personal profiles from LDS Church members in support of women's ordination. Nadine Hansen had been the first to make the case in print in her 1981 essay "Women and Priesthood" (anthologized in this volume); Lorie Winder Stromberg (whose essay "Power Hungry" is anthologized in this volume) and others continued to press the ordination cause throughout the 1980s and 1990s, arguing that without it women would never have access to the LDS Church's all-male hierarchical decision-making structure. A new wave of social-media-powered Mormon feminist activism in the 2010s and the efforts of a new generation of Mormon feminists like Kelly, a human rights attorney, Chelsea Shields Strayer, and Hannah Wheelwright (working with more seasoned advocates like Hansen and Stromberg) brought ordination back onto the Mormon feminist agenda. "As a group we intend to put ourselves in the public eye and call attention to the need for the ordination of Mormon women to the priesthood. We sincerely ask our leaders to take this matter to the Lord in prayer," declared Ordain Women's mission statement. OW organized direct action at the LDS Church's General Conference in October 2013, as more than two hundred women lined up to ask for admission to the Saturday evening men's only "Priesthood" session; more than five hundred women and their allies lined up at the historic Tabernacle on Temple Square to once again ask admission into the gender segregated spaces of the Mormon tradition at General Conference in April 2014. Kelly's speech to the first Ordain Women direct action exemplifies a new sense of directness and vigor in Mormon feminism: a "radical self-respect," as Kelly described it. In June 2014, Kelly was excommunicated, a move viewed by many Mormon feminists as a reprisal against the boldness of Ordain Women's direct action strategy.

Source

Kate Kelly, "Equality is Not a Feeling" (2013), unpublished manuscript.

"EQUALITY IS NOT A FEELING"

My name is Kate Kelly. I am a sister, a daughter and a friend. I am a returned missionary, I was married in the Salt Lake temple. I am a faithful, active Mormon woman and I think women should be ordained.

I want to welcome everyone here tonight. Women have flown in from New York, Florida, Oklahoma, Virginia and even from Germany. Some have driven from Oregon, Arizona, California and Idaho. Some have come at great, great personal and social cost and to you I say, "Thank you."

We have all demonstrated the utmost courage and radical self-respect by showing up here today. It is my privilege to stand beside you.

I have heard from many women, "I see nothing wrong with the status quo. I feel equal." To them I say: you can feel respected, supported and validated in the church, but equality can be measured. Equality is not a feeling.

In our church, men and women are not equal.

Today we are communicating a message to our leaders and to the Lord. We are ready. The 9th Article of Faith states: "We believe all that God has revealed, all that He does now reveal, and we believe that He will yet reveal many great and important things pertaining to the Kingdom of God."

Whatever the outcome today:

We were brave.

We showed up.

We knocked.

Janan Graham-Russell (1989–), "On Black Bodies in White Spaces: Conversations of Women's Ordination and Women of African Descent in the Church of Jesus Christ of Latter-day Saints" (2013)

In this essay, Janan Graham-Russell, drawing from a tradition of womanist theology centered on the concerns, perspectives, and priorities of women of color, calls upon the Mormon women's ordination movement to recognize the experience of Black Mormon women and the intersections of race, gender, and class in shaping the diverse experiences of Mormon women. Some supporters of women's ordination had drawn rhetorical parallels between the gender segregation of the LDS priesthood and its historic racial segregation: although some Mormon men of African descent were ordained to the priesthood in the nineteenth century, such ordinations were discouraged by LDS Church president Brigham Young and were formally prohibited by modern LDS Church policy until 1978. But according to Graham-Russell, those who compared the situation of Mormon women to the situation of Black Mormon men before 1978 overlooked the experiences of Black Mormon women, who before 1978 were excluded from participation in LDS temple rites by reason of the priesthood ban. Black women's experiences, Graham implies, affirm the argument made by historians like D. Michael Quinn and theologians like Margaret Toscano (see her essays anthologized in this volume) that participation in temple rites conferred a form of priesthood on women. While voicing support for the movement for greater equality, Graham-Russell calls on white women to account for their racially privileged access to priesthood long before their sisters of black African descent. Graham-Russell joined the Ordain Women action at General Conference in April 2014.

Source

Graham-Russell, Janan. "On Black Bodies in White Spaces: Conversations of Women's Ordination and Women of African Descent in the Church of Jesus Christ of Latter-day Saints." *A Life Diasporatic* (September 23, 2013). http://alifediasporatic. wordpress.com/2013/09/23/on-black-bodies-in-white-space-conversations-of-womens-ordination-and-women-of-african-descent-in-the-church-of-jesus-christ-of-latter-day-saints/.

References and Further Reading

Bringhurst, Newell T., and Darron T. Smith. *Black and Mormon*. Urbana: University of Illinois Press, 2006.
Newell, Quincy D., ed. "The Autobiography and Interview of Jane Manning James." *Journal of Africana Religions* 1.2 (2013): 251–91.

"ON BLACK BODIES IN WHITE SPACES: CONVERSATIONS OF WOMEN'S ORDINATION AND WOMEN OF AFRICAN DESCENT IN THE CHURCH OF JESUS CHRIST OF LATTER-DAY SAINTS"

What is it like to be hypervisualized and invisible at the same time?

This question has persisted in the historical and present narrative of African-American women in the United States, that is, what is it like to stand in a room and watch yourself become the subject of discussions rooted in flawed perceptions of your existence and identity? From ideas of the "Mammy," or the asexual black woman whose only joy in life comes from tending to her white master and his family, the "Jezebel," an oversexualized black woman, and the "Sapphire," commonly known as the "Angry Black Woman," black bodies, in the physical, spiritual, emotional and mental sense, have been put out for public consumption and discussion for centuries, often without the input of black voices. It is because of these historical and present experiences of African-American women in particular that concern identity politics that I have been left feeling disturbed with recent conversations about the "priesthood ban" by the Ordain Women movement and in blog posts by Margaret Young. The language and facts have excluded the experiences of women of African descent with regards to the priesthood and the temple. They should be addressed.

I write from the perspective of women born women in the African diaspora, specifically African-American women, within The Church of Jesus Christ of Latter-day Saints. Women of African descent are not a monolith and as such, I cannot testify of the experiences of those living in and/or from Africa, those from Africa who have immigrated to the United States or other countries nor every African-American woman in the Church. However, I can attest to the problematic aspects of discussing the Church policy that prohibited people of African descent from fully participating in temple ordinances from 1852 when then-Church President Brigham Young made statements to the Utah Territorial Legislature regarding people of African descent and the priesthood until the 1978 revelation by then-Church President Spencer W. Kimball, without referring to the policy in its entirety.

Often times the ban is referred to as the "priesthood ban" in regards to its effect on men of African descent; however, the term does not encompass the full extent to which it affected the lives of women. In the online article, "Renaming the 'Priesthood Ban,'" anonymously written for the LDS blog *Zelophehad's Daughters*, the author describes this dichotomy and offers thoughts on renaming the policy in which two terms are introduced, "Exaltation Exclusion" and "Priesthood-Temple Ban."* I believe both help describe the effects of the ban. While the term "Priesthood-Temple Ban" addresses the physical implications of the ban, "Exaltation Exclusion" properly addresses the eternal implications the ban had on people of African descent. According to Mormon theology, there are three kingdoms of Heaven: the Celestial, Terrestrial and Telestial. The Celestial Kingdom is the highest. To reach the highest degree of the Celestial Kingdom, that is, the degree closest to God, there are certain ordinances such as the "temple endowment" and sealings of spouses which must be performed in LDS temples. For a considerable amount of the Church's history, people of African descent could not hope to be exalted, or reach the "highest degree of glory."

While I do respect and support the extensive work of both those involved with Ordain Women and the pursuit of equality both within and outside of the Church, as well as Margaret Young, whose work has focused, in part, on Jane Manning James, one of the first female African-American members of the Church, the truth is this: white women have had access to the priesthood and temple in its entirety for much longer than women of color, particularly women of African descent.

For over a century, people of African descent were denied access to the most sacred of ordinances in our faith because of, in my opinion, racist ideologies at the time the Priesthood-Temple Ban was instituted. Even though the ban was lifted in 1978, the memory of those teachings about the question of existence that surrounded people of African descent remained. While it was perhaps the desire of many General Authorities of the Church, that Church members would, as Elder Bruce R. McConkie, a member of the Quorum of the Twelve, stated in his 1978 talk "All Are Alike Unto God," "Forget everything that I have said, or what President Brigham Young or President George Q. Cannon or whomsoever has said in days past that is contrary to the present revelation," people often do not forget teachings that have been commonplace in their lives. Even the words of those whom we consider to be prophets cannot quell the lingering attitudes that regarded any difference between people of African descent and whites as preordained. Though women's ordination would allow for women to have greater access to leadership opportunities throughout the Church as an institution, it does not solve the ever-looming issues that many women of African descent, and presumably women of color, face. Many of these issues concern the benevolent

---

* See Kiskilili, "Renaming the 'Priesthood Ban,'" *Zelophehad's Daughters* (June 8, 2008): http://zelophehadsdaughters.com/2008/06/08/renaming-the-priesthood-ban/.

and overtly racist dialogue that many people of color have come to know so well in our interactions with some Church members. I'm not against asking Church leaders to consider praying about the question of women's ordination, but it is hard to align myself with any group or individual, whether for or against, who does not address the privileges that come with discussing women's ordination or the priesthood as it has existed in The Church of Jesus Christ of Latter-day Saints.

"Woman" is not a universal experience and should never be regarded as such, whether in the Church or outside of it. The course of women within the Church of Jesus Christ of Latter-day Saints is one that has diverged at several points. As an African-American woman and convert to the Church, my deepest connection to the Church lies in the presence of Jane Manning James, Mary Sturlaugson Eyers, Mary Lucille Bankhead, and countless others who challenged and transcended the physical and spiritual restrictions that once kept them from the hope of exaltation to the highest degree of the Celestial Kingdom. Their experiences help to provide strength, for myself at least, in a Church that has a troubling history, and arguably troubling present, with respect to race. For any group or individual to not talk about these experiences, to talk about equality without intersectionality, does a grave injustice to any discussion on the matter.

So again I pose this question, what is it like to be hypervisualized and invisible at the same time? The answer is, simply put: to be both is to be forced into silence. In this, if debates over whether or not women should receive the priesthood include talking about people of African descent, my hope is that all the facts about the ban are presented and there is some recognition of the privileges that come with discussing black bodies in white spaces.

Gina Colvin (1967–), "Ordain Women, But . . . : A Womanist Perspective" (2014)

A vital perspective on equality and gender in the LDS Church came from Gina Colvin, an indigenous Maori university professor, educator, and activist in New Zealand. Colvin's blog, *KiwiMormon*, gained a significant following thanks to its brilliantly incisive criticism of the LDS Church's continued privileging of its white, middle-class North American "center," even though the majority of Mormonism's 15 million global adherents live outside the United States. Like Graham-Russell, Colvin identified as a womanist, drawing from a philosophical, political, and theological tradition centered on the experiences, perspectives, and concerns of women of color. In her writings, she linked rejections of sexist inequality with movements to unsettle racist and imperialist power structures that diminished the well-being, dignity, and happiness of people of color and indigenous peoples. On the eve of the second Ordain Women action, Colvin published a rousing call to think carefully about whether admitting women to Mormonism's lay priesthood would substantially change the misplaced priorities or exclusionary tendencies of the LDS Church hierarchy or would move Mormonism any closer to its ideal of becoming a "Zion" society. The arrival of these powerful voices from global Mormonism to connect resistance to gender inequality within the LDS Church to a broader agenda for human emancipation marked the maturation of the Mormon feminist movement and set out new horizons for its future.

Source

Colvin, Gina. "I'll Be at the Ordain Women Event, But . . ." *KiwiMormon* (April 2, 2014). http://www.patheos.com/blogs/kiwimormon/2014/04/ill-be-at-the-ordain-women-event-but/.

"ORDAIN WOMEN, BUT ... : A WOMANIST PERSPECTIVE"

I'm going to the Ordain Women (OW) action on April 5. I support it. Anytime a group of people get together to lobby for change for women it's worth paying attention. Historical public action to highlight the lack of equality for women has earned some women the right to vote; it has earned women reproductive rights, the right to own property, the right to employment and pay parity. It has challenged the cult of domesticity, the sexual objectification of women, the normalization of patriarchy; it has drawn attention to the plight of domestic violence, and has more recently sought to challenge sexist culture. These are actions that I support.

But while I consider myself nominally a feminist I am mostly a womanist.

So I feel cautious. I embrace OW guardedly. Mostly when I walk with my sisters on Saturday my internal dialogue will be thus:

1. Ordain fewer men.
2. Unordain some men.
3. Stop ordaining male children.
4. Separate priesthood from church leadership, administration and management.
5. Ordain some women.
6. Give both men and women the right to participate in church leadership, administration and management, but don't call that priesthood.

It's a given that women aren't equal to men in the church—and any argument that brawls with this fact is a nonsense. While men are granted the exercise of ecclesiastical and managerial authority over women—that is called a patriarchy. Mormonism is without doubt a patriarchy.

But simply naming it a patriarchy ignores its additional features—because it's not just a patriarchy. It's a colonial patriarchy. It's a white patriarchy. It's a class-based patriarchy. It's an Americentric conservative patriarchy bound to a particular economic and political order that is nearing its "use by" date.

So will the ordination of women necessarily address those ideologies that have normalized a broader and more extensive suite of inequalities? I remain skeptical. Can women in Mormon power be relied upon to initiate an interrogation of all forms of marginalization and oppression? I think not—at least not by virtue of our femininity alone.

But the same can be said for all forms of oppression. Simply changing the face, the class, the colour, or the gender of unequal power structures doesn't alter the fact of those institutional and ideological processes that gave rise to inequality in the first place. Sometimes it doesn't matter who is in charge. If the structures of power are flawed you can put anyone in to row the boat, but it won't change the pull of the rip tide. Whoever has the oars will have to change the currents, or elicit the help of others to pull the boat into shore.

Over time Mormonism has made some terrible concessions for its political and economic gains as it's nestled into successive waves of dominant US ideologies. It has traded its spiritual spontaneity and extemporaneous revelatory culture for a lock-step uniformity. It has exchanged a magnanimous and generous economic system for a cynical corporate culture that lists property development as its "core charitable activity." It has normalized a puerile clothing aesthetic, and has sought to craft a religious identity out of denial, discomfort and sacrifice. In the wake of correlation it has replaced a somewhat colourful, incoherent, chaotic but ultimately interesting religious experience with a dull, tedious, lacklustre Mormonism that has many of us dribbling with boredom. It has given rise to a tide of viciousness and meteoric cruelty from those thinking they are doing the work of Jesus with their spew of vile recriminations. It has replaced a theology of independent divine femininity with an insistence on maleness as the final word.

But more importantly, contemporary cultural Mormonism has evolved without a robust, healthy, healing emphasis on diversity, inclusion, and social justice. Yes, it's mostly big on kindness, charity, purity, and good manners but it is a kind of mannerliness that cracks and shatters quickly, revealing a cruel and nauseating intolerance for change, questioning, collaboration, or even raising the possibility of spiritual wickedness in high places.

Our faith experiences are kaleidoscopic and depend on more than our gender. They depend on our class, our race, our culture and a myriad of other social and human conditions. Asking for power to be expanded sideways doesn't necessarily mean that our spiritual lives will be automatically and collectively expanded to incline us toward unraveling oppressive power structures. It doesn't necessarily mean that poor brown and black women will be represented in the galleries of LDS leadership. It doesn't necessarily mean that poor white, brown and black children will be fed. It doesn't necessarily mean that our diverse cultures, conditions, and practices will be included as we seek to create a global Mormon religious identity that eclipses an American religious imperial culture. It doesn't necessarily mean that we will better clothe the naked, feed the hungry, give shelter to the weary, take in the unwanted, relieve the plight of the oppressed, care for the elderly or hear the voices of the unpopular. It doesn't even necessarily mean that bursts of colour and light will fill the night air as we join together in a symphony of high spiritual feeling.

Ordaining women could mean very little in the grand scheme of things. Or it could be the great symbol of hope for women, and men across the world. Hope that a corporate behemoth can change, that core values can be questioned, that institutional power can be contested, and that ultimately ALL will find the Church of Jesus Christ of Latter-day Saints a magnanimous and empowering home wherein we can sing of Zion with glorious belief.

Notwithstanding, I will be there—with hope.

Lani Wendt Young (1973–), "Rejoice in the Diversity of Our Sisterhood: A Samoan Mormon Feminist Voice on Ordain Women" (2014)

Another perspective on the women's ordination movement came from Lani Wendt Young, a Samoan LDS Church member, mother of five, and author of a successful and popular novel series exploring the indigenous mythologies of Pasifika peoples. In 2013, Young spoke out in the *Samoa Observer* as a survivor of childhood sexual abuse about the need to address violence against women and children in Samoa. "Many women wrote to thank me for voicing what is too often silenced in our communities. They wrote to share their own experiences of rape and abuse, and to engage in dialogue about ways to fight this problem. I wrote from a place of anger, pain, and healing to raise awareness of a widespread issue, and it's incredibly humbling to realize that by doing so, others have been able to speak out about their own personal survivor journeys." Young faced criticism as well for making her courageous public stance, but she continued to write and speak about sexual and domestic violence at her blog and public speaking engagements. In this April 2014 essay, Young expresses support for Ordain Women's efforts to address gendered inequality within the LDS Church but calls on both the Church and the Mormon feminist movement to address issues like sexual and domestic violence that bear heavy costs for women and families in Pasifika communities. Like Janan Graham-Russell and Gina Colvin, Young pushes Mormon feminism to define its agenda on a global scale and to recognize and value the experiences, perspectives, and priorities of Mormon women of color.

Source

Young, Lani Wendt. "Rejoice in the Diversity of Our Sisterhood: A Samoan Mormon Feminist Voice on Ordain Women." *Young Mormon Feminists* (April 19, 2014): http://

youngmormonfeminists.org/2014/04/19/rejoice-in-the-diversity-of-our-sisterhood-a-samoan-mormon-feminist-voice-on-ordain-women/.

References and Additional Readings

Young, Lani Wendt. *Telesa: The Covenant Keeper.* Auckland, New Zealand: Pasifika Books, 2011.

"REJOICE IN THE DIVERSITY OF OUR SISTERHOOD: A SAMOAN MORMON FEMINIST VOICE ON ORDAIN WOMEN"

I was driving home from church one Sunday, when I saw a couple dressed in church clothes, having an altercation by the roadside. The man was shouting, dragging the woman (his wife?) by the hair with one hand. With the other he held his scriptures and was using them to beat her around the face and head as she cowered and struggled. Two small children stood to the side, crying.

It's been a long time now, but that's an image I have never forgotten. The symbolism brutally obvious. A man using the weight of scripture and religious authority to subdue a woman.

My name is Lani Wendt Young. I consider it a blessing and privilege to have been born and raised in the LDS church in Samoa. I was taught from an early age that I am a child of Heavenly Parents and that my elder brother Jesus Christ is to be my example in all things. I am a feminist because my Saviour is. *"He inviteth them all to come unto him and partake of his goodness and he denieth none that come unto him, black and white, bond and free, male and female; and he remembereth the heathen; and all are alike unto God."*[*]

On Saturday April 5th, a woman named Shayla Hudson carried my name with her as she walked with five hundred supporters of Ordain Women (OW) to the Tabernacle in Temple Square and asked for admission to the General Priesthood session of Conference. Because of Shayla, I was able to lend my quiet, faraway voice to those articulating issues of gender inequality in our church. Seeking ordination is not my cause, but I support efforts to ask for change when it comes to women in this gospel.

There are many who find OW offensive and threatening. A common criticism I see across social media is along the lines of: "I'm an LDS woman and I feel equal. I'm happy with the church as it is and I don't want the Priesthood . . . Out of millions of people in this church, there's only 500 of you!"

In other words, *you're in the minority so your experience, feelings and thoughts don't count. Shut up and sit down.* This seems at odds with the teachings of Christ who urged us to seek out the one, to value the needs, hurts, the testimony and faith of even the least among us. I am reminded of the wise counsel of Chieko Okazaki, "Rejoice in the diversity of our sisterhood . . . it is the diversity in our

---

[*] See 2 Nephi 26:33.

circumstances that gives us compassionate hearts." It seems the rejoicing in our diversity is sorely lacking when it comes to critics of OW.

I also challenge this critique because it counts me in the millions; it assumes the agreement of all my Samoan sisters and brothers here in the Pacific and anyone else, anywhere outside the Utah Mormon bubble. Just because we don't walk on Temple Square, doesn't mean we don't support OW, or that we don't want to participate in discussions about the position of women in our faith. And even if we *don't* support women's ordination, it doesn't mean that we too are happy with everything and "feel equal."

The women I serve with are busy trying to live the gospel as they work, raise children and contribute to family and village duties. Their faith is a strength and an example to me. Their testimony nurtures my own. But due to a combination of factors, that include the intersection of culture and religion—many of my sisters are hurting.

Samoans are proud to tell you we are a Christian nation founded on God, *Fa'avae i le Atua o Samoa.* Schools begin each day with prayer, hymns and scripture, and the whole country shuts down on the Sabbath. We have multiple churches in every village and families contribute great amounts of money and time to their religions. Almost forty percent of the country is LDS. And yet, ours is a country rife with abuse. One Judge who sees such cases come through his courtroom every week, said that "the sexual assault of young girls by mature males is becoming an epidemic." One study estimates that over fifty percent of women in Samoa have experienced some form of violence in their families. A disturbing survey showed that sixty percent of women believed that a woman deserved to be hit by her partner (or his family) for a number of reasons, including serving him burnt food for dinner.[1] Almost every Samoan I know has a story to tell of childhood abuse—often relayed amidst much laughter—about beatings from older cousins, parents and even teachers and pastors, using brooms, metal pipes, pieces of lumber, belts and frying pans. These are only the barest hints of a widespread and deeply ingrained attitude that sanctions and normalizes violence—particularly against women and children.

Many of our LDS families are no exception to this attitude. Yes, the gospel teaches us that such behaviour is wrong. Yes, lesson manuals instruct us on how a man who holds the Priesthood should behave, how he should treat the women in his life. But as long as men continue to hold all the leadership positions in this church, as long as women are told in the temple they covenant to the Lord through their husbands, as long as only men sit in judgement on a disciplinary council making decisions about a woman's worthiness, as long as a woman's divine worth is too often assigned to her biological capacity for growing babies, as long as these things "are the way it is" in our church culture and doctrine—then both men and women will continue to use these structures as excuses and rationalization for abuse.

I personally don't want to hold the Priesthood. (Beyond how we women participate in it inside the temple.) But through my various callings and my work I am troubled. I have felt the pain of my sister, a second wife, troubled by questions of our polygamous past and wondering where she will "fit" in the kingdoms to come, because her divorced husband has been sealed to more than one woman. I have seen the strength of my single sister as she struggles to remain faithful in a church that tells her marriage is the highest order of the Priesthood and a woman can only share in the priesthood authority of her husband. I have wept with my sister who can never have children and listened with her as leaders tell us that "men get the Priesthood and women get motherhood." I have felt the shame and discomfort of my repentant sister who must confess her sexual sins before a disciplinary council made up entirely of men. I have been in stake leadership meetings, one of only two women present in a room of twenty men—as they plan how to best serve the needs of several thousand people, where more than half of those thousands are female. I have been horrified when leaders tell a rape survivor that she needs to repent, a beaten wife that she needs to be submissive and have more humility, a teenage girl that she needs to make sure she dresses modestly so she doesn't tempt a boy to sin because she will be "like a plate of raw meat left uncovered that attracts flies." And I have been angry on behalf of my sister who endures an abusive husband as he uses a triple heavy weight rationalization for his behaviour:

1. Religion: I have the Priesthood and God said I'm the head of the family.
2. Culture: I'm a *matai*, a chief. You are just a wife. You serve. And if we are living with my family, then you serve my mother and my sisters too. Because in our society kinship trumps marriage. "*O le tuafafine o le ioimata o lana tuagane.*" A sister is the pupil of her brother's eye. A sister is honoured, respected and listened to by her brothers. But a wife has little or no status.
3. Biology: I'm a man. I'm bigger, stronger, better.

It's not enough to tell these sisters to pray harder, be more patient in their afflictions, and "the Lord's church is perfect but people are imperfect" (so suck it up and smile?) It's not enough to just get a lesson or talk on this issue once a year, employing vague terms and platitudes—especially not in Samoa when physical and sexual abuse are such a widespread problem.

I don't know if priesthood ordination is the remedy for these hurts. But I very much want there to be forums available for us to have these difficult but necessary conversations about gender inequality in the church, conversations that are specific to women's varied cultural experiences worldwide in this growing international church.

Specific to Pasifika LDS women in New Zealand and Samoa, I ask:

Instead of official letters issued from Church headquarters and read in our wards about how marriage equality is a threat to "the family," where are the letters condemning violence in the home, calling on men (and women) to stop beating each other and their children? When the Chairman for the National Council of Churches in Samoa tells women they need to make sure they bite and scratch their rapist because otherwise we will "know that she wanted it" and the reason why there's so many social problems in Samoa is because young people have had "too much education and too much focus on rights," where are the voices of local LDS church leaders speaking out against such harmful counsel from a spiritual leader?[2]

Samoa is in dire need of trained counsellors and treatment programs to help abusers and survivors. The LDS church could take the lead in this area. What if we acknowledged that our families have some serious problems and prioritize church funds to establish an agency similar to LDS Family Services here? Instead of paying to train more missionaries to go convert people, let's put some of those funds into training our Bishops, Relief Society Presidents and other ward leaders how to better respond to and help those in their congregations that are living in abusive families. That way, the next time a woman sports a black eye at church, the Bishop can do more then tell her husband he can't take the Sacrament for three months and encourage them to pray more as a couple. The Bishop can also refer the abuser to a therapist and make his attendance at an anger management program mandatory for future church participation. What would make these changes even more effective is if the Relief Society president was consulted and included every step of the way as individuals, couples and families seek *real* help in their journey of healing.

I do not ask these questions because I am *fiapoto*. Apostate. A man-hater. Or seeking to cause trouble for this church. I ask them because I know we are children of God and our Heavenly Parents love us and want us to be happy. I ask these questions because I believe we can do better. I know our elder brother Jesus Christ wants us to be better at this. This is a church of ongoing, continuing revelation and there is room for change, for improvement.

I may never meet Shayla Hudson and those who walked with her on April 5, I may not be convinced that priesthood ordination is the answer, but I am grateful for the courage and strength of their convictions. Their personal circumstances and possibly their gospel experiences may be very different from mine—a big brown Mormon woman who has five children, writes books and blogs, and lives on an island in the South Pacific. But what connects us is a sincere desire to be better disciples of Christ, better sisters in Zion. I can rejoice in that which unites us *and* that which sets us apart.

I can rejoice in the diversity of our sisterhood.

Can you?

Notes

1. "Most Women Feel Men's Violence Justified," *Samoa Observer* (March 17, 2014). http://www.samoaobserver.ws/other/women/9667-most-women-feel-m ens-violence-justified.
2. "Bite Them Hard, Church Chairman Urges Women," *Samoa Observer* (November 17, 2013). http://www.samoaobserver.ws/other/women/8044-bite-them-hard-church-c hairman-urges-women.

Trine Thomas Nelson (1980–), "Claim Yourself: Finding Validation and Purpose Without Institutional Approval" (2014)

Since the 1980s, white Mormon feminists had sometimes drawn comparisons between the historic ban on Black male priesthood ordination and the contemporary policy prohibiting the ordination of women. Mormon womanists and feminists of color rejected this comparison because, as Trine Thomas Nelson phrased it in this essay for *Feminist Mormon Housewives*, doing so constituted an act of "co-optation" that "subsumed" the experiences of Black Mormons and rendered them invisible. A returned missionary who started blogging for *FMH* in 2005, Nelson urged Mormon feminists to study and learn from Black Mormon experience, offering her own father's example of serving a mission during the years the Church maintained its racial segregation of the priesthood. After attending the April 2014 Ordain Women action, Nelson explains, "I wanted to write about knowing God found you acceptable and worthy of all blessings even if the institution you loved didn't." Nelson's essay offers a strong reframing of the entire ordination movement, calling into question the impulse to ask for institutional permission to act that had eroded many forms of Mormon women's spiritual authority, including healing by the laying on of hands, as Linda King Newell observed in her essay "A Gift Given, a Gift Taken" (anthologized in Part I of this volume).

Source

Nelson, Trine Thomas. "Claim Yourself: Finding Validation and Purpose Without Institutional Approval." *Feminist Mormon Housewives* (May 15, 2014): http://www.feministmormonhousewives.org/2014/05/claim-yourself-finding-validation-and-purpose-without-institutional-approval/.

"CLAIM YOURSELF: FINDING VALIDATION AND PURPOSE WITHOUT INSTITUTIONAL APPROVAL"

While I don't feel called to hold the priesthood, I fervently support those who do. If you desire to serve God, you are called to the work, regardless of gender.

I attended the Ordain Women action, but didn't ask for admission, on that premise. What I witnessed were women and men who feel called to serve and administer to their brothers and sisters.

For women of color, being marginalized, dismissed, and othered comes with the territory. Being involved in Mormon Feminism is often the same thing on a different day. We sigh deeply at the criticism and soldier on, doing what we must. We claim ourselves, we drive ourselves to succeed, and we derive our value from something greater than an institution.

I often have conflicting feelings regarding the movement for ordaining women when supporters equate it with the civil rights movement and the priesthood/temple ban. To me, the ban isn't some event in the past to use as a model for future actions. It's not something that should be subsumed by groups who have similar experiences. That is co-optation. It's about my parents; it's personal, and painful. The ban has been lifted for over 30 years yet its effects can still be felt. As a child, I had primary classmates, and the occasional adult, reassure me that I would be white when I was resurrected. In college friends wondered if I would ever find an eternal companion because, "The Church discourages interracial marriage." Walking the halls at church, or in the temple, it is rare to see images that look like me, or my children, reflected.

Martin Luther King Jr. often recognized Gandhi as one of his inspirations. He called Gandhi, "the guiding light of our technique of non-violent social change." But while he used many of the principles of Gandhi in his own work he was clear to point out the struggles of those who came before him and acknowledged their sacrifices and how it helped propel the movement in the United States forward.

Early in 1959 MLK was provided with the opportunity to visit India. Throughout his trip he had the privilege to see and learn from those who knew Gandhi, recognize their sacrifice, and to witness the progress that India had made towards greater equality. Upon his return, he used his platform not only to discuss what he learned and how it applied to the movement's next steps; he also drew attention to the dire poverty in India and encouraged the world community to respond.

We can all be inspired by moments or movements in the past; however, it's important to acknowledge the pain or experiences of those who came before us or those who still experience the pain of oppression. Credit their wisdom for moving us forward, and then pay tribute to them by mentoring those struggling to reclaim themselves. To do less reduces the struggles of others to an academic discussion, which removes the humanity and sacrifice of those we profess to admire.

My father was a teen and young adult through the civil rights movement. As a teen, he was told by his guidance counselor he would never make it to college. He went on to earn two graduate degrees. He was a Black Panther and served in Vietnam. The man knows conflict, he has experienced oppression, and he has overcome.

He joined the church at a time when he was not allowed to hold the priesthood. He experienced acts of racism from those who should have welcomed him into the Body of Christ. He repeatedly petitioned the leaders of the church to serve a mission and was denied. The burning desire to serve led him to serve an "unofficial mission" with a recognized LDS organization. My father did not hide his light under a bushel, nor did he allow "folk" doctrine to cloud his sense of self. He stopped asking and just followed where the Spirit led him to serve. This led him to meet my mother and touch countless lives with his dedication to the Lord.

My father talks of times where not having the priesthood or access to temple blessing was, "like a slap in the face." In those moments he was comforted by the Spirit and remembered to "Be Still" and recognize his worth as the son of a merciful God who would not bar any of His seeking children from exaltation. That legacy of faith and self-worth, that isn't dependent on an institution for validation, has been passed on to my siblings and me. I intend to pass it on to my children.

My parents didn't wait for the general body of the church to be ready for something that was never theirs to give. They sought their own personal witnesses and acted accordingly.

I use them as a template for how I live my life. I strive to be beholden only to my values, to live with integrity and be of service to my fellow-man. My relationship with the institution has often been precarious. There have been moments of frustration, confusion, and contentment. The more confidence I gain in my inner voice, the more freedom I've experienced and it's allowed me to create meaningful relationships within my community.

How can we claim ourselves, while finding our place in an institution that is moving towards progress slower than we'd like? How can we leave a legacy for our children while paying tribute to those who suffered so we can be in our current place?

I look to my past, to my father, and remember to listen to the Spirit and follow that instruction. Relying on that wisdom has not led me astray. There are many lessons to be learned from those in the past who have experienced oppression and marginalization. I reclaim myself every time I honor those individuals and teach their lessons to my children.

Elizabeth Hammond (1975–), "The Mormon Priestess: A Theology of Womanhood in the LDS Temple" (2014)

Mormon feminist theologians like Margaret Toscano and Valerie Hudson Cassler have explored the power of LDS temple ceremonies, sometimes focusing on archival evidence suggesting that Joseph Smith viewed temple endowment as a vesting of men and women alike with a form of priesthood or on the symbolic potency of women's roles in temple ceremonies. Still, many Mormon women have found persistent gender asymetries in temple liturgy to be a challenge to their faith. In this essay, Elizabeth Hammond undertakes a systematic analysis of LDS temple rites, arguing that they present a coherently gender discriminatory theology reflective of the beliefs and worldview of Brigham Young and his historical cohort. Hammond joined the LDS Church at the age of sixteen. A graduate of Cornell University, she began seriously researching LDS marriage, history, and gender in the Church in 2008 and began writing for the *Feminist Mormon Housewives* blog in 2011. Her essay offers both a frank assessment of features of the temple found discouraging by many Mormon men and women, as well as reasons for hope that the ritual might be updated to reflect more encouraging egalitarian elements of Mormon belief.

Source

Hammond, Elizabeth. "The Mormon Priestess: A Theology of Womanhood in the LDS Temple." *Feminist Mormon Housewives* (April 6, 2014). http://www.feministmormonhousewives. org/2014/04/the-mormon-priestess-the-short-version/.

"THE MORMON PRIESTESS: A THEOLOGY OF WOMANHOOD IN THE LDS TEMPLE"

When attending the temple, some Mormon women report being surprised, confused, or even traumatized by the gender messages portrayed there. The temple ceremonies can initiate dissonance in a woman's spirituality, so she often composes personal narratives that align the temple with her own gospel beliefs. There is no universally-agreed upon interpretation of the temple, but a careful examination of temple wording, structure, and rites reveal a very deliberate and internally consistent theology of cosmological womanhood.

I posit that temple ceremonies reflect pioneer-era perspectives which mainstream Mormonism itself has rejected and outgrown. Thus temple theology and modern doctrine often stand at odds, which is a major cause of dissonance in temple patrons. The bulk of this essay is dedicated to an analysis of the temple's internal logic, after which I lightly contrast temple theology with modern doctrine and contemplate what it could look like to align the two. My goal is to offer insight and interpretive language to the current temple ritual so that women may more proactively define their relationship to it.

Initiation

Female "temple workers" administer initiation rituals to women, in which the body is symbolically washed, blessed, anointed with oil, and dressed in sacred undergarments that reflect temple symbolism. A ceremonial "new name" is bestowed. Men are promised they shall become "priests unto the Most High God," while women are promised to become "priestesses to your husbands." This phrase remains unexplained in mainstream Mormonism, but Priestesshood power is implicitly defined throughout temple rites.

The Law(s) of Obedience

Before changes to the temple ceremony in 1990, Eve promised to "obey" Adam as Adam obeys God, and in parallel, a female initiate promised to obey her husband as he obeys God. Now, female initiates covenant to "hearken to your (Adam's/ husband's) counsel" as he hearkens to the Father. Changing "obey" to "hearken" and "law" of the husband to "counsel" of the husband were considered significant and progressive. However, regardless of the verb in this vow, the relationship between Adam and Eve remains completely unaltered, in the simple fact that Eve covenants with Adam, not with God. In both the old and new rituals, Elohim and Woman are separated by Man in between.

God instructs that if Eve covenants with Adam, and Adam covenants with God, a Savior will be provided for them both. That is, God declares that Eve's redemption is contingent upon her making this vow. Eve/woman disobeyed God in Eden, so to ensure her salvation, God provides Woman a new god whom she can obey and to whom she can be devoted body and soul: the husbandgod. Husband-as-god is a relationship that men enact throughout the temple, as will be discussed.

Men and women covenant to obey the commandments when first baptized and renew that covenant every Sunday via the Sacrament. When a male Mormon is ordained to priesthood, he promises to "obey every word that proceeded from the mouth of God." Later in the endowment temple patrons will covenant to keep the Law of the Gospel.

Given that people covenant to obey God's laws in the baptismal, priesthood, and Law of the Gospel covenants, why is there an Oath of Obedience? The Oath of Obedience is not a promise to obey certain *commandments*, it is the promise to obey a certain *person*. It is a declaration of allegiance and loyalty, the making of master and vassal, and the moment when Woman and Man each identifies the person who will be his or her respective "Lord."

The Covenant of Obedience is the only time in all the temple rites where either Adam or Eve names the person with whom they are making covenants. Every covenant thereafter is not directed at a specific person, but is declared *before* God and/or witnesses. Most Mormons perceive that women covenant with God, but the only "whom" a woman *ever* declares in the endowment is Adam. Men and women make the Covenant of Obedience separately, because men and women ultimately covenant to obey different people.

The pattern is set in the very first temple covenant: throughout the whole endowment, though people typically think Eve/woman is covenanting with

Elohim, she actually makes every covenant (Obedience, Sacrifice, the Law of the Gospel, Chastity, and Consecration) with her future husbandgod. Patrons don't readily see this because in the physical space of their view, Adam and Eve kneel at the same altar with Fathergod (or sometimes the apostle Peter) presiding. Also, all the covenants besides Obedience are made with women and men agreeing at the same time, creating the illusion that their covenants are all directed at God, as the patrons are primed to believe.

However, operationally speaking, there are two different temples in the same room. Men and Women each have their own distinct ritual space, clothing, officiators, covenants, and promises, and as established in the Oath of Obedience, different "Lords."

Women are told they will be priestesses, and they even receive priesthood robes and signs, but their Priestesshood is to their husbands, not God. Women generally cannot have Priestesshood in mortal life because female power comes directly through the husbandgod's future exaltation. Usually, in mortality, the husband is not yet deified, so the woman is not yet a priestess.

In the temple model of female salvation, Eve's Fall and subsequent estrangement from Elohim are healed not through Jesus alone, but also through her husband. Because of Christ's atonement both Man and Woman can overcome death (live forever) and be sanctified (cleansed from sin). Elohim will then resurrect and exalt Man, and thereafter, acting as her god, the deified husband shall resurrect and exalt his wife/wives. It is from the husbandgod's exaltation that she receives her eternal power as his priestess, and it is by the husbandgod that she shall receive her eternal increase (children). By this mechanism Man acts in accord with Christ as savior to his wife. The husband exalting the wife is enacted in the temple during the Matrimonial Veil Ceremony.

Female Exaltation as Motherhood

There is no Mother in the temple account of creation. The male creator gods (Elohim the Father of spirits, Christ the father of spiritual rebirth, and Adam the father of mortal bodies) form humankind without a woman present. Adam is created, not born, and Eve is born of Adam—a biological impossibility. This model for creating human life stands in direct opposition to the Mormon understanding of how children are conceived in the afterlife, an undertaking of husband and wife working together, not father and son. Despite the lack of a Heavenly Mother's involvement in humanity's creation, motherhood nevertheless emerges as the primary identity of Woman in the Eden mythos.

Both Adam and Eve were instructed to keep two commandments in the garden: multiply and replenish the earth and don't eat of the tree of knowledge of good and evil. While the "fruit" commandment could be kept or broken by either Adam or Eve as individuals, the "multiply" commandment could only be kept by Adam and Eve together as a couple. As soon as Eve breaks one commandment by herself (eating the fruit), she concurrently removes Adam's ability to keep both commandments even though he had done nothing wrong. Adam could either keep the fruit commandment, remaining alone in Eden, or else he could break the fruit commandment and have children. Adam is put in a position where he *has* to break a commandment, so he chooses to keep the one he perceives as the most important—he eats of the fruit "that man may be."

Both Adam and Eve choose progeny over paradise—Eve by partaking the fruit, and Adam by following her to keep the two of them together. But according to the temple, Eve was the only one who sinned—her sin being that she obeyed Satan instead of obeying God. Adam's choice was the lesser evil resulting from an impasse of Eve's making. In this light, even Adam's transgression can be interpreted as valiant. Adam's ongoing faithfulness to God is emphasized throughout the endowment as he overcomes temptations and passes loyalty tests.

Since Eve chose children over God, and Eve then covenants to Adam as her new Lord, the Mormon Eden casts the "nature" of woman to be wife and mother as her fullest and deepest identity.

The obvious problem with the temple portrayal of Eve's choice and subsequent eternal submission to Adam is that the atonement of Christ is not powerful enough to redeem Eve from her sin. It depicts that all modern Women are paying for Eve's transgression via an eternal separation from God that can only be ameliorated by marriage to a Mormon priest. Mormonism absolves Mankind from eternal punishment for Adam's Fall, but the temple fully embraces womankind's eternal punishment for Eve's Fall. Thus, though the goal of the temple is to facilitate reunion between mortal and divine, its Eden narrative keeps Elohim and woman eternally apart.

I pause to acknowledge that the LDS Church is developing a new rhetoric of Eve's choice, depicting it as less of a tragedy and more as a heroic act or even a selfless sacrifice. Eve is increasingly portrayed as the wise, initiative-seizing heroine of the Eden tale. Perhaps this widely-adopted heroic Eve narrative offers hope for future innovations to the temple rites.

This analogy, Man is priest and king to Fathergod as Woman is priestess and queen to husbandgod, does not occur just in the covenants and the Eden narrative—indeed it permeates the temple rites throughout.

Tokens

As a cultural motif, the token was a method for identifying a lost heir in order to lay claim to a birthright. The most common version of a token was something made of two halves (or else deliberately broken into parts) which could be tested for a perfect fit. Temple tokens (handclasps) are symbols of testing, recognition, and reunification. The ultimate reunion is enacted at the end of an endowment ceremony, when, at the Veil of the Temple, the tokens are all presented to the Lord, followed by the ritual embrace.

Tokens are given to the audience during the Eden passion play. These days, the Eden drama is usually watched as a movie, so tokens are given by "ordinance workers" between movie or sound clips, and the audience is not able to witness the nuance of how tokens are meant to be transmitted. In a live-acted session it is much more obvious. The man acting as Elohim (or sometimes Peter who is representing Elohim) gives the token to Adam, who gives the token to Eve. Adam then gives the token to the male initiates while Eve gives it to the female initiates. The symbolism is obvious: Eve does not receive her tokens directly from God, just as she does not covenant directly to God. She receives tokens from her future husband, who acts as her god in bestowing them upon her.

Women are not yet sealed to a husband when they receive their endowment. If a woman does not yet have an eternal husband, how is she making promises to him? This works by the Mormon concept of proxy: a person "standing in" for another person during a ritual. The "Adam" in the Eden narrative represents the archetypal man and a woman's *future* husband. A female initiate receives her tokens through Adam—her future husband by proxy—and later gives them to the fiance, the man who will become her actual husband.

Names

Names permeate Mormonism because they define stewardship, reflect spiritual status, and are often used as indicators of time (past, present, and future). Names are central to baptism (to take the name of Jesus Christ), baby blessings (membership records) patriarchal blessings (defining tribal affiliation for access to the blessings of Abraham), family history work (to forge eternal kinship ties), and temple rites (temporal and spiritual identities reflected through the given name and new name).

Naming claims authority. In Eden God named/claimed Adam then invited Adam to name/claim Woman. As he did so, Adam obtained stewardship over Eve just as he obtained stewardship over the earth by naming the animals.

In real life husbands don't get to name their wives like Adam did (fathers as first stewards do this), so instead, a husband learns his wife's covenant name which she had received during the temple initiation. It is at that moment that the groom assumes the bride's stewardship away from her father. The girl's father will NOT use her new name, since he is no longer her steward, and each woman is instructed not to tell her covenant name to anyone except the person at the Veil. God uses the husband's name to resurrect and exalt him, and the husband, as her god and steward, uses the wife's to resurrect and exalt her.

Marriage Rites

The veil ceremony at the commencement of an endowment is emblematic of reunion with the divine, resurrection, and exaltation. Just before being sealed, an engaged couple retires to the Veil of the Temple and performs this ceremony privately.

The immortal behind the veil is simply called "the Lord," not Elohim or Jehovah, as the gods are named in the creation enactment. This is intentional, since "the Lord" is different for women and men as determined during the Oath of Obedience. For men, "the Lord" is Elohim, who gives and later tests the man's names, signs, and tokens. For women, "the Lord" is her husband. This is not obvious in a regular endowment ceremony, where proxies for "the Lord" stand in for all initiates, both male and female. But it becomes obvious in the matrimonial veil ceremony.

The groom stands as "the Lord" behind the veil to test the bride. The bride declares the groom as the specific person to fulfill the role of husbandgod by offering him her signs and tokens, giving him her new covenant name, and allowing him to symbolically exalt her by bringing her through the Veil. This enactment of groom-as-Lord deeply enforces the husband-as-god narrative begun in the Eden drama.

In the sealing ceremony, woman surrenders herself a second time. The vows reflect that Woman gives herself to the groom, but he does not give himself to her. Bride and groom both "receive" each other, but the husband, who belongs to God, cannot give himself. Consistently, in the context of polygamy, a husband cannot give himself fully to any one woman.

Priestesshood and the Second Anointing

The Second Anointing comprises the ordinances in which the promised blessings of the temple endowment are sealed as binding.

First, a prayer circle is conducted by the husband. A General Authority washes the feet of the husband (to cleanse him from "the blood and sins of this generation," a blessing unique to men). The husband is anointed as King and Priest unto the Most High God, and the wife is anointed as Queen and Priestess to her husband. These blessings had been promised during the temple initiation. The anointing rite parallels the original Initiatories in both content and form.

The moment the man receives his initiation into godhood is also the moment when the woman receives initiation into Priestesshood. I would also posit that just as mortal stewardship over the woman had passed from her earthly father to her husband during the marriage rites, it is during the Second Anointing that her eternal stewardship passes from her Heavenly Father to her divine husband. This is when the husbandgod replaces Elohim as a woman's deity, a process begun in the Oath of Obedience.

As the couple had performed the matrimonial veil ceremony alone where the husband acted as god to the wife, the couple now retires to a private room wherein the woman shall act as priestess to the husband. The wife performs a ceremonial washing and anointing of the husband's feet, after the pattern of Mary of Bethany's administrations to Christ shortly before His death. The symbolism of Woman treating Man as Savior is clear. Later, the Priestess-wife lays hands on her husband's head to administer blessings. She does not speak liturgical words, but relies on the Spirit to guide an extemporaneous pronouncement.

Though men are ordained early in life and encouraged to develop their priesthood, the primary Priestesshood training women currently receive is contained in their experiences administering female Initiatory rituals. Intiatories closely resemble healing blessings, Mother's Blessings, and the female role in the Second Anointing. Priestesshood is no longer institutionalized outside the temple, but it used to be freely practiced by some female Saints of the pioneer era, who were openly referred to as "priestesses."

The Second Anointing is very rare in modern times. Most women will probably never hear about, let alone experience, a Second Anointing ritual, so most Mormon women remain unaware of the temple's vision of female destiny.

So what is Mormon Priestesshood? Temple ritual and historical precedent suggest that Mormon Priestesshood consists of the power to administer female temple initiations, to heal, to declare blessings upon women, children, and an woman's own husband, to lead female prayer circles, and to access the husband-god's glorified body for purposes of administering to him and for procreation. Given that there are no revelations—canonized or not—that specifically speak to Priestesshood, there is likely much more to it. Under the current restrictions for anointing Mormon priestesses, there are probably only a relative handful of them on earth at any one time.

Conclusions

The internal logic of the temple as described in this essay may feel foreign to many readers. Because the temple retains vestiges of now-abandoned theology, temple rites often clash with modern LDS doctrine in significant ways.

Modern Mormons are taught that both men and women covenant directly with God, but in the temple women covenant to Adam. Mormons reject actively living polygamy, but in the temple it is structurally accommodated. Members believe Christ's atonement is powerful enough to fully restore every person to God, but in the temple Eve's fate is reminiscent of Original Sin, where daughters assume an ongoing punitive demotion based on the actions of their archetypical progenitor. Mormons actively revere Eve and her choices in Eden as heroic and even necessary to God's plan, but in the temple those choices are the direct cause of her being rebuked, silenced, and eternally separated from God. Mormons of both genders are taught they are gods in embryo, saviors on Mount Zion, and joint heirs with Christ, while in the temple these are privileges only extended to, and enacted by, the brothers.

Women are promised Priestesshood, Queenhood, and Motherhood, but only motherhood is acknowledged as part of female identity in Church development programs, and Heavenly Mother is treated much more as a consort than a Goddess. The temple establishes a God-Man-Woman hierarchy, while Mormons typically understand that, because of the atonement, Jesus is the center of a God-Christ-Humanity hierarchy. The temple suggests Woman shall ultimately recognize her husband as her god, while modern doctrine reflects that women and men worship Elohim alone. Despite the Church emphasizing women's central role in creating human life, no mother is needed in the temple Eden. And while leaders seek to assure women that they enjoy blessings equal to men, the temple portrays only a template of male exaltation and does not address female afterlife or the attributes, activities, image, or name of Heavenly Mother or any other exalted female being. All this misalignment and the emotional energy gathering around it suggest that eventually there will either be movement toward retrenching modern Mormon doctrine to comply with Deseret-era perspectives, or else movement toward overhauling temple rituals to better reflect modern gospel sensibilities.

It is possible to envision an updated ceremony that embraces modern Mormon doctrine. Elohim (which means "gods" in Hebrew) could be represented by Heavenly Parents. Both Adam and Eve could be born of Heavenly Mother, not Eve from Adam nor Adam from a male trifecta. Mothergod's voice could be heard offering her new children wise instruction. The depiction of Eve in Eden could be much more nuanced, revealing her thought process, motives, and heroism. Eve may have more opportunities to display her obedience and pass loyalty tests. She could also bear testimony at the conclusion of the filmed portion. The power of the atonement to fully redeem Eve could be emphasized and make the ritual far more Christ-centered instead of Man-centered. Since Eve's punishment would not relegate Woman to spiritual vassalage below her husband, Woman could covenant directly with Elohim (as Mormons already believe women do) and receive the promise to become a priestess unto the Most High God. She may even use this Priestesshood to administer both inside and outside the temple. To parallel their obedience covenants to Elohim, Adam and Eve could receive their tokens from the Father and Mother respectively. Patron couples could pass together through the Veil of the temple into the arms of Mother and Father, learning each other's covenant names in the process. Reunion and at-one-ment would be ritually communicated in powerful and startling new ways. Is this vision so very far fetched, given Mormonism's modern understandings of gospel doctrine?

I hope Mormon women redirect their energies away from ignoring, agitatedly accepting, or resenting the temple toward envisioning what is possible and the revelations yet to come. If women start to see themselves as fully redeemed from Eve's transgression, as directly linked to Elohim, as Priestesses unto the Most High, and as daughters who shall inherit all their Heavenly Parents have, the temple will be a place of solace and exciting possibility for Mormon women.

Rachel Hunt Steenblik (1984–), "Birth/Rebirth: Welcome Baby, You Are Home" (2014)

Even as many Mormon feminists pressed for full participation in LDS Church decision-making or priesthood ordination, they continued to affirm motherhood as a spiritually profound and transformative experience. In so doing, they rejected the tendency in twentieth- and twenty-first-century LDS discourse to dichotomize the capacities and contributions of men and women into two categories: priesthood leadership and motherhood. Writing about their experiences of giving birth became for some Mormon feminists a way to explore the divinity of their embodied experience as women as well as their own connection to the female divine—their Heavenly Mother. As part of an ongoing series of birth stories at *The Exponent* blog, Rachel Hunt Steenblik recounts her birthing of her daughter, Cora. Steenblik was among the Mormon feminists who opted for home or midwife-assisted births as an expression of confidence in traditional and woman-centered birthways, and she recalls in this essay the strength she drew during labor from remembering powerful figures in Mormon women's history.

Source

Hunt Steenblik, Rachel. "Birth/Rebirth: Welcome Baby, You Are Home." *The Exponent* (January 2, 2014). http://www.the-exponent.com/birthrebirth-welcome-you-are-home/.

"BIRTH/REBIRTH: WELCOME BABY, YOU ARE HOME"

The contractions started on a Thursday afternoon, when the only thing I wanted was to take a nap. I lay in my bed with my eyes closed. One surge came, and then another, every ten minutes. Each lasted approximately 1 minute and 15 seconds. I could feel them grow. They became easier to manage if I stood or walked. At their end, I would climb back into my bed. I called my husband, Spencer, after about two hours of this. He was at work. I asked him to come home soon—though not necessarily immediately—and to please pick up grapes on the way. However, the next contraction was so forceful that it made me throw up. I called him back and said, "Actually I need you to come home right now."

Soon contractions were five minutes apart, and while Spencer was offering kind words and even kinder back support, I needed the care and support of women. More contractions passed, and then the door opened: our doula! She was the most welcome sight. Soon she knelt beside me and asked how I felt I was doing. I just kept shaking my head. She asked me again. Finally I whispered that I was not sure why I ever thought it was a good idea to give birth at home, without medication. She placed her hands gently, but firmly upon my shoulders, and looked me in the eyes. "Rachel," she said, "You can do this." It was simple, and a little silly, but I believed her. She had been at births before—including her own—and her voice was steady and strong. She breathed with me until my breaths were calm again, and low. She helped me get into a better position in the pool. I was leaning over the edge now, with my arms somewhat folded. My legs were opened wide, with my inner thighs pressed against the pool in a deep squat. I rocked back and forth into the contractions.

At each one's close, I would pull away from the pool's edge, but sometimes continued rocking. I signaled each new contraction by uttering, "Oh gosh," and physically repositioning myself. With Aunika's encouragement I would often add, "I welcome you," or "I can't wait to meet you, Cora." I remember Aunika telling me that she loved the way I was breathing, and that I was doing a great job. One time she felt prompted to say that the way I was giving birth was similar to the women I study. I thought of my Mormon forbears, including Patty Sessions, Emma Smith, and my mother. It strengthened me more than my doula could have known. And, even in the midst of immense pain, it made me smile. Occasionally I remembered words or ideas that I had read, like "It is possible to give birth," and "I'm going to get huge," as well as how contractions could not be more powerful than me, because they *were* me. Other times I remembered nothing at all.

A few contractions passed, and my daughter's head began to crown. I was praying very, very hard during this time, because I needed my baby's body to follow quickly. I pictured a friend's birth video that showed exactly that, and pleaded with Heavenly Father to sustain me. I also prayed to feel the love and support of my Heavenly Mother, and for my deceased grandparents to be close. A few more contractions passed before the first part of my prayer was answered: my daughter slid right out. I felt it, but needed confirmation that it was really over. Someone told me that Spencer caught her, and was holding her. I was relieved and overjoyed, but could not turn around. I had nothing left. Strong women reached in to lift me over the umbilical cord, until I faced my daughter.

She was so pretty, and so slippery; I was nervous that I would drop her in the pool when Spencer handed her to me. She was also red cheeked, and had no visible vernix on her, which surprised us. She let out a tiny, hearty cry, but was calm immediately after.

When things were still, I sang my daughter the songs I sang her in the womb, and cried as I welcomed her into my family. We fell asleep together in our own bed, and it was perfect. For me the best part of having a baby at home is that we were home. The second best part of having a baby at home is that it made our home sacred. The third is that I felt (mostly) cared for.

Sometimes when I looked at my baby in those first few days, the only thing I could think was, "The hardest thing I have ever done was for you." And then I would start to cry.

She was born out of my vulnerability and strength.

Carol Lynn Pearson (1939–), "Pioneers"

The nineteenth-century Mormon pioneers who made the exodus across the American plains from their besieged settlements in Missouri and Illinois—or, for those who had immigrated from Europe, their homeplaces across the ocean—in the hopes of building a Zion society where all could flourish and live their faith hold a treasured place in Mormon culture and consciousness. In the 1970s, at the beginnings of the organized Mormon feminist movement, historians like Claudia Bushman, Laurel Thatcher Ulrich, and Linda King Newell had turned to Mormonism's nineteenth-century women pioneers to reconstruct the sense of possibility and opportunity that earlier Mormon women had felt as leaders and builders of a transformative religious movement. The image of the nineteenth-century Mormon pioneer suffragette rekindled in contemporary Mormon feminists a hope that what Claudia Bushman called the "dual platforms" of Mormonism and feminism could indeed align with powerful consequences. Throughout the 1980s, 1990s, and the first decade of the 2000s, the Mormon feminist movement grew, faced institutional reprisals, survived discouragement and hostility, and innovated robust new ways to advance concerns about the status of women and girls in Mormonism. The Mormon feminist community developed tremendous capacity for supporting women in the deeply personal and sometimes painful and protracted process of coming to terms with Mormonism's complicated legacy for women. Mormon feminism offered a unique space where women could claim authority over their spiritual lives, sort out the gendered barriers and contradictions they had encountered in their religion, and interject their own voices into a faith tradition they valued deeply but that provided little space for women's leadership. As this poem by veteran Mormon feminist Carol Lynn Pearson demonstrates, the symbolic figure of the Mormon pioneer honors this deeply personal but collectively lived experience of seeking truth: "I have packed the handcart again / packed it with the precious things / and thrown away the rest." In Mormon feminism's fourth decade, Mormon feminists found themselves still facing familiar obstacles—fear, institutional backlash, community disapproval, racial and class bias, and racial and class privilege—and with a long journey ahead of them, but taking fresh courage in their unprecedented numbers, level of organization and communication, and global reach. Having survived the deep discouragements

of the 1990s, it seemed a good time to say, as did Pearson, "I will be all right: /
My people were Mormon Pioneers."

Source

Pearson, Carol Lynn. "Pioneers." *Sunstone* 132 (May 2004): 40.

"PIONEERS"

My people were Mormon pioneers.
Is the blood still good?
They stood in awe as truth
Flew by like a dove
And dropped a feather in the West.
Where truth flies you follow
If you are a pioneer.

I have searched the skies
And now and then
Another feather has fallen.
I have packed the handcart again
Packed it with the precious things
And thrown away the rest.

I will sing by the fires at night
Out there on uncharted ground
Where I am my own captain of tens
Where I blow the bugle
Bring myself to morning prayer
Map out the miles
And never know when or where
Or if at all I will finally say,
"This is the place,"

I face the plains
On a good day for walking.
The sun rises
And the mist clears.
I will be all right:
My people were Mormon Pioneers.

Glossary of Names and Terms

This glossary offers biographies of individuals referenced in anthologized writings, as well as definitions for key terms in Mormon religious and cultural life.

Aaronic priesthood: lower order of the LDS lay priesthood, named after the Old Testament high priest Aaron, and available to young men aged twelve and older.

Alice Reynolds Forum: organization that met on campus at Brigham Young University in 1978–1981 to discuss Mormon feminist concerns.

Anderson, Lavina Fielding (1944–): author, editor, Mormon feminist, and one of the trustees of the Mormon Alliance, an organization founded in 1992 to monitor abuses of power within the LDS Church.

Anointing: the bodies of the sick are anointed with a small amount of consecrated olive oil in Mormon ritual healing.

Apostle: a quorum of twelve apostles—modeled on the twelve disciples of Jesus Christ identified in the New Testament—is the second highest-ranking leadership body in the LDS Church, reporting to the Church's First Presidency.

Arrington, Leonard (1917–1999): founder of the Mormon History Association and LDS Church historian (1972–1982), who advocated open access to LDS Church archives and new standards of professionalism in LDS history, launching the "New Mormon History."

Ballif, Algie Eggertson (1896–1984): Mormon feminist, member of the University of Utah Board of Regents, and two-term Utah legislator.

Bankhead, Mary Lucille (1902–1994): descendant of Jane Manning James and other Black Mormon pioneers; researcher of Black Mormon history.

Beck, Julie (1954–): fifteenth general president of the LDS Church's Relief Society (2007–2012).

Beehive class: in the church's Young Women's program, young women aged twelve and thirteen are classified as "Beehives" and attend Sunday classes and activities together.

Benson, Ezra T. (1811–1869): member of the LDS Church Quorum of the Twelve (1846–1869) and grandfather of Ezra Taft Benson.

Benson, Ezra Taft (1899–1994): member of the LDS Church Quorum of the Twelve (1943–1985) and thirteenth LDS Church President (1985–1994).

Bidamon, Emma Hale Smith (1804–1879): early Mormon religious leader, founding president of the Relief Society, and first wife of Joseph Smith.

Bishop: congregational lay clerical leader.

Black Priesthood and Temple Ban: For more than a century, the LDS Church practiced racial discrimination in forbidding members of African descent to be ordained to the Church's lay priesthood or to have access to LDS temple rites. Some Mormon men of African descent were ordained to the priesthood in the nineteenth century, but such ordinations were discouraged by LDS Church president Brigham Young and ultimately were discontinued. The same policy was applied to deny participation in LDS temple rites to Mormon men and women of Black African descent. The policy was rescinded in June 1978 by LDS Church president Spencer W. Kimball.

Bloggernacle: the constellation of Mormon-themed blogs on the Internet; it derives from the word "tabernacle," a reference to a historic LDS meeting venue located on Temple Square in Salt Lake City, Utah.

Bushman, Claudia Lauper (1934–): historian, author, Mormon feminist, and founding editor of *Exponent II*.

Cannon, Angus (1834–1915): early Mormon missionary, pioneer, and religious leader. After being convicted of polygamy under the Edmunds-Tucker Act, Cannon appealed his conviction to the United States Supreme Court. He later ran for a seat in the Utah State Senate but was defeated by his first wife, Martha Hughes Cannon (1857–1932), the first woman elected to a state senate in the United States.

Cleveland, Sarah Marietta Kingsley (1788–1856): first counselor to Emma Smith in the founding Relief Society Presidency (1842–1844).

Coltrin, Zebedee (1804–1887): Mormon missionary, pioneer, and patriarch; Coltrin served as president of one of the LDS Church's Quorums of the Seventy (1835–1837).

Deseret Book: LDS Church-owned bookstore chain.

Deseret News: LDS Church-owned newspaper, founded in 1850.

Dushku, Judith Rasmussen (1942–): political scientist, Mormon feminist, humanitarian, and one of the founding board members of *Exponent II*.

Early morning seminary: LDS religious education program for high school students; outside Utah, classes often meet in the mornings before school.

Edmunds-Tucker Act: act of the United States Congress (1887) to criminalize polygamy, disincorporate the LDS Church, and abolish the rights of Utah women to vote.

Endowment: a religious rite performed in Mormon temples that entails the making of covenants and the receiving of new knowledge that marks a higher level of devotion within the faith. As do religious rituals in many world faiths, LDS temple rituals utilize ceremonial clothing. A ceremonial "washing and anointing" of the believer's body constitutes the "initiatory" portion of the endowment rite.

The Ensign: the official LDS Church magazine.

Exaltation: within the context of LDS theology, "exaltation" indicates the spiritual status of those who reach the celestial kingdom.

Eyer, Mary Sturlaugson (1955–): Eyer converted to Mormonism in 1976 and two years later, in 1978, after the rescinding of the priesthood-temple segregation policy, was the first documented African-American woman to serve an LDS mission. See her memoir *A Soul So Rebellious* (Salt Lake City: Deseret Book, 1980).

"The Family: A Proclamation to the World": official LDS Church statement released by President Gordon B. Hinckley on September 23, 1995, asserting the eternal value of gender and reaffirming the doctrinal significance of heterosexual marriage.

Family Home Evening: LDS Church-directed initiative first launched in 1915 encouraging Mormon families to reserve one night a week for study, discussion, or other activities designed to foster family bonds and teach religious principles.

Faust, James E. (1920–2007): member of the LDS Church's Quorum of the Twelve (1978–1995) and First Presidency (1995–2007).

Fiorenza, Elizabeth Schussler (1938–): German Catholic feminist theologian, professor at Harvard Divinity School, and author of twenty books.

Friedan, Betty (1921–2006): first president of the National Organization for Women and author of the landmark book *The Feminine Mystique* (1963), an examination of American women's gender roles in the twentieth century.

Gates, Susa Young (1856–1933): novelist, editor, women's rights activist, and daughter of Brigham Young, Gates was the founding editor of the *Young Women's Journal* (1889–1929) and the *Relief Society Magazine* (1915–1970).

Geddes, Patrick (1854–1932): Scottish biologist, sociologist, and philosopher.

Gentile: Colloquial Mormon term for non-Mormons.

Godbeites: colloquial name for members of the Church of Zion, or Godbeite Church, a Mormon splinter group founded in 1870 by William Godbe (1833–1902) and distinguished by its emphasis on universalism and mysticism. Members of the Church started what would become the *Salt Lake Tribune*.

Gospel Doctrine: adult Sunday School class.

The Gospel of Thomas: Coptic-language text containing 114 sayings attributed to Jesus and unearthed at Nag Hammadi, Egypt, in 1945.

Grant, Heber J. (1856–1945): seventh president of the Church of Jesus Christ of Latter-day Saints (1918–1945).

Hafen, Bruce C. (1940–): Provost of Brigham Young University (1989–1996) and member of the LDS Church's First Quorum of the Seventy (1996–2010).

Hanks, Maxine (1955–): Mormon feminist lay theologian, editor of the landmark volume *Women and Authority: Re-emerging Mormon Feminism* (1993), and one of six Mormon scholars and feminists disciplined in September 1993. Hanks was rebaptized in 2012.

Hatch, Orrin (1934–): United States senator representing Utah, serving continuously from his election in 1976 to the present.

Heavenly Mother: Mormon theology recognizes the existence of a Heavenly Mother, the spouse and co-parent of God the father. In April 1991, Gordon B. Hinckley, then a member of the First Presidency and later LDS Church president, suggested that those who prayed to Her were "well meaning," but "misguided."

High priest: a rank in the Melchizedek priesthood, a priesthood available to all observant male members of the LDS Church over the age of eighteen.

Hinckley, Gordon B. (1910–2008): member of the Quorum of the Twelve (1961–1981), First Presidency (1981–1995), and fifteenth president of the LDS Church (1995–2008).

Holland, Jeffrey R. (1940–): ninth president of Brigham Young University and member of the LDS Church's Quorum of the Twelve (1994–).

Jacques, Vienna (1787–1884): early Mormon convert acknowledged by name in Doctrine and Covenants 90:28–31 for donating her assets to the LDS Church.

James, Jane Manning (1822–1908): Early African-American convert to Mormonism and the first documented African-American Mormon pioneer to cross the plains to Utah. James in 1869 petitioned LDS Church leaders to participate in temple rites and to be "sealed," or married for the eternities, to Walker Lewis, an African-American Mormon man. She was refused. Her second petition for sealing, in 1895, was also declined.

Jenson, Marlin (1942–): member of the LDS Church First Quorum of the Seventy (1989–2012) and Church historian (2005–2012).

The Joseph Smith Papers: a multi-decade project of the LDS Church and Brigham Young University to produce a scholarly edition of the writings and personal papers of Joseph Smith. Its first and second volumes appeared in 2008 and 2011.

Kimball, Heber C. (1801–1868): one of the members of the original Quorum of the Twelve of the Church of Jesus Christ of Latter-day Saints (1835–1868); counselor (1847–1868) to the LDS Church's second president, Brigham Young.

Kimball, Sarah Granger (1818–1898): general secretary of the Relief Society and president of the Utah Woman's Suffrage Association. In her pro-suffrage sermons, Kimball referenced the Mormon doctrine of Heavenly Mother as evidence of the divine equality of men and women.

Kimball, Spencer W. (1895–1985): twelfth president of the LDS Church (1973–1985). Kimball rescinded the LDS Church policy of racial segregation in the lay priesthood and temple rituals.

Kimball, Vilate Murray (1801–1868): early Mormon convert and pioneer.

Kirtland, Ohio: site of a large and significant Mormon settlement and LDS Church headquarters from 1831 to 1838; the first LDS temple was built and still stands there.

Kony, Joseph (1961–): leader of the Lord's Resistance Army, a Ugandan guerilla group known for its use of child soldiers.

"Law of common consent": in the Doctrine and Covenants 26:2, revelation to LDS Church founders Joseph Smith and John Whitmer establishes that the administrative business of the Church should be decided by the "law of common consent," with sustaining votes from the membership.

Liahona vs. Iron Rod Mormonism: from the Book of Mormon; within the context of contemporary Mormonism, these have become symbols for two different approaches to living the faith: "iron rod" Mormonism indicates a more rigid, obedience-focused approach, while "liahona" Mormonism is still faithful but more seeking and intuitive. See Richard D. Poll, "What the Church Means to People Like Me," *Dialogue: A Journal of Mormon Thought* 2.4 (1967): 107–17.

Lewis, C. S. (1898–1963): British Christian philosopher, scholar, and author.

Locke, John (1632–1704): English philosopher associated with empiricism and liberalism.

Lorde, Audre (1934–1992): Black feminist lesbian writer, theorist, and activist. Her essay "The Master's Tools Will Never Dismantle the Master's House" (1984) critiques the exclusion of women of color and lesbians in the mainstream feminist movement.

Lysistrata: Greek comedy performed in 411 A.D., which features efforts by women to end the Peloponnesian War by withholding sex from their husbands.

"Marys, not Marthas": A reference to the New Testament story of Jesus's visit to the home of two sisters, Martha, who works in the kitchen to prepare to feed their guest, and Mary, who instead sits to listen to his teachings (Luke 10:38–42). When Martha criticizes her sister for declining to help, Jesus defends Mary for choosing "the better part."

McConkie, Bruce R. (1915–1985): Member of the LDS Church's Quorum of the Seventy (1946–1972) and Quorum of the Twelve (1972–1985). In 1978, McConkie, who had endorsed racist speculative theology attributing the priesthood ban to the spiritual deficiencies of people of African descent in his compendium *Mormon Doctrine* (1958, 1966), renounced and disclaimed these prior views in an address to a gathering of LDS Church educators.

McKay, David O. (1873–1970): ninth president of the Church of Jesus Christ of Latter-day Saints (1951–1970).

Melchizedek priesthood: Melchizedek is a king and priest mentioned in Genesis 14; the LDS Church's Melchizedek priesthood is a higher order of lay priesthood conferred upon adult men by ordination.

MIA: Mutual Improvement Association, a shorthand reference to the full name of the LDS Church's Young Women's Mutual Improvement Association.

Millet, Kate (1934–): American feminist and author of *Sexual Politics* (1970), a critique of sexism in the writings of major American authors.

More, St. Thomas (1478–1535): English statesman executed for opposing the schism between the Church of England and the Roman Catholic Church.

Moroni: Book of Mormon prophet.

Nauvoo, Illinois: site of a major and historically significant Mormon settlement and LDS Church headquarters from 1839 to 1844.

Nauvoo Relief Society Minutes: Minutes from the founding meetings of the LDS Church's Relief Society were published as The Beginning of Better Days: Divine Instruction to Women from the Prophet Joseph Smith (2012).

Nelson, Russell M. (1924–): surgeon and member of the LDS Church's Quorum of the Twelve (1984–).

Newell, Linda King (1941–): historian and co-author with Valeen Tippetts Avery of *Mormon Enigma: Emma Hale Smith: Prophet's Wife, "Elect Lady," Polygamy's Foe, 1804–1879* (1984).

NGO: nongovernmental organization, or humanitarian nonprofit.

"O My Father" (1845): originally titled "Invocation, or the Eternal Father and Mother," this hymn by Eliza R. Snow presents Mormonism's best-known and most enduring articulation of belief in a Heavenly Mother.

Oaks, Dallin H. (1932–): legal scholar and member of the LDS Church's Quorum of the Twelve (1984–).

Otterson, Michael (1948–): managing director of LDS Church Public Affairs (2008–).

Packer, Boyd K. (1924–): member of the LDS Church Quorum of the Twelve (1970–present). In 1993, he warned against the dangers of the "gay-lesbian movement, the feminist movement, and the . . . so-called scholars or intellectuals" ("Talk to the All-Church Coordinating Council").

Parable of the leaven: New Testament parable found in Matthew 13:33 and Luke 13:20–21.

Penrose, Charles W. (1832–1925): theologian, hymnodist, *Deseret News* editor, and member of the LDS Church's Quorum of the Twelve (1904–1911) and the First Presidency (1911–1925).

Pentecost: in the New Testament, Acts 2:1–31 describes a dramatic outpouring of the Holy Spirit on a gathering of early Christians.

Peterson, Esther Eggertson (1906–1997): Utah-born labor, consumer, and women's rights activist, who served in the cabinets of Presidents Kennedy, Johnson, and Carter.

Peterson, Grethe Ballif (1932–): Mormon feminist, author, founder of the Salt Lake Children's Justice Center, LDS Church Young Women's General Board member, and *Exponent II* managing editor. Peterson is the daughter of two-term Utah legislator and Mormon feminist Algie Eggertson Ballif (1896–1984) and niece of women's and labor rights advocate Esther Peterson.

Peterson, H. Burke (1923–2013): member of the LDS Church's Presiding Bishopric (1972–1985) and Quorum of the Seventy (1985–1993).

Perry, L. Tom (1922–): member of the LDS Church's Quorum of the Twelve (1974–).

Personal Progress Program: the LDS Church's goal-setting program for young women aged twelve to eighteen, focused on self-esteem, religious and secular knowledge, and spirituality.

Phelps, W. W. (1792–1872): early Mormon leader and hymnodist, penned the classic Mormon hymn "The Spirit of God" (1836).

Pinewood Derby: traditional Boy Scout activity featuring the construction and racing of toy wooden cars.

Plaskow, Judith (1947–): Jewish feminist theologian and author of two books, including *Standing Again at Sinai: Judaism from a Feminist Perspective* (1991), the first book of Jewish feminist theology.

Polygamy: While it is difficult to ascertain precisely when Latter-day Saint polygamy began, some evidence suggests that Joseph Smith married a second wife, Fannie Alger, in the mid-1830s. A revelation on plural marriage to Joseph Smith was subsequently recorded in 1841, which year also marked the first polygamous marriage in Nauvoo. LDS Church apostle Orson Pratt would publicly announce the practice of plural marriage in Utah in 1852. The LDS Church officially stopped authorizing new plural marriages in 1890 under tremendous pressure from the United States government. However, the Church has never renounced the doctrine of eternal polygamy—that in the highest levels of heaven a man may be married to more than one woman—as introduced by Joseph Smith. Eternal plural marriages, with one man "sealed" to more than one woman in the afterlife, continue to be performed in Mormon temples.

Prayer policy: Beginning in 1967, women were not permitted to offer prayers during local sacrament meetings. This restriction, a stark change from prior practice, was rescinded in 1978.

Priesthood: The LDS Church has a lay priesthood: authority to conduct religious rites is conferred by ordination on religiously observant Mormon men aged twelve and older. There are two orders of priesthood in the contemporary LDS Church [See *Aaronic priesthood* and *Melchizedek priesthood*.] Priesthood "offices" are ranks—for example, deacons, teachers, priests, elders—that entail specific ritual powers and responsibilities.

Priesthood Correlation: An LDS Church bureaucratic program initiated in 1960 under the direction of future LDS Church president Harold B. Lee. Spurred in part by the Church's global growth, the Correlation program aimed to systematize and regularize Church administration, operations, publications, and teachings and to place all Church programs under the supervision of the Church's all-male priesthood hierarchy. Correlation impacted Mormon women in specific ways. During the 1960s and 1970s, the female leadership of the once-independent Relief Society lost the authority to develop and administer its own programs, finances, and publications.

Priesthood session: a session of the LDS Church's twice-yearly "General Conference" reserved for men aged twelve and over.

Primary: organization within the LDS Church for children aged eighteen months to twelve years. It is the only gender-integrated program in the Church to be headed by women.

Publican: a tax collector; Luke 18:9–14 contrasts the prayers of a Pharisee who prizes and promotes his own righteousness with that of a despised but humble publican.

Rector, Hartman, Jr. (1924–): member of the LDS Church's Quorum of the Seventy, a Church-wide governing council (1976–1994).

Relief Society: The LDS Church's official women's organization, the Relief Society, was founded March 17, 1842, in Nauvoo, Illinois. It was put on hiatus in 1844. It operated in an extremely limited way from around 1854 until 1867, when Brigham Young formally called for its reorganization. During the 1960s and 1970s, the female leadership of the once-independent Relief Society lost the authority to develop and administer its own programs, finances, and publications under an LDS Church bureaucratic initiative known as "correlation." [See *Priesthood Correlation*.]

Relief Society Magazine: In 1914, the *Relief Society Magazine* succeeded the *Woman's Exponent* as the major print publication produced by and for Mormon women. It continued until December 1970.

Returned missionary: beginning in the late 1960s, serving a term in full-time proselytizing missionary service became an expected rite of passage for Mormon men aged nineteen and older; marrying a "returned missionary" emerged in the same decades as a defining priority for young Mormon women.

Reuther, Rosemary Radford (1936–): Catholic feminist theologian and author of nine books including *Sexism and God-Talk: Toward a Feminist Theology* (Boston: Beacon Press, 1993).

Reynolds, Alice Louise (1873–1938): national Democratic activist, author, *Relief Society Magazine* editor, and literature professor at Brigham Young University. [See also *Alice Reynolds Forum*.]

Richards, Emily Sophia Tanner (1850–1929): founder of the Utah chapter of the National Women's Suffrage Association; member of the LDS General Relief Society board.

Richards, Louisa Lulu Greene (1849–1944): poet and writer; founding editor in 1872 of the *Woman's Exponent*.

Rigdon, Sidney (1793–1876): former Baptist preacher, influential early Mormon convert, LDS Church spokesman, and leader of a breakaway sect in 1844.

Road show: a short comedic or dramatic sketch; "road show" social nights were a common element of LDS congregational life in the 1970s and 1980s.

Roberts, Brigham Henry (1857–1933): author of the six-volume *History of the Church of Jesus Christ of Latter-day Saints* (1902–1932), member of the Church's Quorum of the Seventy, and Democratic politician.

Robison, Louise Yates (1866–1946): seventh general president of the LDS Church's Relief Society and founder of Mormon Handicraft, a nonprofit organization selling handmade wares by Relief Society members.

Roosevelt, Eleanor (1884–1962): humanitarian and advocate for the rights of women, workers, the poor, refugees, and people of color.

Sacrament Meeting: LDS congregational Sunday worship service centered around the sacrament, the LDS form of Christian communion.

Sealing: Marriages between observant members of the LDS Church performed within LDS temples. Mormon belief holds that the Old Testament prophet Elijah appeared to Joseph Smith and Oliver Cowdery in the LDS temple at Kirtland, Ohio, in April 1836 to "restore" additional priesthood authority to conduct religious rites in LDS temples that could "seal" mortal family relationships to survive after death into the eternities. Temple marriages promise to "seal" spouse to spouse for the eternities.

Seceders: in 1870, Mormon convert William Godbe (1833–1902) led a faction of reform-minded Mormons known as "Godbeites" in seceding from the LDS Church.

Second Anointing: The second anointing is a religious rite historically performed in LDS temples for a select number of married Mormon couples designated worthy to have their post-mortal exaltation to the highest levels of heaven "sealed," or "to have their calling and election made sure." It was introduced by Joseph Smith in 1842.

Seventy: a rank in the LDS lay priesthood; congregational "Seventies" associations or "quorums" were discontinued in 1986.

Shakers: the familiar name for the United Society of Believers in Christ's Second Appearing, a spiritualistic, pacifist Protestant sect founded in England in 1747.

Shipp, Ellis Reynolds (1847–1939): One of the first women doctors in Utah; in 1875, sponsored by Brigham Young, Shipp left her children in the care of a sister wife to study medicine in Pennsylvania. She later founded Utah's School of Nursing and Obstetrics and served on the boards of Deseret Hospital and the Relief Society.

Silkmaking: in the 1850s, Brigham Young encouraged the establishment of a silkmaking industry in Utah as an economic development effort, fully involving women as silk producers.

Smith, Barbara Bradford (1922–2010): tenth general president of the Relief Society (1974–1984) and a leader in the Church's fight against the Equal Rights Amendment.

Smith, Bathsheba W. Bigler (1822–1910): fourth general president of the LDS Church's Relief Society (1901–1910).

Smith, George A. (1817–1875): early Mormon leader, member of the Quorum of the Twelve (1839–1868) and counselor in the First Presidency of Brigham Young (1868–1875).

Smith, Joseph (1805–1844): founder and first president of the Church of Jesus Christ of Latter-day Saints.

Smith, Joseph F. (1838–1918): sixth president of the Church of Jesus Christ of Latter-day Saints (1901–1918).

Smith, Joseph Fielding (1876–1972): a descendent of Church founder Joseph Smith's brother Hyrum and son of the LDS Church's sixth president, Joseph F. Smith, Joseph Fielding Smith served as the tenth president of the Church of Jesus Christ of Latter-day Saints (1970–1972).

Smith, Lucy Meserve (1817–1892): Mormon pioneer and diarist.

Snow, Eliza Roxcy (1804–1888): second president of the Relief Society (1866–1887), theologian and writer. [See also *"O My Father."*] Among her husbands were Joseph Smith and Brigham Young.

Snow, Erastus (1818–1888): Mormon pioneer, colonizer, and member of the LDS Church's Quorum of the Twelve (1849–1888).

Snow, Lorenzo (1814–1901): fifth president of the LDS Church (1898–1901).

Spafford, Marion Isabelle Sims Smith (1895–1982): ninth general president of the LDS Church's Relief Society (1945–1974).

Stake: an LDS church regional administrative unit, like a diocese; it is administered by a three-member presidency and a twelve-member High Council of male lay clerical leaders.

Standard Works: the suite of canonized LDS scriptures: the Bible, Book of Mormon, Doctrine and Covenants, and Pearl of Great Price.

Stanton, Elizabeth Cady (1815–1902): American women's suffrage and anti-slavery activist and author of the *Declaration of Sentiments*, and publisher of the two-volume *Woman's Bible* (1895, 1898).

Stark, Helen Candland (1902–1994): Poet, author, Mormon feminist, organizer of the Alice Reynolds Women's Forum, and funder of an endowed lectureship and a room at the Brigham Young University library in Reynolds's name. University officials later denied the Forum use of the Reynolds Room for a lecture on the Equal Rights Amendment.

Stone, Lucy (1818–1893): American suffragist and anti-slavery activist and orator credited with convincing Susan B. Anthony to join the suffrage movement.

Sunbeam teacher: within the LDS Church's Sunday program for children under twelve (the Primary), Sunbeams are children aged three and four.

Sunstone Symposium: a national conference convened by the independent Mormon magazine *Sunstone*, which was founded in 1974.

Stake: an LDS Church regional administrative unit, like a diocese.

Talmage, James E. (1862–1933): Mormon theologian, author, and member of the LDS Church's Quorum of Twelve Apostles (1911–1933).

Taylor, Elmina Shepard (1830–1904): first president of the LDS Church's Young Ladies National Mutual Improvement Association (now, the Young Women's Association); in 1888, she was one of the founders with Susan B. Anthony of the National Council of Women.

Taylor, John (1808–1887): member of the LDS Church's Quorum of the Twelve (1838–1880) and third LDS Church president (1880–1887).

Temple recommend interview: All Mormons who participate in temple worship must undergo interviews with local lay clergy to affirm their commitment to live the tenets of the faith, including sexual morality and abstinence from alcohol, tobacco, and drug use. Young men and young women who participate in temple proxy baptisms for deceased ancestors and others undergo pre-screening by interview as well.

Teraphim: small religious figurines representing ancestors or pre-Abrahamic gods and goddesses of the Middle East; see Genesis 31.

Thirteen Articles of Faith: basic exposition of LDS beliefs written by Joseph Smith for Chicago newspaper editor John Wentworth in 1842 and published in 1845 in the LDS newspaper *Times and Seasons*.

Times and Seasons: an LDS Church newspaper published at Nauvoo, Illinois (1839–1846).

Toscano, Margaret Merrill (1949–): Classics and humanities scholar, University of Utah professor, and Mormon feminist theologian.

Tullidge, Edward (1829–1894): progressive Mormon author, whose works include *Women of Mormondom* (1877).

Turner, Rodney: BYU professor and author of *Woman and the Priesthood* (1972), Turner espoused a conservative view of women's gender roles, including opposition to birth control.

Utah suffrage: The Utah territorial legislature granted women the right to vote in 1870. It was revoked by the United States Congress under the Edmunds-Tucker Act (1887).

Wards: local LDS congregations, organized geographically; smaller congregations are called *Branches*.

Weight, Thelma Eggertson (1898–1992): Utah civic leader who served for decades on the Utah County Board of the Department of Public Welfare.

Wells, Emmeline Blanche Woodward Harris Whitney (1828–1921): nationally known advocate for women's suffrage, editor of the *Woman's Exponent* (1877–1914), and president of the Relief Society (1910–1921).

Whitmer, Peter, Sr. (1773–1854): elder member of a family of early converts to the Mormon movement; his Fayette, New York, home served as the Church's organizational birthplace.

Whitney, Elizabeth Ann (1800–1882): early Mormon religious leader, second counselor to Emma Smith in the founding Relief Society Presidency (1842–1844) and, subsequently, second counselor to Eliza R. Snow in the Relief Society Presidency (1866–1887).

Widtsoe, John A. (1872–1952): scientist, author, theologian, and member of the LDS Church's Quorum of Twelve Apostles (1921–1952).

Woman's Exponent: Independent newspaper (with close ties to LDS Church leadership) founded in 1872 and produced by and for Mormon women. The *Exponent* voiced adamant support for woman's suffrage and mounted a candid defense of Mormon polygamy. It ran until 1914.

Woodruff, Wilford W. (1807–1898): fourth president of the Church of Jesus Christ of Latter-day Saints (1889–1898).

Young, Brigham (1801–1877): second president of the Church of Jesus Christ of Latter-day Saints (1847–1877) and first governor of Utah territory (1850–1857). After the death of Joseph Smith, Young led the Mormon movement's westward migration and directed the building of its physical, political, economic, and religious institutional infrastructure.

Young, Zina Diantha Huntington Jacobs Smith (1821–1901): third president of the Relief Society (1888–1901), midwife, and teacher; among her husbands were LDS Church founder Joseph Smith and LDS Church president Brigham Young.

Zoramites: in the Book of Mormon, the Zoramites are a Nephite sect associated with pride and idolatry.

Additional Resources

For further reading in Mormon feminism, in addition to the works listed or referenced in the introduction and the anthology, see the following periodicals, blogs, books, and articles.

Blogs And Websites

By Common Consent (http://bycommonconsent.com/)
Doves and Serpents (http://www.dovesandserpents.org/wp/)
Exponent (http://www.the-exponent.com/)
Feminist Mormon Housewives (http://feministmormonhousewives.org/)
Feminist Mormon Women of Color (http://www.femwoc.com/)
Modern Mormon Men (http://www.modernmormonmen.com/)
Mormon Matters (http://mormonmatters.org/)
Sistas in Zion (http://sistasinzion.com/)
Young Mormon Feminists (http://youngmormonfeminists.org/)
Zelophehad's Daughters (http://zelophehadsdaughters.com/)

Periodicals

Exponent II (http://www.exponentii.org/)
Dialogue: A Journal of Mormon Thought (https://www.dialoguejournal.com/)
Segullah (http://journal.segullah.org/)
Sunstone (https://www.sunstonemagazine.com/)

Organization Websites

LDS Wave (http://www.ldswave.org/)
Mormon Women's Forum (http://66.147.244.239/~girlsgo6/mormonwomensforum/)
Mormon Women Project (http://www.mormonwomen.com/)
Ordain Women (http://ordainwomen.org/)

Books

Allred, Janice. *God the Mother and Other Theological Essays.* Salt Lake City: Signature Books, 1997.
Anderson, Lavina Fielding, and Janice Merrill Allred. *Case Reports of the Mormon Alliance.* Vols. 1–3. Salt Lake City: Mormon Alliance, 1996–1997.
Barber, Phylis. *How I Got Cultured: A Nevada Memoir.* Reno: University of Nevada Press, 1994.
Barber, Phylis. *To the Mountain: One Mormon Woman's Search for Spirit.* Wheaton, IL: Quest Books, 2014.

Beecher, Maureen Ursenbach, ed. *Personal Writings of Eliza Roxcy Snow.* Logan: Utah State University Press, 2000.

Beecher, Maureen Ursenbach, and Lavina Fielding Anderson, eds. *Sisters in Spirit: Mormon Women in Historical and Cultural Perspective.* Urbana: University of Illinois Press, 1987.

Bell, Elouise. *Only When I Laugh.* Salt Lake City: Signature Books, 1990.

Bradford, Mary Lythgoe. *Leaving Home: Personal Essays.* Salt Lake City: Signature Books, 1987.

Bradford, Mary Lythgoe. *Mormon Women Speak: A Collection of Essays.* Salt Lake City: Olympus Publishing, 1982.

Bradley, Martha. *Pedestals & Podiums: Utah Women, Religious Authority, and Equal Rights.* Salt Lake City: Signature Books, 2005.

Bradley, Martha Sonntag, and Mary Brown Firmage Woodward. *4 Zinas: A Story of Mothers and Daughters on the Mormon Frontier.* Salt Lake City: Signature Books, 2000.

Brooks, Joanna. *The Book of Mormon Girl: A Memoir of an American Faith.* New York: Free Press/Simon & Schuster, 2012.

Burgess-Olson, Vicky. *Sister Saints: Studies in Mormon History.* Provo, UT: Brigham Young University Press, 1978.

Bushman, Claudia L., ed. *Mormon Sisters: Women in Early Utah.* Logan: Utah State University Press, 1997.

Bushman, Claudia, and Caroline Kline. *Mormon Women Have Their Say: Essays from the Claremont Oral History Collection.* Salt Lake City: Greg Kofford Books, 2013.

Compton, Todd M. *In Sacred Loneliness: The Plural Wives of Joseph Smith.* Salt Lake City: Signature Books, 1997.

Cornwall, Marie. "The Institutional Role of Mormon Women," in *Contemporary Mormonism: Social Science Perspectives,* ed. Marie Cornwall, Tim Heaton, and Lawrence Young, 239–64. Urbana: University of Illinois Press, 2001.

Daynes, Kathryn M. *More Wives Than One: Transformation of the Mormon Marriage System, 1840–1910.* Urbana: University of Illinois Press, 2001.

Derr, Jill Mulvey, Janath Russell Cannon, and Maureen Ursenbach Beecher. *Women of Covenant: The Story of Relief Society.* Salt Lake City: Deseret Book, 2002.

Dew, Sheri, and Virginia H. Pearce, *Beginning of Better Days: Divine Instruction to Women from the Prophet Joseph Smith.* Salt Lake City: Deseret Book, 2012.

General Board of the Relief Society. *History of the Relief Society.* Salt Lake City: Church of Jesus Christ of Latter-day Saints, 1967.

Gordon, Sarah Barringer. *The Mormon Question: Polygamy and Constitutional Conflict in Nineteenth-Century America.* Chapel Hill: University of North Carolina Press, 2001.

Hanks, Maxine, ed. *Women and Authority: Re-emerging Mormon Feminism.* Salt Lake City: Signature Books, 1992.

Howe, Susan Elizabeth. "A Dream for Katy: A Celebration of Early Mormon Women." Provo, UT, 1992.

Howe, Susan Elizabeth. *Stone Spirits.* Provo, UT: Redd Center for Western Studies, 1997.

LDS WAVE. *Words of Wisdom: A Collection of Quotes for LDS Women.* 2011.

Madsen, Carol Cornwall. *An Advocate for Women: The Public Life of Emmeline B. Wells, 1870–1920.* Provo and Salt Lake City: Brigham Young University Press and Deseret Book, 2006.

Madsen, Carol Cornwall, and Cherry Silver. *New Scholarship on Latter-day Saint Women in the Twentieth Century: Selections from the Women's History Initiative Seminars, 2003–2004.* Provo, UT: Joseph Fielding Smith Institute for LDS History, 2005.

McBaine, Neylan. *Women at Church: Magnifying LDS Women's Local Impact.* Salt Lake City: Greg Kofford Books, 2014.

Menlove, Francis. *The Challenge of Honesty: Essays for Latter-Day Saints.* Ed. Dan Witherspoon. Salt Lake City: Signature Books, 2013.

Newell, Linda King, and Valeen Tippetts Avery. *Mormon Enigma: Prophet's Wife, "Elect Lady," Polygamy's Foe, 1804–1879.* New York: Doubleday, 1984; Champaign: University of Illinois Press, 1994.

Pearson, Carol Lynn. *Daughters of Light*. Salt Lake City: Bookcraft, 1973; 1986.

Pearson, Carol Lynn. *Women I Have Known and Been*. Placerville, CA: Gold Leaf Press, 1992.

Peterson, Esther, and Winifred Conkling. *Restless: The Memoirs of Labor and Consumer Activist Esther Peterson*. Washington, D.C.: Caring Publications, 1997.

Quinn, D. Michael. *Same-Sex Dynamics among Nineteenth-Century Americans: A Mormon Example*. Urbana: University of Illinois Press, 2001.

Smith, Tamu, and Zandra Vranes. *Diary of Two Mad Black Mormons: Finding the Lord's Lessons in Everyday Life*. Salt Lake City: Ensign Peak, 2014.

Sorensen, Virginia. *A Little Lower than the Angels*. Salt Lake City: Signature Books, 1998.

Thayne, Emma Lou. *A Woman's Place*. Salt Lake City: Nishan Grey, 1977.

Thayne, Emma Lou. *The Family Bond*. Salt Lake City: Nishan Grey, 1977.

Thayne, Emma Lou. *The Place of Knowing: A Spiritual Autobiography*. Bloomington, IN: iUniverse, 2012.

Thayne, Emma Lou. *With Love, Mother*. Salt Lake City: Deseret Book, 1975.

Thayne, Emma Lou, and Laurel Ulrich Thatcher. *All God's Critters Got a Place in the Choir*. Salt Lake City: Aspen Books, 1995.

Toscano, Paul, and Margaret Toscano. *Strangers in Paradox: Explorations in Mormon Theology*. Salt Lake City: Signature Books, 1990.

Waterman, Bryan, and Brian Kagel. *The Lord's University: Freedom and Authority at BYU*. Salt Lake City: Signature Books, 1998.

Van Wagenen, Lola. *Sister-Wives and Suffragists: Polygamy and the Politics of Woman Suffrage*. New York: New York University, 1994.

Whipple, Maureen. *Giant Joshua*. Salt Lake City: Western Epics, 1976.

Williams, Terry Tempest. *Refuge: An Unnatural History of Family and Place*. New York: Vintage, 1991.

Williams, Terry Tempest. *When Women Were Birds: Fifty-Four Variations on Voice*. New York: Picador, 2013.

Essays

Anderson, Lavina Fielding. "A Voice from the Past: The Benson Instructions for Parents." *Dialogue: A Journal of Mormon Thought* 21.2 (1988): 103–13.

Anderson, Lynn Matthews. "Issues in Contemporary Mormon Feminism." *Mormon Women's Forum* 6.2 (1995): 1–8.

Bennion, Sherilyn Cox. "The Woman's Exponent: Forty-Two Years of Speaking for Women." *Utah Historical Quarterly* 44 (Summer 1976): 222–39.

Bentley, Amy L. "Comforting the Motherless Children: The Alice Louise Reynolds Women's Forum." *Dialogue: A Journal of Mormon Thought* 23.3 (1990): 39–61.

Bradford, Mary L. "The Odyssey of Sonia Johnson." *Dialogue: A Journal of Mormon Thought* 14.2 (1981): 14–26.

Bushman, Claudia L. "The Lives of Mormon Women." *Foundation for Apologetic Information and Research, Sandy, UT, August 2006*. www.fairmormon.org.

Bushman, Claudia L. "Should Mormon Women Speak Out? Thoughts on Our Place in the World." *Dialogue: A Journal of Mormon Thought* 41.1 (2008): 171–84.

Evans, Vella Neal. "Woman's Image in Authoritative Mormon Discourse: A Rhetorical Analysis." Ph.D. diss., University of Utah, 1985.

Hanks, Maxine. "Explorations in Feminine Theology." *Sunstone* 133 (July 2004): 40–41.

Harrison, Kent, and Mary Richards. "Feminism in the Light of the Gospel of Jesus Christ." *BYU Studies* 36.2 (1996–1997): 188–99.

Hoyt, Amy. "Beyond the Victim/Empowerment Paradigm: The Gendered Cosmology of Mormon Women." *Feminist Theology* 16.1 (2007): 89–100.

Kantor, Jodi and Laurie Goodstein. "Missions Signal a Growing Role for Mormon Women." *New York Times*, March 1, 2014. http://www.nytimes.com/2014/03/02/us/a-growing-role-for-mormon-women.html.

Kline, Caroline. "The Mormon Conception of Women's Nature and Role: A Feminist Analysis." *Feminist Theology* 22.2 (2014): 186–202.

Lyon, Tania Rands, and Mary Ann Shumway McFarland. "'Not Invited, but Welcome': The History and Impact of Church History on Sister Missionaries." *Dialogue: A Journal of Mormon Thought* 36.3 (2003): 71–101.

Newell, Linda King. "The Historical Relationship of Mormon Women and Priesthood." *Dialogue: A Journal of Mormon Thought* 18.3 (1985): 21–32.

Paulsen, David, and Martin Pulido. "'A Mother There': A Survey of Historical Teachings about Mother in Heaven." *BYU Studies* 50.1 (2011): 70–97.

Pearson, Carol Lynn. "'Dear Brethren'—Claiming a Voice in the Church." *Dialogue: A Journal of Mormon Thought* 36.3 (2003): 201–206.

Petrey, Taylor G. "Toward a Post-Heterosexual Mormon Theology." *Dialogue: A Journal of Mormon Thought* 44.4 (2011): 106–41.

Quinn, D. Michael. "Mormon Women Have Had the Priesthood since 1843," in *Women and Authority: Re-emerging Mormon Feminism*, ed. Maxine Hanks, 365–409. Salt Lake City: Signature Books, 1992.

Radke-Moss, Andrea. "The Place of Mormon Women: Perceptions, Prozac, Polygamy, Priesthood, Patriarchy, and Peace." *Foundation for Apologetic Information and Research*, Orem, UT, August 2004. www.fairmormon.org.

Toscano, Margaret Merrill. "If I Hate My Mother, Can I Love the Heavenly Mother? Personal Identity, Parental Relationships, and Perceptions of God." *Dialogue: A Journal of Mormon Thought* 31.4 (1998): 31–51.

Toscano, Margaret Merrill. "Is There a Place for Heavenly Mother in Mormon Theology?" *Sunstone* 133 (July 2004): 14–22.

Toscano, Margaret Merrill. "'Are Boys More Important Than Girls?': The Continuing Conflict of Gender Difference and Equality in Mormonism." *Sunstone* 146 (June 2007): 19–29.

Ulrich, Laurel Thatcher. "A Pail of Cream." *Journal of American History* 89.1 (2002): 43–47.

Ulrich, Laurel Thatcher. "Mormon Women in the History of Second-Wave Feminism." *Dialogue: A Journal of Mormon Thought* 43.2 (2010): 45–63.

Study Group Guide

1. What did you think about Mormonism and feminism before reading this anthology? Did this book change your thinking? Was there one essay or poem that particularly resonated with you?

2. One hundred eighty-eight women are mentioned by name in the Bible, compared to six in the Book of Mormon. Carol Lynn Pearson points out that prophets in the Book of Mormon regularly address their words only to men, even when women are present. Do you ever feel ignored when reading holy texts or participating in your faith or worship? If the roles were reversed, and the scriptures were predominantly about women, what effect would that have on men and on society at large? What can be done to counterbalance the effects of women's absence from the scriptures?

3. Claudia Bushman describes how some Mormon women in the 1970s were first attracted to feminism: "We looked for diversity because, in all honesty, we are not always completely satisfied with our lives as housewives. Our families are of primary importance to us, but they do not demand all our time. . . . Our educated intelligence, which we have been taught is the glory of God, sometimes cries out for a little employment." How have you worked out the balance between serving others and caring for your own social, emotional, and intellectual needs?

4. Linda King Newell documents the history of women in the church giving healing blessings to others. The practice of women washing, anointing, and healing the sick went from being an established, cherished practice to one that was challenged and then slowly disappeared in the twentieth century. Why would a practice that was once common fall out of favor? Have you ever wanted to receive a blessing from a woman? How would receiving a blessing from a woman be different from receiving one from a man?

5. One of the most differentiating points of Mormon doctrine is the belief that God the Father is not and cannot be single: If we have a Heavenly Father, we must also have a Heavenly Mother. Why do you think our Mother in Heaven is not more present in Mormon scripture and teachings? How does her absence affect you? Jesus taught that the first great commandment is to love God. Does that apply equally to both our Heavenly Parents?

6. In her years in the General Relief Society Presidency, Chieko Okazaki said she often saw situations where men in leadership positions didn't think to include women in the decision-making process, and women didn't ask to be included because they had been taught it was not their place. "[W]hen women get the message that their job is to be supportive and just agree with the decisions of the bishop, they become clams." Have you seen women clam up because they did not think their contributions would be valued? If women want to be more involved in decision-making in the church, should they ask for those changes themselves, or wait for men to invite them?

7. Nadine Hansen writes, "Having an all-male priesthood affects our attitudes toward women and men much more deeply than we realize. Many people sincerely believe that granting priesthood to men while denying it to women in no way influences their egalitarian ideals. But would we still feel the same if instead of an all-male priesthood, we had an all-female priesthood?" What would it be like if most General Conference talks were given by women? If women presided at every meeting? What if female leaders told men how important they were? Can men and women ever be separate but equal?

8. While some feminists argue that women need to have the priesthood in order to achieve full equality in the church, others assert that although men and women have different roles, those roles are equally significant. What unique roles do women currently play in the church? What about women who are not mothers? How could women's contributions become more visible?

9. Laurel Thatcher Ulrich tells of time when a blunt bishop countered one of her earnest complaints with this statement: "The Church is a good place to practice the Christian virtue of forgiveness, mercy, and love unfeigned." It hadn't occurred to her that her Church might not be a place that exemplified Christian virtues so much as a place that required them. Is that your experience of religious practice or community-based worship? How do you show real love and mercy to those with whom you disagree?

10. The Internet has brought an opportunity for women throughout the world to voice their concerns about women's issues that they feel are not being addressed or taken seriously in their own communities. They are writing about issues like abuse, racial inequality, inadequate training in counseling for lay clergy, and so on. What issues would you add to this list? What are the women's issues you see as most pressing in your community?

Suggested Readings By Topic

Claiming Spiritual Authority

Lorie Winder Stromberg, "Power Hungry"
Meghan Raynes, "Now I Have the Power"
Neylan McBaine, "To Do the Business of the Church"

Collective Action

"White Roses Statement"
"What Women Know"
What Women Know Collective, "All Are Alike Unto God"
Kate Kelly, "Equality Is Not a Feeling"

Diversity

Joanna Brooks, "Invocation/Benediction"
Janan Graham-Russell, "On Black Bodies in White Spaces"
Gina Colvin, "Ordain Women, But . . . : A Womanist Perspective"
Trine Thomas Russell, "Claim Yourself"
Lani Wendt Young, "Rejoice in the Diversity of Our Sisterhood"

Feminism And Mormonism

Claudia Lauper Bushman, "Women in *Dialogue*: An Introduction"
Elouise Bell, "The Implications of Feminism for BYU"
Sonia Johnson, "The Church Was Once in the Forefront of the Women's Movement"
Laurel Thatcher Ulrich, "The Pink *Dialogue* and Beyond"
Mary Lythgoe Bradford, "Across the Generations"
Linda Sillitoe, "an elegy in lower case (for president spencer w. kimball)
Cecilia Konchar Farr, "Dancing Through the Doctrine: Observations on Religion and Feminism"
Joanna Brooks, "Where Have All the Mormon Feminists Gone"
Lorie Winder Stromberg, "Power Hungry"
Chieko Nishimura Okazaki, "There Is Always a Struggle"

Feminism In The Early Church

Claudia Lauper Bushman, "*Exponent II* Is Born"

Judith Rasmussen Dushku, *Mormon Sisters*: "Feminists"
Carol Cornwall Madsen, "Mormon Women and the Struggle for Definition"

Gender Complementarity

Margaret Merrill Toscano, "The Missing Rib"
Margaret Merrill Toscano, "Put on Your Strength, O Daughters of Zion"
Valerie Hudson Cassler, "Two Trees"
Neylan McBaine, "To Do the Business of the Church"

Gender Roles

Nadine McCombs Hansen, "Women and Priesthood"
Carol Lynn Wright Pearson, "Walk in the Pink Moccasins"
Elouise Bell, "The Meeting"
Lynn Matthews Anderson, "I Have an Answer"

Marriage/Polygamy

Carol Lynn Wright Pearson, "Millie's Mother's Red Dress"
Judith Rasmussen Dushku, *Mormon Sisters*: "Feminists"
Judith Rasmussen Dushku, "The Day of the Lamb and the Lion"
Violet Tew Kimball, "Wife #3"
Carol Lynn Wright Pearson, *Mother Wove the Morning*
Lani Wendt Young, "Rejoice in the Diversity of Our Sisterhood"

Mormon Culture

Claire Whitaker Peterson, "Hide and Seek"
Elouise Bell, "When Nice Ain't So Nice"
Gina Colvin, "Ordain Women, But . . . : A Womanist Perspective"

Mother In Heaven

Margaret Munk, "First Grief"
Sonia Johnson, Excerpt, *From Housewife to Heretic*
Linda P. Wilcox Desimone, "The Mormon Concept of a Mother in Heaven"
Lisa Bolin Hawkins, "Another Prayer"
Carol Lynn Wright Pearson, "Motherless House"
Carol Lynn Wright Pearson, *Mother Wove the Morning*
Margaret Merrill Toscano, "Put on Your Strength, O Daughters of Zion"
Janice Merrill Allred, "Toward a Mormon Theology of God the Mother"
Chelsea Shields Strayer, "Dear Mom"

Motherhood

Carol Lynn Wright Pearson, "Millie's Mother's Red Dress"
Cherie Taylor Pedersen, "Expanding the Vision"
Sonja Farnsworth, "Mormonism's Odd Couple: The Priesthood-Motherhood Connection"
"What Women Know"
Rachel Hunt Steenblik, "Welcome Baby, You Are Home"

Patriarchy/Church Leadership

Sonia Johnson, Excerpt, *From Housewife to Heretic*
Lavina Fielding Anderson, "The LDS Intellectual Community and Church Leadership"
Kynthia Taylor, "The Trouble with Chicken Patriarchy"
Gina Colvin, "Ordain Women, But . . . : A Womanist Perspective"

Personal Journeys

Reva Beth Russell, "A Purple Rose"
Laurel Thatcher Ulrich, "Lusterware"
Laurel Thatcher Ulrich, "Border Crossings"
"What Women Know"
Carol Lynn Wright Pearson, "Pioneers"

Political Activism

Dixie Snow Huefner, "Church and Politics at the Utah IWY"
Sonia Johnson, "The Church Was Once in the Forefront of the Women's Movement"
Sonia Johnson, "Patriarchal Panic: Sexual Politics in the Mormon Church"
Cecilia Konchar Farr, "I Am a Mormon, and I Am for Choice"

Priesthood

Linda Kind Newell, "A Gift Given, a Gift Taken: Washing, Anointing, and Blessing the Sick among Mormon Women"
Carol Cornwall Madsen, "Mormon Women and the Struggle for Definition"
Nadine McCombs Hansen, "Women and Priesthood"
Margaret Merrill Toscano, "The Missing Rib"
Sonja Farnsworth, "Mormonism's Odd Couple: The Priesthood-Motherhood Connection"
Margaret Merrill Toscano, "Put on Your Strength, O Daughters of Zion"

Scriptures

Nadine McCombs Hansen, "Women and Priesthood"
Lynn Matthews Anderson, "Toward a Feminist Interpretation of Latter-day Saint Scripture"
Carol Lynn Wright Pearson, "Could Feminism Have Saved the Nephites?"

Sexuality

Lisa Butterworth, "Thirteen Articles of Healthy Chastity"

Temple

Carol Cornwall Madsen, "Mormon Women and the Struggle for Definition"
Margaret Merrill Toscano, "The Missing Rib"
Margaret Merrill Toscano, "Put on Your Strength, O Daughters of Zion"
Elizabeth Hammond, "The Mormon Priestess"

TEXT CREDITS

Credits are noted in chronological order, per the appearance of the works in the anthology.

Claudia Lauper Bushman (1934–), "Women in *Dialogue*: An Introduction" (1971), originally published in *Dialogue*. Courtesy of Claudia Lauper Bushman.

Claudia Lauper Bushman (1934–), "*Exponent II* Is Born" (1974), originally published in *Exponent II*. Courtesy of *Exponent II*.

Carol Lynn Wright Pearson (1939–), "Millie's Mother's Red Dress" (1974), originally published in *Exponent II*. Courtesy of *Exponent II*.

Claire Whitaker Peterson (1928–), "Hide and Seek" (1974–1975), originally published in *Exponent II*. Courtesy of *Exponent II*.

Elouise Bell (1935–), "The Implications of Feminism for BYU" (1975). © *BYU Studies,* used by permission. The full version of this article was originally published in *BYU Studies* 16.4 (1976).

Judith Rasmussen Dushku (1942–), "Feminists," originally published in *Mormon Sisters: Women in Early Utah* (1976). Reproduced with permission of Utah State University Press in the format Republish in a book via Copyright Clearance Center.

Margaret Rampton Munk (1941–1986), "First Grief" (1978), originally published in *Exponent II*. Courtesy of *Exponent II*.

Dixie Snow Huefner (1936–), "Church and Politics at the Utah IWY" (1978), originally published in *Dialogue*. Courtesy of Dixie Snow Huefner.

Sonia Johnson (1936–), "My Revolution," originally published in *From Housewife to Heretic* (1981) (Wildfire Books).

Sonia Johnson (1936–), "The Church Was Once in the Forefront of the Women's Movement": Speech to the Senate Constitutional Rights Subcommittee (1978). Courtesy of Special Collections Dept., J. Willard Marriott Library, University of Utah.

Sonia Johnson (1936–), "Patriarchal Panic: Sexual Politics in the Mormon Church" (1979). Courtesy of Special Collections Dept., J. Willard Marriott Library, University of Utah.

Linda P. Wilcox Desimone (1939–), "The Mormon Concept of a Mother in Heaven" (1980), originally published in *Sunstone*. Courtesy of Linda Wilcox.

Lisa Bolin Hawkins (1954–), "Another Prayer" (1980), originally published in *Exponent II*, and "Let My Sisters Do for Me" (1980), originally published in *Dialogue*. © 1980 Lisa Bolin Hawkins. All rights reserved.

Carol Lynn Wright Pearson (1939–), "Motherless House" (1980), originally published in *Mother Wove the Morning*. Courtesy of Carol Lynn Pearson.

Linda King Newell (1941–), "A Gift Given, a Gift Taken: Washing, Anointing, and Blessing the Sick among Mormon Women" (1981), originally published in *Sunstone*. Courtesy of Linda King Newell.

Index

CPSIA information can be obtained
at www.ICGtesting.com
Printed in the USA
BVOW03s1201290917

495915BV00004B/4/P